ELIZABETHAN
AND
METAPHYSICAL IMAGERY

ELIZABETHAN
AND
METAPHYSICAL IMAGERY

RENAISSANCE POETIC
AND
TWENTIETH-CENTURY CRITICS

BY

ROSEMOND TUVE

THE UNIVERSITY OF CHICAGO PRESS

CHICAGO · ILLINOIS

THE UNIVERSITY OF CHICAGO PRESS, CHICAGO & LONDON
The University of Toronto Press, Toronto 5, Canada

TO

THE FIRST SCHOLAR

AND TO

THE FIRST LOVER OF BOOKS

THAT I KNEW

❂

A. G. T. AND I. M. L. T.

FOREWORD

THIS is a study of images in the nondramatic poetry of the English Renaissance. To a writer of this period, genre was so important a factor in the making even of very small artistic decisions that my division is not in reality an arbitrary one. Yet, of course, many of the critical principles discussed apply, and were applied, to images as dramatists use them.

The most difficult problem for any writer on images is that created by the fact that whole poems may not be quoted. All comments on images taken in isolation seem to me invalid. I have therefore made none; although the process of analyzing whole poems is too lengthy to include (except infrequently), each image discussed here has been so studied. There is an important—and awkward—corollary to this statement. I use no image in this discussion without counting upon the reader's familiarity with the whole poem, very often his close familiarity. Yet no one can or will read this book turning constantly to Hebel's Drayton, Martin's Vaughan, Margoliouth's Marvell, and all the rest. I have tried to counter this difficulty by using as often as possible poems which can be found in a convenient anthology edited by scholars, Hebel and Hudson's *Poetry of the English Renaissance* (referred to throughout as HH), and by consistently appending page references to that book. However, I have followed the text of the editions from which any scholar would normally and properly quote, have cited these in an appended list, and have given whatever reference is necessary to users of those editions (page, first line or number). Where variant readings affect images, I have said so. *U*'s and *v*'s have been regularized without comment, but no other modernizations have been made.

The somewhat unorthodox procedure of constant and rather striking reference to another text in addition to that actually used seems to me justified by the end to be attained: that comments made on so scattered a group of poems might be tested conveniently by the critical reader, in the light of knowledge not only of the poem's point and general structure but of the tone, particular context, and other images surrounding the single image quoted. In the case of Donne, from whom frequent and widely scattered quotations were required because he is a central figure in most of the critical controversies discussed, I have not attempted to cite any other edition than Grierson's; similar exceptions are made where long sections use exemplification almost entirely from the work of some one poet.

Similarly, in the case of critical treatises, I have used whenever I could the critical works in such collections as G. Gregory Smith's *Elizabethan Critical Essays;* in one outstanding case the latter's text is incomplete—Puttenham—and I have therefore given page references throughout to the edition by Willcock and Walker cited in the Bibliography.[1] In a study requiring such frequent but short quotation from many and scattered texts it was necessary to reduce footnotes to a minimum by a strict and often ugly conventionalizing of references, but the textual authority for any phrase or citation should be immediately clear upon reference to the hand-list of editions which appears at the end of the book.

I have given dates in parentheses especially for lesser critical writers or rhetoricians, or for some poets (like Yeats) where date has important bearing upon the nature of the imagery and might not be recalled; I do this merely to provide a convenient aid to a reader's memory and do not attempt to enter controversies regarding date (especially of composition), although I have taken cognizance of such matters when the point at issue is affected. The use of critics of widely varying date to support the same general position is intentional. This study is not concerned with minor differences in poetic which shifted over small periods of years. It was in part written to uphold the contention that there were no major shifts in aesthetic during the period

---

[1] However (as elsewhere wherever possible), references are so made that passages may be found in either edition if they occur in both.

treated, but that such shifts have occurred since and have served to distort our reading of these poets.

Another slight unorthodoxy appears in the use of italics. In order to emphasize pertinent phrases in critical pronouncements or in images under discussion, I have used italics fairly freely; they are mine *unless* I append the note 'Author's italics' (appearing in the critical editions used, that is).[2] In most cases, then, italics are my own without further remark; the customary reverse practice would have been both awkward and tedious.

The Appendix of Longer Notes, following the main body of the discussion (referred to in the appropriate footnote, thus: "See Appendix, Note A"), contains such matter as disagreements with particular critics, especially if they involve lengthy analyses of specific poems or of minor aspects of some critical principle; documentation consisting of further examples; references to scholarly studies which would provide supporting data; etc.

In so wide-ranging a discussion, however, references to secondary materials or critical and scholarly work in the field had necessarily to be kept at a strict minimum, and I may not claim that my many debts can even be conjectured from my footnotes. I have used the careful critical apparatus supplied by the work of editors without remark or expressed gratitude (other than the usual acknowledgment); the number of articles, even books, upon one problem after another herein considered, which would deserve citation as general background for such problems but which I do not attempt to cite, is very great. A note is appended recognizing the kindness of publishers in allowing the quotation of copyrighted materials.

I wish to thank Professor John F. Moore for a reading that saved my readers certain special discomforts; and, without attaching responsibility to them for flaws in this study, I should like to thank readers of my manuscript, in whole or in part, who may be understood to have done all they could to save me from the inadequacies which remain: Professors Josephine W. Ben-

---

[2] In a very few cases of italicized proper names or foreign phrases I have not interrupted the discussion to insert this distinguishing phrase.

nett, Dorothy Bethurum, Leicester Bradner, Robert Penn War-
ren, and H. S. Wilson; and Professor Allan Gilbert, for an interest spread over long years, and for a criticism giving me the
benefit of his minute knowledge of Renaissance poetic.

My thanks are due to publishers whose generous permissions
have made it possible for me to quote from copyrighted materials (the uses of such materials having necessarily been especially frequent in the case of editions listed in my bibliography): To
the American Book Company, for quotations from A. H. Gilbert, *Literary Criticism: Plato to Dryden* (1940). To Basil Blackwell (and Basil Blackwell for the Shakespeare Head Press), for
quotations from *The Works of Michael Drayton*, ed. J. W. Hebel,
K. Tillotson, and B. H. Newdigate (1931–41); *The Poems of
Ben Jonson*, ed. B. H. Newdigate (1936); C. Day Lewis, *A Hope
for Poetry* (1935). To the Cambridge University Press (quotations by permission of the Macmillan Company, publishers,
New York), for quotations from Crashaw, *Steps to the Temple
. . . . and Other Poems*, ed. A. R. Waller (1904); Sidney, *The
Last Part of the . . . . Arcadia, Astrophel and Stella and Other
Poems*, ed. A. Feuillerat (1922); Puttenham, *The Arte of English
Poesie*, ed. G. Willcock and A. Walker (1936). To the Claren-
don Press, Oxford, for quotations from *Campion's Works*, ed.
P. Vivian (1909); *The Poems of John Donne*, ed. H. J. C. Grier-
son (1912); G. Gregory Smith (ed.), *Elizabethan Critical Essays*
(1904); *The Poems English and Latin of Edward Lord Herbert
of Cherbury*, ed. G. C. Moore Smith (1923); *The Works of George
Herbert*, ed. F. E. Hutchinson (1941); *The Poems and Letters of
Andrew Marvell*, ed. H. M. Margoliouth (1927); *The Works of
Henry Vaughan*, ed. L. C. Martin (1914); *Wilson's Arte of
Rhetorique, 1560*, ed. G. H. Mair (1909). To F. S. Crofts and
Company, for quotations from J. W. Hebel and H. H. Hudson
(eds.), *Poetry of the English Renaissance* (1938). To Faber and
Faber, Ltd., for quotations from Herbert Read, *Collected Essays
in Literary Criticism* (1938). To Harcourt, Brace and Company,
for quotations from T. S. Eliot, *Collected Poems, 1909–35* (1936);
T. S. Eliot, *Selected Essays* (1932); T. E. Hulme, *Speculations*,

ed. H. Read (1924). To the Harvard University Press, for quotations from Daniel, *Poems and A Defence of Ryme*, ed. A. C. Sprague (1930). To Houghton Mifflin Company, for quotations from *Complete Poetical Works . . . . of John Keats*, ed. H. E. Scudder (1899); Archibald MacLeish, *Poems, 1924–1933* (1933); *The Poems of Sir Walter Ralegh*, ed. A. M. C. Latham (1929). To the Macmillan Company, for quotations from K. E. Gilbert and H. Kuhn, *A History of Esthetics* (1939); *The Autobiography of W. B. Yeats* (1938); W. B. Yeats, *Essays* (Vol. IV of *The Complete Works*) (1924); *Collected Poems of W. B. Yeats* (1941). To Methuen and Company, Ltd., for quotations from *Marlowe's Poems*, ed. L. C. Martin (1931). To the Modern Language Association of America, for quotations from *The Poems of George Chapman*, ed. P. B. Bartlett (1941). To the Nonesuch Press, for quotations from *The Poems of Bishop Henry King*, ed. J. Sparrow (1925). To the Oxford University Press, for quotations from F. O. Matthiessen, *The Achievement of T. S. Eliot* (1935); I. A. Richards, *The Philosophy of Rhetoric* (1936); *The Poetical Works of Edmund Spenser*, ed. J. C. Smith and E. de Selincourt (1932); *Letters on Poetry from W. B. Yeats to Dorothy Wellesley* (1941). To the Princeton University Press, for quotations from *Boccaccio on Poetry*, trans. C. G. Osgood (1930); T. M. Greene, *The Arts and the Art of Criticism* (1940); Hoskins, *Directions for Speech and Style*, ed. H. H. Hudson (1935). To Charles Scribner's Sons, for quotations from J. C. Ransom, *The World's Body* (1938); Allen Tate, *Reactionary Essays on Poetry and Ideas* (1936); Edmund Wilson, *Axel's Castle* (1932). To the University of Illinois Press, for quotations from Fracastoro, *Naugerius*, trans. Ruth Kelso ('Illinois Studies in Language and Literature,' Vol. IX, No. 3 [1924]). To the University of North Carolina Press, for quotations from Cleanth Brooks, *Modern Poetry and the Tradition* (1939).

Although the reading of early books to which they assisted me is by now a decently buried substratum rather than overtly apparent in this study, I should like to thank the staffs of the Folger, Bodleian, and Huntington libraries, the British Museum, and the libraries of Yale University, Harvard University, and Connecticut College, for many courtesies óver a long period. And for courtesies over a shorter but more agitated period, the staff of the University of Chicago Press.

ROSEMOND TUVE

CONNECTICUT COLLEGE
October 1946

CONTENTS

PART I

SENSUOUSNESS AND SIGNIFICANCY
AS FUNCTIONS OF IMAGES

CHAPTER I

THE PROBLEM AND WHAT IT INVOLVES

CRITICAL comment on the imagery of Spenser's period has shown a marked shift in the last century and a quarter. During a century of loud praise, and a quarter-century of rising disfavor, one function of images has been especially in the foreground, and it is one which no Elizabethan mentions except in passing: the accurate conveying of the sensuous qualities of experience.

It is obvious that images carry into poetry the sights and sounds of the physical world. The theorist of the Renaissance is likely to remark upon this one of their powers when he treats of mere descriptive detail—the naming of concrete particulars. He takes far greater care, however, than do the authors of modern discussions of poetry, to preserve the important logical distinction between such imagery and imagery introducing the element of metaphor and similitude. Especially when he talks of or uses the latter sort, the Elizabethan, unlike the modern, appears to be little interested in the capacity of an image to all but reproduce sensations. This is the simplest function an image can have: the accurate transliteration of a sense impression.[1] Yet not even the schoolboy of the sixteenth century is told to keep his eye on the object.

Of course this silence on the question of sensuousness in images would in itself prove little. The ultimate declaration of poetic intention in any age is to be found in the poetry itself. One of our critical commonplaces has been that Elizabethan and early seventeenth-century imagery was deliberately and richly sensuous; perhaps any reader who knows the poetry has already

[1] This is Geoffrey Bullough's phrase, used of Edith Sitwell in *The Trend of Modern Poetry* (London, 1934), p. 113.

3

called up an army of evidences for the commonplace—like these, for instance:

> Far from the town (where all is whist and still,
> Save that the sea, playing on yellow sand,
> Sends forth a rattling murmur to the land,
> Whose sound allures the golden Morpheus
> In silence of the night to visit us)
> My turret stands. . . . .
>
> (Hero and Leander, i, 346; in HH, p. 177)[2]

> Upon a bed of Roses she was layd,
>   As faint through heat, or dight to pleasant sin,
>   And was arayd, or rather disarayd,
>   All in a vele of silke and silver thin,
>   That hid no whit her alablaster skin. . . . .
>
> (FQ, II, xii, 77)

> Where, like a pillow on a bed,
>   A Pregnant banke swel'd up, to rest
> The violets reclining head. . . . .
>
> ('The Extasie,' p. 51; in HH, p. 465)

> With how sad steps, o Moone thou clim'st the skyes,
> How silently. . . . .
>
> (Astrophel and Stella, xxxi; in HH, p. 110)

> Ha' you felt the wooll of Bever?
>   Or Swans Downe ever?
> Or have smelt o' the bud o' the Brier?
>   Or the Nard in the fire?
> Or have tasted the bag of the Bee?
> O so white! O so soft! O so sweet is she!
>
> ('Her Triumph,' from Jonson's Poems, p. 92;
in HH, p. 504)

These and the dozens they are meant to recall would not, at first sight, seem to argue any different conception of imagery's virtues and uses from that which resulted in

> 'Mid hush'd, cool-rooted flowers fragrant-eyed,
>   Blue, silver-white, and budded Tyrian,
> They lay calm-breathing on the bedded grass. . . . .
>
> (Keats, 'To Psyche,' 13)

---

[2] Attention is called to the conventions of quoting outlined in the Foreword, and to the bibliography of editions used, at the end of the book.

or

> The Autumn moon floats in the thin sky;
> And the fish-ponds shake their backs and flash their
>   dragon scales
> As she passes over them.
>
> (Amy Lowell, 'Wind and Silver,' from
> *What's O'Clock*, p. 221)

But the problem is not so simple; is not to be solved by easy comparisons between isolated images.

If these are adventitious likenesses, where does the likeness begin and end? If not, would these earlier poets, or any poet between 1570 and 1630, have indorsed Keats's comments in the *Letters* or signed under any single one of the tenets of the Imagist Manifesto? Much commentary on Elizabethan imagery is based on the assumption of such common aims. Yet if one makes an honest attempt to read the latter document with the eyes of Edmund Spenser—or John Donne—one must read it with deep dissatisfaction. Any differences between the responses of these last two I am prepared to examine as part of the problem.[3] Even if we grant large differences, would Donne, or any Metaphysical poet, have understood T. S. Eliot's attribution to him of a 'direct sensuous apprehension of thought,' or have recognized himself in that intellectual poet who 'feels his thought as immediately as the odour of a rose'? Would this somewhat obscure differentia have seemed to him to mark off truly his imagery from that of the earlier Elizabethans? Or, for that matter, would any poet writing under Elizabeth have been satisfied with that string of laudatory adjectives fastened upon the imagery of his era by a century of attention to the sensuous function of imagery—rich, graphic, brilliant, colorful, exuberant, decorative, concrete, picturesque, precise, robust, full-blooded? Would his own likelier adjectives—apt, pleasing, artificial, lively—be evidence of similar or of different criteria governing the nature and use of imagery?

It is necessary to ask these questions, partly because we have

---

[3] Donne comes closest to the fifth tenet, though for reasons that would not entirely please its propounders; this recommends that poetry be hard and clear and not blurred or indefinite.

become discontent with the poetic aims which made these nine-teenth-century adjectives laudatory ones. They wear their Ro-mantic heritage in their faces. The Elizabethans themselves do not commonly descant upon these virtues in poetry or in one another's verses. The nineteenth-century explanation for this silence—that the Elizabethans, with sublimely right instincts albeit small intellectual consistency, wrote good Romantic po-etry in despite of a sterile and imitative pseudo-classical poetic —grows less flattering with the years.

We are concerned, however, not only to scrutinize this gap between early practice and theory, although if it existed it offers an interesting problem in the history of aesthetics. But nine-teenth-century admiration has been in many quarters replaced by discontent, and present critical discontent with the imagery of Spenser's period goes so deep as to offer a still more pressing reason for our scrutiny. Modern criticism shows a growing tendency to forsake Elizabethan for Jacobean poets—precisely on grounds of the greater adequacy of later imagery. Not that modern taste has ceased to desire sensuous particularity in po-etry. But such a demand is a very narrow one to make of images. That an image should all but give us an immediate sense experi-ence is, logically and imaginatively, the simplest function we can ask it to serve. So simple is it that only some passages in some poetry show it in purity, and no poetry has been able to go long upon such fare without starvation. Having got very hungry going down the late nineteenth-century no-thorough-fare ourselves, and anxious that images should serve a more complicated imaginative function, we have come to see in the Elizabethan facile and painted plenty a malnutrition something like our own. We have seen in the earlier poets a decorative poetic diction and an unfunctional use of sensuous images for pure exuberance of ornamentation, and have seen them as evi-dence of barriers erected between the poet and reality. Modern poets fled with Yeats from painted symbolic object to symbol; modern criticism fled from Spenser as the painter of the poets to Donne. We have given the same reasons for both flights, with how much justice I am not entirely sure. Certainly a very

great deal of the justification of the shift in our taste from Elizabethan to Jacobean poetry has found its basis in differences seen
between the two periods as regards the relation of imagery to
reality.

In the process of justification, moreover, there have been
made, in all seriousness, not only some damaging accusations
but also some very interesting limitations which touch all imagery. I would prick the solemnity with which we have made this
shift in taste only to that modest extent possible to one who has
shared in it. I, too, take a more immediate pleasure in Donne's
Anniversaries than in Spenser's *Muiopotmos*, pick up Marvell
oftener than Daniel. But I am not satisfied with *the reasons why*
as so far advanced. The reasons fit single images; they do not
fit whole poems. They are too small to cover the problem; they
would have a dozen Elizabethans 'murdered with a spot of ink'
—and indeed one's skeptical historical sense suspects that the
devil did not come into the study at all. Moreover, the proponents of the reasons censure earlier imagery on grounds that
would put too much of the world's poetry out of countenance.
For the earlier Elizabethan imagery is said to go wrong in ways
so fundamental and so characteristic of the long tradition of
great English poets, and the definition of imagery that goes
right has become so narrow a one, that it is difficult to see what
kind of poetry is to satisfy the conditions, if the criteria advanced for the satisfactory use of imagery in poetry are the
tenable ones.

They seem tenable if we do not read with an unwise breadth
of interest, that is, if we keep to certain kinds within the poetry
that remains to us or certain areas within the work of any one
man. But to account for all that is left over cannot but cause
one embarrassment. Certainly both Elizabethan and seventeenth-century poetry, or the complete work of any single poet
in either time, bulges out on all sides if we try to force it into the
narrow pattern defined by modern criteria. If it slips from the
level of the concrete to that of abstraction and of statement—as
it constantly does—it offends one critic; if it loses sensuous immediacy in a labyrinthine rhetorical patterning, it offends an-

other; where it speaks to the Will, it will offend a third, and in all probability lose its power to unify the adult modern sensibilities of a fourth; in that it habitually (and seemingly without regret) sacrifices rich texture for clear logical structure I do not see how it can fail to fall out of the line of vision of yet another. Our best modern criticism seems to me to leave little *Lebensraum* for Elizabethan poetry, and it is time we examined that function of imagery which is most immediately concerned in these judgments.

Good poetry will live without being given any room; nothing has been oftener demonstrated, unless it be that other fact of literary history, that no one who leaps to his feet to announce a critical error ever sits down without adding some new one. Revolutions in taste are so harmless in their way that there is no particular reason to tamper with this one, if that is what it is. But a curious and interesting aesthetic problem is offered by the fact that both swings of the pendulum, the admiration quite as much as the repudiation, seem to depend on ideas about imagery which differ greatly from those held by the writers who created the images. To my knowledge, those writers' ideas upon imagery have never been isolated and examined; I know of no strict and constant attempt to interpret images contemporary with those critical ideas by their light, and with conscious differentiation between earlier and modern assumptions about imagery. I should like to know what difference such an understanding will make to our actual aesthetic response to those images.

I am less concerned, then, to re-establish orthodox Elizabethan poets in a high place in our modern hierarchy of taste than to detect and examine assumptions about the essential character of sensuous images and their function in poetry; the ideas and practice of the earlier period should be set over against some of our own, where that would be clarifying, and in this respect the discussion is in as much need of illustration and criticism from the reader's knowledge of Yeats or Eliot as from his knowledge of Drayton or Herbert. I have found it impracticable to point up every comment with illustrations or qualifications suitable to two such different frames of reference, but my own practice has been to study, with the same methods and at the same time, the imagery of the major Elizabethans and of all the Metaphysicals, and that of Eliot and Yeats and MacLeish (entire) and of Pound (in part). No comment is made without the implied hope that the reader will make application, comparison, and objection from within the field of modern poetics and poetry as well as from his fund of experience with all the sixteenth- and seventeenth-century images I am unable to quote. All earlier images have been explicitly chosen (from among hundreds of examples) for their typicalness, both of poet and of period. It goes without saying that judgments of the value or beauty of images from one period may not be made on the basis of critical postulates accepted only in the other; nor do I intend to make an exhaustive comparison of the imagery of these two eras, nor to show that of one as more 'beautiful' than that of the other.

I am interested in this Part I in the *nature* of imagery that appears to serve a predominantly sensuous function, in any era, but primarily in the *modifications* of that nature resulting from critical tenets held in one particular era—roughly that from Sidney to Marvell—with any shifts in intention during that time as marked by shifts in practice.

1. *Complications*

In its primary form the sensuous function of images could be defined as the straightforward transliteration, with or without the aid of metaphor, of a sense impression.

I will clarify the function in a summary fashion by illustration. Common or proverbial phrases often exhibit it; proverbs usually go beyond it ('raining pitchforks'); cf. 'It never rains but it pours,' which states a concept). Slang phrases depend often upon it but commonly use connotation for a heightening which is not sensuous heightening ('She's a honey'). This function oftener induces comparisons than metaphors (early Yeats's 'pearl-pale,' but also Spenser's 'stony eyes'—Terwin's in *FQ*, I, ix). When the comparison is of one sensuous quality in a physical object to a similar quality in another object, we have the type in its purest form ('wine-dark sea,' 'the nut-brown maid'; whereas 'he is as hard as nails' is outside the pure type, and the image has a further function). Obviously, epithet frequently has this function ('rosy cheeks'); and epithet's logical basis, 'a qualitie by way of addition,' is recognized by the Elizabethan rhetorician. Yet, characteristically, the theorist does not single out sensuous vividness to recommend in the figure *epitheton*, but rather advises, as Puttenham does, for instance, that 'he must be apt and proper for the thing he is added unto.'[4] It is interesting that, although this detection of sensuous comparableness is now thought of as native to poetry, it is easier to find in prose or common speech than in pre-Romantic poetry.[5]

It will be immediately obvious that to examine images in isolation is to give the problem a false simplicity. Two kinds of poetic aim, *raisons d'être* for whole poems, appear to impel poets toward the use of images with a sensuous function.

The first such poetic purpose is so severe that it is seldom found pure: the representation of a sensuous experience, or series of sensuous experiences, without comment or other unmistakable indication from author to reader of value or generalized meaning.

This is so very narrow a poetic subject that it is possible that the modern attempt to isolate it was foredoomed to failure. A fair number of modern poems (some of H. D.'s may occur to the reader) appear to have this end.[6] I can find no Elizabethan poem

[4] III, xvi, p. 182 (1589) (for conventions adopted to simplify references see the Foreword). Peacham similarly gives only this advice; though epithet 'garnishes' and provides 'grace' and 'majesty,' its functions are value-stating, not descriptive (pp. 146–47 [1593]). When Puttenham says further that epitheton must not be 'disagreable or repugnant,' he means, of course, not out of agreement with the thing compared to (pp. 182, 176). The criterion is decorum, not prettiness.

[5] A related fact is also interesting: the less the poetic literacy of a reader, the less he will be content with this form of poetic pleasure. No evolutionary conception of poetry underlies this remark about a contemporary form of poetic sophistication; I find myself less able than many to regard the reader of 1590 as poetically illiterate.

[6] It is not necessary or possible in this book to give a systematic exposition of either Symbolist or Imagist theory. Modern images used represent, of course, wide variations within modern poetic theory and widely differing stages of chronological development within the work of single poets. They are used here with awareness of, but without

which attempts it. One must, of course, allow that in any poem
the poet's selection of details induces a unity of mood which restricts, although it does not unequivocally state, the interpretation which the obedient reader may place upon the author's
sense impressions, made his own through the medium of the
images (assisted, of course, by metrical control of tone). Pound
writes:

Alba

As cool as the pale wet leaves
of lily-of-the-valley
She lay beside me in the dawn.

This fences off a corner of the speaker's experience in such a
manner that the reader will make some vaguely similar interpretation of sharply felt sensuous detail. But the distinction between this and the firm assertion of meaning by the Renaissance
poet will be clear if I juxtapose a poem by Herrick on a similar
situation:

To Anthea lying in Bed.

So looks Anthea, when in bed she lyes,
Orecome, or halfe betray'd by Tiffanies:
Like to a Twi-light, or that simpring Dawn,
That Roses shew, when misted o're with Lawn.
Twilight is yet, till that her Lawnes give way;
Which done, that Dawne, turnes then to perfect day.

(No. 104)

Herrick's meaning is perfectly unequivocal, and the metaphor
which notes his evaluation of the lady in the last line is an entirely public one. It would be an ill-read Renaissance reader
indeed who could make other than the intended inferences from
this conventional *judgment—lady:day*. Herrick is not concerned
to give the reader any choice (or any puzzle); he may agree

---

comment on, these variations and stages, since the modern examples are presented as
typical not of particular poets but of currents that have been important in modern
poetry and criticism. If one adds what has appeared since in the important critical
journals, the citations of, for example, René Taupin, *L'Influence du symbolisme français
sur la poésie américaine* (Paris, 1929), furnish a reasonably full bibliography on the
subject—information I must count upon rather than offer here. Pound's poem next
following occurs in *Lustra*, dated 1915 in *Selected Poems*, ed. T. S. Eliot (London, 1933)
(poem, p. 89).

about Antheas in their beds, or he may write another poem, but he cannot very well read an equivoke into this one. After line 4 the imagery ceases to be merely sensuous; but, although the intention of the poem is not revealed until line 6, the progressive character of the image and the rhetorical patterning show that its logical structure was planned from the beginning as climactic in nature.

It will be noted that Herrick introduces no sensuous detail which is irrelevant to the logical structure of his poem and that this structure stems from the evaluation to be conveyed. This last is the directive force governing his imagery. One's pleasure in Pound's poem is due to the acute and delightful fidelity with which experience is represented. The subject matter of Herrick's poem is a sensuous experience; but its 'cause'[7] is not the representation of that experience.

In this connection I wish to make one further qualifying distinction. I have tried to keep out of this category poems which portray sensuous experiences with marked accuracy but which clearly have another and further aim that is yet more important to the poet. Hence I use the phrase '*representation* of a sensuous experience' in the sense in which we use the word in speaking of the element of 'representation' in painting—in Dutch genre painting, Currier and Ives' landscapes, Landseer's dogs. That is, in the sense of a careful, loving attempt to reproduce, to record as seen, with a view to lifelikeness. I shall not use the word 'represent' to mean 'stand for the reality or concept behind.'[8] These two kinds of meaning indicate two very different conceptions of the function of images and, ultimately, of poetry.

[7] I shall occasionally use this untranslatable Elizabethan term because it combines the meanings of 'poetic subject' and 'poet's intention' so economically. Although close to the Aristotelian 'final cause,' it has, as used by Elizabethans, less of self-conscious calculation than our words *aim* or *purpose*. *Subject* is open to confusion with 'subject matter,' and in both Latin and English critical treatises *subject* and related words (*object, subjective* reality) are troublesome to translate, retaining implications taken on through scholastic usage even, evidently, as late as Descartes.

[8] Except, of course, in the sense, assumed throughout, that all formal media of art are capable only of providing us with signs of real things. The distinction I intend is this: my name at the bottom of a check represents me, the delegate I vote for represents me, but not as a 'life-like,' carefully drawn portrait of myself 'represents' me. I use here the latter sense. If the portrait were of Hitler or Lincoln, it would take on also

It will presently appear that the crux of the matter, if we are to understand the Elizabethan conception of the relation of sensuous experience to poem, lies in what the Elizabethan understood by the concept of 'Imitation.' If, as is frequently stated, he understood it to imply that relation between art and reality which the representational painter intends we shall enjoy, then the absence of poems with the aim which I have here isolated is very curious. So also are his choices of subject matter— seldom of a kind favored by genre painters. So also are his methods of imitating. That unity of impression which a Vermeer interior, a Breughel landscape, a nineteenth-century descriptive poem, can alike offer, or that unity of mood which holds together a Monet or an Imagist poem—these are not the Elizabethan's primary vehicle of meaning (though he may enhance his stated meaning so). He does not confine himself to those instrumentalities for the conveying of meaning to which the Impressionist painter or the Imagist confines himself: selectivity and accuracy. When he appears to have so done, stricter examination reveals his method to be rather that of the emblem or of representationally inaccurate symbolic schools of painting like the Byzantine or Sienese—using public symbols without equivocation for the conveyance of unmistakable general meanings.

To distinguish between poetic images written under these differing attitudes toward the reality imitated is far more difficult than to distinguish naturalistic from symbolic images in painting. All these matters stand to be examined as we proceed. What I am here concerned to make clear is that if neither the Romantic nor the Victorian nor the modern admiration of accuracy in sensuous images is matched by any similar admiration on the part of the sixteenth- and seventeenth-century poet, then

---

the first kind of representation of meaning, to those who knew what the men stood for. Some pertinent distinctions, in the visual arts, are interestingly made in R. Bernheimer's contributions to *Art: A Bryn Mawr Symposium* (Bryn Mawr, 1940).

To avoid confusion I shall state at once another assumption: that no poet of the stature of those I speak of, in any period, is unaware of basic differences between 'copy' on canvas and 'copy' in a reader's mind. Artists can pose similar aims for arts in different media without denying differences in the media. I am not concerned with the extreme cases in which the first of these has led to the second.

we must revise our understanding of what art's imitation of nature meant to him.

The second purpose for whole poems which makes for emphasis upon the sensuous function of images is much more inclusive: the accurate representation of an author's emotional experience or state of mind, the communication of that state or experience in all its sensuous fulness being regarded as a sufficient aim for a poem (without, for example, further indication by the author of an intended general meaning).

Two modern preoccupations have strengthened this aim for poems, with its attendant sharpening of sensuous perceptions conveyed in images. The first is our interest in the description of single moments of consciousness, single mental experiences seized and carefully represented for their own interestingness, inducing extremely delicate and precise recording of sensuous impressions involved in the experience (early Eliot). A second is the modern unwillingness to make generalizations involving statements of absolute values or implying acceptance of such values—obviously the more uneasy an honest writer feels about presenting his own experience even as a particular which is significant of a universal, the more he is driven to communicate almost solely in particulars (see certain types of Yeats's poems). We must confront throughout the discussion the question of whether or not these typical modern interests and reluctances are found in sixteenth- and seventeenth-century poems. Whether Donne's poems, for example, show these aims (this is pretty generally accepted by modern criticism).

A few illustrations may usefully limit this second type of poetic subject. One would expect, despite Sidney's notorious defense even of the lyric on moral grounds, that songs would be most likely to show images used simply to assist the representation of a state of mind.[9] This ought to fit love songs at least, which permit 'the many moodes and pangs of lovers, throughly

[9] It has been a universal expectation for a century and a half that lyrics should show a peculiarly direct relation to sensuous reality and should reveal primarily the 'emotions' of an author rather than his 'ideas'—a distinction drawn frequently with some pugnacity. Various forms of this expectation pervade modern criticism, but see, e.g., Herbert Read's essay on the 'Nature of Metaphysical Poetry,' reprinted in *Collected*

to be discovered' (Puttenham, I, xxii [1589]). Suppose one reads through Bullen's *Lyrics from Elizabethan Song-Books*, for example, with this natural expectation. One finds few poems which can have been chiefly intended to show us just how their writers felt, and few images which fit in with modern notions of the function of sensuous imagery in lyrics.[10] Interestingly enough, the examples which I believe would come nearest to modern expectations turn out to be Campion's.

They do not come very near. The climax of 'When to her lute Corrina sings' (in HH, p. 447; in Bullen, p. 157) is the announcement 'And as her lute doth live or die, / Led by her passion, so must I,' but Campion leaves to us all particular elucidation of that element of dependence in a lover's state of mind—nor does the poem lead us on to any such private pursuit. He confines himself to an image whose parallelisms can evoke only the most general notion of the speaker's feelings, as though he were interested rather in praise of Corinna neatly elucidated through the parallel he draws. The emotion is so little particularized that Corinna might indeed be the Elizabethan analogue of the latest Carnegie Hall concert sensation, if it were not that we know enough about the conventions of Elizabethan love poetry to deduce another state of mind in the speaker than musical enthusiasm. The images reveal a man moved, but writing what the rhetorics call 'a praise' of the lady and the music, rather than examining the nature of his emotional experience. The ambigu-

---

Essays in Literary Criticism (London, 1938): 'A lyric is simply a perception'; '. . . . those poems the world agrees to call lyrical are exclusively concerned with the record of sensibility' (not defended in the essay).

[10] Two reasons help to explain this: the wide difference between Renaissance and modern theories of the lyric, and the fact that virtually all lyrics were influenced by an accompanying musical structure (those from plays as well). This influence is perhaps the most important single factor overlooked in our asethetic judgments of Elizabethan lyrical imagery. I cannot possibly examine its influence upon the nature of single images chosen by the poet, since this is only demonstrable with actual performance from the musical scores. Luckily, the three lyrics here discussed happen to have been reproduced with their music by M. M. Kastendieck, in *England's Musical Poet: Thomas Campion* (New York, 1938), pp. 140, 144, 152. Any doubting reader might pursue the subject of the accepted sixteenth-century relation between lyrics and music in Minturno's *L'Arte poetica*, Book iii (1564), or in Campion's own remarks, or note how it is taken for granted in treatises up and down the period.

ity in 'My thoughts enioy a sodaine *spring*,' picking up the suggestions of 'Her voice *revives* the leaden stringes,' the worn unparticularized image of heartstrings (its nature probably governed by the identity of the musical phrase to which lines 6 and 12 were sung), less metrically felicitous than its musical parallel, 'Ev'n with her sighes the strings do breake'—these do not describe; rather they invest with new interest a perceived analogy, cunningly patterned to make the most of the repeated musical pattern.

'When thou must home to shades of under ground' (in H H, p. 449; in Bullen, p. 94) leaves as its final impression not an insight into a writer's emotion so much as a perception, subtle and only half-smiling, of the general ironic discrepancy between Beauty's triumphs and Beauty's proud cruelty. This occurs despite the individualized form given to the irony in 'When thou hast told these honours done to thee, / Then tell, O tell, how thou didst murther me'; it occurs, indeed, because the images are instruments to such a result. The slyness of 'that smoothe toong whose musicke hell can move,' the very generalized detail, including the lovely 'White Iope, blith Hellen, and the rest,' and the rhetorical *ironia* of 'beauteous spirits' where 'beautiful shades of erstwhile proud spirits' is meant—not only are these images not sensuous in function, but they lead the poem toward generalized reflection rather than toward the more exact understanding of the writer's emotion as peculiar to him. Again, in 'Follow your Saint, follow with accents sweet' (in HH, p. 447; in Bullen, p. 8), the images, though moving, do not succeed in the representation of a state of mind. I do not believe that Campion intended them to.

We know from Campion's two Prefaces to the Reader (in HH, pp. 444–45) his declaration, 'I have chiefely aymed to couple my Words and Notes lovingly together,' and his characterizing of his airs of 1601 (whence all three examples come) as 'earepleasing rimes without Arte.' We know from his *Observations in the Art of English Poesie* (1602) the basis of his praise of poetry —that it is the 'maintayner of eloquence,' 'raysing the mind to a more high and lofty conceite'; we know also his scorn of rhyme

in greater poems, as 'unarteficiall,' a mere *figura verbi* 'sparingly
to be us'd, least it should offend the eare with tedious affectation' and force a poet to 'extend a short conceit beyond all
bounds of arte' (in Gregory Smith, II, 327, 330, 331). Clearly,
Campion with his emphasis on conceptions and on 'art' and on
the ear does not think of poetic imitation as the *representation*
of an emotional experience.

Compare the local particularity and sensuous function of
these images and the assistance they give in representing exactly
a state of mind:

> The winter evening settles down
> With smell of steaks in passageways.
> Six o'clock.
> The burnt-out ends of smoky days.
> And now a gusty shower wraps
> The grimy scraps
> Of withered leaves about your feet
> And newspapers from vacant lots. . . . .

(T. S. Eliot, 'Preludes,' pp. 24–26)

And all the other particularized local details: the lonely cab-
horse steaming, the early coffee-stands, the yellow soles of feet,
the 'fancies that are curled around these images.'

I do not juxtapose these to force a comparison without examination of the many factors, but only to indicate that the distinctions do need to be made. There is little critical gain in heaping together images so different, as though all were intended to
achieve the 'sense of particularity.'[11] The Elizabethans, like
later poets, were writing from within their own poetic.

---

[11] The phrase is taken from Eliot's 'Note on the Verse of John Milton,' in *Essays and Studies for the English Association*, ed. H. Read (Oxford, 1936), pp. 32–40. Milton's recommendation of Mazzoni in his *Of Education* is not the only reason why a reader cannot but find Eliot's discussion less conducive to sensitive aesthetic judgments of Milton's imagery than is Mazzoni's 'della Particolarizatione' in Book iii of his *Difesa* (pp. 677–89 [1587]). His analysis stands on common Renaissance positions (most like to Sidney's, perhaps, in English), and his delicate distinctions between genres on grounds of differing purposes, his definitions of the limits and purposes of particularity and of the other functions to be simultaneously served by imagery, illuminate some of the reasons why Milton's images are as they are. To Eliot's comparison with images from *Macbeth*, which 'convey the feeling of being in a particular place at a particular time,' Mazzoni would simply give the answer in Milton's phrase in the *Of Education*—a reminder of

Again it becomes clear that the crux of the matter lies in the Renaissance poets' understanding of 'Imitation,' their commonly accepted aim for poetry. It appears that their criteria for imagery will have to be examined in the light of how they understood and attempted to follow this aim or of how in practice they redefined, limited, or rejected it.

One further general observation emerges from any attempt to read a large number of Elizabethan lyrics with the expectation that they will show the commonly accepted modern aims for lyrical poetry. Song is supposedly the least deliberative of forms, the least interested in the statement of general truths in general terms. Yet to read through Bullen's *Lyrics* (any collection does quite as well) is to reap a harvest of maxims, generalities, and blanket statements which would do credit to a conduct manual.[12] These songs show writers irresponsibly, blithely addicted to arriving at conclusions of that general nature usually considered proper to reasonable discourse. They have no slightest hesitation in proclaiming that 'true pleasure / Lives in measure' (p. 11), that 'Wealth prized in itself no outward value needs' (p. 16), that 'Securer lives the silly swain' (p. 198). Ladies are sung to in proverb or epigram, are told that 'Easy praise quits easy pains' (p. 196), that 'the honies of our youth / Are oft our age's gall' (p. 22); they are advised to 'Never love unless [they] can / Bear with all the faults of man' (p. 37), while their lovers meditate upon the rash generalization that 'Love is sweetest seasoned with Suspect'(p. 10).

I have not culled out the bad or the forgotten poems; these are songs we have all remembered for grace and melodious lightness. It is undeniable that the Elizabethan writer of lyrics does just what the Victorians, for example, have been mocked for

---

'what Decorum is, which is the grand master-piece to observe.' The same answer would apply to Eliot's discontent with the images in *L'Allegro* and *Il Penseroso* because they are all 'general'; this is simply the *brevità* which replaces *particolarità* in some genres. The imagery in the two poems is very sensitively adjusted to the *purposes* of the especial kind they represent.

[12] See Appendix, Note A, for remarks on the variations resulting from special functions in conventional forms like the *pastourelle* or *aubade*, whether in the sixteenth century or in Yeats.

doing; his normal method includes, we must admit, the drawing of most unwarrantable conclusions of just the sort exemplified by 'God's in his heaven / All's right with the world.'[13] True, his conclusion may be, instead, 'There is underneath the sun / Nothing in true earnest done' (p. 213). But we should not be put off by differences in the proposition stated. Either offends equally against the nature of poetic discourse on the basis upon which the condemnation is offered by modern critics: the intrusion into poetry of the methods of reasonable discourse, with a high degree of irrelevancy between the particulars advanced and the general conclusion stated. Whatever we find to have been the reasons for it, the use of such methods directly affected the nature and amount of sensuous or local detail which writers felt to be poetically necessary.

So much reference has been made to differences between earlier and modern poetic that it is wise to suggest here that this part of the problem will not admit of a simple chronological solution. Suppose one reads through the songs alone in the volume of Yeats's collected verse. One finds unexpectedly that song as a kind frequently appears to lead him to generalized imagery, highly traditional in character and somewhat out of keeping with the poetic purposes generally assigned to him (of which accurate representation of states of mind is certainly one).

'A man may put pretence away / Who leans upon a stick' (metonymy for 'an old man') would be quite usual in a sixteenth-century song; so would the generalized groupings of particulars like 'All that silk and satin gear' ('Those Dancing Days Are Gone,' p. 305 [1931]). The imagery of 'Lullaby' (p. 304 [1931]) is not unlike that of early lyrics in function; similar also is the willingness to begin with the general meaning under which the particulars are subsumed: 'may your sleep be sound / That have found it where you fed.' The 'great *honey-coloured* / *Ramparts* at your ear' might possibly distinguish 'For Anne Gregory' (p. 282 [1929]) from early poems, yet the metonymy

[13] See J. C. Ransom, 'Poetry: A Note in Ontology,' in *The World's Body* (New York, 1938), p. 121. I take no pleasure in this lyric either. But if I must find my reason in the nature of the relation between images and idea, I am dismayed at the number and the beauty of the songs I must send into the discard after it.

of the single salient detail and the turn of the last stanza are in keeping with long-used conventions. The logical structure of 'The Fool by the Roadside' is strictly traditional (p. 254 [1928]); and long-followed traditions sanction the imagery of foil and burning heart ('A Song,' p. 158 [1919]), as well as the use of a synecdochic generalized refrain, 'O who could have foretold / That the heart grows old?' All these poems, it would seem to me, exceed in intention the aim we have examined—the representation of a state of mind. They exceed it in exactly the same way as the Elizabethan and seventeenth-century songs exceed it, with the same effect upon imagery.

Generalizing statement is not the only element to look for when we wish to detect whether or not a poem goes beyond this intention. The straightforward particularity of many modern poems, left to the reader to interpret or not, is to be distinguished from a more traditional use of sensuous particulars deliberately summed up into what amounts to, but in form is not, a generalizing statement. Elizabethan examples are everywhere, but I will quote Yeats instead, italicizing the generalizing additions to the actual image-making words:

> That is *no country for old men*. The young
> In one another's arms, birds in the trees,
> —Those dying generations—at their song,
> The salmon-falls, the mackerel-crowded seas,
> Fish, flesh, or fowl, *commend* all summer long
> *Whatever is begotten, born, and dies.*
> Caught in *that sensual* music. . . . .
> ('Sailing to Byzantium,' p. 223; from *The Tower* [1928])

Yeats, like all earlier poets, frequently indicates the significance of his images by such directive summaries. This distinction between two ways of using sensuous imagery is closely related to the question of 'obscurity,' in the Symbolists and in the Metaphysicals. Obscurity in the latter does not generally result from unwillingness to exceed, as any generalizing would, the strict limits imposed by the aim of representation of a state of mind.[14]

---

[14] Modern criticism of modern poets contains many excellent descriptions of the part played by imagery in effecting poetic aims such as this; it seems to me that they

Again we see that the nature of the imagery and the intention of a poem are indissolubly connected. Only the rest of the poem can tell us why the image is there; and, unless we know that (in our partial way), we shall only lump together images that are really very different. The more we tend simply to assume in earlier poems purposes which now happen to be congenial to us, the more we shall overlook in the rest of the poem those subtler indications of purpose which explain why the imagery is as it is. The more wilfully we misread earlier imagery, the fewer fields of poetic pleasure we leave open to ourselves. This seems wasteful. Even the consideration of Renaissance poetic, into which we are drawn by the nature of the problems, seems less so.

All this is mere posing of the problems. None of the above will go far as proof of the different nature and purposes of Elizabethan imagery. Too many variables have been unavoidably ignored. Exact date is one of them. The possibility of warring theories of poetry within the period is another. Genre is another. Possibly sonnets come closer, for example, to modern notions of the aims of lyric than do songs—considering the fact that even Donne will put whole stanzas of generalized sententious statement into a 'Song':

> O how feeble is mans power,
>   That if good fortune fall,
> Cannot adde another houre,
>   Nor a lost houre recall!
>   But come bad chance,
> And wee joyne to' it our strength,
> And wee teach it art and length,
>   It selfe o'r us to' advance.

> (p. 19)

But whatever these significant variables turn out to be, there yet remain vast numbers of sensuous images in Elizabethan and

---

sharpen one's perception of the differences between earlier and modern images even when, as frequently, they are part of a discussion attempting to relate Metaphysical to modern poetry in method. For an example, take F. O. Matthiessen, *The Achievement of T. S. Eliot* (Oxford and London, 1935), pp. 28, 42, and many passages in the chapter on Eliot's 'objective correlative' (pp. 57, 61, 62, 66, 78).

Jacobean poems whose character does not seem explicable according to modern conceptions of the nature and functions of sensuous imagery.

2. *Necessities*

I have tried to demonstrate my reasons for thinking that there is little hope of our making valid critical remarks about Elizabethan and seventeenth-century images unless we use all the tools we have to find out what they are in the poems *for*. I shall therefore begin boldly at the theoretical end.

Nothing is more difficult than to make sure inferences about the intentions of other minds than one's own. Yet criticism is based on such inferences—often more gracefully hidden than mine will be. There is no choice but to make them. I think that the difficulty will be minimized by attempting a sympathetic understanding of the criteria which Renaissance images were written to meet, and therefore still do meet, whether we take the pains to observe it or not. Luckily this involves only the large, sweeping, generally accepted tenets of sixteenth- and seventeenth-century poetic; differences sufficient to affect functions of imagery did not (it seems to me) take place until a couple of hundred years after the period, and there are still more similarities than differences. Nevertheless, because of these slow changes, a modern reader runs more risk of misjudging the functions of Elizabethan imagery by ignoring changes in poetic than did a Renaissance reader of misjudging medieval imagery. It is in literary situations where such changes have intervened that historical criticism is helpful—even necessary. Understanding of the problems does not, of course, constitute enjoyment of the solutions. But the responsibility of establishing a working contemporaneity with the Elizabethans still lies with us; much modern criticism seems to show that it cannot in this instance be carried alone by the poetry itself. Hence, despite the opposed dangers of doctrinaire interpretation of the poetry and subjective interpretation of the doctrines, I shall organize the discussion around the commonplaces of Renaissance theory.

Even in a preliminary consideration it became apparent that

the sensuous imagery of the simplest song plunges one immediately into the problem of what Renaissance writers understood by the concept of 'the imitation of nature' in poetry. To consider that avowed end is, by definition, to consider what to them constituted 'functional' imagery. Theoretical declarations can be checked by observing the ends toward which actual images do function. One has chiefly to take care (as not all modern criticism has done) not to assume for these writers intentions they did not profess, and then call their images 'unfunctional.' There is a remarkable constancy in poetic intentions as they are declared in theory and betrayed in practice throughout the entire period.

An inquiry into the relations between images and current interpretations of Imitation will not, however, reach into all the corners of the question, and we must go further. Two great commonplaces of the theory of ornament in the Renaissance are peculiarly related to the question of functions and character of imagery—'poetry as a speaking picture,' and 'style as a garment.' It seems necessary that we should try to understand how these commonplaces would affect sensuous imagery especially and should try to observe whether the images of the period show poets putting into practice these general concepts. And, upon the bases so established, it would seem wise to inquire of Renaissance theory and substantiate from Renaissance practice: What were the Elizabethan's specific criteria for imagery, especially as these concern images predominantly sensuous? This will include a constant questioning of whether or not these criteria adequately explain the nature of early seventeenth-century images, and it will include the relation of these criteria to the pertinent Renaissance commonplaces—'embellished Nature' as poetic subject; 'delight' or pleasure as part (or all) of the poet's aim; the demand for 'significancy'; the acceptance, for poetry, of certain aims (the didactic) and certain methods (abstract 'statement') of reasonable discourse; the demand for rhetorical efficacy; and, most pervasively influential of all critical concepts, 'Decorum' as a regulative principle.

The first of all these matters—the ways in which elements in the conception of Imitation[15] influenced images—is not simple; and I should perhaps preface the examination proper with a bare schematic statement of the conclusions to which I have been led. Quarrels over the interpretation of this concept were many, and they have not been ignored. But the broad, widely proclaimed interpretations of the concept are what influenced images, and these are common to the many schools of thought whose acrimonious disagreements on lower levels enliven the period.

Elizabethan imagery is frequently thought of as not functional because its artificial, decorative elements seem so much in evidence; it does not seem to imitate the real. But this may be because we predetermine the meanings of 'imitation' and 'real.' It is true that functional imagery under a definition of Imitation as representation—whether of things or of states of mind—will be rhetorically simple, will be full or inclusive (often shocking and homely in order to be faithful), will be sensuously accurate or precise. If the Elizabethan and seventeenth-century poet so understood Imitation, then his imagery is certainly unfunctional, for it is rhetorically artful, decorously selective, and sensuously often imprecise. We may, of course, beg the question by saying that these poets were dishonest in their representation of reality—prettifying it, by using 'poetic diction' in obedience to a requirement called Decorum, and by imposing an 'unreal' ethical order in obedience to the didactic requirement. Of this they are frequently accused, but one would prefer a less presumptuous explanation if there is one.

There is an explanation in certain generalizations consistently proclaimed in theory, and demonstrated in the practice of poets of all schools (and many languages, for that matter), whatever their lesser quarrels. Current notions of an admirable poetic imitation of nature appear to me to have demanded that images achieve excellence on each of three levels, if we may so schema-

---

[15] I speak here obviously of Elizabethan notions of the relation of art to reality. The actual word 'Imitation' was, of course, frequently used to signify one of the processes by which students supposedly learned to maintain that relation justly—i.e., the imitation of Latin authors as an aid to the forming of a decorous Latin style; the tie lies in the meaning of Decorum. See below, chap. vi, n. 2; chap. ii, n. 27.

tize it, of poetic intention. The qualities of 'artificiality,' decorous selectivity, and relative sensuous imprecision are in fact the
very qualities which mark Renaissance images as functioning
toward Imitation as Renaissance writers conceived it.

The 'artificiality' is explicable by their intention to imitate by
making an artful construct, an artifact (to wrench the word
somewhat). This artifact was designed to please on grounds of
its formal excellence rather than by its likeness to the stuff of
life—a relatively formless subject matter not to be identified
with the poetic subject and evidently not even loosely identified
with 'reality.' On this level Renaissance writers and readers
judged images as an element of artistic form. This 'right artificiality' (Harvey's phrase) is a necessary but not a sufficient
criterion for excellence on a second level.

On this second level images must assist in Imitation conceived
as involving the artist's *ordering* of Nature, and his interpretation must have coherence. Art as coherent ordering is connected
above all with the artist's capacity to select images on grounds
of their appropriateness. Images so selected must be 'significant'; they will generally be consistent, apt, particular but not
local or singular.

Coherence in the images, again, is a necessary but not a sufficient criterion for excellence on a third level: Imitation as truth-
stating, as didactically concerned with the conveying of concepts—not simply orderly patterns, but what we should commonly call 'ideas' and 'values.' The second and third levels are
carefully distinguished only rarely. Most poems all through this
period and considerably later 'imitate nature' on all three levels.
On this third level the correspondence of the artist's 'truth' with
truth as it might by other approaches be apprehended or conveyed, the validity of his concepts and values, was subject to
appraisal. It is clear that images designed to assist in the poetic
statement of values would not succeed in this by virtue of their
sensuous precision. Poets well understood the role of a credible
vividness in accomplishing such intentions, especially in certain
genres; but profound suggestiveness or logical subtlety is likely
to displace sensuous accuracy in the images.

The fact that Renaissance notions of valid 'causes' for poems were such as I have indicated had far-reaching and deep and intricate effects upon the nature of the images used by Renaissance poets. The real reasons for the character of their images lie not in Renaissance poetic but in Renaissance philosophy. What is truly operative here is their definition of the real, and that definition is not precisely ours.

It would be unwise to stress only the differences. Modern critical comment has far outdistanced even the most rebellious of modern poems in revolt against some of these ideas; and careful restatement and exemplification will reveal their closeness to some ideas of our own.

CHAPTER II

'IMITATION' AND IMAGES

1. *Imitation and Images as Artifice*

O N THE level of formal excellence, images were expected to please readers looking specifically and with well-trained eyes for formal beauty rather than for a faithful description of a section, however small, of the world of fact. Formal beauty as far as images are concerned meant design given to the natural (otherwise inadequately expressive), through the admirable craftsmanship of the maker; and men of the Renaissance, like their predecessors, thought of the discipline of rhetoric as affording the poet necessary training in this respect.[1] Every sixteenth- and seventeenth-century image quoted will exemplify this kind of formal beauty, for this primary expectation is basic to the other criteria for images, and it was as well met by the carefully paired terms of Donne's similitude of the compass as by the *carmen correlativum* of Spenser's island of Phaedria—'No tree, whose braunches did not bravely spring; / No braunch, whereon a fine bird did not sit: / No bird, but did . . . .' (etc., *FQ*, II, vi, 13). The most seemingly ingenuous of Renaissance images are not formally artless; the images which would fail to meet this first expectation would be some of Whitman's enumerations, or Sandburg's casually piled modifiers, or that hill of moss beside Wordsworth's *Thorn*, 'Just half a foot in height.'

Extreme pleasure in poetry as a craft probably closed Elizabethan eyes to kinds of poetic pleasure which the Romantics

---

[1] Appendix, Note B, gives the most important of the bibliographical helps to an understanding of the incredible (to us) extent to which rhetorical training affected every Renaissance writer with a grammar-school or a university education. For England, virtually no writer except Deloney lies outside these influences, and his attempts to obscure that fact furnish some of the most amazing images in *Thomas of Reading* or *Jacke of Newburie*.

placed very high; it certainly operated to make this age impatient of artless reportage. As Gascoigne tells writers, 'if you do . . . . never studie for some depth of devise in the Invention, and some figures also in the handlyng therof, it will appeare to the skilfull Reader but a tale of a tubbe.' For the method of avoiding this insupportable result, he advises poets to make things-as-they-are more expressive by the use of some 'covert meane,' some rhetorical figure less obvious, more shadowed, than mere descriptive epithet:

If I should undertake to wryte in prayse of a gentlewoman, I would neither praise hir christal eye, nor hir cherrie lippe, etc. For these things are *trita et obvia*. But I would either finde *some supernaturall cause* wherby my penne might walke in the superlative degree, or els I would undertake to aunswere for any imperfection that shee hath, and thereupon *rayse the prayse* of hir commendacion. Likewise, if I should disclose my pretence in love, I would eyther make a strange discourse of some intollerable passion, or *finde occasion to pleade* by the example of some historie, or discover my disquiet in shadowes *per Allegoriam*. . . . .[2]

These are not so much remarks on style as on poetic subject, although they are sometimes quoted as illustrative of the 'quaint' early Elizabethan affection for ornamental trimmings. The two intentions posited—a 'praise' and a 'persuasion'—are typical intentions for lyric in the Renaissance;[3] of the two resulting poems, one would be an evaluation of the lady, and the other would be an argument with her. Only artificial heightening will successfully imitate the real subjects indicated by these intentions, for neither subject is simply a segment of actuality, either physical or psychological, and neither intention is merely descriptive, either of the lady or of the lover's feelings. Writers and readers who decline or suspect the pursuit of 'supernaturall causes' in poems will find a sufficient and convincing image of the beauty of a loved girl in MacLeish's 'And you stood in the door and the sun was a shadow of leaves on your shoulders / And a leaf on your hair' ('Not Marble nor the Gilded Monuments,' p. 48). But one will find, rather, images like those I have quoted earlier (Campion's lute and heart, or Herrick's

---

[2] *Certayne Notes of Instruction* (1575), in Gregory Smith, I, 48. The Latin phrases are italicized in the text.

[3] See below, chap. v, pp. 84 ff.

metaphor fetched from the dawn) in writers who pursue causes beyond the natural with that 'curious Imitation' which Harvey says is learned only in the 'apprentishood' of 'Arte' (*Pierce's Supererogation* [1593], in Gregory Smith, II, 276).

Elements of formal beauty in images are not to be thought of as added on but as intrinsic. We may quarrel with some poets' interpretations of the requirement of formal excellence. But at least Puttenham is not talking about adding detachable 'beauties' to a subject when he says that the writer must make use of 'figurative speaches the instrument wherewith we burnish our language fashioning it to this or that *measure and proportion*' (III, iii, pp. 142–43 [1589]). Thus poems come to possess that quality 'the Greeks called *Enargia*[4] . . . . because it geveth *a glorious lustre and light.*' This resultant 'light' is simply that 'illumination'—revealing harmony, order, proportion—which had been indicated time out of mind as an attribute of works of art achieving formal excellence, by Cicero, by Augustine, by Aquinas.[5] The metaphor was constantly and unself-consciously used by all manner of writers on poetry in the early Renaissance

[4] *Enargia* is not quite conveyed by 'a style vivid with images.' It was a favorite recommendation in the Renaissance, perhaps because of Quintilian's fairly full discussions in vi. ii. 32 and viii. iii. 61, where he equates it with Cicero's *illustratio et evidentia* and discusses its relation to the stirring of the emotions, and to mere lucidity, which does not 'thrust itself upon our notice.' It was sometimes confused with *energia;* see Chamard's note to Du Bellay's recommendation of *energies* (n. to i, chap. 5 [1549]). Sidney praises *energia*, that 'forciblenes' which betrays the writer's own feeling (I, 201; Gregory Smith's note gives references to Aristotle and Scaliger, who equates it with *efficacia*, a criterion I discuss in chap. viii). Puttenham's distinction between these two is not usual; his close relating of both to figured language is. Mazzoni's discussion is perhaps more typical, e.g., *Della difesa*, iii, esp. p. 686 (1587); the warnings against *soprabbondanza* follow in the next chapter.

[5] See K. E. Gilbert and H. Kuhn, *A History of Esthetics* (New York, 1939), pp. 135–44 and note. Thomas Aquinas' statement there quoted is as clear as any: the clarity of the beautiful is that property of beauty which is 'the shining forth of the *form* of a thing, either of a work of art or nature . . . . in such a manner that it is presented to the mind with all the fullness and richness of its perfection and order.' Through it the elements of beauty in things manifest themselves with clearness. Like Sidney, sixteenth-century writers generally use some such locution as 'figure forth,' 'make evident'; they were perfectly aware that the relation between what we call 'aesthetic effect' and form and conceptual content was not a simple one, and their theories on the formal qualities of images exhibit that awareness. Here, as elsewhere, the Renaissance made fruitful use of ideas inherited from or through the Middle Ages; I could frequently take citations quite as well from medieval as from later poetic and rhetoric and could illustrate equally well with images from Chaucer or Machaut or the Gawain poet.

and seventeenth century, and it was used to indicate the desirability—simultaneously—of qualities of imagery frequently set in opposition by modern critics of the two periods.

For example, 'illumination' is connected simultaneously with splendor, majesty, and with perspicuity, *clarté*, *chiarezza*. This has come to seem contradictory only as modern usage has stressed the relation of perspicuity to plainness, and omitted what Renaissance writers generally mention in the next breath: that this clearness is a matter of *fitness* in images and words, so that the manner of achieving it will vary as subjects vary. It is characteristic that Minturno's long discussion[6] beginning 'How can that be luminous which is hidden?' does not even warn against difficult conceits but simultaneously praises splendor and warns against crowding with ornaments, since a work cannot be illuminated if it is *less splendid by virtue of the number* of ornaments. Moreover, ornaments must be 'members,' not 'pieces.'

That is to say, 'clearness' is set in opposition not to intellectual difficulty but to confusion, and lustrous splendor is not praised instead of, but as an accompaniment of, structural lucidity. We all remember that Jonson, in speaking of perspicuity as the 'chiefe vertue of a style,' translated Quintilian's 'nothing so vitious in it, as to need an Interpreter' (*Discoveries*, p. 98; Quint. i. vi. 41). We should remember as well, however, that Sidney's famous sentence about the illuminating power of poetry is concerned with the power of images in all arts to bring a man 'to a iudicial *com*prehending' of matters; Sidney, too, is concerned that the grounds of wisdom should not 'lye darke before the *imaginative and iudging powre*' (in Gregory Smith, I, 165). Both poets are talking about an effect of art directly upon the 'inward conceits' of those who see, hear, and read; both are interested in 'true lively knowledge' and the functional use of art-ful writing to convey it with immediacy.

To ask for the aesthetic quality of *clarté*, then, is not to ask for a special type of style. And although Jonson talks about 'pure

---

[6] Appendix, Note C, defines further this conception of 'luminous' imagery by citations from Minturno, Sidney, and T. S. Eliot, making certain distinctions by means of images from Eliot.

and neat language,' and Sidney about language not too abstract and generalized, and Minturno about language 'non humilis, non abiecta,'[7] all three seem to recommend a kind of luminous immediacy, a formal *clarté* that was not called in question until long after the seventeenth century. Such a poetic might see as a flaw Donne's crowding of his tropes, but it would have to censure him for his failure to illuminate the subject for his reader rather than for his lack of mere expository lucidity. By the criterion of *clarté*, both early critics and late would have to admit praiseworthiness alike in the 'illustrious' majesty of Spenser's fourth *Hymne* and in the fiery clarity of 'Batter my heart, three person'd God,' with its three traditional 'shadowes *per Allegoriam.'*

Attempts to achieve 'clearness' so defined produced, in fact, both openly resplendent and artificially shadowed images; their common denominator was the art with which they were designed to convey a poet's exact and whole meaning, with force, to a reader. Chapman claimed 'clearness' for his covert figures, on the usual ground of fit and expressive clothing of high invention:

> That, *Enargia*, or *cleerenes of representation*, requird in absolute Poems is *not* the perspicuous delivery of a lowe invention; but high, and harty invention exprest in most *significant*, and unaffected phrase; it serves not a skilfull Painters turne, to draw the figure of a face onely to make knowne who it represents; but hee must lymn, give *luster, shaddow, and heightening;* which though ignorants will esteeme spic'd, and too curious, yet such as have the iudiciall perspective, will see it hath, *motion, spirit and life.* . . . .
>
> Obscuritie in affection of words, & *indigested* concets, is pedanticall and childish; but where it shroudeth it selfe in the hart of his subiect, utterd with *fitnes* of figure, and *expressive* Epethites; with that darknes wil I still labour to be shaddowed: . . . . [p. 49; prefatory letter to *Ovids Banquet of Sence* (1595)].

This understanding of the place and purpose of the shadowed image is not at all unlike Gascoigne's. It covers the kind of obscurity we looked at above in Yeats's 'Sailing to Byzantium' (st. 1), in which the poet's invention is high and complex but

[7] 'De perspicuitate,' *De poeta*, vi, p. 447; like Quintilian viii. ii. 2 (*sordida et humilia*). Or see Tomitano's three manners of writing a *narratio: Brieve, Chiara, Verisimile*, and his examples from Petrarch—differing in fulness of detail (*Ragionamenti della lingua Toscana* [Venice, 1546], Book ii, p. 156).

delivered in images whose connection with his interpretation is not left vague or tenuous to a careful reader. Chapman's defense of such darkness is as old as the discipline of rhetoric; his shadowing is an art-ful means to *clear* expression of the very life of a subject.

Chapman's connection between clearness or luster and painting a subject with motion, spirit, and life is also traditional; Quintilian discusses it at length.[8] And Minturno's and others' discussions lead one to suspect that *chiarezza* has more to do with poetry's power to *realize clearly* than with facile lucidity.[9]

I do not believe that there was any relaxation, in the early seventeenth century, in poets' sense of their responsibility for achieving *clarté* by formal artifice. If the characteristics thought of as opposed to *clarté* were those of inadequately perceivable *form*, and lifeless insipidity, surely the Metaphysicals neither desired nor exhibited them. Their 'obscure' images are as cunningly framed to achieve the eloquence that accompanied formal excellence as any in the period. Through all these discussions of 'illumination' and of the artistry which assists it, the rhetorical ideal of eloquent communication persists. The ingenious images of Metaphysical poets offer no evidence that they disagreed with Quintilian's insistence on the need for art in achieving what he defines, from the verb *eloqui*, as 'the production and communication to the audience of all that the speaker

---

[8] He adds that *perspicuitas* 'results above all from *propriety* in the use of words'; one form of this, deserving highest praise, is 'employment of words with the maximum of significance.' In Sherry's handbook of 1550, perspicuity is expressly identified with clearly realized description: '*Enargia*, evidence or perspicuitie called also descripcion rethoricall, is when a thynge is so described that it semeth to the reader or hearer y^t he beholdeth it as it were in doyng' (sig. E i^v). We see that these meanings suit with those of Jonson and others (emphasizing intelligibility), when we remember that 'light,' not prosaic plainness, is in question. It is not possible to think Jonson so ignorant of rhetorical tradition that he would use this weighted word to mean merely what most moderns mean by 'clearness.'

[9] See Minturno, *L'Arte poetica*, i, p. 22 (1564); see also *De poeta*, p. 118 (1559); Tasso, *Discorsi*, iv, p. 186 (1594) (treating of metaphor). Hoskins' (1599) list of figures used for 'Illustration' shows that his understanding of this technical term was far from the flattened modern notion of mere exemplification. The requirement of *clarté* by Du Bellay, the Spenserians, and others must be interpreted against the background of these uses. Certain oppositions posed between the Spenserians' lucidity and the Metaphysicals' intensity, supposedly resulting from their 'different' aesthetic, are accordingly suspect (see, e.g., R. L. Sharp, *From Donne to Dryden* [Chapel Hill, N.C., 1940], chap. i).

has conceived in his mind' (viii. Pref. 15). The typical modern objections to clearness and eloquence had not yet arisen, and commands like that of Verlaine's 'Art poétique'—'Prends l'éloquence et tords lui son cou!'—would have stifled the Metaphysicals' voices along with the rest.

Rhetorically figured language is not the sole instrument for achieving pure formal beauty, but it had the most immediately distinguishable effect upon images. This effect was not toward making them 'purely decorative.' Modern misrepresentations of the Renaissance writers' theory of the didactic usefulness of poetry have intervened to blind us to the extreme complexity and flexibility of their definitions of the functional image. That theory did not operate to divide images into the formally beautiful and the logically useful, with tolerance for the first and respect for the second.[10] The whole vast store of figures classified in the rhetorics (some producing images and some modifying their character) was used with the subtlest possible understanding of their effectiveness upon a reader's sensibilities. The enhancement of eloquence through rhetorical skill did, however, make images 'artificial' and carefully patterned:

> Call not these wrinkles, *graves;* If *graves* they were,
>   They were *Loves graves;* for else he is no where.
> Yet lies not Love *dead* here, but here doth sit
>   Vow'd to this trench, like an *Anachorit.*
> > (Donne, 'Elegie IX,' *The Autumnall,* p. 93)
> > (Author's italics)

Much of the vigor, clarity, and impressiveness *of the image in its functional relation to the whole* results from the use of the initial *catechresis,* a short *allegoria* needing a metaphor and a simile, with two more recherché types of figure, two common ones, and at least two or three schemes.[11] The Elizabethans were respon-

---

[10] See Appendix, Note D, for a more careful statement of the absence of opposition between the 'logical' and the 'imaginative'; and for certain possibly unhappy effects of this modern dichotomy upon modern criticism of Renaissance poetry.

[11] The figure *concessio* in the granting and remolding of the sense—inducing two *distinctio* or figures of difference, and epanalepsis in the second line; plus a mild apostrophe and a conventional personification, and several repetitive schemes which I shall not call by their complicated names.

sive to these delicacies of relationship between the eloquence and the poetic integrity of a poem, whether we are or not.

This is merely to say that part of the 'harmony' which was enjoyed was the skilful fitness of the figures, their relation to a luminous whole design. The extent to which response to this was conscious must have varied greatly, as it does among readers of all eras. When E. K. remarks appreciatively of Spenser's January eclogue, line 61, 'a pretty Epanorthosis . . . . and withall a Paronomasia,' he is saying what any educated reader might say; part of his pleasure, as sentence after sentence in his Prefatory Epistle would show, is that aesthetic pleasure of marking the *fitness* with which formal beauty of design has been imposed upon the natural.[12] With the eye fixed upon this *relationship*, it is as inadmissible to neglect formal beauty for matter as the other way around. 'Ye know not what hurt ye do to learning,' says Ascham, that most moral of critics, 'that care not for wordes but for matter, and so make a devorse betwixt the tong and the hart' (*Scholemaster* [1570], in Gregory Smith, I, 6). Neither are we told to care more for words; we are told not to make the separation.

Readers as well as poets are to attend to this warning. We forget it most easily if the subject has led the poet to heightening of an opulent rather than an ingenious kind. Modern readers are prone to think, for example, that either ineptitude in narrative or naïve pleasure in merely decorative ornament must have produced a long, slow, rhetorically ornate and sumptuous description like that of Mortimer's tower in Drayton's *Mortimeriados* (1596). But an artist's images are not likely to assist the aims we set for swift and faithful narrative of happenings if his intention is that his images should go far beyond naturalistic fidelity in expressiveness and should be part of a design which by its formal beauty heightened the significance of his matter. When

---

[12] I choose this well-worn example partly because H. D. Rix's analysis of the January eclogue enables a modern reader to see the kind of observant reading we would give to rhetorically patterned writing if we were Elizabethans (*Rhetoric in Spenser's Poetry* ['Pennsylvania State College Studies,' No. 7 (1940)], pp. 64 ff.). One of the most striking things about the very numerous notes by E. K. which presuppose rhetorical training is the evidence they give of a kind of reading pleasure which modern readers are not prepared to share easily and immediately.

Drayton re-wrote the piece six years later as *The Barons Warres*, he made change after change in the imagery. These changes show not a simple outgrowing of 'rhetoric' but rather a maturer attention to the Decorum which governed the relation of ornament to subject.[13] In Donne's image above and in Drayton's tower, the artifices used differ as they properly should according to matter, genre, cause of poem. Donne's image is ingenious and Drayton's is florid, but either poet exemplifies the normal methods used to satisfy that primary requirement of formal design which is here discussed. The images quoted in other chapters will exemplify these methods dozens of times over, in endless variety, up and down the entire range of the period.

Another difference between Elizabethan notions and ours I may not omit from this section—the absence of opposition between the 'artificial' and the 'natural.' The reasons for this carry us into Renaissance conceptions of the reality to be imitated through the help of images. One of Tasso's statements will explain very quickly why 'art' in Renaissance images was formally rather than naturalistically conceived, and yet was not divorcible from subject, also conceived formally as idea (equated with *res*, in Scaliger's Book iii). The poet makes likenesses of 'cose sussistenti': 'But what sort of things shall we say subsist? Are they the intelligible or the visible? Certainly they are the intelligible.'[14] This is the extreme of the position, but later citations will show how widely accepted was the general position, in various forms which all had the same effect upon

[13] A very few examples: Drayton cuts, later, the pun on Orwell (or ill), the apostrophe to Thames and Isis (*Mort.*, 1338, 1604; cf. *BW* iv; he is stern even with lovely images like 'Nor let thy Ships lay forth their silken wings'). He cuts the *accumulatio* of apostrophes to the letter of Mortimer received by the Queen (2758; cf. *BW* vi, losing 'pretty' and 'radical' images alike, e.g., 'Pully which draw'st the curtaine of the Day'). Compare the change of image from the soft wax kissing her fingers to red wax sticking to them like a portent of blood (*BW*, st. 90). On the other hand, there are consciously rhetorical additions to *BW*: an *icon* of Mischief, a *descriptio* of the potion, *sententia* deliberately set off, 'A Metaphor from Timber' and other expanded analogies (*BW* ii, 5; iii, 7, 41). There is constant interplay between all Drayton's reasons for revisions—stylistic, politic, structural; see K. Tillotson's excellent notes in Vol. V of the Hebel edition, where variants in editions of *BW* may be found (1603 to 1619, too complicated to notice here).

[14] *Discorsi*, Book ii, p. 50; in Gilbert, p. 477.

imagery. To put it too bluntly, the poet who imitates not the visible world but the intelligible as manifested in the visible will not consider that the use of artifice to emphasize form makes imagery less 'true to Nature.'

Instead of thinking about differences between images in that they offer, respectively, 'artificial' or 'natural' likenesses of the visible world, we must think about differences between images in that they imitate the different aspects poets see of the intelligible world. The following four images happen to deal with a similar phenomenon or content—a flush brought to the cheek. This is unimportant; what is important is the difference in the four poetic subjects (the 'intelligible' things) illuminated by the images. Those differences were a most potent factor in producing great differences in form, much as the blushes must have resembled each other when they took place.

> As after pale-fac'd Night, the Morning fayre
> The burning Lampe of heaven doth once erect,
> With her sweet Crimson sanguining the ayre,
> On every side with streakie dappl's fleckt,
> The circled roofe in white and Azure deckt,
> Such colour to her cheekes these newes do bring. . . . .
>> (the news brought to Queen Isabella, of Mortimer's
>> joining the faction against Edward II [Drayton's
>>> *Mortimeriados*, vs. 141])

> And ever and anone the rosy red,
> Flasht through her face, as it had been a flake
> Of lightning, through bright heaven fulmined;
> At last the passion past she thus him answered.
>> (Britomart when describing Artegall to
>> her companion [*FQ*, III, ii, 5])

> wee understood
> Her by her sight; her pure, and eloquent blood
> Spoke in her cheekes, and so distinctly wrought,
> That one might almost say, her body thought. . . . .
>> (Donne, *The second Anniversary*, 243, p. 258)

> And troubled bloud through his pale face was seene
> To come, and goe with tydings from the hart,
> As it a running messenger had beene.
> At last resolv'd to worke his finall smart,
> He lifted up his hand. . . . .
>> (Red Crosse, in the Despair canto [*FQ*, I, ix, 51])

All these are 'artificial,' no one more than any other. Of the
many factors which have operated to make them differ as to
formal qualities, none is more important than the widely differing purposes which accompany the four *differing* choices of
aspects of nature to be imitated (for 'art' stands in the same
relation to 'nature' in all of them). Drayton magnifies the
Queen's beauty and her guilty love, using an exalted simile that
requires ornate sensuous elaboration; Donne clarifies the notion
of the relation between a fair body and a fairer soul through the
use of a combined synecdoche and metaphor, based on the
rhetorical commonplace of the relation of eloquence to thought
and drawn out to a logical conclusion; Spenser uses in the first
case a simile based on common qualities to assist a dramatic but
simple narrative purpose; and in the second, a comparison,
based on common purpose, to assist the purposes of psychological
narrative (the heart is the seat of the will, and the next lines
indicate Red Crosse's decision to accept despair's subtly in-
sinuated advice to self-destruction).

The four images assist the poets' attempts to trace out four
different structures of meaning; of each meaning the outer appearances of things (though similar to the eye) are a true expression, but without the poet's art an insufficiently luminous
or striking one. In this sense 'le naturel' is not 'suffisant,' as Du
Bellay says (ii, chap. 3) in a famous passage bewailing the fact
that there is no sleep for poets. The task of imposing form was
not assumed to be easy, but neither was it assumed to set the
poet in opposition to 'nature,' the mother of forms within the
poet's mind as without it. The qualities of all four passages
quoted rest on a conception of naturalness in images which is
far removed from any Romantic equation of the most natural
with the most artless—as far removed as is Quintilian's definition: 'No, that which is most natural is that which nature permits to be done to the greatest perfection.'[15] Similarly, Tasso

---

[15] 'Verum id est maxime naturale, quod fieri natura optime patitur' (ix. iv. 5). The
discussion is a mine of Renaissance commonplaces (whether language in the rough is
more manly—*virilem;* why train the vine, then? why not continue to live in huts? etc.).
See n. 22 below. Spenser, in a famous passage in defense of the natural life (*FQ*, II, vii),

tells the poet to seek his subject among things disposed to receive form (p. 32). This is advice, of course, which no poet of any
time can help trying to follow. In addition, however, definitions
of nature at the time these poets wrote encouraged them to see
no enmity between her and an order-imposing art.[16] For such
reasons as these, then, the Renaissance image could be extremely and carefully artificial without being thought of as unreal, as
not natural, or as mere decoration.

Although the opposition did not lie between artificiality and
artless naturalness, there was, of course, a vicious opposite to
true art. Renaissance emphasis on the difficulty of the art of
poetry is a commonplace, and it is frequently accompanied by
an emphasis which is equally a commonplace—disdain of false
art. Both emphases are as characteristic of Sidney as of Jonson, present equally in Du Bellay or in Carew's elegy on Donne.
And none of them thinks true art need be confused with that
'feigned art with pompous words' which Giraldi Cinthio says
leads writers to 'swelling words and strong epithets,' to 'bloody
dead men' in laments and nothing but flowers, caves, waves, soft
breezes, if gladness is written of ('An Address to the Reader by
the Tragedy of *Orbecche*' [1541], in Gilbert, p. 245). The Muses'
garden was not to be purged of such soft melting phrases and
pedantic weeds by a return to Nature as the last century and a
half has defined her. Not in Carew's eyes, at least; he does not
praise Donne for a return to the natural, but for true and right
artificiality. He is as scornful of mere ballad-rhyme, not 'refined,' as of the exiled trains of gods and goddesses. 'Nature with

---

has Guyon make pronouncements against adding 'superfluities' to 'Untroubled Nature,'
but he shows no sign of regarding this as including a condemnation of elaborate similes;
the sacrilege of digging up gold and silver for Mammon's uses did not cover the mining
of the jewels of rhetoric. There is no inconsistency here. Spenser is talking about in-
temperance and pride—falsity of ends, not elaborateness of means; licentious and
pompous-proud language would come under the same ban, as an offense against Nature.
But not artificial language.

[16] Art is the 'coadiutor to nature,' 'a surmounter of her skill' (her expressive skill, not
her pleasing prettiness; Puttenham, III, xxv, p. 303). These two are inescapably co-
operative 'conjurateurs' (see Thomas Sebillet, *Art poétique françoys* [1548], ed. Félix
Gaiffe [Paris, 1910], i, chap. 3, p. 25; *L'Art poëtique du Jacques Peletier* [1555], ed.
André Boulanger [Paris, 1930], i, chap. 2, p. 73).

fit ornament'—the phrase is Giraldi Cinthio's, but it indicates that which is set over against false art, throughout the period.[17]

Feigned or pedantic or lifeless art does not find its opposite, then, in the natural feeling of the heart, rebelliously bursting through the trammels of form. Sidney says 'look in thy heart and write,' but he is talking about 'inventing' or finding matter; and, anyhow, no one gives as poetic advice the Elizabethan analogue to what this counsel means to most moderns—no one bids the poet look into his liver to find words. No school advocated as desirable poetic imagery 'that naturall stile' for which Harvey taunts Nashe so unmercifully. Harvey's snorts of ironic scorn for him who calls carelessness 'nature' show how far both he and his enemies were from a poetic in which 'spontaneous' meant praise for an artist:

It is for Cheeke or Ascham to stand levelling of Colons, or squaring of Periods, by measure and number: *his* [Nashe's] penne is like a spigot, and the Wine presse a dullard to *his* Ink-presse. There is a certaine lively and frisking thing . . . . that scorneth to be a booke-woorme, or to imitate the excellentest artificiality of the most renowned worke-masters that antiquity affourdeth. The witt of this & that odd Modernist is their owne. . . . . Whuist Art! And Nature advaunce thy precious Selfe in thy most gorgeous and magnificent robes![18]

Those who substituted vigor for art continued to be laughed at. The 'terrible gunpowder' of the pamphlet style did not find

[17] This does not quarrel with the evidence of widespread distrust of the vanities of rhetoric (adduced, e.g., by R. F. Jones in 'The Moral Sense of Simplicity,' *Studies in Honor of F. W. Shipley* [St. Louis, 1942], pp. 265–87). Current rhetorical theory recognized the plain style as proper to many purposes, certainly to those of the theologians and scientists whose disclaimers of 'eloquence' are so numerous; and vain eloquence was berated on all hands—while then, as now, men disagreed on the line dividing 'true' from 'false' elaboration. When these disclaimers occur in prefaces, the centuries-old epistolary convention of including them as part of a *captatio benevolentiae* must be remembered.

[18] From *Pierce's Supererogation* (1593), in Gregory Smith, II, 277. Harvey's entire discussion is in the vein of ironic satire—including those references to the marvels of the new style, 'the nippitaty of the nappiest grape' (p. 250), which R. L. Sharp interprets without this reservation (*op. cit.*, p. 37; in n. 9 above). We may find some of Harvey's applications pedantic, but the fundamental tenets in his theory continued to be accepted as sound—hence the power of his irony. In verse, the newer writers do not pour themselves out in artless images; they turn from some types of rhetorical art and choose others, equally orthodox. Their images do not show them as repudiating what Boccaccio calls *exquisita locutio* (*De geneal. d.*, XIV, vii; the whole chapter is congenial to Renaissance ideas).

adherents in any poetic school; and what is analogous, in imagery, to 'squaring of Periods' in sentence structure continued to characterize all but mere ballad wits. Applications of the principle of Decorum were to vary, most with genres, less with date. But neither Spenserian nor lover of 'strong lines' was to relinquish as a first requirement for images that proper artificiality which characterized the parts of a construct designed to satisfy laws of formal excellence.

This is only a first expectation for images. They may be either openly illustrious or ingeniously shadowed; they will always be eloquent. Although this eloquence is a function of form, the constant in all eloquent images is their expressiveness, that inescapable relation to the poet's subject by virtue of which they vary infinitely as poets' subjects vary.

2. *Imitation and Author's Ordering*

The requirement of right artificiality, strictly defined, was not a sufficient criterion for images in so far as they assisted—on the second level of aesthetic intention—in expressing the author's interpretation of nature, the meaning to be conveyed by his reordering. This conception of what Imitation involved led to a careful selection of images on grounds of their decorous relation to the coherent pattern which is the author's subject.[19]

This rigorous selectivity according to the concept of Decorum[20] has caused great difficulty to modern minds. Although we have balked most at the way it functions with respect to characterization in fiction or drama, it functions in a precisely similar way with respect to images. Hoskins commends Sidney's *Arcadia* because Philoclea shows always 'mild discretion,' and Mopsa, 'proud ill-favored sluttish simplicity'—'wherever you

[19] The effect of principles outlined in this section upon the character of specific images is illustrated in sec. 1 of chap. vii, 'The Criterion of Significancy.'

[20] Since fitness or Decorum was the basic literary desideratum during the Renaissance, it had manifold aspects which I must define gradually throughout Part I, and I shall treat it in a culminating chapter (ix) as a specific criterion for images. Here we are concerned with it only in that it was the regulative concept which held the writer's images (and his characters and his incidents) to his chosen subject or interpretation.

find them';[21] and Spenser introduces no lovely thing into his Bowre of Blisse that we can feel to be quite innocently lovely. The modern eye is quick to see in this an irresponsible disregard of the complexities of human character and experience. The Elizabethan answer to such a charge of irresponsibility is Donne's answer to Ben Jonson's complaints against his *Anniversary:* 'that he described *the Idea of a Woman*' (see chap. vii, n. 4, below). This intention once accepted, Donne's 'blasphemies' were entirely decorous, and decorous in the same sense and for the same reason as Sidney's 'perfect expressing' of qualities and affections in his characters.

We do not find Renaissance writers offering either the defense 'But I described *my* idea of a woman' or 'But I described how *that* woman was.' These phrases—they would be the modern answers to Jonson—do not seem to fit their intentions. Elizabethan poets were far more likely to be concerned with imitating Cicero's 'intellectual ideal by reference to which the artist represents those objects which do not themselves appear to the eye' (*Orator* iii; a Ciceronian commonplace in the Renaissance, in various phrasings). Or, as a result of the pervasiveness of Platonic and Neo-Platonic conceptions of reality, they were more likely to be concerned with imitating Plotinus' ideal form and order, or the very pattern and concentrated essence of Love, or Anger (or Variety—see Donne's 'Elegy XVII,' p. 113). Or (if one prefers Aristotelian terms for a point of view which affected the practice of poetry similarly, however different its metaphysical implications) they were more likely to be concerned with what Fracastoro calls 'imitat[ing] not the particular [that is, "the object exactly as it is"] but the simple idea clothed in its own beauties, which Aristotle calls the universal'

[21] Hoskins' notion of how one goes about creating real characters is quite the opposite of the naturalistic writer's: one first learns to 'set down an humor' truly, then fixes names; each character 'expresses' an affection throughout 'with steadfast decency' (decorum, of course; *Directions for Speech and Style* [1599], pp. 41–42). This affected imagery especially in narrative poetry; it was, of course, a commonplace (see, e.g., Minturno, *L'Arte poetica*, i, 45 ff., on the dispositions of the mind). The Elizabethans were no more naïve than we are in their observation of human character; they regarded the whole piece as the unit, and we look at the single character. Appendix, Note E, comments on the possibility of a critical change of heart.

(*Naugerius* [1555], fol. 158ᵛ; trans., p. 60). The commonly held conception is phrased in dozens of ways, of which the most familiar to us perhaps is Sidney's discussion of embellished nature. Probably equally familiar to the Renaissance Englishman were Scaliger's many statements concerning the poet's imitation of the perfect pattern, not the imperfect particular object.[22]

As we shall see, imagery was bound to be affected when such ideas as these watched over poets' putting-in and their leaving-out. Elizabethan poets differ most from modern ones perhaps in what they thought it quite truthful to excise; but the range and treatment of what was put in were affected as well. Techniques vary extremely; what is shared is the common refusal to narrow the task of images to that of a truthful report of experience. Even when he writes on 'Going to Bed,' Donne is ready to desert the particular for the personified universal, and apostrophizes the idea of 'Full nakedness!' for full fifteen lines, with three analogies to demonstrate why 'bodies uncloth'd must be, / To taste whole joyes' ('Elegy XIX,' p. 119). Instead of confining himself to the story of Malbecco's experience of jealousy, Spenser transcends the novelist's method with a piercing and sudden daring, and Malbecco 'Yet can never dye, but dying lives,'

> woxen so deform'd, that he has quight
> Forgot he was a man, and *Gealousie* is hight.
>
> (*FQ*, III, x, 60) (Author's italics)

The Elizabethan poet simply has no nervousness about dealing overtly with universals (perceptual, affective, and conceptual). By rare good luck, Fracastoro illustrates his statement of the theory with an image. A heightened visual image from Virgil serves as an example of how the poet writes when he 'seeks all the adornments of speech, all the beauties' which can be given, not to some particular, but to this 'different idea' he makes 'for himself, of untrammeled and universal beauty.' The 'adornments' which Fracastoro isolates for comment do not chiefly

---

[22] Later objectors do not call these basic tenets in question, when the particular critics here cited ceased to be the fashionable authorities. See Appendix, Note F, for other citations and for helps to interpreting the thirty-five meanings of the equivocal word 'Nature' which may be isolated in Renaissance writing on poetry.

individualize; they select such particulars as will best indicate the intended universal. Such is the common intention of Elizabethan and early seventeenth-century imagery.

This does not force the poet to omit apparently discordant elements of experience; it does force him to make up his mind, and subtly indicate, why he chose to admit them. The coherence is imposed by the author's meaning, by subject and not by stuff. Although such ideas have not ceased to affect poetic imagery, the writers of the Renaissance, as they were more comfortable in the acceptance, were more bold in the application of them.

This recognition of author's *interpretation* as controlling subject must be distinguished from the modern author's portrayal of his own *process* of interpreting or feeling, of 'the very movement of thought in a living mind,' the 'interplay of perception and reflection' (these phrases come from F. O. Matthiessen's and Edmund Wilson's essays on Eliot).[23] The earlier author's subject was different, however similar his stuff; his subject was still 'his meaning,' not 'himself-seeing-it.' One finds the choice of the images made upon different grounds, and their structural function differently affecting their nature, if one reads first Eliot's 'Prufrock' (p. 11) and then even a difficult border-line case like Donne's 'Elegy XI, Upon the losse of his Mistresses Chaine, for which he made satisfaction' (p. 96). Eliot shows us a man having a thought. Donne arranges the thoughts a man had, upon losing his mistress' property, into a carefully logical and hence wantonly witty exposition of the 'bitter' and disproportionate cost of ladies.

The measure of the difference is the strict logical coherence of Donne's images. This does not mean that the images are not sensuously vivid; only that they are not primarily so. Each is chosen and presented as a 'significant' part of an ordered pattern, and every care is taken to make that order rationally

---

[23] *The Achievement of T. S. Eliot* (Oxford, 1935), p. 13; *Axel's Castle* (New York, 1932), p. 107; these are modern critical commonplaces. One might use equally well phrases from C. Brooks's discussion objecting to Wilson, in which he stresses the similarities between Metaphysical and Symbolist poetry, denying the importance of logical unity in either, and comparing Donne's poetry to Yeats's, whose symbols are 'nothing but concrete and meaningful images in terms of which the play of the mind may exhibit itself' (*Modern Poetry and the Tradition* [Chapel Hill, N.C., 1939], pp. 59 ff.).

apprehensible. The relation of each image to the point in hand is as clear, to us, as logical association can make it—the relation of circumcis'd French crowns and unlickt Spanish bear-whelps to bad money, the relation of martyred angels in the fire to wasted good money. Eliot's 'lonely men in shirt-sleeves, leaning out of windows' are no less clearly seen than Donne's 'lowd squeaking Cryer,' but their attachment to their author's meaning is; for Donne's crier is a perspicuously logical part of his suggestion that the lady might save more than money by letting him out of the restitution.[24]

The fact that Donne's images and his logical pattern lead us to an unconventional and satirical conclusion (what lady is worth *good* money?) is neither here nor there. It would not operate in the least to make his subject or images indecorous either to his contemporaries or to his predecessors. The Elizabethan demand for a unified and coherent meaning does not confuse coherency with moral orthodoxy. The requirement that images be 'significant' of a coherent meaning rationally imposed by the author and rationally apprehensible by the reader holds in Donne's poem, with just the same kind of effect upon images, as it holds in poems that state the more usual conclusions made about ladies during this period. Sensuous images, like others, were scrutinized for their decorum in this respect.

3. *Imitation and Didactic Intention*

At this level of intention, Imitation involves the presentation of valid concepts about the order and operation of nature in its most inclusive sense. This 'useful' purpose of poetry receives attention not alone in discussion of aims but in one treatment

[24] This is not an especially typical Donne poem, but, even so, it would seem to me that Allen Tate's phrase 'the poet's dramatization of his own personality' indicates for it a modern subject-and-intention which will not account for what is left out, nor for the order of what is put in (*Reactionary Essays* [New York, 1936], p. 72). If we speak as psychologists of ultimate motivations, and thus weaken this statement into something that fits all expression in any medium in any era, then it will (if true) fit Donne also.

For the differences we feel between this kind of poem and, e.g., the Drayton and Spenser passages quoted in sec. 1, I should urge both more numerous and more complicated reasons, and the reader will find more of them perhaps in chap. ix than anywhere else.

of ornament after another. Renaissance poetic is so universally
adamant on the question of the importance of Wisdom as well
as Eloquence that I need only take up here certain possible mis-
applications of Renaissance didactic theory.

It leads to fatal misinterpretations of the didactic aim in
Renaissance poetic to speak of it unconnected with that other
universally accepted requirement, the decorous relation between subject and style. The preoccupation with this relationship shows that the theorists were more aware than were the
poorer poets of the period that the didactic aim can be vicious
if matter be considered a good separable from the expressing of
it. Ascham saw this danger fully as clearly as those modern critics
who fear the overdidactic reader. 'They be not wise therefore
that say, "What care I for a mans wordes and utterance, if his
matter and reasons be good" ' (in Gregory Smith, I, 6). Such
men generally have an ax to grind, some 'private and parciall
matter,' some propaganda to spread. But Ascham does not
therefore see 'the didactic aim' as the enemy of poetry. He at-
tacks instead such a reader's arbitrary division between matter
and utterance. Obviously, the principle of Decorum rules out,
as an understanding of the didactic aim, any idea that one
should be able to reduce a poem to some paraphrasable message. Thus to restate 'a poem's ideas' is simply to deny those
ideas their fit and decent form. Above all the many disagreements on the exact definition of poetry's aims there runs this
constant theme of pleasure in a fit relation, and critics are as
quick to imply that mere enjoyment of a content is an enjoyment not possible in poetry as to assert that there must be sound
matter to enjoy.

Of course, critics were at variance as to *what* constituted wise
matter, what concepts were valid and valuable, what images
demonstated imperfect integration of meaning and ornament. A
rebel like Castelvetro states firmly that the end of poetry is to
'delight and to recreate the minds of the crude multitude'; he
objects to versified natural philosophy; his statement of the
various conceptual universals which give pleasure to the spectator of a tragedy might not have satisfied an Ascham (*Poetica*

d'Arist. [1576]; trans. in Gilbert, pp. 307, 351). But such disagreements do not mean that a Castelvetro is to be placed with
modern antididactic critics who relinquish the criterion of an
intended rationally coherent meaning to be examined for its
validity.

Some types of disagreement conceivably draw in the question
of imagery. Castelvetro scores Scaliger for the 'absurdity' of
seeing in Aeneas a constant moral perfection (*ibid.*, p. 317).
But Scaliger does what the didactic theory does *not* ask a reader
to do: praises a certain specific moral meaning which he is determined to find as a primary aim in the poem—and hence he
mistakes his author's subject. This is easy to do. It occurs frequently, and irrespective of a reader's search for didactic meanings, since it is caused rather by insufficient attention to the
decorum to which the poet has held his images.

Modern readers are more likely to mistake the author's
meaning by forgetting that there may be a controlling didactic
aim than by hunting for one, like Scaliger. For example,
Spenser, in Una's lament for the supposed death of Red Crosse,
chooses not poignantly simple or particularized images, but instead a high-flown and lengthy apostrophe to the sun:

> O lightsome day, the lampe of highest *Iove*,
> First made by him, mens wandring wayes to guyde, ...
> Henceforth thy hated face for ever hyde,
> And shut up heavens windowes shyning wyde:
> For earthly sight can nought but sorrow breed. . . . .[25]

This may seem to us, for one thing, a lamentable failure in the
precise communication of emotional experience. But the poet's
subject is not 'how the girl Una felt at the loss of her lover'; it is
the infinite sadness of the breach between right Truth and Red
Crosse, the representative of human kind, and the image must
hold all the heavy weight of all the ways and times that breach

[25] Etc., *FQ*, I, vii, 23. (Author's italics.) The parallel with *I Tamb.*, V, 2, does not
affect my remarks. Borrowings often (as here) demonstrate the extreme sensitivity of
Renaissance poets to points of decorum; the astrological point of the image in Bajazeth's
curse, and the relation between the obscuring of God's Light and man's severance of connections with Truth in Una's *lament*, are proper, respectively, to the differing purposes
of the authors. W. B. C. Watkins, 'The Plagiarist: Spenser or Marlowe?' *ELH*, XI
(1944), 249–65, gives citations to previous discussions.

has been made. The heightening of the style is one with the conveying of the matter. Spenser makes here no division between style and matter, but we do—if we demand, much like Scaliger, our own preferred meaning.

The acceptance of conceptually definable aims for poetry meant stress on the ideational element even in sensuous images. This meant often the use of images with known significances, like those of myth. The image unsuited to didactic poetry is, however, not the image drawn from unconventional or 'low' matters, but the malproportioned or the irrelevant image. The poet's images to be decorous must keep close to the heart of his subject. The precise local particulars so congenial to modern taste are absent from sixteenth- and seventeenth-century poems; nevertheless, any homely particular which could take on symbolic or ideational significance could be as decorously admitted to a poem as Una's lamb. Such reservations and discriminations in the use of images proceed from an acceptance of poetry's responsibility to convey the poet's ordering of the world of values and meanings.

Neither all poets nor all critics would have agreed with a Sidney's or a Lodge's statement of didactic aims. But I cannot find that early or late objectors to overnarrowly defined didacticism take any one of three characteristic modern ways out: the substitution of nonlogical ('imaginative') truth as poetic subject; or the substitution of naturalistic representation as a poetic aim; or the notion that one may look on and understand how a certain poet might believe what seem to him to be truths, withholding judgment the while on the truth or falsity of concepts conveyed. Eliot's discussion on 'entering the world' of Dante, 'suspending both belief and disbelief,' states this last and common attitude of modern criticism with more delicacy than most. The whole vast body of Renaissance defense of the ancients shows how inconceivable such an attitude would have been to these men, with their very different conception of poetic belief. Their approaches to older poets show also how the habit of thinking in metaphor (partly inherited from the Middle Ages) operated to remove difficulties of 'belief' that loom much larger to the more inflexible modern mind, primarily trained to be literal.[26]

These three commonest modern forms of revolt against didacticism do not find Elizabethan or seventeenth-century exponents. Nevertheless, abuses of didacticism could be fought on quite as firm a ground by the Renaissance judge of imagery as by any modern critic, for as the law of decorum was stern in ruling out beautiful non-sense, so was it equally stern in ruling out non-beautiful sense. The position where careful statement enables one to examine it to the bottom seems to be that neither of these is really possible in good poetry; it is everywhere accepted that neither is commendable.

Thus, on all three levels of poetic intention—of formal construct, of coherent ordering, of artistic statement of truth—divorce between poetic subject and image is inadmissible. This is recognized in the humblest corner of the first level; the vices of style as the rhetorical handbooks describe them are some form or other of such a divorce (*tapinosis, bomphiologia, et al.*, if any reader wishes to pursue them). This is quite out of line with the currently received opinion, to which I cannot subscribe, that the Elizabethan stress on rhetoric normally produced such a divorce. Emphasis on technique does not produce 'ornament for ornament's sake'; foolish technicians who have nothing to say by means of the technique produce it. The Elizabethan period exhibits the normal number of foolish writers.

It is quite possible that we add to the category some who do not belong there by misjudging the matter their images were meant to illuminate, or by disagreeing with its validity, arguing thence a disproportion between their heightened style and their matter (to us trivial or unprepossessing). For it is true that, outside the drama, that matter does not satisfy the peculiar modern humility (arrogant enough) which thirsts for presentation of the whole baffling, ironic, conflict-filled complex of life. In so far as this thirst is just the special modern form of avidity for the

---

[26] See below, chap. vii, sec. 2. The Eliot quotation is from *Selected Essays* (New York, 1932), p. 219.

particular, we tend even to prefer reading around the resolutions of the ironies, giving our attention to that presentation of conflict which is often the first step in the dialectical method favored by later poets. Even our honest discontent with their concepts we do not like to call by just that name, the whole matter of the poetic statement of 'truths' having got such a shady reputation by reason of its blander adherents.

If we cannot lend ourselves sympathetically to these understandings of imitation and of reality, however, we shall read sixteenth- and seventeenth-century images with a certain inner hostility.[27] Our suspicion is waked when we find that the Elizabethan was not generally writing (rarely even for the length of a single image) 'here is the thing that happened, here the object, the landscape, the human being that was seen.' It still more wakes our suspicions to notice that he was not generally writing 'this is how *I* felt about the experience, how *I* saw the object, the landscape.' A Renaissance poet's conception of the subject of poetry and of the nature of truth allowed him to seek to present true meanings of things without looking first to the local particularities they exhibited (which the Romantic and late Romantic did not dare to do); and his conception of poetry's aim and of the nature of truth led him to stress the 'conceipt' without stressing the conceiver (which the modern does not care to do). This distribution of pressures removed the necessity for support in the shape of imagery with a sensuous function as we see it most commonly used in modern lyric, short narrative, or reflective poem.

[27] Although my organization of Renaissance principles was made on the basis of their own theory and practice before the appearance of T. M. Greene's *The Arts and the Art of Criticism* (Princeton, 1940), the aesthetic orientation of these principles will be more clearly seen by reference to a modern restatement of the problems of aesthetics such as Professor Greene's. See Appendix, Note G. In response to his suggestion that critics deliberately seek more common ground by agreement as to categories discussable, I have occasionally substituted his terms for similar ones of my own or for Elizabethan ones.

CHAPTER III

UT PICTURA POESIS AND FUNCTIONAL SENSUOUS IMAGERY

THE Renaissance tag that would seem most indicative of a theory of ornament commending purely decorative images is that Horatian half-quotation, *ut pictura poesis*, so scornfully pointed to by twentieth-century criticism and so frequently traced and discussed by modern scholarship. Despite the latter aid, it is very difficult to determine exactly what practicing poets would have understood by this counsel and, hence, exactly what types of images we are justified in declaring it to have produced.

It would seem, and it is generally assumed,[1] that the injunction 'poetry should be like painting' would lead to ornament like pigment applied to meanings to decorate them. There are three imputations here, all laid at the door of sixteenth-century poets with respect to their use of 'painted' imagery: (1) the choice of pleasing matter lending itself to pleasing detail; (2) the pleasure in mere resemblance to the actual, resulting in facile expansion of detail; and (3) the separableness of 'colors' from meaning.

These results seem to me implied in the dictum only *in case* we think of painting as 'a decorative and hence pleasing copy of the external qualities of a real (usually pleasing) object.' In other words, painting as not even a good representational painter would define it. It is not at all certain that Renaissance poets so thought of painting and hence so understood the comparison. Suppose one substitutes—and then re-reads the counsel *ut pictura poesis*—'Painting is the art of significant form'; or

[1] Partly through the influence of Irving Babbitt's discussion of later use of the dictum, in *The New Laokoön* (Boston, 1910); this stimulating treatment appears to have disturbed the proper historical focus in, e.g., R. Tuve, *Seasons and Months: Studies in a Tradition of Middle English Poetry* (Paris, 1933), chap. iii. In discussing Renaissance uses of the comparison, I must choose to remain as pre-Lessing as possible, despite undoubted connections.

'Painting is an art which must avail itself of "individual and perceptible means in representing" the subject.'[2] The odium of meaningless ornament and of separable-decoration-stuck-on vanishes. Now it is extremely difficult to be sure that we are justified in omitting just such overtones of meaning from the Renaissance poet's practical understanding of the comparison.

I do not wish to take Sidney, who overtly states that he includes such meanings. It may illuminate the question of what poets thought this dictum demanded of their imagery if we consider what some other poets themselves praise in graphic works of art. I choose three; the three are chosen either because they are suspect or because modern criticism assumes that they differ in their poetic as to just this point. The passages are Drayton's painted tower, in *Mortimeriados* (1596) (2311 ff.), revised in *The Barons Warres* (1603) (vi, 233 ff.); Spenser's House of Busyrane, III, xi; and Donne's 'His Picture' (p. 86).[3]

It is, of course, a commonplace that Elizabethans wished pictures to be 'lifelike.' We may break down this general commendation into what such a demand would require of images, with the help of Drayton's phrases: the sledge seeming still to

[2] The quoted phrase is Mazzoni's, in a section on the necessity of credibility; he is speaking of Dante's use of *Idoli e imagini* and of contemplative teaching by the poet (*Della difesa*, intro.; see trans. in Gilbert, p. 365). An earlier discussion relates the dictum to the *particolarità, evidenza, chiarezza* of narrative poetry especially (intro.).

In using in this chapter the phrase made famous by Clive Bell, I do not suggest that Renaissance painters, writers, and public would have subscribed to all his statements in *Art* (New York, [1914]). They would not. They would disagree on the irrelevance of the representational element (pp. 25, 225), with the definition of what is significant (pp. 8, 12, 53), and so on. I do suggest that we falsify matters when we apply *ut pictura poesis* as though the Renaissance had a mid-nineteenth-century understanding of that phrase, and that mid-nineteenth-century enthusiasm for naturalistic representation omits from consideration some ideas of the nature and function of art which both Renaissance thinkers and artists and some modern schools try to pursue (e.g., Bell, pp. 69, 81–82, 112–14, 220). It should perhaps be mentioned that Burckhardt's emphasis upon naturalism in defining 'humanism' and 'the Renaissance' is not always evaluated against the background of the enthusiasms of Burckhardt's own period.

[3] Others, like Herrick's 'To the Painter,' No. 108, or Carew's (ed. Vincent, p. 147), would show us similar emphases. The fact that Spenser speaks of tapestries affects not the point at issue but the divisions of scenes and a few details praised as peculiarly suited to the medium. In the Drayton passage I keep to commendatory phrases which do not owe their origin to the *Metamorphoses;* variants in *BW* (1603 to 1619), though interesting, do not materially affect my points. Readers will be aware of similarities to ideas espoused by Renaissance painter-theorists, but the documentation is lengthy, and it is more prudent to keep here to evidence nearer home.

make the wound (in *BW*, '*T'expresse whose Act*' Art showed her best); the nymphs combing their hair 'As *living*, they had *done it actually*' (in *BW*, 'So strove the Painter *to content the Eye*'); Phaeton's fire 'Drawn *with such life*, as some did much desire / To warme themselves, some frighted with the fire'; the Heliades, seeming truly women, seeming yet truly trees, 'Done . . . . with *such exceeding Life*' (*BW*; the art consisted in expressing their double nature). In the later version Drayton makes more particular comment in appreciation of artifice used for aesthetic effect: the windows that gave 'sure Colour' by the proportioned reflection of 'condensated and grave' beams of light on every figure; the planning of a border near what is 'By Architects called the Cornish,' to afford a finer apprehension of difference in focus—'That lent the Sight a breathing, by the space / 'Twixt things neere hand, and those farre over head.'

Drayton finds three causes for praise: skill in the craft of painting, the simple content of the eye, and a conveying of the very vitality of sentient and acting beings. The first criterion as a praise of painting is equivocal when applied to poetry. The second is not applicable except at two removes, and I do not find it otherwise applied. The third is simply that expressiveness of images which has already been discussed as a requirement. It is well phrased in a picture which Drayton did not take from Ovid but invented; he adds in *The Barons Warres* Mercury sprinkling drops on Hebe by a fountain:

> Wherein the Painter so *explain'd their Joy*,
> As he had meant the very Life to limne. . . . .

What is here recognized is the attempt to bring credibly into art the intangible 'Joy,' the essential vitality of which the external detail is a manifestation. One may well inquire whether poetic images that strove, for example, to 'explain the joy' of lovers, their very life in a moment of action, would be either carefully accurate copying of external particulars or pigments laid on to decorate a subject. The line between praise for accurate transcript of particulars and praise for *expression through particulars of the essential significance* of a subject may look to us like a thin one, since the development of naturalism. The fact that Spenser and Donne also hold to it firmly but without self-consciousness may indicate that the possibility of the confusion was not then envisaged. It may have become a matter for excited partisanship only since the development of certain world-views loosely termed 'scientific.'

Spenser's passage is too familiar to require much quoting. His praise is for the way Europa's 'tender *hart* / Did lively seeme to tremble'; for Apollo 'lively seene,' breaking quite his garland ever green, 'with other *signes of sorrow*,' for the border with its symbolic river of blood 'So lively and so like.' As an intrinsically *pleasing* detail, even in paint, this last is perhaps on a par with those blood stains (of slain lovers) with which Marlowe decorates Hero's blue kirtle (i, 16). Neither is intended to, or can, please by being seen as faithful copy; they please only by virtue of the habit (in both writer and reader) of seeing the intelligible in the visible—a habit shared by most of the arts in an era like the Renaissance, and of which the extreme example is the emblem. Spenser, too, praises the fit use of significant detail, as in the Leda:

> O wondrous skill, and sweet wit of the man,
> That her in daffadillies sleeping made. . . . .

Again, what Spenser praises in graphic images furnishes a perfectly sound criterion for poetic images. A Cézanne or a Yeats or a Leonardo makes a similar effort to emphasize such detail as will convey his sense of the living essence of his subject. Aspects of reality chosen for presentation differ; modes of directing emphasis differ. These passages simply indicate the recognition that painting (like poetry) achieves excellence on the levels of formal loveliness and significant ordering. To read Spenser's passage in its context in Book III is to see that he goes some distance toward claiming for the visual arts the power of conveying values; here Cézanne would leave him, but Yeats might not. Probably none of the three earlier poets would see anything to boggle at in Yeats's statement: 'I now see that the literary element in painting, the moral element in poetry, are the means whereby the two arts are accepted into the social order and become a part of life and not things of the study and the exhibition.'[4]

Donne, too, obviously has reference to a lifelike picture of himself. But it mirrors 'That which in him was faire and delicate'—and it is this significance which allows him to make poetic use of it. It is a 'shadow'; it 'shall *say what I was*'—as in another Drayton passage an 'image' figures forth that which a thing verily is: 'See wofull Cittie, on thy ruin'd wall, / The verie *Image of thy selfe* heere see, / Read on thy gates in charrecters thy fall, / In famish'd bodies, *thine Anatomie*' (*Mortim.*, 1569).[5] When Donne paints another picture to set by the side of that first, the effect upon his imagery is the normal one (I believe): the introduction of sensuously *apprehensible* detail with the further *function* of indicating in sum an abstraction.

The poem's need of an *icon* makes Donne use imagery of exactly the same logical simplicity which we may find more frequently in images of the genres chosen by Spenser and Drayton.

---

[4] Revealing in this connection is Yeats's whole discussion of the revolt against the literary element in painting and the parallel revolt of the 'Aesthetic School,' and his statement that this 'revolt is coming to an end, and the arts are about to restate the traditional morality. . . . . Supreme art is a traditional statement of certain heroic and religious truths, passed on from age to age, modified by individual genius, but never abandoned' (*The Autobiography of W. B. Yeats* [New York, 1938], pp. 418–19). See also his discussion of Spenser's Phaedria (pp. 266–68); his remarks about Milton, including the extraordinary statement (for *ca.* 1909, even in its context), 'Having no understanding of life that we can teach to others, we must not seek to create a school' (p. 422); and his explanation of the place, in the historical process, of that generation which substituted a spiritual for a physical objectivity, demanding, like science, the 'right of exploration of all that passes . . . . and merely because it passes' (p. 277). Like many of Yeats's prose statements, these are dangerously conclusive taken in isolation; his own later poems, though illuminated by such statements, offer a more delicate comment on the problem.

[5] Both *image* and *anatomy* (by synecdoche) are commonly used in this sense of 'sign (structural framework) that figures forth the essence (whole).' Cf. Donne's name in the window being his 'ruinous Anatomie.' See *NED*, *image*, esp. meanings 4, 3; *anatomy*, meanings 4[b], 5[b], 10. The latter used as a trope appears even in Aristotle; Donne's use here is No. 4[b], the '*pop.*' one. It is semantic considerations such as these that make deductions about a poet's personal interests, from imagery, so dangerous a game. Such choices do indicate something, very vaguely and generally, about changing popularity of words due to shifts in the general information common to some cultural group. But it would be just about as relevant to list the anatomy image under 'medical' as to classify the American slang phrase 'I put my John Hancock to it' under its user's 'interest in constitutional history.'

Icon and the various kinds of *descriptio* are figures especially useful in narrative poetry, and Donne quite properly uses them infrequently. The subjects and the forms which he ordinarily chose do not admit of so leisurely a movement, or demand the painter's kind of *illustratio et evidentia*. When occasionally they do, he provides us with crashing *Storme* or feather-motionless *Calme*, or with the thirteen-line *allegoria* of his famous and uncharacteristic river-image, with all its justly observed painter's details (pp. 175, 178, 87).

In that one of his poems which has most nearly a narrative structure, *The Progresse of the Soule* (*Metempsychosis* [1601]), the images are again logically simple and, like the painter's images, 'lively' and 'like.' Witness the wantoning whale, breaking the sea with his brazen fins, the elephant with careless-lying proboscis like an unbent bow, the ape lifting Siphatecia's kid-skin apron with his russet paw, the sparrow just out of its small blue shell with bones mere threads, the plant pushing for its growing-space as in our streets the great will find passage through crowds so thick a weasel scarce could pass.[6] These images show 'poetry like painting' in the simpler sense in which theorists advise it, the sense in which 'painted' imagery was so frequently suitable to the purposes and form of the *Faerie Queene*. When, at intervals, the latter poem too becomes 'Poêma Satyricon,' its imagery is repellent in precisely the same way as Donne's. The power and repulsiveness with which Donne paints the obscene and the grotesque are scarcely to be referred to that libertine skepticism evinced by the last three lines of the poem, however attractive such a connection is to the modern skeptic. They are rather to be referred, like the disrobing of a Duessa or the orgiastic lust of a Hellenore, to an entirely traditional use of images to convey the poet's notions, impressions, or judgments with such graphic convincingness as served the painter in the conveyance of his.

Though the use of accurate visual detail was proper to some

[6] Stanzas 32–33, 39–40, 48, 19, 14. Donne had written many poems full of logically subtle conceits prior to 1601, so that an explanation in terms of 'poetic development' is precluded.

poetic purposes, we have seen that what is praised in painting goes far beyond this. It is always the power of the 'images' which is praised; their accuracy is but the means of it. The Renaissance recognized as clearly as we do (or as the ancients did, or the Middle Ages) the power with which meanings may be conveyed in the individualized frame of reference[7] which both poets and painters use. Mazzoni says substantially this. Such an emphasis in poetry leads to a useless parade of decorative or merely accurate particulars only if the individual's importance resides in its particularity. And this is precisely what both poet and critic in the period seem not to believe.

Writers of various times, places, and opinions show understandings such as I have indicated, in their references to painting in its relation to poetry. Ascham puts aside that workman who can merely make an adequate copy of a body, for him who can give to man, woman, or child 'the right forme, the trew figure, the naturall color, that is *fit and dew to the dignitie* of a man, to *the bewtie* of a woman, to *the sweetnes* of a yong babe' ([1570], in Gregory Smith, I, 22). Peacham, treating of the 'exornation' of persons, says that like the cunning painter one so manages proportion and color that he '*compoundeth* as it were *complexion* [i.e., temperament] with *substance* and life with countenance'; thus the persons represented not only make a show of lifelikeness 'but also by outward countenance of *the inward spirite and affection*' ([1593], p. 134). There is nothing original or unusual about such ideas; I am simply trying to examine whether or not *ut pictura poesis* was so understood by the general as to tie poets to a barren technique of imagery.

Chapman declares for significancy in both arts (1595; see above, chap. ii, sec. 1). Sidney is, of course, perfectly clear on the matter, with his 'meaner sort of Painters,' who counterfeit, and 'the more excellent' who paint in outward beauty an inner quality. Fracastoro's distinction between two different kinds of painters, undervaluing those who merely imitate the object, would similarly direct a poet to emulate the artist who sees in particulars 'the universal and supremely beautiful idea' of their

---

[7] T. M. Greene's phrase; see Appendix, Note G (chap. ii, n. 27). See n. 2, above, for Mazzoni's words.

creator.[8] Mazzoni says that Dante represents 'with idols and beautiful images before the eyes of everyone all intellectual being and the intelligible [as cf. the sensible] world itself,' 'images fitted for making the people *understand the quality of* the supercelestial world.'

Whatever else they would lead to, these understandings of the ways in which poetry may resemble painting would lead to neither slavish copy nor decorative unfunctional image. It would indeed not be an untenable hypothesis that the function of ornament as conceived by the Elizabethans was comparable to the function of distortion in modern art. There is a ground of difference in the amount of emphasis upon the artist himself and upon contrasts between his and other men's view of the world. Where the modern says, 'A work of art conveys the ARTIST's vision,' the Elizabethan proclaims and reiterates, 'A work of art conveys the artist's VISION.' Yet the understanding of the functional use of artifice is not dissimilar, and it seems to me that we come closer to what *ut pictura poesis* would do to the images of a poet writing in 1600 if we think of a Seurat or a Picasso than if we think of a nineteenth-century representational painter. But the modern swing back toward meanings that are not identifiable with faithful copy-of-the-actual has been deflected and disturbed by entanglement with various modern worries about meaning in the universe which did not trouble the Renaissance. Roger Fry's description of the artist's passionate apprehension of certain emphatic rhythms of line and color is not unsuited to the Renaissance poet's repatterning of the actual through that rhythmical emotional heightening which he called rhetoric; but the two eras part company as soon as the kinds of 'meaning' which prompt such reordering are spoken of. And any Renaissance exponent of either art would be in open and incredulous disagreement by the time Fry arrived at 'a man's head is no more and no less important than a pumpkin.'[9]

[8] Fol. 158ʳ, trans. p. 60 (1555). 'Some beauties are real [*verae*], some apparent. The poet is he who is moved by the real.' Hence the 'unlimited and incomparable' usefulness of poetry; 'if there were no poets, no one would know the beauties of the world' (fol. 163ᵛ, trans. p. 71).

[9] *Vision and Design* (London, 1928), pp. 51–52.

In Renaissance poems the meaning which dictates the re-ordering of the images from actual life is even likely to be overt-ly stated; there is no feeling against this, as being prosaic. How-ever, certain categories of aesthetic effect depend upon mean-ing remaining implicit; the meaning is not for this reason less clear—merely less obvious. Recognition of the incompleteness of explicit statement is, moreover, the traditional explanation for the *necessity* of metaphor. This acceptance of the co-opera-tive rather than competitive functioning of statement, meta-phor, and graphic detail runs straight through the period, from the earliest Elizabethans through the Metaphysical poets. Al-though it depended similarly in all of them upon the unabashed acceptance of clear meanings as poetic subjects, it also pre-vented *ut pictura poesis* from vulgarizing 'a poem' into 'an idea plus a little picture.'

No study is more fruitful as a clarification of the relation of 'picture' to 'poem' than careful observation of the interplay be-tween statement and image throughout a fairly long passage in any of the greater poets. Spenser's judgments of when overt statement is necessary in an image are extremely subtle, and his degrees of explicitness are consciously and most delicately varied. The 'motto' of an emblem may be introduced in an Alexandrine at the highest moment of a represented action, as the rushing and yet insidious movement of the winding, leap-ing monster in I, i, 18 is brought to a standstill by 'God helpe the man so wrapt in *Errours* endlesse traine.' On the other hand, in the description of the same creature, the painful aptness of the recurrent symbol of half-darkness, 'Where plaine none might her see, nor she see any plaine,' is left to the alertness of the reader. But if he be metrically sensitive and rhetorically trained to have expectations roused by *sententia*, then Red Crosse's dangerously secure 'Vertue gives her selfe light,' four stanzas earlier, will start echoes that sound through the mourn-ful cadences and half-lit images of the following stanzas with a kind of fragile and ironic bravery.

In yet another way, in the House of Pride canto, the 'pic-tures' of Idleness and Avarice and Envy 'speak' out against the

vices of a sick commonwealth only by virtue of the psychological acumen with which they are drawn. They are 'complexion compounded with substance,' as Peacham's phrase quoted
above has it; persons of like complexion who are counselors
in our own commonwealth present in the flesh no more unified a
compounding. Spenser's compression is such that it is hard for
the mind to be as quick as the eye. Less well trained to this interpenetration of meaning and image, one oversimplifies the
text; it is taxing to catch not only the bouzing can'of Gluttony
but the foreign-policy implications of 'from his friend he sel-
dome knew his fo.' It is not the alert eye which remarks the suggestion of masked emptiness under the last phrase describing
the money-getter's life led 'unto him selfe unknowne.' Or hears
the tone of voice concealed in Envy's slur at the almsgiver, the
familiar muttered malice of 'Bosh! conscience money.'

These are statements; the painting, the image, has slipped
insensibly onto the level of generalized abstraction, where response to it draws on the reader's fund of experience, not on his
pictorial imagination. But no greater violence to the *poetry* of
Spenser could be done than, by separating the two, to turn the
poem into one vast picture gallery. I do not find this separation
possible, nor valid, nor intended, even in Spenser's (or Marlowe's, or Drayton's) most vividly sensuous 'paintings.'

It must also be allowed, however, that the part played by
conceptual statement is much greater in these than in modern
writers. An early or late Renaissance reader would expect such
a picture as the following to be interwoven with explicit statement or its equivalent:

> They are rattling breakfast plates in basement kitchens,
> And along the trampled edges of the street
> I am aware of the damp souls of housemaids
> Sprouting despondently at area gates.
>
> The brown waves of fog toss up to me
> Twisted faces from the bottom of the street,
> And tear from a passer-by with muddy skirts
> An aimless smile that hovers in the air
> And vanishes along the level of the roofs.
>
> (Eliot, 'Morning at the Window,' p. 31)

This imagery is untraditional in what is missing rather than in what is present. One would not expect the most orthodox 'Spenserian' of the 1590's to mind the *catachresis* (a 'desperate' metaphor) of the *damp souls;* it is in perfect decorum. The synecdoche of the twisted faces, the possible double metaphor in 'bottom of the street,' would delight him, if one is to judge by what was written and praised. But to him, and for many years after him, a poem for which such an image-technique was chosen (a congeries of vivid and significant particulars) would normally have the purposes if not the form of an emblem; though no motto need appear, I believe he would ask its significancy to be pointed up by generalizing turns of phrase capable of sure interpretation. The isolated images satisfy the dictum we have been examining.

It seems just to conclude, then, that we must disentangle *ut pictura poesis* from 'word-painting' when criticizing images. Other purposes are implied in that critical tag as the Renaissance apparently understood it. When we recognize the demand for expressiveness that lay behind their demand for lifelikeness, and remember the parallel demand for significant abstractions portrayed through the vivid concretions in a poem, it does not seem to me that we can think of *ut pictura poesis* as inducing either decorative or appliquéd images. *Ut pictura poesis* emphasized the 'individual frame of reference' which characterizes both these arts, and it emphasized graphic liveliness in poetry when that was proper to the poet's ends. I see nothing to quarrel with in this. It is possible that the Elizabethan 'decorative' image, mere 'separable' ornament, is a reader's rather than a writer's phenomenon, and that it is the child not of *ut pictura poesis* but of nineteenth-century expectations and of twentieth-century rebellion against them.

CHAPTER IV

THE 'GARMENT' OF STYLE AND FUNC-
TIONAL SENSUOUS IMAGERY

ONE other accepted Renaissance commonplace adumbrates a whole theory of ornament: *the metaphor of 'style as a garment.'* Such a conception could be vicious. Like the analogy with painting, it would seem to tempt poets to think of imagery as something added onto meaning, and of 'embroidered' prettiness as a desideratum, with one added temptation—to make garments that could stand alone, so stiff with 'external Gorgiousness' that they needed no body within. This is only one way of understanding the metaphor, the one responsible for most modern aspersions cast upon it. Another traditional meaning seems to help explain the character of much Elizabethan imagery, both bad and good: the notion of style as a garment in the sense that the flesh is the soul's garment, its bodying-forth or manifestation. The separableness of ornament from meaning would obviously be the chief differentia here between two somewhat different conceptions implied in 'style as a garment of thought.'

Any understanding of the metaphor would have been almost subconsciously acted upon by practicing poets, and our approach must be the indirect one of deducing from the results—actual images—just how and in what sense the ornament in typical poems and passages is the 'garment' of the thought. This is a long process, and I shall only exemplify here, by various demonstrations, the kind of inquiry one must make before one can call images 'embroidery.' Since the basic problem of all imagery is in question—its relation to poetic meaning—whole poems are involved, and I choose sonnets as more manageable.

Drayton devotes a whole sonnet to the image 'Like an adventurous Sea-farer am I' (new in 1619; No. 1). Did Drayton think of an image as a piece of literary drapery with which to trim up a fragment of psychological biography? (The subject is presumably his comment on how 'Thus in [his] Love' he made tedious travels and met oft-varying Fate.) If he had, the image *could not have been written as it is.* If he had, he would not have chosen an *allegoria,* whose purpose is to give intellectual pleasure by a meaning half-concealed, as no seventeenth-century reader trained in rhetoric could fail to know; he would not have increased the emotional tension by putting off statement of the meaning until the last two lines; and he would not have made understanding of that meaning dependent upon the reader's seeing in adjunct after adjunct of a sea voyage just what it was that happened in his love-travels. Port of departure, compass, pole, capes, gulphes, calms, rocks—through these his attitude toward what happened is stated, and in no other wise is it stated. It is only by his creating this expressive body in our presence that we have any sight of the spirit that is his thought.

Perhaps he learned this late? From the Metaphysicals? Take 'Cleere Ankor,' written in 1594 (Amour 13), kept throughout (1619: No. 53), with no image-changes—and this poet was not lazy about revisions. Drayton liked to write 'descriptio' of place in narrative, where it has a function that it still has in any novel. But this is not one; these silver-sanded shores, crystal streams, myrrh-breathing zephyrs, dew-impearled flowers, have the same *relation* to the meaning as do the particulars of the seafarer image: they state it. They are the only way we know wherein Arden is his Tempe, by virtue of what sweet Ankor is his Helicon. These are very different images from those of the later sonnet, but I do not think that they differ on the score of separableness from the poem's full conceptual meaning (always left incomplete by mere explicit statement, as the discipline of rhetoric insistently declared).[1]

---

[1] Both sonnets praise his lady, and in both he has taken Gascoigne's advice on artful invention (see above, chap. ii, sec. 1); the later one has a spice of persuasion. The milk-white swans which adore the brook because it is made lovelier by Idea's looking into it are a metalepsis—Puttenham's *farrefet* (III, xvii, p. 183 [1589]); by this figure we leap over the heads of many words and 'take one that is furdest off, to *utter our matter by*' (Puttenham's example is Medea's cursing the mountain that bore the mast that brought Jason).

We may not enjoy in 'Cleere Ankor' the hyperbole of Drayton's meaning, may object to the absence of irony in the magni-
tude of his praise. Nevertheless, we may only object to the
pretty decorativeness of the images by objecting to the meaning of which they are the incarnation; subtract them and the
praise is not there at all—we should just have to make it up
ourselves out of what happens to be in our minds about Helicon.
This is one way of writing poems, but it is not the only way;
and even Eliot adds notes to his to get around some of its dis-
advantages. This poem is about Drayton's notions of his lady,
not about the ones we wish he had had, although on another
level of criticism the Elizabethans would see our objections to
those notions as quite within our rights as critics. At any rate,
we must concede that if the decorative qualities of the images
had resulted from a conception of style as an embroidered garment put on over the meaning, then the body underneath would
be less affected by taking the garment off; it would at least be
there.

Roughly this is the test we have always to apply. But it may
clarify matters to take a demonstrably weak sonnet and inquire
whether its faults possibly result from an attempt to dress up
meaning—Spenser's *Amoretti* xli, for example, which retreats
after the octave into easy conventionalities of imagery. He begins with saucy, metrically irregular question and sly, rhetorically patterned suggestion for improvement: 'Is it her *nature* or
is it her *will?*' He breaks the meter harshly to play on 'that she
will plague the man that loves her most,' and pulls in to a concluding sudden flattery based on her *nature*. But then he abruptly leaves this little psychological puzzle and embarks on a new
set of meanings, a discussion of the misuse of nature's gifts.
This is embodied in a fishing-in-a-tempest image and ends in an
ejaculatory conclusion that does not follow from the argument
of the poem, although the use of four different figures of repetition fortifies the statement of it. The weaknesses of this sonnet
come from weak logic, not from zeal for decorating. The poor
sestet is neither more nor less decorative than the better octave,
and both similarly present meanings inseparable from orna-

ments; it is the later *meanings* which are irrelevant to the main structure, not the ornaments of style. It becomes clear that, in discussing embroidered style, we must distinguish between irrelevancy of ornament and basic structural flaws.

Perhaps we should take one of the *Amoretti* whose peculiar fault is a tiresome stringing-out of rather pretty sensuous particulars—No. xv. It begins with a variant of the image Donne uses in 'The Sunne Rising' (p. 11). Why look in 'both the Indias' for riches? asks each poem; they are all here in my love. But Spenser goes on to list the cargoes merchants bring thence:[2] if sapphires be desired, her eyes are they, if rubies, pearls, ivory, gold—anyone could fill out the parallels with the lady, all based on similarities in physical properties, and all perfectly relevant logically. But this is dull; we do not see why Spenser felt it necessary. It has been easiest for modern criticism to answer that he did it because some writers and readers of 1595 enjoyed the mere mention of such pretty things, relevant or not; but this does not in the least follow from the evidence. Again, it is the purport of these entirely relevant and functional images with which we are dissatisfied; we do not care to hear just how Spenser's lady is beautiful. Our conclusion, however, is not a conclusion about imagery—decorative in Spenser, functional in Donne.

We are led to conclude that, when a writer chooses a simpler subject, he is content with a simpler logical structure, fit enough for praising his lady's physical beauties, but not fit for a subject like Donne's: the praise of Love itself in that it can make two human beings constitute the world in little. Such a subject takes argument, not pointing-to, and the images in each poem obey the logical need imposed by the poem's intention. If the subject in No. xv were typical of the *Amoretti*, they would miss that tone of delicate mockery which is the charm of so many of them (Nos. x, xviii, xx, xxiiii, xxvii, xxxii, xxxiii, xliii, xlvi, liiii, lvi,

---

[2] These are not 'the same image,' despite parallel content. One difference in the tone of the image results from Donne's adjuring the sun, a typical *aubade* motif, while Spenser instructs merely 'Ye tradefull Merchants,' who fetch from, rather than look upon, 'both the 'India's of spice and Myne.' The germ of Spenser's expansion lies in this difference.

lvii). But there is no poetic law against Spenser's simpler subject; it is less interesting to us as a psychological phenomenon.
Both these poems seem to me to attempt and largely to maintain the same relation between meaning and ornament. Spenser
needs a less tight logical organization—though, indeed, I do not
think that Donne would ever allow himself the logical jump of
Spenser's conclusion.[3] The inadequacies are still not those which
would result from a conception of ornament as something to be
irrelevantly draped around meaning for the sake of decorative
qualities it possessed in itself. It becomes clear that we cannot
decide about the decorativeness of images by noting their pretty
content; we must look to the demands made by the poem's
subject.

The fact of the matter seems to be that any understanding
of this accepted and widely influential critical tag would lead to
unfunctional ornament *only* (1) if 'style' were thought of as
sharply divided from 'matter'; and (2) if, as a result, one found
that legislation about ornament recommended some as intrinsically beautiful, arranging the colors of rhetoric in a
hierarchical value series from blush pink to deep coral, admitting little pleasurableness in grubby brown or pale gray. The
first was sternly guarded against by emphasis on the principle
of decorum; I do not find the corollary even in the most schematized lists of ornaments, with their complete disregard of the
object-content of images, and their acceptance of the rhetorical
axiom that figures are chosen for their efficacy toward an end.
Puttenham's language may shock us somewhat: 'figurative
speaches . . . . be the flowers . . . . that a Poet setteth upon his
language by arte, as the embroderer doth his stone and perle,
or passements of gold upon the stuffe of a Princely garment'
(III, i); but the same sentence warns that the stuff will only be
disfigured unless decorum be observed, hammering the chapter
to a finish with *discreet* using, in *measure*, in *proportion*, *aptly*
bestowed. Apt to what? These phrases ask that language be

3 Her-vertuous-mind is allowed to destroy the parallel, and the poem is correspondingly weakened.

made more beautiful through art, but they talk about a *relation*, not about the charms of pearls.

Puttenham's whole discussion has reference to the level of formal excellence (see also another use of the metaphor in III, xx, p. 247). He accepts the fact that quite artless clothing is less agreeable than that showing the skill of the maker, and thinks that a limb should not be left naked and bare, and unclad in 'his *kindly* clothes' (natural as ordained by 'custome and civilitie'). The Renaissance acceptance of this postulate is part of the very meaning then given to the word *art;* to object to such civil custom in an art is like objecting to fugal treatment of a theme because the design obscures a tune people might otherwise hum about their work. Puttenham proceeds, through several following chapters, upon the generalizations apparently universally accepted about ornament: that its *character* varies infinitely and subtly with *function*, which derives from *genre* (as the ornament of epic properly differs from that of love elegy) or which derives from *subject* (as light causes differ from weighty causes) and from certain lesser variables. I find grounds such as these to be the ones used throughout the whole period for recommendations about the nature of images. This is a very different thing from legislation about the very stuff of figures, based on some intrinsic decorative virtue which that content might have.

If the Renaissance critic did base his approval even of primarily sensuous images upon the latter ground, it seems odd that we find such continual warnings against excess. That admonition has no meaning except in relation to some other controlling factor. Warnings against excessive addition of particulars (including, presumably, charming ones) are everywhere found. Hoskins, for example, may well have thought that Spenser's *accumulatio* of sapphires and rubies ran the risk he points out in treating the figure, that it may become mere superfluity of words, 'like a schoolmaster foaming out synonymies.' Nevertheless, 'the practice of it will bring you to abundance of phrases, without which you shall never have *choice, the mother of perfection*' (pp. 24–25 [1599]). Flexibility is quite different from floridity as an artistic reason for seeking abundance of

phrases. Pretty images are not to my knowledge exempted from
the general stricture against excess. It would certainly be extraordinary to find even the shoddiest of the rhetoricians advising
poets not to use an excessive number of images unless they were
all pretty. Hod-carriers of criticism these may have been, but
their instructions to 'beautify' carry quite different implications. Those implications will be examined in chapter vi, but one
may be swiftly indicated because it has already been noted. It
assisted poets in regulating the definition of 'excess.' I refer to
the artist's task of making a work of art more 'luminous'
through more expressive formal ornament.

Quite typical are Hoskins' comments on the value of metaphor 'to *express* a thing with *more light* and *better note*' (p. 8).
Time and again he emphasizes this same traditional attribute
of beauty ('illumination'; see above, chap. ii, sec. I). As, for
example, in his short introduction to two functions of figures
which are responsible for two of his three main divisions:

> To amplify and *illustrate* are two the chiefest ornaments of eloquence, and
> gain of men's minds two the chiefest advantages, admiration and belief.
> For how can you commend a thing more acceptably to our attention than
> by telling us it is extraordinary and by *showing* us that it is *evident?* There is
> no looking at a comet if it be either little or obscure, and we love and look
> on the sun above all stars for those two excellencies, his greatness, his *clear-
> ness:* such in speech is amplification and *illustration.*[4]

Accordingly, when Spenser uses three images instead of one to
give 'more light and better note' to the fall of the dragon (I, xi,
the fourfold 'So downe he fell'), this surely need not be because

---

[4] P. 17. Both *amplify* and *illustrate* exhibit semantic changes, of course. Hoskins'
'gain of men's minds' is reflected in our common phrase 'a convincing image.' It is
easiest to notice imagery's part in this small motion of the mind on the level of very simple images, like Donne's 'Drawing his breath, as thick and short, as can / The nimblest
crocheting Musitian' ('Elegie I,' p. 79). Or like those found in clusters almost anywhere in Spenser (for imagery to assist a reader's realization of an imagined action is
needed fairly infrequently by Donne, constantly by Spenser). For example, these from
V, vi: Talus outside the door 'Like to a Spaniell wayting carefully' (26); the knights that
lay 'here and there like scattred sheep' after his depredations (30); 'Streight was the
passage like a ploughed ridge' (36); Britomart's eyes that through her bever 'did
flash out fiery light, / Like coles, that through a silver Censer sparkle bright' (38). Of
the five, the last is the only one that uses metaphor, and also the only image that functions toward amplification as well as convincing realization or 'illustration' of this
simplest type.

each facile ornament was a gain in itself, each stitch of embroidery a beauty because of some pleasing color it introduced.
It is quite as plausible that he found these images not excessive
because he thought that no other garment could suitably clothe
the fall of that massive body (to use the phrase not as comparison but as metaphor, as the Elizabethans commonly did). That
is, because he thought that the importance of that fall could no
otherwise take on before us significant form.

It may seem that there is no sure way of knowing how poets
understood these terms—excess, more light, a beautiful garment. Certainly the poetry shows that the subjective judgments
involved in applying them differed then as now.[5] But our problem is: in practice as distinct from theory, did notions like 'style
as a garment' encourage the admission of images which were
simply intrinsically attractive, on the ground of their being thus
more inherently 'poetic'? Everyone is aware that this question
has been answered with 'yes' for the Spenserians, 'no' for the
Metaphysicals, thus erecting adherence to this criterion for
images into a differentia between two 'schools' of poets. We need
to discover whether this did in truth operate as a criterion, and
that is very difficult.

However, there are ways of watching poets in the act of
choice. When extensive revisions give us special opportunities
for watching the poet at work, we can judge fairly certainly
whether 'more pleasing or less pleasing image-content' is one of
his grounds for making changes.[6] When we concentrate on what
the poet himself judged to be acceptable, the part played by our
prejudices as to what a good image should be will at least be
at a minimum, which is the best that can be done. Only large
bodies of revision offer scope for trustworthy conclusions, for
many factors enter any poet's decision to omit or to retain any

[5] For I do not deny, of course, that there were silly, pretentious, excessively orna-
mented poems written by Elizabethans (these are also precisely the faults of bad seventeenth-century poems). I deny that they were written with the blessing of Renaissance
poetic.

[6] That this was one of his criteria would become evident regardless of whether he
were in favor of or in rebellion against 'poetic diction,' images traditionally accepted as
pleasant, Petrarchan image-conventions, and the like.

image; knowledge of many of those factors being irrecoverable, conjectures would in many instances be more vicious than idle.

I have chosen to examine the revisions of a poet who is supposed to have undergone a sort of conversion or development with regard to precisely the tenet of poetics which is here in question. Drayton's sonnet revisions between 1594 and 1619 should be revealing, since by the latter date his imagery is by common consent admitted to be more concise, colloquial, and original, more like that of Shakespeare or the Metaphysicals. Since his images do show this change in nature, we should expect these revisions to be evidence for the generalization that Drayton outgrew an earlier admiration for intrinsically decorative images, an admiration often seen as a point of difference between 'Spenserian' and seventeenth-century poetic.

So far as I can discover from an examination of every cut, change, or addition of an image in the six editions of the sonnets, the evidence does not allow this generalization but some very different ones. Two are pertinent to a consideration of images especially distinguished for their sensuous nature or function.

One generalization is that Drayton's general basis for keeping or cutting seems to be: is the logical structure of the sonnet clear, and do the images sharpen or blunt the meaning? He rejects or retains or adds seemingly without regard to the decorative or undecorative stuff of the figures. If sonnets with Petrarchan conceits, rhetorical elaborations, images using conventional poetical objects, do not successfully unite these elements into poems with clear meanings, they are thrown out. But if sonnets with intellectually complicated conceits, dissonant images, and harsh, surprising, learned, scientific, homely image-content, fall short of a similar structural success, those sonnets are thrown out too. That is to say, Drayton learns a good deal about keeping decorum, about that more excellent integration of form with poetic subject which theorists had praised time out of mind, and he becomes increasingly aware of the sonnet's proper differences from other genres. But with direct regulation of content of images this developing artistry seems to have had little to do.

Drayton does develop certain moods which are less apparent in earlier sonnets, does appear to become increasingly convinced of certain general truths about love and ladies in the statement of which pretty images would be of no great help. This leads to the second observation on the revisions as a whole. Quite regardless of the content of the images, the defiant sonnets, or those in which he would rather cure his love than keep it, impress us as sonnets containing 'metaphysical' imagery. When one stops to examine them, one frequently finds the new element to reside not in images but in concept, syntax, meter (especially arrangement of pauses). These newly accentuated moods seem to induce the choice of certain poetic subjects—a satirical comment on this, a mocking argument about that—which make Drayton find use sometimes for a kind of imagery resembling that of the Metaphysicals in structure and tone. It would be hard to make a case for image-*content* as the changing factor. But the correlation between changing points of view, on Drayton's part, and an impression of likeness to the Metaphysicals, on ours, is marked and provocative.

Neither of these observations about Drayton's revisions seems to me to fit into the shift in poetic usually postulated, from a sixteenth-century acceptance of imagery as decorative embroidery to a later more functional conception of imagery, born of rebellion against 'poetical' objects and diction. The point is a point not only about Drayton but about what really happened to imagery during this period. For we cannot say that there was such a shift but that he did not share in it; his poems *do* show the changing character to account for which this fundamental shift in poetics has been argued by critics. Unless I particularize at some length, the distinction between a poet changing his aesthetic creed and a poet developing his logical skill and changing his evaluations of life will not be clear. There is no way around the fact that these comments will be entirely understandable and interesting only to those who read them edition in hand.[7] Any reader who already believes me may skip three pages.

---

[7] I have chosen to support rather than simply to announce my opinion; and there is no other possible way of investigating such a point about images—except this of viewing

Drayton's eye does not seem to be on the intrinsic nature of images. Those of 1594 which he approved sufficiently to *keep* until 1619 include all sorts of contents: alike the tear-floods and the registration-in-a-volume of 2; the lady-sun-eagle conceit of 3; the mythological commonplaces of 18; the dry-brained lunacy of 43.[8] On the other hand, indiscriminately tossed *out* in 1619 are types of image-content ranging from tears stamped with his lady's face to pearl-paved wells.[9] Cheerfully *cut* as early as 1599 are not only the lukewarm tears but also the triplicity and ascendant of 16, the mithridate and loadstone of 23, and various other images like *or* unlike Donne's in content.[10] He may cut expanded images ending in dissonant conceits and cheerfully dispense with a harsh dramatic rhythm.[11]

He does not do anything he ought when it comes to images from science. He may *put in* scientific images in 1599 (11; careful similitudes with the elements; Hebel I, 486), and take them *out* in 1619. (We must, of course, not make the error of seeing as 'scientific and dissonant' only those seventeenth-century images which make use of what we post-Copernicans think of as 'science.')[12] Drayton may put in a 'poetic' Prometheus image or a

---

very many images in very many whole poems. The sonnets are referred to by number; the edition will be clear from the context. For those of 1594 see Hebel, I, 98 ff.; for those of 1619, II, 311 ff.; for those appearing only in the intervening editions, I, 485 ff. All variants affecting images have been considered. A 'Finding-List,' by first lines, appears in V, 302 ff.; K. C. Tillotson's notes, in the same volume, are essential helps to an understanding of Drayton's sonnets; an article by F. Y. St. Clair is of interest ('Drayton's First Revision of His Sonnets,' *SP*, XXXVI [1939], 40–59).

[8] And the blotted abstracts of 1; the phoenix hyperbole of 6; the dew-empearled flowers of 13; the anvil and bellows of 44 (all 1594; kept 1619).

[9] The well of 9; the diphthong-consonant conceit of 11; both the 'anatomize' metaphor and the conceit of his tears stamped with her image, in 14; the poets' hills and floods of 20; the isle peopled with armies of pale jealous eyes of 22; both the crystal quivers of her eyes and the peevish saint of 26 (all 1594; not in 1619).

[10] Invention stalled treading a maze in 17; the lady:daystar of 29; the bastard of 40; the abortion and sighs as symtomas of woe in 41; the besieged fort of 42 (all cut in 1599).

[11] E.g., the tormentor-and-crucified of 1594:15 (see notes, Hebel, V, 16); or the childbirth and poor orphan of 16, with its harsh ending.

[12] The assumption that images using the natural sciences were seen by the sixteenth or the seventeenth century as dissonant or daring stands to be questioned in any case; it is most familiar in modern critics who see likenesses between Metaphysical and modern poetic on the ground of similar anxiety to amalgamate inharmonious materials into a poetic unit. C. Day Lewis (one example among a dozen) says that 'the wit of the

star of beauty with graces sitting on her eyelids, in 1600, and
leave them ([1619] 14, 4); or he may put in spheres and prime
mover in 1599 and later *cut* them (23; Hebel, I, 486). Or he may
put in scientific images in 1594 (23) and take them out in 1599,
evidently because they are part of a hyperbolical *accumulatio*
with a paradoxical but not tightly articulated conclusion. The
same reason, with its attendant relation to tone, may partly account for the removal of 'Blacke pytchy Night' ([1594] 45); certainly only a sternly self-disciplining author could part with
the luminous suavity of 'Nor Moone nor stars lend thee their
shining light.'

Nor does Drayton tinker with the images he does keep in
order to make them intrinsically either more 'poetic' or more
homely, either to rip out or to add embroidery; the variant
readings generally turn on matters of meter or of logical clarity.
This is quite natural in case he had never intended to embroider.
Perhaps the fact that his changes do not fall in with modern
generalizations about rebellion against poetic diction argues
that it is a mistake to interpret what happened to images in the
1600's in terms of what has been said between 1798 and 1940
about imagery's relation to the 'real' world. So far as one can
deduce Drayton's reasons for his omissions, additions, and
alterations from 1594 to 1619, they are seen to be varied, complicated, and quite in line with accepted poetic as of 1585 or
1590.

Certain sensuously ample images are greatly affected by
changes he makes. He learns to avoid the leisureliness of epic,

---

metaphysicals was pointed with the tough iron of science' (*A Hope for Poetry* [Oxford,
1935], p. 61); this is true, but it is also perfectly traditional—in medieval poetry, for
example. Loose notions of what should be classified under 'science' are responsible for
much of the modern tendency to see this as new; the same unconscious acceptance of
our own definitions lies behind much comment on 'poetic' diction. An example would
be E. J. Sweeting's characterization of a passage from Skelton's *Garlande of Laurell*
(using many astronomical terms) as 'aureate language,' far removed from the language
of everyday life (*Early Tudor Criticism* [Oxford, 1940], p. 16). Language may not be
thought of as inkhorn, hybrid, aureate, when one set of scientific theories is made use
of, and thought of as daring, surprising, and contributory to an ironic tone when another
set (now more acceptable to scientists) is made use of. The use of the tough iron of
science is not the differentiating factor.

which had good reason for using *icon* or *descriptio;* he may cut these or even the simple and widely used *pragmatographia* (a 'counterfait action').[13] As early as 1599 he cuts the Actaeon sonnet, 35, and the ship *icon* of 34. But he could have learned from the rhetoricians that these were figures not easily made decorous in a form like the sonnet; this is clear from definitions of usefulness or type of example in one after another manual or schoolbook—Sherry in 1555, or Peacham in 1577, or their earlier Latin sources, or Puttenham's perfectly clear treatment, or Peacham's overt warnings in 1593.[14] Perhaps he was still young enough to wish to show the sharp wit, great reading, good memory, and art of the workman which recommend the *icon* to Peacham, and learned only reluctantly not to overweight a short poem with a figure supposed to be used sparsely as a 'singular iewell' (p. 146).

He shows a clearer understanding of means to ends when he uses the figure *mimesis* to do just what Peacham (pp. 138–39) gives as its special value—to deride or 'deprave'; compare the mimicked conversation of his anti-critics sonnets ([1619], 31, 24), or the dialectic of 19. Donne's famous 'conversational tone' most frequently results from just such a keeping of rhetorical decorum; he does precisely what rhetoricians advise in the literary situations he chooses. Two expanded figures (conventional *parabola*) were added by Drayton in 1599 and kept in 1619 (7, 23)—Love the drunken prodigal at a feast, and Love the ungrateful lodger. Both have their *haec fabula docet* neatly and wittily drawn as a conclusion, and both, I think, were kept for their delicately mocking tone. This last is also the reason why

---

[13] Puttenham distinguishes these conveniently, III, xix, pp. 239–46. The edition of 1619 sees the excision of the eagle's Icarus-like story in 22, of Beauty drowned in the well, 9, although they were kept until 1605.

[14] For particular figures, I use Peacham's phraseology rather oftener than that of others because his 1593 edition gives a 'caution' and 'use' for each figure. His major source is the textbook by Susenbrotus, *Epitome Troporum ac Schematum* (?1540), who in turn depends on the widely used pseudo-Ciceronian *Ad Herennium* (both are treated in T. W. Baldwin's book, cited in Appendix, Note B). The *Epitome* had several English editions after its first in 1562, and Susenbrotus was set as a required author in grammar schools. It was probably the text from which Puttenham drew heavily for examples (see Appen. III in the edition by Willcock and Walker).

we do not notice them as rather outmoded in *method* for poetry written in this form, appearing between 1599 and 1619.[15]

A few other examples from 1619 will serve to show how easy it is to mistake a difference in tone chiefly resulting from a different conceptual base for the poem, for a new kind of imagery. The lighthearted paradoxes of 'You not alone, when You are still alone' (11 in 1619; put *in* in 1599) are not different in method, or in the interplay of abstractions rather than concretions, from 'If ever wonder could report a wonder' (No. 17 in 1594 but rejected within four years). The same rhetorical elaboration and the same absence of sensuousness in the half-buried imagery characterize both, but the one which 'sounds seventeenth century' states a very different attitude toward the lady, and quite properly differs in tone; in addition to the effects of a different poetic subject upon logical structure and syntax, there appears a plain, simple development of skill, touching these and meter. In the anti-critics sonnets an argumentative intention leads to homely or violent images,[16] as it does in all satire—a commonplace of theory that was hoary with age by the sixteenth century. A very old-fashioned *icon*, but aptly chosen for its end, in the catalogue of the effects of age ([1619], 8), shows sensuous detail approaching the violence of some of Donne's descriptions, as in Elegies ii and viii. Such detail was traditionally decorous for the type of subject in all three poems.

All these sonnets differ in conceptual point and in tone, but not in the nature of the poetic techniques favored, from commendatory early sonnets which we tend to think of as exhibiting 'sixteenth-century decorativeness.' Most of the sonnets which say 'Love is rather a sell' instead of 'Love is an admirable thing' impress us as similar to the work of later poets; but though the imagery sometimes differs by virtue of a sternly logical aim for the whole piece, it is most frequently similar in method, except for certain rhetorical lessons which Drayton learned. He could have learned them equally well earlier, and, once he has, he ap-

[15] The same applies to the anvil *icon* ([1594], 44, and kept, mythological commonplaces and all [1619], 40).

[16] E.g., 49, added in 1599.

plies the principles he has learned to all types of subject. Occasional possible differences in image-content do appear to bear some relation to the mocking type of subject increasingly favored by Drayton, but it would be dangerous to speculate about it. I should be unwilling to erect generalizations about the relation of poetic subject to imagery on this narrow base. The fact that there are innumerable unrecorded factors in such choices restricts us to a few general principles.

Keeping of decorum, for example, undoubtedly caused certain large, vague differences. The murderer-image and the dissection-image of 46 and 50, for instance, may appear to draw on a new and different sort of content (both appear first in 1605). But both are witty and slyly ironical and use the time-worn rhetorical-logical method of a similitude introducing and supporting a general proposition; the proposition is not at all flattering to the lady, and neither may the image be, if it is to be decorous. One sonnet, new in 1619, lists the ingredients of a recipe for a remedy for love, and it is pungent and sharp; an earlier one lists the adjuncts of a lover so perfect he would decline the remedy with a tear, and it is fervent and at once serene' and plaintive.[17] The later sonnet, however, differs from the earlier not by virtue of a new type of imagery or a changed idea of poetry but by virtue of opposed conceptual meanings and certain developed logical skills. The objects mentioned in the lists actually overlap; but the sighs and tears of the first, by a normal law of language, simply are not the same objects as those of the second, when such different things are said *of* them in order to say different things *through* them. This interpenetration of object with meaning in obedience to the nature of the evaluation being expressed, whether or not recently discovered by the semanticists, was so accepted a rhetorical axiom that no Elizabethan I can find seems to think in terms of some objects being 'poetical.' The rule of decorum is rooted in such understandings of the fundamental nature of language. It aided a poet to adjust his tone to the kind of evaluation—of love, or death, or man, or event—he was enunciating.

[17] These two are No. 15 in 1619 and No. 38 in 1594, cut in 1599.

To conclude: I do not think we can say that the accepted metaphor of 'style as a garment' implied the acceptance of 'applied' decorative images as a good, in Elizabethan thinking about poetry. Style *is* the garment of the thought in too true a sense, in good sonnets and bad: the images state the meaning; the images derive their prettiness from their task of stating some simple commendatory meaning. Legislation on the stuff of figures does not appear; legislation on their decorous fitness to their function does. The typical warning is against excess; the typical praise is for luminous significancy. These statements are exemplified and reinforced when one studies the revisions of a poet who is supposed to have undergone a typical change of heart regarding images between 1594 and 1619; one finds a poet who learned to apply to a developing form—the short reflective poem—certain principles which had been traditional for generations, and one finds a poet who, as he changes his ideas, changes his tone of voice. He comes to put logical clarity ahead of certain other virtues poetry can have (or perhaps comes just to discover that it need not quarrel with them). Intrinsic content of images (of whatever kind) does not seem to be of moment to him as he weeds the bad from the good in his garden, over those twenty-five years. Perhaps he did not think of image-content as a ground of judgment for pleasingness in images, because it must be an equivocal ground for men who thought of images as irrevocably parts of meanings. There is beauty in garments certainly, but suitability will be (and is) mentioned as the chief law of that beauty when the garment of imagery is so undeniably related to the bodies it clothes.

In this long consideration of the larger theoretical concepts of Renaissance poetic, and of how they appear to have been interpreted by writers of images, I have indicated but not examined several specific criteria for imagery. Such an examination is the task of the rest of Part I.

So much harm has already been done by trying to make neat, clear, and succinct statements of Elizabethan poetic creeds that I am unwilling to add to it by a summary of the above pages. I

am willing only to suggest certain principles arising from the
investigation so far, which every reader of sixteenth- and seventeenth-century poetry may prove or disprove as he reads the
poems themselves. One of these principles is that the secret of
the nature of an image lies in the 'cause'[18] of the poem. Era, intellectual climate, personality, exact subject matter—all are
secondary considerations, important and to be talked of (in explaining images) only in so far as they affect the poet's general
intention. We shall understand why an image has the character
it has only as we come closer to knowing why the poem was
written at all. Since the aims of poems are not only manifold
and hidden but differ in this earlier era from many typical subjects and purposes in our own era, affected both by the Romantics and by increased respect for a straightforward report of
objective reality, it is easy to mistake early images for something their authors never intended them to be. In particular, we
shall look in vain for our own type of precise sensuously accurate image.

Another principle which seems to operate is that the relation
of imagery to statement, including that of 'particulars' to
'meaning,' can be, and then was, somewhat differently conceived than we conceive it. If one looks in earlier poetry for a
world in which these could be sharply divided, one will only
diminish their images into mere examples, their symbols into
mere counters, their allegory into barren diagram, their analogies into facile proofs, their pursuit of truth through dialectic
or speaking picture into self-conscious exhibitionism or priggish
exhortation. In all this poetry the extent to which the universe
and the particulars within it are instinct with meaning is alarm-
ing to a modern mind; but much of the imagery turns either to
naïve inanity or witty bravado if one forgets to read all images
with a quickened sense of what they may stand for. 'Poetry
deals with universals' operated to make of images something
which one must always be at least ready to read as synecdoche
rather than as description. Reading on the figurative level has to
be sustained rather than intermittent. I do not speak merely

[18] See above, chap. i, n. 7.

of the earlier part of the period or of the Platonists among the poets.

I have accepted it as a principle that the great commonplaces, like *ut pictura poesis* or the 'garment of style,' which sum into comparison or metaphor a whole theory of ornament, embody the serious aims of intelligent men and that the poems can show us what they meant. So, too, if we find that 'Imitation' was seriously and carefully defined to include formal excellence in design, coherent ordering, statement of truth, then that definition was in all probability useful and regulative, and we shall do well to consider every image as possibly explicable in terms of it. In so far as such intentions are shared, they affect every image, if the poet be master of his medium. I think that it is more likely that we misunderstand the theory or misread the poems than that there existed any great gap between the two. There is much that is common to all poetic, and much that is common to all poetry, in each.

CHAPTER V

THE CRITERION OF SENSUOUS VIVIDNESS

IT IS not easy to draw up a list of criteria for images in the Renaissance. They sit on no branch ready for plucking, for theorists do not isolate 'images' as an element in poetic technique, and the poets' own criteria may be deduced only by scrutinizing innumerable single images in relation to whole poems. However, there are not very many, as there are not in any age. And they do not appear to vary greatly, even over a wide range of dates and personalities. Moreover, it is so difficult to find quarrels between critical assumptions and actual practice that we must assume some coherence between the two.

This relationship is not of the kind where particular influences of this critic upon that poet can be demonstrated, nor am I in the slightest degree interested in such currents within the whole stream. Helps to the better understanding of practice are rather to be found in the assumptions and general positions common to critic after critic, rhetorician after rhetorician; judging by the images produced, these were also common to poet after poet. The level at which the relationship to practice obtains is that at which changes do not occur each decade, but every few centuries, and, although I give dates consistently, it should be justifiable to use any critic during the period whose phraseology enables us to spy out how the typical current generalizations were understood and put to practical use. The criteria to be examined and illustrated in the following chapters derive from the general principles already outlined, variously combined; but our business now is to make these derivations, to watch the functioning of specific criteria on the level of that small poetic unit, the single image, and to see if this approach does in truth make the characteristics of images throughout the period not only explicable but especially enjoyable.

The evidence of the images will, I think, combine to give us a respectful understanding of the poetic under which these poets worked. It will also suggest certain other generalizations which there will not be space to examine or time to prove but which may be illuminating so far as they go—generalizations especially about differences between modern and sixteenth- and seventeenth-century poetic, generalizations about the likenesses currently advanced between Metaphysical and modern imagery, between Metaphysical and Symbolist poetic.

1. *Sensuous Vividness: Images Which Describe or Amplify*

Images which satisfy the criterion, 'Is it representationally accurate and convincing in its sensuous detail?' find a certain justification in sixteenth-century theory. The place accorded them is small, and is so narrowly restricted by warnings about excess, appropriate genre, and especially fit use toward an end, that I am not certain that any Elizabethan would have accepted this as a sufficient criterion even for single images. In Peacham (1593), for example, figures which would demand this sort of excellence form one of four sub-suborders, of one of three suborders, of one of three divisions. The criterion's direct application would be practically confined to figures like *icon* or *imago*, prosopopoeia (when to animals or things without life we frame an action), and various kinds of *descriptio: topographia, topothesia* (a *feigned* place), *cronographia, pragmatographia* (actions, such as a battle), etc. Metaphor, like all tropes, has quite other and larger demands made of it, a point upon which no rhetorician shows the slightest wavering.

The least problematical of these figures are *icon* (picture; usually in the form of a similitude), *descriptio* of person, and *topographia* (description of place). Each is frequent in nineteenth-century and some modern poetry and is difficult to find with any show of accuracy except in Elizabethan narrative or inset narrative. If one considers the requirements of fiction, it is easy to see why such figures occur as set pieces in early prose fiction as well; Spenser or Sidney are easily outdone in precision

of observation by Nashe or Lodge, writing in low or middle style
without the added requirements of heroic or reflective poetry.
But all narrative poems need these figures, and such examples
as these from Drayton's *Endimion and Phoebe* (1595) appear to
intend vividness and convincingness of sense detail:

> An Azur'd Mantle purfled with a vaile,
> Which in the Ayre puft like a swelling saile,
> Embosted Rayne-bowes did appeare in silk,
> With wavie streames as white as mornings Milk:
> Which ever as the gentle Ayre did blow,
> Still with the motion seem'd to ebb and flow:
>
> (111–16; part of a portrayal of Phoebe)

> Shadowed with Roses and sweet Eglantine,
> Dipping theyr sprayes into this christalline:
> From which the byrds the purple berries pruned,
> And to theyr loves their small recorders tuned.
>
> (51–54; *topothesia*)

The attention to sensuous vividness in all such figures is clear
from examples and remarks in any of the rhetorical handbooks.[1]
Treatises on poetic clearly presuppose such knowledge.[2]

The shorter the poem, and the less innocent of deeper emotional intention, the less careful the elaboration, but even tiny
fictions see fit to begin with descriptive figures:

> Beauty sat bathing by a spring
>   Where fairest shades did hide her;
> The winds blew calm, the birds did sing,
>   The cool streams ran beside her.
>
> (Munday, 'To Colin Clout,' from *England's
> Helicon* [1600]; HH, 203)

Marlowe's descriptions of Hero and of Venus' temple are famous
examples. Metaphysical poets show few of them; they did not
write in the genres or the lyrical forms to which such figures
were naturally proper—except satire, where the base style made

---

[1] In Fabri, Sherry, Wilson, Rainolde, Peacham, Puttenham, Day, Hoskins, Barton,
or their various Latin sources from Cicero to Susenbrotus, or for that matter in their
late imitators or borrowers like Blount in 1654 or Hoole in 1660 or Johnson in 1665.

[2] As do Minturno's remarks about *descriptio*, *De poeta*, ii, p. 115 (1559), or Tasso's
familiar lists, with his warnings about excess, and his advice on when to stress *l'efficacia*,
l'affetto, and when verisimilitude (*Discorsi*, ii, pp. 81–82 [1594]; in Gilbert, p. 490).

for a homelier kind of accuracy, as it always had. On the other hand, every genre in which Spenser wrote requires such figures, except for the sonnet. We have seen Drayton in process of learning that they are not especially well suited to sonnets. Spenser attempts only one or two in the *Amoretti*.[3]

The natural need for such figures in narrative was strengthened by time-honored rules for the use of inset narration in other types. Here consistent rhetorical training over a period of years was bound to exert some influence on poets. The 'oration demonstrative' included a *narratio* as one of its parts. Since the aim of such a piece of writing was *to praise or dispraise*, the well-learned rules for its general structure were frequently and justifiably used for poems with that aim; the basic structure is: *exordium, narratio* (or statement of the facts, divided into persons, acts, time, place, etc.), *confirmatio, confutatio, conclusio*.[4]

The naturalness with which conventions of rhetorical structure were used and appreciated in poems is exemplified in Hobbinol's 'prayse' of Eliza (*Shep. Cal.*, April). The stanza beginning 'Ye dayntye Nymphs,' E. K. remarks, 'is, as it were an *Exordium* ad preparandos animos,' and the image of Phoebus thrusting out his golden head 'A sensible *Narration*, and present view of the thing mentioned.' The small poetical fictions used 'to praise or dispraise,' like Greene's 'Old Menalcas on a day' or Lodge's 'Love in my bosom like a bee,' seldom take time for

---

[3] Number lxiiii makes a disastrous effort to use an *icon*, with the usual 'distribution of circumstances'; 'Comming to kisse her lyps,' he found a garden, with a list of flowers ingeniously paired off with various parts of the lady. Number lxvii ('Lyke as a huntsman after weary chace') is more nearly successful because the basic similitude, being more apt, is capable of greater reflective as cf. sensuous elaboration.

[4] Everywhere found, of course, but of Wilson's *Arte of Rhetorique* there is a convenient modern edition (pp. 11 ff., 29, 106 [1560]). Or see Cox, *ca.* 1530, who happens to depend upon Melanchthon; most interested persons in the Renaissance would be familiar with Quintilian's treatment (iii. viii). Rainolde's rhetoric, cited in the next paragraph, is now out in a modern edition by F. R. Johnson; I use it partly because H. D. Rix cites more largely from it in analyzing a fable in Spenser's February eclogue (*op. cit.*, p. 80; in chap. ii, n. 12, above). Widely used handbooks like Farnaby's get the whole matter into the compass of a few easily learned diagrams which presumably served as a basis for exercises of the type described by schoolmasters like Brinsley (Thomas Farnaby, *Index rhetoricus* [1625]—many editions, of which I have seen 1646). Such rhetorical handbooks, of course, did not cease to be taught and used as years went on, though I cite early texts.

the expansively descriptive figures of proper narrative; they get on to a point or two of confirmation or confutation, or immediately declare some fanciful *conclusio* (HH, pp. 154, 156). In Carew's 'A Fly that flew into my mistress' eye,' the *confirmatio* takes the form of a play on the conventional conceit, lady:sun (p. 52).[5]

The interest of mentioning such rhetorical conventions here does not lie only in the fact that notions of the type of imagery proper to certain types of pieces came to be imbedded in poets' minds through long practice (for they wrote dozens of such pieces as schoolboys). Readers' tastes also were formed on the same training. Such readers were bound to read with rather more nicety of observation than do we an 'oracion by fable' such as Wyatt's version of the field-and-town-mouse story (in HH, p. 21), or 'narrations poetical' such as Herrick's frivolities concerned with how-violets-came-blue. A rhetoric like Rainolde's *A booke called the Foundacion of Rhetorike* (1563) would give us the scheme for either. Rainolde stresses in the first type (as does Wyatt) the 'reasoning of the things contained'—his example, introducing a very introspective ant and grasshopper, requires considerable use of dramatic *sermocinatio* or feigned speech; he notes also the application of the moral (by Wyatt satirically addressed to 'my Poynz'). Rainolde's example for the second is the story of how roses became red by the blood of Venus' feet (fols. iv,[v] xvi[r]). Wyatt's and Herrick's readers read such poems with recognition of conventions they had themselves labored over, studying perhaps Rainolde's sources, Cicero and Aphthonius, or the latter's prototype, Hermogenes, or any one of a great many others. Recognition has its own pleasures.

Recognizing the propriety of the imagery is among them. Wyatt's homely and base-style[6] sensuous details are typical of the 'fable': the swimming furrows, the cat's 'stemyng Ise / In

---

[5] Any lyric mentioned or quoted, if it was meant to be sung, will show pronounced differences in the imagery from lyrics which were not sung. This holds regardless of date or authorship; the former had conventions of their own to utilize, and the various musical types (e.g., madrigals, airs) produced special lyrical forms, most of which declined rapidly during the seventeenth century.

[6] See below, chap. ix, sec. 5: 'Decorum and the "Three Styles." '

a rownde hed with sherp erys,' the setting of dragnets for hares or 'hay for Conys over Ryvers'; typical also is his down-to-earth dialogue. No conclusions may therefrom be drawn as to whether he would or would not have put, in the place of such homely detail, elaborate *icon* and *cronographia* into a poem of a different sort—one on Acrasia in the Bowre of Blisse, for example. The imagery is proper to the kind; we cannot tell for sure whether it is especially proper to the poet.

The second of the three basic types of rhetorical structure—demonstrative, deliberative, and judicial pieces—also lent itself to poetic adaptation, simply because its aim was that of a good many shorter poetic forms, especially love poems. Various such forms (especially as they came not to be sung) developed in the direction of the 'oration deliberative,' whose aim was *to persuade or dissuade*, and which used the *loci* or topics of *confirmatio*, arguing the honesty, profitableness, difficulty, etc., of something, or their opposites. Donne's normal structure resembles this, though other influences have also intervened. It is obvious that such an aim would frequently combine with the simpler mere 'praise' (oration demonstrative). Poets were not tied to the distinctions or the rules; what carried over and influenced imagery was a sort of residue of training.

This particular connection between rhetorical types and Renaissance lyrics or other short pieces has received no notice, to my knowledge, but it has a great deal to do with the nature of the sensuous imagery in such poems. In fact, this connection largely explains why we do not find in them the sensuous particularity to which we are accustomed in modern lyrics. It even helps to explain why that characteristic is not a common one in Metaphysical imagery. Hence it is necessary before examining this criterion further to make clear this especial relation between rhetorical and lyrical theory.

It is sometimes said that the Renaissance had no well-defined lyrical theory, because the domination of Aristotle's *Poetics*, and of epic, pushed critical discussions pre-eminently toward other interests. It is true that there are fewer long systematic discussions of the lyric, and fewer controversies about it. But I should like to suggest that it is rather we who have neglected the ideas of Renaissance writers on lyrical poetry, and the intimate connection of those ideas with contemporary productions, under the double influence of our greater attention to Elizabethan dramatic literature and of our own different ideas about the lyric, which have made theirs antipathetic to us. Their lyric theory seems to me both well defined and able to inclose without any Procrustean losses the wealth of varied lyrical productions of the age. Characteristically, they developed theories that had their base in certain classical ideas and were yet generously adapted to the vast lyrical developments during the Middle Ages; these developments had formed the conventions that were the living tissue of lyrical writing during the Renaissance. Also, characteristically, their theories show a free collaboration between rhetoric and poetic. As is usual both in the Middle Ages and in the Renaissance, theorists and writers saw what was common to these two arts of expression through language, and were singularly skilful and original in making each serve the other without loss of integrity.

The major concept in Renaissance lyric theory is, as we should expect, concerned with aim. The general intentions of lyric are to praise and to plead. The converse of the first is always included—vituperation, dispraise. Sidney's emphasis is especially upon 'praises': of virtuous acts or persons (in Gregory Smith, I, 178), of God (I, 201); but before he has finished the latter paragraph he is talking of the *Energia* which is necessary if any writer is to persuade his mistress that he is in love. This emphasis upon power to move the affections is usual;[7] it is perhaps the link which accounts for the close relation between aims for lyric and those we have noted in the two kinds of 'oration.'

The similarity seems to me a natural one rather than a 'borrowing' showing the domination of rhetoric over poetic, though treatments in poetic theory generally use phrases that recall rhetorical discussions of these aims, in addition to phrases that recall Aristotle's mentions of hymns, encomiums, invectives,

---

[7] See also Puttenham's discussions of lyrical pieces (I, xx–xxvi); they commend or lament, celebrate, or complain (in practice the latter means plead or argue with).

and Plato's praise of the gods. Sebillet remarks that the 'lieus de demonstration' of the Greek and Latin rhetors will serve, in 'blasons,' to write praise or dispraise, 'prière ou detestation.'[8] The sonnet has more of gravity (ii). *Laudare, pregare*, are Minturno's emphases in treating of the *materia melica*[9]—not only praise of gods but things, places, abstractions like innocence or liberality (p. 171 [1564]). He, too, thinks of the formal pattern in a lyric in the usual rhetorical terms, with his 'il Proemio, la Narrazione, e l'Uscita' (pp. 179–80).

Although, as in rhetoric, there is more stress on moving the affections than on revealing them, poetry of this genre is expected to be especially 'simple, sensuous, and passionate.' The note of emphasis upon an appraisal, an evaluation, and thence frequently upon undisguised persuasion, is even so the note which is never lost. This explains in part the presence of so much general statement in songs, for, instead of being personal revelations, they are praises or dispraises of some person, attitude, condition, idea, affection, outcome of events; or they plead for or against something. All this may not fit very well with notions of the lyric as revelation of emotional experience, or outburst, or cry, or record of nuances of feeling, or notation of delicate movements of the sensibility. But it does fit very well a body of lyrical literature that includes such different things as medieval trope, sequence, and religious lyric, Provençal *chanson* and the *dolce stil nuovo*, Chaucerian compleynt, Petrarchan sonnet, villanelles by Du Bellay, odes by Ronsard, motet and madrigal, Carew's 'Ask me no more,' Donne's 'Message' or 'Confined Love', Herbert's 'Vertue' or 'Discipline.' Of course, such lyrics *do* reveal emotion, *do* record delicate movements of the sensi-

[8] Discussed with the song, II, chap. vi, x (1548) (*op. cit.*, above, chap. ii, n. 16). The epistle has a 'stile plus populaire' than the elegy, though both often treat of love (vii).

[9] In Book iii of *L'Arte poetica*. English lyric for a number of decades fits very well into Minturno's assumptions, and as in shorter treatments by others, control through formal patterning is by no means thought to interfere with the importance given to the *affetti* (see esp. pp. 175 ff.). One might mention also his recognition of the dramatic element in lyrics—no new technique of Donne's, as some modern commentary implies, but familiar in medieval lyrics in most languages.

bility. It is simply that there is another important element in them, answering to a further demand.[10]

These two aims of praising or dispraising and of pleading or persuading were as natural to lyric as to the two basic rhetorical structures which they also characterized. Once the similarity in aim was openly recognized, as these and other Renaissance theorists show that it was, conventions learned in rhetorical practice were the more freely used in the writing of lyrics. The first type of rhetorical structure habitually makes more use of sensuously vivid imagery than the second; the same difference can be noted in lyrics with the first or the second intention. The differing effects upon the sensuousness of the imagery may be quickly exemplified by examples of each from Herrick.

It would be easiest to take some fanciful invention used to praise, like the robin-story delicately complimenting 'Mrs Eliz: Wheeler' (No. 130). But I shall take 'The Vision' (No. 142), in which an ostensible light reproach to himself is ironically turned upon the lady.[11] He does this, as any good rhetorician does such things, by so coloring the *narratio* of the facts of the case that by the time we reach the conclusion in 'Herrick, thou art too coorse to love' we are delighted to set down this particular Diana as somewhat of a precisian, and entertained to speculate upon the general question of just how coarseness is to be defined by the loved, when she is unwilling to make a Diana's flat repudiation. Even so short a complimentary fiction as this of the lady appearing in a vision and chiding him for his kiss produces a figure that is like *icon* in its care for color and shape, in its classical reminiscences used as a short cut to visual amplitude—the silver bow with green silk strung, the buskins shortened like Diana's 'to descrie / The happy dawning of her

[10] Moreover, theory is entirely cognizant of the importance of music. The short 'demonstration' which was simply a 'praise' is familiar in the songbooks or the miscellanies, and in plays. It is in the lyrical kinds which were, or became, less tied to the requirements imposed by musical setting that an emphasis on the 'deliberative' was to develop.

[11] The text of the poem is printed in the Appendix, Note H. It is possible, if one prefers, to read this as a simple 'praise,' without irony; but Herrick was an accurate marksman, and not only are all the arrows shot one way in the exonerating charm of the images, but also the ambiguity of the last line would be wasted, which is no habit of Herrick's (to love me? or, for me to love?).

thigh.' *Topographia* has shrunk to 'Close by a Silver-shedding Brook,' but the epithet is characteristically sensuous in function. Poems like this can be (and have been) written without knowledge of rhetorical theory, for the conventions got into the theory only because they are such natural accompaniments of this type of aim. Nevertheless, when a type of structure and a type of imagery not otherwise favored in short forms consistently recur together throughout a period, there is generally some reason. This is a 'demonstrative' lyric with inset narrative; its imagery should and does satisfy the criterion of sensuous vividness.

One may contrast the image-conventions adhered to in 'To his Mistresse objecting to him neither Toying or Talking' (No. 38), which has persuasion as its end:

> You say I love not, 'cause I doe not play
> Still with your curles, and kisse the time away. . . . .
> *Small griefs find tongues:* Full Casques are ever found
> To give, (if any, yet) but little sound.
> *Deep waters noyse-lesse are;* And this we know,
> *That chiding streams betray small depth below.*
> So when Love speechlesse is, she doth expresse
> A depth in love, and that depth, bottomlesse.
> Now since my love is tongue-lesse, know me such,
> Who speak but little, 'cause I love so much.
>
> (Author's italics)

What one notices about the imagery here is the use of *sententia* in the form of images, the use of apt but dissonant analogy, of a possible pun in *sound*, of sensuous epithets chosen (like *chiding*) for the slight shadow they cast upon the reader's evaluation of what they modify—the reader is being asked to disapprove of shallow streams of much-protesting Love. The poet here is suavely and delicately pushing a reader toward an opinion; not simply praising, but standing to a position. This is a 'deliberative' lyric, and sensuousness is at a minimum.

Such differences in imagery do not indicate laborious following of some *recherché* theory; as is usual, the theory classifies and regularizes the natural, normal results of differing intentions. The differences are evident to some degree in any poet who writes toward the two differing aims which the differing images assist. But in these earlier poets the aims are so universally favored, the distinctions so finely made, and held with such subtle consistency, that it is pertinent to remember that such habits were at that time deeply engrained by long training. The poet could count upon the same training in his public.

Against a background of such theories of the lyric it is easier to see why figures like *icon* and *descriptio* came more usefully into other genres, and with them their emphasis upon credible sensuous detail. That we find narrative poetry sowed with such figures, that Marlowe or Drayton are correspondingly rich and florid in a way Bishop King or Ralegh have no need to be, simply demonstrates the truth of a fact Puttenham comments on. He says: 'In that which the Poet speakes or reports of another mans tale or doings, ... he is as the painter or kerver that worke by imitation and representation in a forrein subiect'; this is the closest the poet comes to being 'onely a bare immitatour of natures works, following and counterfeyting her actions and effects.'[12]

Thus we see that the place found by Renaissance poetic for sensuously accurate images is a narrower one than we should expect. Moreover, other considerations override accuracy. One such consideration is implied in the very classification of such figures. *Icon* is ordinarily written as a type of similitude; by such figures, as Puttenham says, we not only beautify our tale but very much enforce and enlarge it (III, xix, p. 240). *Enlarge* has a special meaning. For most of these figures come generally under the heading of 'amplification,' a word which means something very different from our modern 'expanding' or 'dilating upon.'[13]

I must here make this distinction clear, for it affects a great

---

[12] III, xxv, pp. 307, 304. See Mazzoni's long chapter on particularization in poetry (Book iii, pp. 677 ff. [1587]). It is typical of the Renaissance habit of mind that Mazzoni feels called upon to defend at length the claim such poetry can have to be called 'imitation,' since it is seemingly a mere transcript of the actual. His grounds for defense are like Sidney's and Minturno's—such poetry also reveals universals, albeit by methods peculiarly fitting to narrative.

[13] It is indeed distinguished from dilation by Hoskins, p. 24.

many images I shall quote, and no lingering tendency to identify amplification with 'trimming up,' or stretching out, must remain in our heads. Figures under amplification are not used to expatiate; they are used to magnify, to make more impressive, more worthy of attention. The metaphor is not spatial; amplification may frequently be used in the interest of brevity. The basic function is heightening or intensification; if extension will achieve it, well and good.

Figures which serve this function frequently must satisfy the criterion of sensuous vividness; generally they must go beyond precision and accuracy alone to achieve what Quintilian says amplification requires, 'the gift of signifying more than we say' (ix. ii. 3). Its fundamental connection is with the *moving* power of poetry. It is related to the stress on *admiration*,[14] prominent in Minturno, Castelvetro, Sidney; it is related to the poet's ability to excite wonder, talked of by Pontano, or Polydore Vergil. Dozens of very different figures 'serve to amplify'; they occupy this place because it has been discovered that they accompany that curious phenomenon recognized by every reader —that the manner in which the language has been used has somehow moved him to an active state of mind regarding whatever is the subject of the poem. The term 'amplify' does not imply making a thing appear admirable, in our sense; it may cause us pleasure, or dejection, but it must appear noteworthy. 'Useful for amplification' says nothing about the length of a figure; it says something about its capacity to make a subject impressive; and as full sensuous detail frequently impresses us, so, too, does the surprise of apt and brief significancy. The connotations strengthened by modern radio uses of the term are applicable ones; these figures are loud speakers.

[14] On *meraviglia*, on astonishment. An appendix to Sidney, on admiration, in Gilbert, p. 459, gives citations. A relevant extract from Pontano's *Actius Dialogus* (*Opera*, II, fols. 150ᵛ–3ᵛ [1518–19]) is printed by R. Kelso (with Fracastoro's *Naugerius*); some of his examples are images, and he distinguishes between orator and poet with respect to this capacity. Minturno also thinks of it as 'la rara laude del Poeta, che aumenta le cose di lor natura grandi, o miserabili, o pure odiose' (iv, p. 282; in Gilbert, p. 294; see Cicero's *De orat.* iii. 26. 104). Polydore Vergil's *De rerum inventoribus* (chap. 8) treats the idea more summarily, but the book had extraordinarily wide circulation (translated into all the vernaculars, appearing in a couple of hundred editions from 1499 on; see W. Ringler, 'Poeta nascitur non fit,' *JHI*, II [1941], 499).

The Renaissance takes more care, however, for the requirement of decorum; only that which merits loud speech is to be
amplified. One may, of course, take issue with the poet's judgment of his subject's importance; in that case it is to be remembered that one's quarrel is with his subject, not with his
imagery. Drayton's eight-stanza *descriptio* (so labeled, *The
Barons Warres*, vi, 433), of the Queen in her chamber, may
seem to modern taste a needlessly expanded and not even very
realistically precise set-piece. The narrative function it is meant
to achieve, and does, is the amplifying of the almost oppressive-
ly amorous mood of this meeting of guilty lovers; we may, of
course, count the motivation of Queen Isabella's betrayal of
Edward II as less worthy of note than did Drayton and his
readers.[15] The Queen and Mortimer comment upon the loveliness of the paintings in the chamber and see in them analogies to
their own lives. The rich descriptions of the paintings are also
meant to be organic, however much they might be enjoyed for
their contribution to the texture of the piece; they fulfil a function comparable to that of the description of the concerto in
Proust's *Swann's Way*, of the Beethoven Fifth in Forster's
Howard's End, or of the El Greco in Maugham's *Of Human
Bondage* (of course, the medium for long narratives is no
longer verse).

Some sensuous additions result from a change of stanza made,
as Drayton says, because the 'often Harmony' of the seven-line
stanza of 1596 'softned the verse *more then the Majestie of the
subject would permit.*' He says in the preface 'To the Reader'
that the eight-line stanza of 1603 has, on the other hand,
majesty, perfection, and solidity, like the Tuscan pillar in
architecture. This subject is meet matter for tragedy, and 'the
dignitie of the thing was the motive of the doing.' The dignity
of the thing is also the motive behind his amplifications.

[15] The relation of this love to the deposition of a king is more strongly emphasized in
this version than in the earlier *Mortimeriados*, and accordingly other less immediately
functional amplifications of the Queen's beauty are cut. Some image-changes since
1596 (*Mortim.*) put details amplifying the amorousness in the place of mere description; for example, lines on her breasts, with references to Venus' swans and doves,
supplant the smock description. A few sensuous details added in *BW* (like her hand
'So white, so soft, so delicate, so sleeke') appear to be due to the changed stanza form.

Exactly similar in motivation are the amplifications of Donne's 'The Calme,' though they magnify not a subject of tragic majesty but one intended to convey the maddening impotence of man, always in disproportion, for nothing fit (p. 178). This poem shows Donne using the kind of *descriptio* (of a 'time') called *cronographia*, a rare figure with him. The simplicity of this figure is somewhat obscured by Donne's extreme fondness for interlarding with tropes, and by the fact that the figure happens to assist in amplification of a negative type—that is, he is 'diminishing' his subject, a perfectly orthodox variant of amplifying. The ships languishing like Bajazet encaged, like slack-sinewed Samson; the sailors swimming in the brimstone bath of ocean, and returning like parboiled wretches; the still-lying dust and feathers—all these are quite in order as amplifications. They force us to attend to man's powerlessness. The poem abounds also in sparer figures proper to the mean or base style of a verse letter of satiric intent. In both Drayton's poem and Donne's, the sensuous images, because of their amplifying function, must show a care for other considerations besides precision; in each poem, the images are in decorous relation to the respective subjects. The two subjects are in almost diametric opposition; the images are very different.[16]

The fact that amplification involves the satisfaction of a criterion to be examined later—significancy—is responsible for much of the sensuous imprecision of Elizabethan images. It may mean that we cannot list even such basically descriptive figures as those examined, under a criterion of 'accurate representation.' Even painting was done less for the eye than for the evaluating mind and emotions; sensuous precision seems to be viewed primarily as instrument or by-product. Obviously, few poets, modern or ancient, paint just to paint. In modern poetry, however, even where amplification of a subject to affect a reader's judgments is an underlying motive, there seems often to be an assumption that precision of detail will of itself provide that amplification. This assumption is basically naturalistic, but its

[16] There are further reasons for this, but they are not pertinent here.

effects have become so widespread that they seem to characterize the modern manner rather than the style of a school. The
cinematographic method and the nature of the detail in a poem
like MacLeish's 'Cinema of a Man' (p. 36) may be a case in
point. The gas jets, the brown honey, the rhododendrons; the
bare straightforward details which stanza by stanza evoke one
country after another to the reader, who recognizes that a true
(though not necessarily a significant) fact about each has been
mentioned—all these achieve in sum an emotional effect against
the contrast of the first and last stanzas, in which the camera's
focus abruptly shifts. But an Elizabethan poet would have accomplished such an effect by an ingenious tissue of magnifications and 'diminishings.'

It will point up the difference to recall Herrick's 'Julia's
Petticoat' (No. 175), because the poem is startlingly precise for
its date, yet traditional. It too is exact, especially in the detail
given by verbs of movement: "two'd pant, and sigh, and
heave, / As if to stir it scarce had leave,' then wildly fling, then
cling to the thighs. But even the verbs are comparisons, chosen
to point to a single unstated comparison, and the tropes (unlike
MacLeish's figurative additions) are pure amplifications, clear
in purpose—'Celestiall Canopie,' 'a flame growne moderate,'
'That Leading Cloud.' If one has missed the significance of the
'conceit' that Herrick says melted him down, the conclusion is
unmistakable: 'sho'd it move / To Life Eternal, I co'd love.'
The more sensuous part of Herrick's image is a tiny *icon*, and
its subtlety lies in the fact that it embodies an unstated similitude (to the lady herself—wishful thinking). Herrick gives us
with especial fineness and charm the sensuous precision to which
poetry of the last hundred and fifty years has accustomed us,
though cunningly interwoven with traditional amplifications.
But I do not think that we may demand this precision of Elizabethan images, if their creators choose to amplify by other
means.

Amplification is not the only extra-sensuous function served
even by figures which merely express things plainly and copiously so that the reader seems to see them as though painted lively

in a table.[17] Hoskins brings in such 'evident and lively descriptions' under *Illustration*, the third function—besides *Varying* and *Amplifying*—which he distinguishes for figurative language.[18] We have seen that Hoskins considers Amplification and Illustration to be channels through which come, respectively, admiration *and belief*; they make men give their minds to a subject, being brought to wonder at it because it is extraordinary and to credit it because it is clear (see above, chap. iv, n. 4). A vividness so firmly instrumental will not make for descriptive images judged merely upon their vividness, even though they are bound to bring in 'life and lustre' by representing 'some unexpected strains *beside the tenor* of your tale' and by 'act[ing], as it were, your meaning.'

This last is Hoskins' note of the function of another sensuously descriptive figure, prosopopoeia (pp. 47–48). His remarks fit, for example, Marvell's many uses of the figure, quite as accurately as the more extended uses that come first to mind, like the speaking animals of Spenser's *Mother Hubberds Tale*.[19] Marvell's 'Dialogues', or his 'Mower's Song,' or the long passage on the oaks 'Upon the Hill . . . . at Billborow,' have certain of their qualities as a direct consequence of the structural use of this figure. One of the consequences is the compressed indirection by which he commends Fairfax's early retirement through the whispering speeches of the oaks; this figure is the device which allows and illuminates his own witty answer as conclusion: 'nor he the Hills without the Groves, / Nor Height but with Retirement loves' (p. 58).

If a poet chooses to use concretions to 'act out his meaning,' we shall have a peculiarly vivid form of interplay between ab-

[17] This characterization is Sherry's heading for various figures he groups under 'demonstration': *characterismus*, *mimesis* and *sermocinatio* (feigned dialogue and gestures), description of a place, time, person, affection, or perturbation (fols. xlv–xlvii [1555]). Puttenham groups them as 'counterfaits' (III, xix, 238–40).

[18] That the word 'illustration' when used in poetics has more than its modern meaning is substantiated by the fact that Hoskins goes on to recommend apt definition and careful making of distinctions as 'other *sparks* of figures' 'for *special lights* in every sentence' (p. 42).

[19] Or the figures of avarice and envy in the *Romaunt of the Rose*, to which Puttenham points as examples of the figure, 'whereby much moralitie is taught' (p. 239).

stractions and concretions—that lighting-up which Hoskins called Illustration; if the poet chooses to use such a figure in conjunction with fairly abstruse ideas (as in Donne's expostulation to 'The Sunne Rising,' p. 11), or in a brief reflective love poem (as in both Donne and Marvell), it will be so foreshortened that we shall have what seems like the 'direct sensuous apprehension of thought.'[20] It is obvious that sensuous detail springing from the use of prosopopoeia simply will not remain on the plane of sensuous description, because of the nature of its function, which dictated its use and which makes images not essentially but only instrumentally sensuous. Detail engendered by the use of this figure cannot help turning into something else before our eyes:

> Bind me ye *Woodbines* in your 'twines,
> Curle me about ye gadding *Vines*, ...
> But, lest your Fetters prove too weak, ...
> Do you, O *Brambles*, chain me too,
> And courteous *Briars* nail me through.
>
>   ('Upon Appleton House,' vs. 609, p. 78.
>   [Author's italics.] See also the address to
>   the meadows in 'The Mower's Song')

Such figures are traditional in nature and use; the foreshortening, however, induces a gnomic quality not so evident in earlier uses in different genres. Like others, Peacham recognizes this double nature (vividness combined with sharp point) in his

[20] This famous phrase of Eliot's has come to be used by modern criticism almost as an explanation of the peculiar nature of Metaphysical poetry (from 'The Metaphysical Poets,' in *Selected Essays* [New York, 1932], p. 246; also see below, chap. vii, sec. 3). I think that any Elizabethan or Jacobean would have found it obscure and psychologically untenable; their own orthodox explanations of the operation of metaphor and its variants illuminate Metaphysical tropes more simply and clearly. Other almost equally famous phrases, from Eliot's essay on Marvell, are pertinent to the present discussion: 'what we have designated tentatively as wit, a tough reasonableness beneath the slight lyric grace' (p. 252); 'structural decoration of a serious idea' (p. 255). Cf. the examination of the fountain image in the dialogue between Clorinda and Damon: in this image—though the poem 'because of its formal pastoral machinery, may appear a trifling object'—'we find that a metaphor has suddenly rapt us to the image of spiritual purgation' (p. 259). But transformations of this kind are expected of images, in pastoral. Marvell is using the double level of meaning which orthodox theory recognized as typical of this form (and of prosopopoeia). All metaphors are sudden; in the short forms favored by later poets they are given the violence of miracle. We simply see more of the situation in which the water becomes wine, in a *Mother Hubberds Tale*, or a *Parlement of Foules*, or a *Colin Clouts Come Home Againe*; the relation in their images between *thought* and the world of *sensation* is precisely the same.

discussion of prosopopoeia (p. 136), which an author uses to 'confirme and make his cause *evident*.' It may complain, accuse,
reprehend, commend (Marvell in the poems noticed above ac-
complishes, respectively, the fourth, third, and first of these).
Drayton's Endimion addresses the sweet leaves which tremble
as do his half-fearful loving thoughts, with considerable elaboration (vs. 345). Drayton, however, turns myth into symbolism
in a tale of 1,032 verses; Marvell in 'The Mower's Song' writes
a love-elegy in five short stanzas. The earlier poet, too, conveys
the particular feeling of a character, through paradox and pun
which use the obscurely felt relation between man and inanimate things. Prosopopoeia is an economical means for calling
into play the immemorial human impulse to see such connections, analogies, sympathies, or instructive parallels. The later
images are of no strange new kind; the later poem's form, point,
and tone differ.

It is by no accident that in poems set in a pastoral frame
Marvell finds especial use for figures of this type. He employs
those traditionally favored in this kind: the short *descriptio* of
time or season (as in 'Damon the Mower'); the *descriptio* of
place, with unelaborated circumstances befitting the 'low'
style of pastoral; the feigned dialogues—direct, held to homely
terms, yet pointed and significant (like those between Thyrsis
and Dorinda, Clorinda and Damon). I scarcely need to point
to less sensitive uses of these same figures in Googe's eclogues,
or itemize Breton's black-haired conies and leaping fishes. Because the combination here pursued, of simple vividness with
sharp point, is so firmly rooted in received theory touching this
kind, a typical statement of the reason for both is perhaps worth
quoting. Puttenham, like others, is

perswaded that the Poet devised the *Eglogue* . . . . not of purpose to counterfait or represent the rusticall manner of loves and communication: but under
the vaile of homely persons, and *in rude speeches to insinuate and glaunce at
greater matters*. . . . . These Eglogues came after to containe and enforme
morall discipline, for the amendment of mans behaviour, as be those of *Man-
tuan* and other moderne Poets.[21]

[21] I, xviii, p. 38; second italics mine. Cf. the statement of the commonplace in
Webbe's *Discourse*, in Gregory Smith, I, 262 (1586).

Pragmatographia, the description of an action, is perhaps the most used of all this group of figures and the most productive of sensuous accuracy. The peculiar assistance herein rendered by onomatopoeia is recognized. Peacham (p. 15) pulls in, as similarly useful, archaisms, compounding, and the *provignement* commended by Ronsard and Du Bellay. This last, the composition of words by adding suffix or prefix or by wrenching the grammatical nature of words, is especially familiar in Spenser. It has been commended in modern poets—as an unorthodox license.[22] It received much sixteenth-century commendation, and is a figure in good standing in rhetoric, *enallage.* The perceived relation of archaisms to apt, brief, and convincing description of actions illuminates one of Spenser's motivations for his use of them; with more space I could show that in the epic genre he uses them largely in images which have a sensuous or descriptive function, rather than in images which persuade, make distinctions, or elucidate.[23] The relation of archaisms to vividness is lost on the modern ear; not so, however, the use of onomatopoeia to convey sensuous qualities of experience.

Pragmatographia could not but bring sensuous detail into poetry, for it described 'any busines with the circumstances belonging thereunto' (Puttenham, p. 239). But it brought, quite properly, 'circumstances' rather than figurative language. Literal language characterizes both the description of action, and of action*s*, like a battle, a feast, Spenser's jousts and Herrick's 'Hock-Cart' (No. 251). Drayton uses circumstances rather than tropes to describe a procession (*E. and P.,* 766 ff.).

[22] C. Day Lewis comments upon this aspect of a modern 'revolution in language' (*op. cit.,* p. 71; in chap. iv, n. 12, above). Since the point is well brought out as it touches Spenser and the Pléiade in W. L. Renwick, *Edmund Spenser* (London, 1925), chap. iii, I may as well exemplify from Yeats instead of an orthodox Elizabethan: 'Lives that lonely thing / That shone before these eyes / *Targeted* ....' ('Quarrel in Old Age,' p. 291 [1933]); 'A *rivery* field spread out below' ('Vacillation,' p. 289 [1933]). It is only polite to notice that the *provignement* functions as Peacham says it will.

[23] The fact that Peacham mentions in 1593 the *Calender* and not the *Faerie Queene* may signify something about the impression the latter made upon contemporaries—how archaic did it seem to them? It may also signify something about the deceptive effect of orthography, in *FQ,* even to a fairly critical modern reader, and against his will. The discovery of Wyatt's 'Metaphysical' qualities followed hard upon the Tillyard, not the Foxwell, edition. What Spenser's images furnish of pithiness and apt significancy has perhaps been most neglected.

Marlowe keeps to literal language when Hero 'Being suddenly betrayed, div'd down to hide her. / And as her silver body downward went, / With both her hands she made the bed a tent' (ii, 262). The preceding simile, 'Like chaste Diana,' amplifies lady, not action.[24] These differences are not laboriously planned; they happen, when functions of images differ. But, as so often, rhetorical theorists had observed this, ages before, and such differences were implied in the very definitions which had furnished 'prentice-work for all these poets as students.

Similarly, it is when Drayton advances to the complicated or symbolical Platonic meaning of his myth, to the enigma of human relations with the divine, or to considering certain states of mind thence resulting in Endimion, that his imagery changes. He introduces cosmological similes in careful terminology (660 ff.), complexities of sacred nines and threes (881), technical physiological discussion of the 'effects of Melancholie,' with the senses radically compared to tired travelers (459). That is to say, when action is no longer the first consideration, the images become more complex and more metaphysical.

These shifts and changes are found in any type of poem which has some use for the longer and simpler descriptive figures. Donne's epithalamia are full of descriptive circumstances. We find the *cronographia* of dawn, of evening, that are conventional in this kind (even the sun's horses); the 'action' of the bride's dressing, with conventional amplifying references to Flora and Inde ('Lincolnes Inne,' p. 141), the time-worn prosopopoeia of Bishop Valentine's bird-filled diocese, the lists of jewels that blaze upon the bride ('Lady Elizabeth,' p. 127). But as he leaves description for point, that blazing turns swiftly to a blazing-star that signifies 'That a Great Princess falls, but doth not die.' In so far as epithalamia are lyrical 'praises,' they find considerable room for ample sensuous figures, as does Spenser's; but, although they are themselves *pragmatographia*

---

[24] So does the simple comparison *silver*. Marlowe's comparisons are likely to be conventional when action is being described: Leander 'scales' the ivory 'mount' of her breast (273); the parenthetical witty simile is introduced in the author's own voice not to describe precisely but to make a generalization on love, '(a globe may I term this, / By which Love sails to regions full of bliss).'

of a sort, being studies in expectation they are bound to have less action than emotional intensity, and Spenser's, too, exemplifies that fact by its imagery.

It is apparent from this discussion that to examine sensuous vividness as a criterion for images, in its practical workings, is to be continually forced away from it into recognizing others. It applies pre-eminently in narrative. We find certain fairly ample sensuous images in lyrical writing, but the very reason for their presence lies in certain accepted 'rhetorical' aims for lyrics which in the main do not induce sensuous precision. Or rather, such poems leave the latter far behind, pressing toward intentions either of praising or dispraising or of covert persuading. The amplification toward which even simple figures function forces us by its very definition toward a criterion of significancy or evaluative connotation for images. When one scrutinizes examples of single descriptive figures praised by the theorists for sensuous vividness, like *icon* or prosopopoeia or *pragmatographia*, one finds that one unexpectedly holds in his hand a persuasive similitude, or a double-edged figure used to enforce a point or to clarify a state of mind, or a set of literal circumstances frankly used to advance a narrative or otherwise operate as a springboard for diving into meanings. So far we have looked only at very simple images. A far more important matter is the relation of complex figurative language—of tropes—to this first criterion.

2. *Sensuous Vividness: Its Relation to Trope*

The absence of complex figurative language in images describing action is not characteristic merely of Elizabethan poetry; no images could better exemplify it in fact than Dante's. The main reason for this lies in the nature of tropes, which I believe no Elizabethan or medieval poet ever thought of as chiefly assisting sensuous exactness. To notice their nature before we leave this first criterion is necessary, however, because an understanding of the consistent emphasis upon sensuous imagery in a vast body of poetry—allegorical poetry—depends upon a clear understanding of trope. The relation is one which still obtains, and if the bases for Yeats's continued-metaphors were more universally understood and accepted, his poetry would offer very clear examples.

T. S. Eliot has glanced at these matters, in a comparison between an image of Dante's and one of Shakespeare's.[25] Dante's attempt to make us see more definitely what he saw is exemplified by his image of the crowd in Hell peering at him in a dim light 'like an old tailor peering at the eye of his needle' (*Inf.* xv). This is juxtaposed by Eliot to an image in which Shakespeare '*adds* to what you see,' conveys the strength of Cleopatra's fascination even in death:

> she looks like sleep,
> As she would catch another Antony
> In her strong toil of grace.

It will be noticed immediately that Dante within this figure is using language literally—they peered as the tailor peered. There is no trope here, none of what rhetorical theory calls 'translation'—the actual wresting of signification so that each word means something it does not ordinarily say, by virtue of its 'improper' application to two things which are similar but not the same. Shakespeare's *strong toil* is such a *translatio;* it operates immediately to furnish many meanings—which are possible, not compulsory, suggested, not stated, uncountable, not limited. They are not even any longer under the poet's own control, except as he reins them in with the tiny threads of the co-operating words. All tropes give the reader his head in this fashion. But it is precisely because they open all these dangerous possibilities that metaphors are so powerful an aid (as is Shakespeare's) to suggesting the significance of appearance, to in-sight as compared with sight. These two images exhibit a normal variation in form; and theory of either of the periods concerned carefully distinguishes the differences both in form and in purpose.

Images with such different functions could not possibly be similar in nature. Try clumsily to turn Dante's figure into meta-

[25] 'Dante' (1929), in *Selected Essays* (New York, 1932), p. 205. Author's italics.

phor, with 'tailor-eyed crowd' or 'needle-threading gaze,' and the exactitude he wanted is crowded out by unwanted suggestion and conjecture, and in so far as these are metaphorical they are not what he meant. Change the form of such an image, and we stop looking to think, to condemn, to marvel, exult, pity, or judge.[26] Dante's figure is one of the simplest classified in rhetoric—a *comparison* used to describe action; no competent poet would use it to direct a reader into the realm of values, concepts. He would know that he would not succeed. At least it would seem to me that no poet trained as either medieval or sixteenth- and seventeenth-century poets were trained could fail to perceive this distinction in purpose and its relation to form.

The rhetoricians from Quintilian on persistently note that metaphor is *necessary*, because there are no words for naming things, and that it *enhances* by including more of the significances of things. One may not name the 'leg' even of a rustic bench by saying 'stick of wood'; the supportingness is left out. Metaphor directs the mind inward to supply from remembered experience what is unstated. Tropes were not commended as suitable to clear visualizing of object, act, place, person; they were commended as a means of getting around the inadequacies of language economically, of making the reader think connections which language does not actually say.

It seems to me that no writer of this time, including Donne, would even have comprehended T. E. Hulme's remarks on metaphor (fairly typical of Symbolist and Imagist *theory*). He says in the *Speculations*[27] that only by metaphor can poetry be made not a language of counters but a visual concrete language, a compromise for a language of intuition which 'would hand

[26] One has only to read on in Canto xv and encounter images of a different form to have this happen to one: 'both parties will have *a hunger* of thee'; 'when the *nest* of so much malice was made'; '*banished* from human nature.'

[27] Ed. H. Read (London, 1924), pp. 134 ff.; on p. 138 occurs another phrase which has since been much applied to Metaphysical poets, especially Donne: 'the exact curve of the feeling or thing.' T. S. Eliot's warning that Hulme's book does not intend a complete general theory of poetry is pertinent here (*The Use of Poetry and the Use of Criticism* [Cambridge, Mass., 1933], p. 142); so are I. A. Richards' objections in *The Philosophy of Rhetoric* (London, 1936), pp. 127 ff.

over sensations bodily'; that figurative language endeavors to arrest you, 'to make you continuously see a physical thing, to prevent you gliding through an abstract process.' On the contrary, the earlier writers use metaphor (and the theorists commend metaphor) to fairly push one into an abstract process. We have just looked at images which illustrate this. Dante desires to do no such thing. Shakespeare does. Far lesser poets observe with care the line between two such differing functions, if their choice of images be any guaranty of their awareness of distinctions.

This needs illustration, though only a reader's lifetime of reading could suffice as proof. The Elizabethans are, of course, quite capable of 'handing over sensations.' The narrative poet may use a *topothesia*, full of circumstances largely literal—as Spenser's cave of Morpheus must be at once as literal as Gulliver's reports and as remote as myth, to convince us simultaneously that the dream of Una's falsity literally took place *and* that powers great beyond his human strength were arrayed against Red Crosse.[28] Or, poets may use simple metaphors involving mere comparison of qualities: Herrick's 'For Health on Julia's cheek hath shed / *Clarret*, and Creame commingled'; or Donne's 'Her who still weepes with *spungie* eyes, / And her who is *dry corke*, and never cries.' They may use similes whose logical simplicity holds the reader to one obvious likeness, mutes the string because overtones are not desired:

> Even as a bird, which in our hands we wring,
> Forth plungeth, and oft flutters with her wing,
> She trembling strove. . . . .[29]

But we note that in all these figures the physical properties or the ways of acting do actually pertain both to thing and thing

[28] The sound of the rain, the comparison to the bees, the negative comparison to the unquiet walled town with its noises of London at night, are a contrast but a reinforcement to the more complicated amplifying images: the world of waters wide and deep, Cynthia with her silver dew, low in the bowels of the earth where the cheerful normal sun never enters to make tenantable this eternal dark silence (*FQ*, I, i, 39–41).

[29] 'Upon Julia's Recovery,' No. 9; 'The Indifferent,' p. 12; *H. and L.*, ii, 289. Simple as is Marlowe's figure (a 'bare similitude'), it has a trace of conceptual function; it illuminates the generalization 'Love is not full of pity . . . . but deaf and cruel where he means to prey' (ii, 287).

compared to. These hand over sensations; that is why they are so simple. That function, far from being the reason for using metaphor, is the reason why it has been used so restrictedly.

When 'sensation' is left behind for a less concrete subject, like the motive of a described action, or the emotion felt, then the reader who tries to see continuously a physical thing, or to avoid gliding through an abstract process, is in bad case. This is true even of the simply constructed sensuous figure—the epic simile with careful choice of pertinent detail, or the large rather loosely drawn analogy:

> For as a hot proud horse highly disdains
> To have his head controll'd, but breaks the reins,
> Spits forth the ringled bit, and with his hooves
> Checks the submissive ground: so he that loves,
> The more he is restrain'd, the worse he fares. . . . .
>
> (*H. and L.*, ii, 141)

This horse (he is Leander) is introduced not to be looked at but to point four times at an abstraction. If amid these pawings and stampings we keep our eye on the other physical object, the lover, we step still farther away from the author's meaning, from irrelevancy into bathos.

Spenser compares the joy felt by Una, and by the disguised Archimago, at seeing each other, the first to that of the beaten, burnt-tawny mariner merrily making port, the second to that of the merchant who sees his profitable ship come in and hurls out vows to Neptune. If we watched any of these four persons and avoided gliding through several abstract processes, we should quite miss (for one thing) the sly unspoken dig which defines the nature of an Archimago and foreshadows his victimizing of Una. Exactly such reading of Spenser is in part responsible for his decline in prestige in certain quarters. The Elizabethans expected part of a reader's pleasure to come from the economy with which nice distinctions are suggested rather than stated. There is no need for Spenser to speak of what an alert reader is bound to grasp as *in*sight because of the nature of the figure; if *sight* were being spoken to, a simpler figure would have been used, and it would not have included a metaphor of the type of *hurls*.

If we leave story-telling poetry for poetry that (like *Antony*) has little business with description, we find that the retreat of the images from sense detail toward trope is still more noticeable. The simple form of Dante's figure asks me to keep to what is there said about both tailors and the damned, but I should be poorly equipped for understanding Donne or Spenser if I read these images in the same fashion:

> Blest *order* that hath him! the losse of him
> Gangreend all *Orders* here; all lost a limbe.
>> (*Epicedes* . . . . ; on Hamilton, p. 289 [Author's italics])

> Ere flitting Time could wag his eyas wings
> About that mightie bound, which doth embrace
> The rolling Spheres. . . . .
>> (*Hymne of Heavenly Love*, 24)

The *catachresis* (violent metaphor, *abusio*) is stronger in Spenser's young hawk than in Donne's amputation metaphor, just as the wit upsets more important concepts in order to rearrange them. This figure rings too loud a bell to be used for simple sensuous tasks. Nashe startles us with a synecdoche into the contemplation of abstractions that make the heart weep. 'Brightness falls from the air.' By definition, in every rhetoric, the very nature of this figure means that if I do not supply something not in the word, the poem remains in part unwritten.

There is no trope but makes this demand. I find no confusion about the recognition of this fact, either in Elizabethan theory or in Elizabethan images; I find merely some poetry which needs to make such demands oftener and more profoundly. There is an infinite number of degrees (requiring different types of trope) in which such a demand is made of me, as poets have an infinite number of purposes; the figure itself will indicate the degree, unless I am inattentive. Or unless the poet himself has mistaken it—but certainly the theory of the day gave such assistance as it could, always meager perhaps. As surely as I mistake a figure which tries to hold me to the page for one which sends me, guided only by the poet's suggestions, down whatever paths of experience may help me to understand what is not said—so surely I misread the poem. But again the formal nature of the figure is generally an unerring index, as it is in the Dante and Shakespeare examples.[30] This is not nastily self-conscious; I do not have to know what I am doing; I simply have to do it.

Any trope departs in some tiny degree from the sensuous function toward what we should call, I suppose, suggestion; but what it suggests is an interpretation, not more and more empirical data, however precise. We are familiar with the emphasis of Symbolist poetic on intimation rather than plain statement, on suggesting, which creates, rather than naming, which destroys. This is the same emphasis which one finds in Renaissance rhetoric and poetic when tropes are discussed. There, however, it is not introduced in revolt against plain statement. Some modern criticism seems to imply that 'science' *could* state the poets' meanings but that that would not be poetry; the Elizabethan seems content to assume that the universe is so full of barely capturable significances that any helps to adequate 'naming,' including metaphor, are to be prized.

We are led by Eliot's comparison to another pertinent point: the relation of this image-difference to allegory. There is no question but that allegory tends to use sensuous figures of little complexity. Eliot uncovers and comments on the practical fact of the matter; again, I think, no medieval or sixteenth- or seventeenth-century poet would have been at a moment's loss for the reason. The first and basic distinction in any rhetoric he used as a schoolboy—that between tropes and schemes—would give him the fact itself, for *allegoria* does not use metaphor; it is one.[31] By definition a continued metaphor, *allegoria* exhibits

[30] This is not to say anything so easy as that all use of tropes produces figures functioning like that from *Antony*. They vary greatly, even within the same poem. Herrick in his 'Nuptiall Song' (No. 284) holds us fairly closely to a physical object with his 'proud Plumpe Bed,' swelling like a cloud, brustling like a swan, tempting and wooing (even so, try to subtract *plump*, leaving the quoted image tropical). We are not forced far into *translatio* of the words until: 'throw, throw / Your selves into the mighty over-flow / Of that *white Pride*, and *Drowne* / *The night*, with you, in floods of Downe.' The tropical language here varies in function from simple amplification to the most nice and intense communication of an *état d'âme*. Nor is the difference simply a matter of denotative cf. connotative language; swans and clouds are quite as connotative as floods. The secret seems to me to lie in the type of logical basis for the relation perceived —but that is a matter for Part II below.

[31] Schemes arrange words; tropes actually wrest their signification. Tropes may be used within schemes. Together they constitute 'figures of words'; and 'figures of sen-

the normal relation of concretion to abstraction found in metaphor, in the shape of a *series* of particulars with further meanings. Each such concretion or sensuous detail is by virtue of its initial base *already* a metaphor; and a poet desiring full comprehension will be chary of introducing double metaphors.

I will exemplify. Suppose Donne had been writing an *allegoria*—of the ship of state, for example—with the 'bed-ridde ships' of 'The Calme' (p. 179). The normal development of the figure would be toward sensuously apprehensible details from the 'circumstances' of one bed-ridden, and of the ship, relatable to circumstances of the state: the forced inaction of idle oars like an impoverished commons; the unused brain, an unserviceable sextant like a debased clergy; the gradual rotting of the empty sails of an idle nobility. The more embracing the allegory, the more likely we should be to find vivid 'representational' detail. Donne would probably have wisely cut out the 'bed-ridden' metaphor and kept to a nautical frame of reference. He would certainly not have introduced *within a metaphor* additional new such frames with each detail (like his comparison to Samson), for he is uniformly eager to assist rather than to block our comprehension of his meanings, a tiring quality which has received the name of obscurity from the tired. He is not even willing to intrust to an *allegoria* the simpler (though deeper) meaning of his poem as it stands; he states with complete baldness the relation between this becalmed state and man's metaphysical situation.

We perceive thus that, by definition, none of the 'literal' comparisons adduced (like Dante's) *is* literal if it comes out of allegorical writing. The tropical nature of the details comes from their being parts of a larger figure. That figure is often so large or so primitive that it is universally comprehensible, like the

---

tence' (or thought) will necessarily contain figures of words, usually both tropes and schemes. The classifications become much entangled, but in so far as they reflect *purposes* of various figures, I have not observed damaging misunderstandings even in the hire-and-salary kind of rhetorician. Hudson's introduction to Hoskins' *Directions* has a lucid statement of the major lines of classification. I keep as clear as possible of multiplication of names for figures and of differences in classification which do not affect criteria for imagery; I also confine myself to figures which either are or would produce images.

great elemental tropes—Love:Flame, or Evil:Darkness, or Life:Voyage, or Form:Masculine. No wonder, then, that, as Eliot remarks, Dante's image is more translatable than Shakespeare's. Shakespeare's is already a *translatio*. Detail in allegory, *at the really figurative level of its meaning*, is equally difficult to translate completely from language to language, shades of meaning in words differing so subtly as they do. But the level at which the allegorical figures of Dante or Spenser are untranslatable is the level on which myth enables us to communicate by symbols rather than by naked words. If there is a word for *cross* in the second language, I can translate 'the cross towers over the wrecks of Time' and be understood, *provided* my reader knows the myth. The writer of an *allegoria* breaks down his figure for me into that which my senses can apprehend; it is hence perfectly possible to translate the statement that Una's face 'made a sunshine in the shadie place' (I, iii, 4), while at the level of the *translatio* that Light is Truth I encounter a symbol common to many myths and many languages. If all metaphor could not count upon some degree of such shared understanding, no reader would ever have understood any poet. Even 'it's a daisy' requires a hearer to whom daisies are not merely troublesome in a lawn, like dandelions. Obviously considerations such as these do not make images in allegorical writing 'simple' except in a restricted sense. They do make such images more sensuously ample.

An example I consider bad will show the necessity, in allegorical writing, of a circuitous and seemingly verbose routing of ideas through the slow channels of expanded sensuous imagery. The images must be long-winded in order to assist brevity in the whole piece—a necessity not always appreciated in Spenser criticism. The metaphorical base being a 'given,' economy and profundity in conveying meaning (which characterize metaphor) are achieved by elaboration of the terms of the metaphor. The following *allegoria* is too brief. It is too stingy to be economical. Googe is describing the careless gallant, who makes

> Pleasure . . . . his Mariner,
> to row in vyces Barge,

Then up the Sayles of wilfulnes.
    he hoyses hie in hast,
And fond Affection blowes hym forth,
    a wynd that *Pluto* plast,
Then cuttes he swyft, the seas of sin,
    and through the Chanell deape, ...

(Eighth Eclogue, p. 66)

Googe has read his rhetorical theory carelessly. The enrichment
by apt affinity of things compared which is the *raison d'être* of
the trope *allegoria* is disregarded; the bare statement destroys
the covert darkness which is its strength. Peacham says justly
that this figure serves to *engrave* the lively images of things, 'and
to present them under deepe shadowes to the contemplation of
the mind, wherein wit and iudgement take pleasure, and the
remembrance receiveth a longlasting impression' (p. 27 [1593]).
Where a metaphor is a star, 'in respect of beautie, *brightnesse*,
and *direction*,' allegory is a constellation. But Googe omits the
details which are the poet's means of directing his reader with
exactness toward a meaning, and his lantern for conveying that
clarté, 'illustration.' His meaning is correspondingly muddy and
dim.

This is peculiarly wasteful, since allegory with its sharp-
etched detail as of vision or dream should be one of the least
intellectually vague of figures if the wit and judgment are alert.
It can convey distinctions within a large concept with extreme
brevity. Googe does better in the figure of Excess in 'Cupido
Conquered': a great lubber, as much as six horses could draw,
with a broad flat face, a nose like a turkey cock, and a huge
belly (quoted in note).[32] *Allegoria* may sometimes be squeezed
down into a metaphor, but usually only if the poet is willing to
add much bare statement; 'drunk turkey-nosed Excess' would
shear down the *definition* by the omission of three attributes.
One turns to another Excess—Spenser's in *FQ*, II, xii; conceptual nuances that in unfigured discourse would require a
vermiculate dialectic are directed into one's mind with deft

[32] 'Muche nosed lyke a Turky Cocke, / with teth as blacke as Get. / A Belye byg,
full trust with guts, / and Pestels two, lyke Postes, / A knave full square in every poynt,
/ A Prynce of dronken Oostes' (p. 123).

brevity. The peculiar undiscriminating will-lessness and passivity of Excess, for example (sts. 56–57), would be entirely sacrificed in any metaphor that must highlight solely the disordered garments, or the deceptive daintiness, or the wanton and riotous colors, of earlier stanzas. Thus the paradox of this trope is that economy is dependent upon a leisurely sufficiency of detail.

Readers with more nearly the same sort of training *in reading*, as the poet's, would have been more aware than we are of the skill with which Spenser uses an *icon* or an emblem rather than an *allegoria* for simpler concepts, when he desires immediate emotional response rather than careful perception of distinctions. The loathsome description of Duessa's uncovering (I, viii) is an example; here each detail of dugs like bladders, rough maple-bark skin, fox-tailed rump, is not meant as a metaphor. 'Such is the face of falshood' sums up all the details of disproportion and decay or travesty of the natural. *Icon* is not a continued trope like *allegoria*, but a scheme, and is properly a descriptive scheme, meeting the criterion of accurate representation in its parts, and meeting a further criterion only in sum.

It is not by chance, then, that poems with many and complicated ideas to convey (like Dante's) make much use of *allegoria;* the conveying of the same subject in a mode that does not continuously take the short cut of metaphor would require so much bare philosophical statement that the work could scarcely be a poem at all. The figure must meet all the criteria for metaphor, and they are stringent. But also it must be read as metaphor and not as picture. There is no confusion whatsoever in Elizabethan theory on this point.

3. *Sensuous Vividness: Descriptive Ornament and 'Meaning'*

The last problem I wish to indicate before leaving this first criterion for a second, concerns the Renaissance answer to a question of poetics still very much alive. It is the basic question touching all use of ornament; hence it must be asked and re-asked in every connection, in the limited form suitable to that connection. To what extent did the Elizabethan regard these descriptively sensuous figures as necessary to the conveyance of his meaning? Could the 'meaning' be conveyed some other wise, or without them, and, if so, on what grounds was such ornament justified? This question did not trouble the Renaissance man in quite the same terms as it troubles the modern, who has been pricked by the developing autonomy of one group of disciplines—'science'—into greater sensitivity to the problem of how to differentiate and defend poetical discourse over against other modes.

Elizabethan theory is not particularly bedeviled by that difficulty which hounds so much modern criticism—the relative importance of 'content' and 'form.' These earlier theorists customarily make or imply a different division, and it is one which fits their poems admirably; it might not fit ours. Their ultimate critical questions are not 'What does the poem say?' and 'How is it said?' but 'What is the poem for?' and 'How has that been accomplished?' That is, they consider a poem with respect to end and with respect to means, a consideration which does not bifurcate it. They need not make the murdering division which we nervously make 'just for purposes of discussion,' for they do not identify *end* with *content* and *means* with *form*. In so far as there is any division, it cuts across in a different way.

When the end of poetry is spoken of, the poem does not seem to be conceived of as a unit made up of 'logically stateable structure of meaning' plus 'ornament,' but as a unit in which 'cause' is manifested by 'mode of operation.' Figurative language, ornament, is conceived of as one of the modes through which a purpose operates, but so, too, are any overt statements the poet makes of his 'idea'; so, too, is the matter or argument whose invention probably led him to the conceiving of his purpose. A poem's content is not its end; it is the first choice of instrument made by the poet. One might boil down the poem's statements-and-images into a paraphrase, a sort of core or structure, but that paraphrase would not state the meaning of the poem until one included in one's statement what the poet was using that structure *for*. Ideas stated and texture of ornament had precisely the same relevancy to the end of the poem—

the relevancy of instrument. The meaning of the poem is what-
its-ideas-in-that-form-do.

At the risk of oversimplification—for the conception is not
naïve—one might try to state this in the context of some of
Sidney's famous examples (in Gregory Smith, I, 165, 157, 195).
Sophocles' Ajax gives one, he says, 'a more familiar insight into
anger.' A poem may *say*, as the Stoics say, that Anger is a short
madness; but this paraphrase will not sum up what the poem
means, for its meaning is rather: herein is seen with an 'apparent shyning' how foolishly mad a short madness anger is. Sidney
naturally puts such ideas in terms of poetry's concern with
universals. A poem about Cyrus may say, as may a history of
him, that Cyrus was and did thus and so. But a poem will *so* say
this that this is not all it means, for through the artist's 'fore-
conceite' a man will see 'why and how that Maker [Nature]
made him,' will newly understand and evaluate all Cyrus-like
qualities in man. A poem has in it the germ of a reader's active
understanding of what it 'says,' and any discussion of the
poem's meaning must take cognizance not only of what ideas or
images it may be said to contain but of what those ideas and
images are doing, put together in that form.

They are not always stating some moral notion or advocating
some virtuous action. The understanding toward which those
ideas and images operate may sometimes be distinguished only
with reference to some larger frame of which they are a part. In
sung lyrics their operation is not to be understood without the
music. What they do in passages within longer pieces may sometimes be simply to amplify or point up a mood—as with songs in
plays, which are part of the whole complex web that is being
woven. For example, 'Full fathom five thy father lies' is not a
single poetic unit; it is heard by persons in a drama, and part
of its meaning is the effect it has in the context of the play both
upon us and upon Ferdinand ('This is no mortal business, nor
no sound / That the earth owes' [I, ii]). *Where* such a lyric is, is
part of what it does, and the meaning its author intended and
we receive cannot be equated either with some idea it states or
with the images it gathers together. Elizabethan comment

would, I think, like Ferdinand's four remarks on Ariel's two songs, mark straightway a poem's seeming 'cause'; commentary then frequently proceeds to consider how this was made manifest by content and by form.

On the level of such minutiae of poetic technique as the use of ornamental descriptive figures, acceptance of the common relevance of both 'ideas' and stylistic texture to a poem's meaning meant that such figures were seen *neither* as delightful irrelevancies nor as mere servants of the idea-structure. A useful example is furnished by Peacham's praise for one of Virgil's *cronographia:*

> Midnight an example of Virgill: It was night, and all weary creatures tooke their sweet slumber, both woods and raging seas had left their sounds, and starres now sliding in the midst of the night, when every field is husht, both beasts and painted birdes, ... and such as keepe the wide and wilde country are fast in sleep, when cares were slaked, and harts had forgot their labours.[33]

Peacham's comment is typically unself-conscious: 'Here the poet describeth the dead time of the night, *to amplifie the dolorous sorrow of Dido,*' who alone could find no rest. As Peacham sees it, this figure is neither a chance for Virgil to get in a beautiful though irrelevant description of his perception of night's qualities (though it gives delectation to the mind of the hearer because it describes night beautifully) *nor* a laboriously purposeful way of saying Dido was sorrowful (though it helps to say that). It rather offers a way of magnifying the *depth and importance* of Dido's sorrow. Our participation in that passion, made thus more active, operates to give us 'a more familiar insight into' all sorrow, for, as Sidney says, it is 'so in [its] own naturall seate layd to the viewe, that wee seeme not to heare of [it], but cleerely to see through [it]' (pp. 165–66).

One may find one variant after another of this praise of, or use of, 'texture' in terms of its relation to 'structure.'[34] But this

---

[33] P. 142; trans. from *Aen.* iv. 522 ff.; see the continuation of the passage. I am not concerned to indicate Peacham's sources, but this particular example and comment are used to exemplify 'Temporis Descriptio' in Erasmus' *De rerum copia (Opera omnia*, I, col. 82). In connection with extensive use of the latter as a schoolbook see the *ca.* 180 editions listed by H. D. Rix, 'The Editions of Erasmus' *De copia,*' *SP*, XLIII (1946), 595–618.

[34] Since I wish to utilize these terms of J. C. Ransom's, I shall cite essays in which he makes particular use of them, although here, as elsewhere, the differences which I

relation is not that of subordinate to chief, for both work toward an aim which is not to be equated with either, but dictates both. The notion of ornament as relevant to the poet's total purpose is sometimes explicit, sometimes implicit. Practice suits with their theory rather than with ours, where these differ. I mention this whole matter of the relation of ornament to meaning now in order that the reader will watch the phraseology of both images and quoted critical comment throughout the book. I cannot seem to discover that this era departed from a conception of 'texture' as unquestionably *logically* relevant. But the logic is the logic of the poem's unified conceptual and affective purpose, not of its paraphrasable ideas.

If ornament is not an irrelevance, neither is it a particularly clever kind of machinery which the poet can at will apply or not apply to contents or matters, its sole function being to 'get them over.' Completeness rather than simply palatableness is in question. Sidney says that the end of speech is 'the uttering sweetly and properly the conceits of the minde' (204). Utter the conceit in the manner 'proper' to it—as nearly as the medium will allow—and the resulting poem will manifest the true nature of that conceit through its 'texture'; try to boil down the poem's 'matter' into some quicker though less seductive statement, and you will not have 'the conceit' but only another attempt at utterance of the conceit, this time a far from proper utterance of it. The difficulty involved in 'properly,' the difficulty of making one's whole intention manifest, was assumed to be very great. No figure seems too humble or too mechanical to be thought of as instrumental to this figuring-forth of total mean-

---

indicate between modern and Elizabethan critical positions are so broad in nature, and so widely diffused in modern criticism, that the citation of single critics is inconsistent and even inaccurate. I utilize here Ransom's distinction between the *logical structure* and the *local texture* of poems; readers who do not know the careful and delicate argument through which he arrives at it must not lay at his door the bluntness it may here seem to take on. See 'Criticism as Pure Speculation,' in *The Intent of the Critic*, ed. D. A. Stauffer (Princeton, 1941), and *The New Criticism* (Norfolk, Conn., 1941) (iii, iv). Phrases utilized a few paragraphs hence are also for convenience taken from the same critic, as well as the example from *The Tempest*, and may be found in *The World's Body* (New York, 1938), pp. 116, 118. Although I have attempted it, I despair of putting the different-rather-than-opposed Elizabethan notions into modern phrasing; all the words one wishes to use have undergone semantic changes.

ing. The notion underlies discussion of the most ornamental, the most seemingly meaningless, of figures.

With certain types of poetic subject, the poet will receive special help from descriptive figures giving a sense of visual reality. The modern apologia for these would probably be that they convey the very *Dinglichkeit* of things in their 'rich and contingent materiality,' satisfying the desire for 'a plenum of qualities' which science does not satisfy (to use Ransom's phrases).[35] Renaissance poets and theorists alike attend closely to Aristotle's recommendations in the *Rhetoric* (iii. xi. 2) to put subjects before the eyes; they intend to achieve his *energia* (getting action and vigor through 'audace et variété de figures', as Du Bellay says, Book i. chap. 6); they strive for *enargia*, in writing that will exhibit the scene to the eye—which many commend in terms borrowed from Quintilian. But in all this cry for putting down the very substance of life, one can never detect praise of poetry on the ground of having achieved a presentation of just that. This period is incorrigibly interested in understanding, evaluating, taking some attitude toward the 'substance.' There seems to be common agreement upon this different attitude toward the nature of the poetic subject.[36]

There is also common agreement on the fact that figures inevitably lend to the poem a richness and depth which is the poet's surest instrument of power, of delight, and of completeness in his communication. He does not appear to value this power in order that he may say simply 'the world is thus' through images; even *icon* and *descriptio* always help to add at least 'alas!' or 'Hurrah!' This purposefulness is antipathetic to us; but I do not think that there is anything gained by blinking the fact that the sixteenth and seventeenth centuries wrote very purposeful poetry. (Purposes could develop as a

[35] Above, n. 34.

[36] Perhaps it is responsible for the fact that in Hoskins, for example, where there is an attempt to divide figures according to function, we find no group of figures designed to achieve the conveying of reality so defined in all its substantialness. Not even under the heading of Illustration, or vivid realizing. Rather, we find figures that *do* achieve this, scattered through his three functional divisions: Varying, Amplifying, Illustrating.

man wrote, then as now, of course.) Poets of the early seventeenth century wrote quite as willingly and unself-consciously
as those of the sixteenth under a conception of the poet's intention and subject as 'the uttering sweetly and properly the conceits of the minde.' Genres change, and typical conceptual
structures change, but the relation of both ornament and structure to meaning is similarly understood. At least this is true if
the manner in which that relation is maintained allows us to
judge of how it was understood.

The examination of this first criterion almost amounts to a
demonstration that Renaissance theory does not see the contribution of sensuous vividness as a sufficient contribution for
any image to make to a poem and that practice does not show
images functioning toward that end alone. The very figures
praised outright for satisfying this criterion are used for purposes which show that the vividness was regarded as instrumental to some further function served *by those images*. A general
term frequently used for it in Elizabethan criticism is 'significancy.' Various other considerations all point in the same
direction: the demands of Renaissance lyric theory, the functioning of figures toward amplification, the closeness of some
sensuous figures like prosopopoeia to the realm of symbol, the
tropical basis of sensuous detail in allegory. Elizabethan theory,
unlike some modern theory, does not consider tropes to be
especially suited to the task of conveying sensuous experience
vividly, and even descriptive schemes are seen as instruments
without which meanings would be less adequately conveyed.
   In the importance given to that 'conveying' one must notice
the undeniable relation which poetic bears to rhetoric in the
Renaissance; but in the careful definition of that 'adequately'
lay the distinction, delicately and surely maintained, between
rhetoric and poetry. Rhetoric does not need to be 'planetary
music' to be adequate to its ends; the service of the orator's
more immediate ends requires an agent who is something less
than a philosopher. The place given to nonutilitarian 'contemplating' in some modern theories of aesthetics is not unlike

the Renaissance notion of the poet in love with truth. But, even so, poet differed from propagandist less in aim than in the depth and scope of his vision, and his methods differed less in kind than in subtlety and power. There are in Renaissance thought reasons why logically useless sensuous imagery was seen as poetically insufficient (not mistaken), just as there are reasons why modern critical theories of the image as 'objective correlative' would have been seen as insufficient (not mistaken). The reasons lay in conceptions of the end of poetry, and of human life, for that matter, which are both more daring and more humble than modern conceptions. But that is the business of a later inquiry.

CHAPTER VI

THE CRITERION OF DELIGHTFULNESS

A SECOND criterion which images were asked to meet will seem to fly straight in the face of the paragraphs which concluded the last chapter. It was demanded of them that they be 'delightful.' An adequate definition of this word would require an extended treatment of the whole understanding of poetic 'pleasure' in the Renaissance. However, although I have tried to overlook no hints given in such discussions, I think that one may make a rule-of-thumb definition of what was meant by delightfulness in *images* by observing what characteristics are praised as delightful, meanwhile turning to images of the period to see if the qualities they possess are indeed explicable by assuming that the poets were trying to give the kind of delight praised by theorists. If the two conceptions of delight do not seem to jibe, we shall know that either the theory was incomplete or the poets incompetent. The chief pitfall which this method should avoid is the assumption that whatever we (or the Romantic critics) happen to find delightful is what the Elizabethans meant when they made this demand of images.

A chapter on delightfulness as a criterion can scarcely be quite self-contained, for this whole book is simply an attempt to discover the kinds of delight images were thought to give. Renaissance writers and readers do, however, isolate certain characteristics for this especial praise. The major characteristic is one which I shall treat as a third criterion: significancy. Moving profundity or logical aptness are commonly thought of as delightful, and we shall not be able to keep out of their way. But I shall search out primarily Renaissance ideas regarding imagery which appear to us to involve 'delight' only, and perhaps rather lax notions of delight, inducing images which simply seem to get in on their faces.

There are two holes in the critical fence that especially rouse our suspicion. The praise of 'variety,' 'varying,' makes us suspect that delightful imagery could mean mere exuberant multiplication of particulars to achieve 'copie.' And the praise of 'beautifying' makes us suspect that delightful imagery could mean simply gracefully elegant imagery. Modern comment habitually accuses late-sixteenth-century imagery of both these inadequacies, contrasting it with seventeenth-century imagery. I should like first to come at a better understanding of how these two emphases, which seemingly have only superficial 'delight' to recommend them, touched imagery; thereupon to notice what safeguards were set upon the requirement of delightfulness. Then we can probably trust the other and profounder meanings of 'delight' to arise under other criteria.

1. *The Criterion of Delightfulness: 'Varying'*

I know no better demonstration of the effect which the exhortation to 'vary' might have upon imagery than Carew's string of ways to say 'get out,' in his putting-forward of copiousness as part of 'The Excellency of the English Tongue':

. . . . neither cann any tongue . . . . deliver a matter with more varietye then ours, both plainely and by proverbes and Metaphors; for example, when wee would be rid of one, wee use to saye *Bee going, trudge, pack, be faring, hence, awaye, shifte,* and, by circumlocution, *rather your roome then your companye, Letts see your backe, com againe when I bid you, when you are called, sent for, intreated, willed, desiered, invited, spare us your place, another in your steede, a shipp of salte for you, save your credite, you are next the doore, the doore is open for you, theres noe bodye holdes you, no bodie teares your sleeve,* &c. . . . .[1]

Such praises as these seem to imply delight in mere inventive facility as such.

It must be noted, however, that Carew is adducing these 'prooffes of our copiousnes' in order to show that the author who writes in English will be able to choose, out of such a variety, the word or image which conveys his meaning with

---

[1] In Gregory Smith, II, 292 (?1595–96). Author's italics.

exactly the right overtones. The praise of *copie* throughout this period needs study, but it is so frequently found in this context —of praise for *plenty that provides choice*—that I am not at all sure we have been justified in interpreting it to mean simply 'Elizabethans admired plentiful imagery.'[2] When the Elizabethan studied Erasmus' *De copia* in school, did he learn to admire copiousness in poetry, or did he learn how to invent copiously so that he could be exact and forceful? These are two very different things as far as poetics is concerned.

Something may be learned from typical practical counsel about figures that especially aid facility. One may look at the most *copie*-producing figures—distribution by circumstances, *synonimia*, *periphrasis*, the heaping figures like *congeries*, or climax. Anyone who will read Puttenham's discussions[3] of these figures will note that images formed in line with his commendations would not be multiplications of particulars, but additions to amplify, to enforce persuasion mightily, to enforce the cause and renew the memory. We find him objecting to a *periphrasis* on spring that 'blabs out' the day and month, because it leaves the reader nothing to study on. Sherry has a section of 'ungarnished' figures.[4] They are vices of style, but I can distinguish

---

[2] The reservation applies especially when this praise is found in an *ars poetica*. Semantic changes in the word *art* have been responsible for various confusions of sixteenth-century counsels for *learning the techniques of an art* with notions of the *nature of a work of art itself*. An example touching imagery is the frequent misinterpretation (it seems to me) of Ascham's attitude toward Imitation. Ascham's directions are to assist a student to learn his craft; they are not expected to produce as their result 'a poem,' but 'an exercise, by which its author shall have learned the methods and the decorum an artist may follow in creating.' Faithfulness in copying is hence a criterion for excellence only in a very special sense.

It is to avoid this type of confusion that I have tried even with each figure to abstract the *criterion on grounds of which* advice was given; this is the meeting-point between a technique and a work of art. So read, the rhetorical manual can lay claim to being part of poetics. I think that the intelligent Elizabethan user read such manuals not as recipes for poems but as helps toward putting one's poetic criteria into practice. Hence I cannot find myself agitated (as is C. S. Baldwin, e.g., in *Renaissance Literary Theory and Practice* [New York, 1939]) at the Renaissance 'confusion' between rhetoric and poetic. 'Varying' also is, of course, a rhetorical school term, used to designate the processes by which students were taught to achieve the many kinds of variety which delight us in literature; see T. W. Baldwin, esp. Vol. II, chap. xxxvi (*op. cit.*, in Appendix, Note B).

[3] Pp. 222, 214, 193, 236, 208 (1589).

[4] 'When eyther there lacketh order, or beautifying in the wordes' (fol. ix [1555]).

in them only two definitions of viciousness: indecorous disproportion of style and matter, and overcopiousness. Peacham's
warnings against excess, in the especially copious figures, are
exact and practical; *divisio* and *partitio* will enrich, and are apt
to open the bosom of nature, but it is a vice to 'part' as did
that fool who divided into *why? wherefore? for what cause?* and
to what end? (p. 125 [1593]). *Synonimia* (150), a 'rich and plentiful wardrop,' delights for its variety, but most because it *maintains the worthiness* of a word or thought that deserves such
repetition in changed habit. *Periphrasis* arose first from necessity, then from the desire of *copie* and facility by which the thing
is made *more evident and lightsome* (p. 148). It is really difficult
to quarrel with forcefulness, suggestiveness, emphasis, and
luminousness as desirable poetic aims. We may quarrel with the
application of these notions, and protest that the Elizabethan's
copie produces our tedium. But that is quite different from objecting to his poetic on grounds of its advocating mere multiplication of figures for variety.[5]

Something may also be learned from examining overt commendation of variety to see whether facile inventiveness in turning out images is deemed sufficient.[6] One may find specific advice applicable to imagery in Hoskins' division devoted to *Varying*.[7] The first shock one receives comes from the nature of the

[5] Harvey distinguishes between *redundantia* and the *copia* of the true Ciceronian
(*Gabriel Harvey's Ciceronianus*, ed. H. S. Wilson and C. A. Forbes ['University of
Nebraska Studies,' No. 4 (1945), p. 56]). Infelicitous attempts at *copie* were doubtless
rife; they usually are. See Jonson's comment on some such, in *The Alchemist* ('To the
Reader').

[6] Tasso, in his somewhat general discussion, is clearly thinking of the values of contrast and f true diversity in one's imitation of diverse nature; and his safeguards are
the preservation of an equally true unity (complex rather than facile or obvious) and
the maintaining of an unconfused clarity of effect (see *Discorsi*, iii, p. 125 [1594]; trans.
in Gilbert, p. 499). An accusation commonly leveled against the 'Spenserians' (influenced by Tasso) is that they were willing to sacrifice vigorous singleness of effect for
copie. Perhaps we are less well trained than the sixteenth century in perceiving unity
in multiplicity. Such values with such safeguards would not produce a spate of *unfunctional* images, and their authors cannot have thought them so.

[7] Which may have taken some suggestions from the *De copia*; see Hudson's ed.,
p. xx, note. One may find in Erasmus a great number of the emphases, methods, and
conceptions which I have chosen to quote from later writers in English: the understanding of perspicuity, of 'evident' realization (through *icon*, for example), discussions of
amplification, and decorum, of the various kinds of *descriptio*, etc. (see esp. Book ii of
the *De copia*).

figures included; the second, from the kind of achievement Hoskins expects from them. As we should expect, he takes up several figures using repetition or shifts in syntactical order, but the
delight they furnish is not poetically negligible; like other men
of this period, Hoskins is sensitively aware of the relation between subtle musical and rhythmical variations and poetry's
moving power. But the chief evidence against a poetically lax
definition of 'varying for delight' is Hoskins' inclusion under this
heading of four major tropes, including metaphor and synecdoche.

The delight furnished by these figures (as traditional theory
itself describes it) is entirely inconsistent with any equation between 'delightful imagery' and 'pleasurable multiplication for
copie.' Our next task must be to inquire more closely into just
why the Elizabethan persistently refers to them as 'delightful.'
For Hoskins is far from alone in thinking that tropes as well as
copious schemes are delightful ways of providing variety; the
phrase is worn with use. Such judgments quite prevent us from
concluding that this criterion gave safe-conduct to any image
that simply furnished another pleasant way of saying the same
thing. What sort of images *did* it then recommend?

The first part of the answer is: images are delightful if they
make for a greater intellectual richness. This is one of the most
important implications of the demand for variety. Metaphor is
the major trope for the accomplishment of this end. Two characteristic sixteenth-century assumptions regarding metaphor
which find little room in modern comment are here involved:
one dealing with the nature of the figure and one with its usual
purposes.

I have encountered no early discussion of metaphor which
falls into the modern habit of emphasizing the nature of *that to
which* the comparison is made; the emphasis even in the most
pedestrian of handbook-writers is upon pleasure in the nature of
the 'affinity' seen. Discussions from the *De copia* on, and before
it,[8] dilate upon types of relatedness which are fruitful—*trans-*

[8] Sources for Elizabethan remarks upon metaphor are much too complicated to
trace here, ranging from Aristotle and Quintilian through medieval rhetorical treatments to the standard fifteenth-, sixteenth-, and seventeenth-century schoolbooks,

latio from the realm of animate to that of inanimate nature, from the realm of men's doings to that of abstractions, etc. Sherry stresses the 'strength & power of the signification' (fols. iii^v, xxiii^r [1555]). Peacham talks at length of the pleasure obtained from aptness of proportion and nearness of affinity; metaphors are ready pencils to line out and shadow any manner of proportion in Nature (pp. 3–14 [1593]). Assumptions that relate metaphor-making to the logical place *similitude* underlie his and others' discussions of it, rather than the modern assumption that metaphor-making is especially related to the play of association and to subconscious prepossessions for certain contents. (Such modern assumptions underlie studies of imagery like C. F. E. Spurgeon's.)

Emphases like these obviously bear intimate relation to the nature of the delight which the sixteenth century expected metaphors to give. One claim made for them has been discussed by so recent a writer as I. A. Richards.[9] I give it in Hoskins' phraseology: 'Besides, a metaphor is pleasant because it enricheth our knowledge with two things at once, with the truth and with similitude' (p. 8). Unlike various modern critics, Hoskins does not seem to think of the notion that anyone would find an image delightful because two *items* were mentioned; like other theorists, and like all the poets, he expects readers to experience greater intellectual pleasure because simultaneously some true thing is conveyed and a *relatedness* is seen. All Elizabethan and seventeenth-century metaphor tries, it seems to me, to provide primarily this pleasure. Consequently, poets throughout the period (including the Metaphysicals) take a

---

and the treatises on rhetoric and poetic written in many countries other than England. Elizabethan and seventeenth-century chance remarks are equally of a piece with this whole long tradition; there is no gap between the learned and the workaday attitudes.

[9] See esp. Lecture V in *The Philosophy of Rhetoric* (New York, 1936). Richards' invented terms, though they are to be welcomed, do not suffice for a statement of the sixteenth-century emphasis. An orthodox discussion would neglect the *vehicle*, mention the *tenor*, but concentrate upon a third element: the nature of the relationship seen—its aptness, proportion, illuminatingness, analogical force, profundity, witty tenuousness, etc. Sixteenth- and seventeenth-century rhetoric and logic (like what they sprang from) stress precisely that for the absence of which Richards rebukes 'the traditional theory'—metaphor as a 'transaction between contexts' (p. 94).

very considerable responsibility toward giving the reader whatever he needs to enjoy not the content of the simile but the
similar*ness* of its two terms. The pleasure is generally a highly
conscious one, and the enrichment intellectually stimulating,
but puzzle value is at a minimum.

One short statement from Peacham will relate a kind of delightfulness consistently claimed for metaphor to certain ends of
poetry already discussed.[10] A poet will 'vary' with a metaphor
'for the grace sake of the similitude, and also for the cause of
perspicuitie of the thing expressed' (p. 2). This praise of perspicuity is universal in treatments of metaphor.[11] To Hoskins,
translatio is the 'friendly and neighborly borrowing of one word
to express a thing with more light and better note.' Du Bellay
protests against metaphorical epithets which are cold or lazy
('oysifz,' ii, chap. 4; 'ou froids ou ocieux,' ii, 9); one must use
those of such a kind 'que sans eux ce que tu diras seroit beau-
coup moindre.' The intellectual richness gained through perception of apt affinity was not, in other words, expected to give
merely the cool pleasure one has in logical lucidity, which is
something less than 'perspicuity.'[12]

The expectation of this kind of delight from metaphor does
not in the least rule out the suggestiveness and play of the mind
which modern discussions of metaphor's effect and origin prefer
to emphasize. Other remarks in Hoskins' section on it are il-

---

[10] The complicated subject of the ends seen for metaphor involves all the ends seen
for poetry and can receive no summary treatment here, being rather confronted in
section after section as various criteria and functions of imagery are examined.

[11] In this, as in other connections, one is led to suspect modern labeling of 'clearness' as a pseudo-classical element in some Elizabethan poetic when one sees how often
the shade of meaning intended is not 'metaphors that are lucid and plain and direct'
but 'metaphors that will help to realize *the poetic subject* for the reader.' See above,
chap. ii, n. 8.

[12] However, the emphasis upon delight afforded by metaphor's power to illuminate
did have one important corollary which does not loom large in modern discussions of the
figure. All these remarks look toward a richer texture for poetry. But pleasure precisely *in* the logical relevance of the ornament to the total meaning is not only accepted
but accepted *as a criterion* for 'delightful' metaphor.

The *maker* of a metaphor had best then have prompt wits and perfect logic (universally emphasized). Peacham discusses the 'principall efficient' of metaphor; the
qualities of mind that come into play are exact or discreet judgment, and memory the
'retentive power' of the mind (past experience furnishing the material for new connections seen).

luminating. In addition to noting its functions of *clarté* and emphasis, he says:

> though all metaphors go beyond the signification of things, yet are they requisite to match the compassing sweetness of men's minds, that are not content to fix themselves upon one thing but they must wander into the confines; like the eye, that cannot choose but view the whole knot when it beholds but one flower in a garden of purpose; or like an archer that, knowing his bow will overcast or carry too short, takes an aim on this side or beyond his mark.[13]

These are shrewd remarks on the nature of all metaphorical language and some of the reasons for it. I take Hoskins' figures to be in praise of that richness of all figurative language which goes beyond mere indicating of things to convey them whole, as configurations of meaning. The relevance, finally, even the useful necessity, of this richly textured language is accepted by Hoskins—his archer figure would have no meaning else. It is not that the poet's eyes, and hence his metaphors, note irrelevancies in the garden, but that his mind can no more confine itself to the poverty of literal significations than his eye can remain upon one marigold when the whole knot combines to shout 'oh LOVELY flowers.' The poet does not shoot without a mark; he is in control, and his metaphors will be relevant, but with the relevance of a *poetically adequate* means. There is nothing niggling, barren, or didactically slavish about conceptions of metaphor such as these. Also, however, they are tied down firmly to requisites which prevented Elizabethans from equating 'delightful imagery' with easy and fulsome variation.

These two assumptions about the nature and end of metaphor—that it gave delight by the intellectual agility involved in a double mental act and by the enrichment of the signification—combined to make it a figure especially delightful to the judgment, however pleasing to the senses. Pages of examples would go but little way toward proving this; I hope that the reader will hold it up against any metaphor he meets throughout the book, whether it be pre-Spenser or post-Donne.

Obviously, metaphors vary infinitely within the limits set by function. I shall risk the accusation of blurring such minute and

---

[13] P. 8, under the function *Varying*.

exquisite differences, in order to illustrate these somewhat arid theoretical points by five metaphors from very different poets— Sir John Davies, Donne, Spenser, and Yeats. I have taken passages all of which concern themselves with the power yet the inadequacy of the senses or affections, but just for entertainment.[14]

Sir John Davies questions the power of the senses to apprehend truth, since reason's lamp that spread her beams through man's little world is become a sparkle, half-extinct:

> What can we know? or what can we discerne?
> When *Error chokes the windowes* of the minde,
> The divers formes of things, how can we learne, ...
> How can we hope, that through the eye and eare,
> This dying sparkle, *in this cloudy place*,
> Can recollect these beames of knowledge cleere. . . . .
>
> (*Nosce Teipsum*, I, p. 18; in HH, p. 359)

Donne is answering the same question:

> In this low forme, poore soule, what wilt thou doe?
> When wilt thou shake off this Pedantery,
> Of being taught by sense, and Fantasie?
> Thou look'st *through spectacles;* small things seeme great
> Below; But up unto the watch-towre get, ...
> Thou shalt not peepe *through lattices of eyes,*
> Nor hear through Labyrinths of eares, ...
> In heaven thou straight know'st all, concerning it,
> And what concernes it not, shalt straight forget.
> There thou (but *in no other schoole*) maist bee
> Perchance, as learned, ...
>
> (*The second Anniversary*, 290, p. 259)

Our pleasure in these images is obviously intended to be almost independent of the sensuous experiences suggested by their terms. One pleasure is that we realize man's predicament of obstructed vision with sudden clearness (perspicuity) by thinking of his senses as choked windows or as insufficient eyeglasses or as lattice-covered peepholes. Another pleasure is 'in similitude'; the ways in which a *cloudy place* is related to man's narrow unlighted little inner world are suggestive and emotionally

---

[14] Subject matter is not a determinant, though the effects of different subject matters upon general intention can confuse the issues.

just, whereas the unrelated aspects of windows, lattices, cloudiness, do not obtrude and would not enrich our pleasure. Neither poet makes the slightest move toward bringing these aspects into our vision.

Spenser in the following passage is writing an *allegoria* (continued metaphor) of the killing of Maleger, that strange bodiless captain of the affections of man's mind. I do not choose the incredibly subtle descriptions of his nature, but the moment when Spenser dramatizes the notion of the endless rebirth of this 'dead-living' enemy, buried in his mother earth only to return with greater strength. The reflection is Arthur's ('his' is, of course, 'Maleger's'):

> He then remembred well, that had bene sayd,
> How th' Earth his mother was, and first him bore;
> She eke so often, as his life decayd,
> Did life *with usury* to him restore,
> And raysed him up much stronger then before,
> So soone as he *unto her wombe* did fall; . . . .
>
> (*FQ*, II, xi, 45)

The latent inconsistencies between Earth as mother's womb and earth as compounder of interest do not arise because metaphor keeps the mind to relevant suggestions with a magnet's invisible force; the two combine harmoniously to clarify and enrich our conception of the relation of the affections to the dust we are made of.

In the first passage below, Yeats happens to use one of the oldest of metaphors, but this is not unlike him. We experience different kinds of pleasure from the two figures; in the first we neglect irrelevancies for delight in a clear relation between two sets of terms, as in all traditional use of metaphor:

> An aged man is but a paltry thing,
> A *tattered coat upon a stick*, unless
> Soul clap its hands and sing, and louder sing
> For every *tatter in its mortal dress*,
> Nor is there singing school but studying
> Monuments of its own magnificence;
> And therefore I have sailed the seas and come
> To the holy city of Byzantium.
>
> ('Sailing to Byzantium,' p. 223 [1927])

But in the second we explore irrelevancies and delight in ambiguous suggestions:

> The *unpurged images of day* recede;
> The *Emperor's drunken soldiery* are abed;
> *Night resonance* recedes, night-walkers' song
> After great cathedral gong;
> A starlit or a moonlit dome disdains
> All that man is,
> All mere complexities,
> The fury and the mire of human veins.
>
> ('Byzantium,' p. 285 [1930])

For a poem (the first) in praise of 'the artifice of eternity,' this scarecrow variant of the metaphor of body-as-garment is so apt, so superbly decorous, that it puts into shadow all the earlier examples, on grounds of just what earlier poetic demanded— luminousness. The slight ridiculousness, the curious secretly frightening quality—all suggestions which the poet wilfully evokes—contribute to the logical structure that which could not otherwise be contributed; and our minds are more complete- ly under his control than in the Donne example, where we obey by willingly looking in the direction indicated rather than im- mediately as by magic. The magic is chiefly logic; Yeats's image is more carefully formed (prepared for and delimited) than any of Donne's five.

The second Yeats passage, on the other hand, gives a type of delight that I do not think Renaissance writers strove to give with metaphor, either early or late. They might easily have used such details, but these would not have been metaphorical; if part of an *allegoria*, either the similitudes would have had the public character of symbol, or some indication would assist the reader to enjoy clearly perceived relatedness and such sugges- tions as fell in therewith. All metaphor uses suggestion, and goes beyond a name, as Hoskins says. But the Elizabethan, and cer- tainly the Metaphysical poet, characteristically put his sugges- tions into logical harness and enjoyed the very strength with which they helped to draw the cart. We may, of course, learn from other works of Yeats's what logical harness these sugges- tions (e.g., of day and of purgation) wore in his mind, and thereby complete our understanding of the 'affinities' between the terms of his metaphors; our pleasure is not however contingent upon this.[15]

It is clear that 'varying' through metaphor would make for 'delightful' images not primarily sensuous in function, though plentiful in the mention of particulars. Donne's style, for example, highly tropical rather than schematic, is jammed with concretions, but no one could call it sensuous. Such a fact would cause nobody in the Renaissance any embarrassment, for that era did not share the modern antirational bias which has led us to seize with relief upon phrases like Eliot's 'sensuous apprehension of thought.' The Renaissance poet was perfectly willing to reveal and to cause reflection. An unabashed emphasis upon the role of the judgment in poetic pleasure is found in another quality generally thought to satisfy primarily the criterion of delightfulness. It is a quality regularly asked for, early and late: intellectual subtlety.

Considered with respect to images, this kind of delight was supposed to lie genuinely in their subtlety and not in either of two near neighbors to that quality—neither in unresolved ambiguity nor in mere dressing-up of the ordinary. Puttenham calls this delightful quality 'a certaine noveltie and strange maner of conveyance,' disguising the poet's language and style no little from the ordinary and accustomed, yet 'decenter' (more fitting) than that would be. This will delight and allure 'as well the mynde as the eare' of any 'civill' reader (III, i, p. 137). Poetical clothing is to be 'kindly' (natural), but nevertheless convey the limbs 'somwhat out of sight, that is from the common course of ordinary / speach and capacitie of the vulgar iudgement.' There is no implication that the possession of limbs was intended to remain matter of conjecture. These counsels and the many we find like them do not advise the prettifying of reality by vicious 'poetic diction,' nor yet the wilful obscuring of reality through overingeniousness; the pleasure lies in the

---

[15] It should be noticed, nevertheless, that the suggestions we enjoy are those the poet allows to play upon us; he calls the tune in both cases—perhaps this is one of the differences between Yeats and his imitators.

mental excitement of seeing *through* the strange manner, not in seeing *it*, and in seeing more through it, not more dubiously. Various figures are expressly devised with this kind of delight as their end.

Such covert or wittily subtle figures need illustration rather than discussion. The tissue of synecdoche and metonymy in Herrick's 'Upon Silvia' (No. 62) will illuminate the critics' comments which follow. The cool tone of detached incivility depends almost entirely upon the use of these 'dark' images, especially when accompanied by the bland pretense of literalness in the last line:

> When some shall say, Faire once my Silvia was;
> Thou wilt complaine, False now's thy Looking-glasse:
> Which renders that quite tarnisht, which was green;
> And Priceless now, what Peerless once had been:
> Upon thy Forme more wrinkles yet will fall,
> And comming downe, shall make no noise at all.

We do not think of this as florid, but, of course, it is quite as flowered as any other heightened poetic speech. The wit resides in Herrick's reduction of a thing to its quality (*tarnisht*), his representation of a general by a special (*wrinkles*), his possibly tropical use of *Looking-glasse*, and so on. The flowers grow double, as in the metonymy grafted on metaphor in *green* youthfulness—a kind of compression which Herrick found particularly useful, in his short restatements of axioms or conventions. As usual, the texture by means of which such structures are made manifest determines the exact meaning they carry to us; Herrick, like any good rhetorician, is quite aware of the relation between tone and logical meaning.[16]

[16] I am not unaware of the connections possible between several problems considered just here and various discussions in Kenneth Burke's critical writings; see esp. *Philosophy of Literary Form* (Louisiana State University, 1941) and 'Four Master Tropes,' *Kenyon Review*, III (1941), 421–38 (it is amusing to find him in agreement with Mazzoni on how the number of tropes can be boiled down; see *Della difesa*, i, chap. 18 [1587]). He makes points of considerable interest, even when (as frequently) they seem to me to be those explicit or implicit in most traditional writers on rhetoric. For example, these last seem to me to assume and build upon, as a fact about language, what he discusses as 'poetic meaning.' It is a temptation to state in their phraseology his remarks about 'neutral' and 'weighted' words, or his entertaining example of two hypothetical words for the neutral *shoe: bims* for Communist ones and *bams* for

Peacham warns against using synecdoche among the ignorant or the captious. The latter might boggle at the jump from *tarnished* to *green*. Puttenham, calling synecdoche the 'figure of quick conceite,' rightly relates it to 'speeches *allegoricall*, because of the darkenes and duplicitie of his sence' (p. 195). Metonymy is similarly praised for serving to variety, brevity, and signification (Peacham, pp. 22, 18). *Catachresis* is the most dangerous among the dark figures delighting by their subtlety. Some discussion of its nature will repay us, for it has had a peculiar modern history.

What modern criticism calls the 'radical' or the 'dissonant' or 'conical' image[17] is the traditional rhetorical figure *catachresis*. 'Somewhat more desperate than a metaphor,' as Hoskins says, it expresses one matter 'by the name of another which is incompatible with it, and sometimes clean contrary' (p. 11). This figure combines neatly with hyperbole when one is cheerful, and with 'diminishing' when one is disgruntled. Diminishing is the negative form of amplification; since *catachresis* is a tersely powerful (and often ironic) aid in the 'enlargement' of disapproval, Spenser, for example, uses it in cantos on Braggadochio or Malbecco. Description of the figure elicits an occasional comment on content of image, extremely rare in early critics. Even so, Hoskins' examples show that he was thinking primarily not of dissonant *additional* suggestions of the metaphor's second term (as would a modern commentator on Eliot's 'evening . . . . like a patient etherised') but of *relatedness* a little difficult to see. This strangeness, or intellectual

---

Fascist ones. The rhetoricians are entirely aware of the distinction he makes, and when Spenser prefers to have Cuddie speak of his *galage* instead of his shoe, he is simply choosing—according to accepted theory—to have bim-wearers call their shoes bims (*S.C.*, Feb., 244 and gloss, or Sept., 131).

In general, it seems to me that Elizabethan theory, built on Aristotelian logic and on classical and medieval rhetoric, is pretty completely in possession of the major discoveries of what is presently termed semantics, as those discoveries have been so far used to illuminate literary criticism.

[17] The first term was especially popularized by H. W. Wells's *Poetic Imagery* (New York, 1924); it has been taken on by modern criticism of Metaphysicals especially. For the others see esp. J. B. Douds, 'Donne's Technique of Dissonance,' *PMLA*, LII (1937), 1051–61.

high jump, was the merit of the figure. That is, it could be a merit, if one escaped the danger of exhibitionism to which it could lead. Drayton in revision combed out some of his strings of catachretical hyperboles, probably on the latter score. The mixture of senses favored by Edith Sitwell (shrill green grass) is another form of it; involving a logical subtlety, it may sound labored when used with a sensuous function, and rather quickly runs the risk of affectation.

When earlier poets use the figure, the reasons for their need of it can generally be readily seen. Religious, and notably mystical, poets are forced toward *catachresis* by the transcendental nature of what they are attempting to convey through metaphor. Many religious symbols would be catachretical if tradition had not taught us to remark compatible terms rather than dissonant suggestions (*agnus dei*).[18] Simpler *catachresis* is much used for far less complicated functions. The nature of the subject and the conventions of satire would indorse Marston's use of the figure in the first of the following images:

> My spirit is not *puft up with fatte fume*
> Of slimie Ale, nor *Bacchus* heating grape.
> My minde disdaines the *dungie muddy scum*
> Of abiect thoughts, and Envies raging hate.
>
> ('To Detraction,' *Scourge of Villanie*, ed.
> G. B. Harrison, p. 2; in HH, p. 366)

The *scum* image, however, is just a metaphor, a normal 'diminishing' of a base subject (meiosis). On the other hand, Donne needed the violence of a *catachresis* to aid in a similar function—swift lowering of the value or importance of something:

> To know and feele all this, and not to have
> Words to expresse it, *makes a man a grave*
> Of his owne thoughts; I would not therefore stay
> At a great feast, having no Grace to say.
>
> ('Ecclogue,' 93; p. 134)

[18] Similarly, images like Crashaw's have a deceptively sensuous character which promotes misreading if the intellectual process of abstracting is relaxed. In kindred images the second term or vehicle of the metaphor is frequently also a metaphor, a complication which makes them still more 'desperate.'

To some readers *grave : silence* would come so quickly that this would be simply metaphor, without the 'abuse' of the word which gives *catachresis* its other name (*abusio*). Since the distinction from metaphor depends on the quickness or slowness of the mind which is apprehending the logical 'affinity' in the figure, poets with minds of extreme logical agility would overuse the figure without knowing it. *Catachresis* is dark, but not shadowy like synecdoche; sharp, rather. Only the prick of the point of connection is to be felt, whereas in synecdoche what is unmentioned is meant to be half-glimpsed. The effect of this figure upon tone is marked. More violent than varied, and more intellectually than emotionally subtle, it is particularly decorous in satire, in lyrics of dispraise, or in ironically persuasive deliberative pieces where compression is at a premium. That it should be favored by the Metaphysical poets is a foregone conclusion.

Much modern use of the figure is to be expected on similar grounds. In addition, much modern imagery resembling this figure has been produced through experiments in giving free rein to 'association,' and through the prestige given by Symbolist poetic to half-caught suggestions and obscure, often trivial, private relations perceived between things. Such modern imagery is different from the traditional figure by reason of its lesser logical strictness. Both Elizabethan and Jacobean poets use *catachresis* with sharp logical relevancy; the delight truly lies in its observed subtlety of point, and it is clear, when one reads whole poems rather than culled images, that the poets expect the reader to shear off irrelevant suggestions with a keenness approaching their own. Modern pleasure in alogical figurative language has caused (it seems to me) a considerable amount of misreading of Metaphysical images of a deceptively similar character.

The distinction is demonstrable only with modern examples. It has some importance not only because popular modern notions of certain relations between Metaphysicals and Symbolists have been erected on the ignoring of it, but because it will clarify our definition of the criterion of delightfulness. The first two Eliot figures below use true *catachresis* in the traditional manner. But a third, also catachretical, is unlike pre-nineteenth-century imagery in effect and in method:

> The eyes that fix you in a formulated phrase,
> And when I am formulated, sprawling on a pin,
> When I am pinned and wriggling on the wall. . . . .
>
> I have measured out my life with coffee spoons. . . . .
>
> ('The Love Song of J. Alfred Prufrock,' pp. 14, 13)

> Among the windings of the violins
> And the ariettes
> Of cracked cornets
> Inside my brain a dull tom-tom begins. . . . .
>
> ('Portrait of a Lady,' p. 19)

The different type of pleasure afforded by the first two will serve to underline the fact that traditional tropes of this kind, whether early or modern, evoke delight by their logical rather than their sensuous subtlety and thence by controlled rather than free suggestions. I think it would be hard to find a *catachresis* in the Metaphysicals which is, like Eliot's third, delightful less for covert but sure indication of a tenuous 'affinity' than for the possibly irrelevant suggestions released in the reader's mind.[19]

For the incontinence with which many modern poets use *catachresis* they would probably be rebuked by Renaissance writers, yet one reason for this excessive use is quite orthodox and is not far to seek. *Catachresis* is a powerful figure in the exploration of a certain few types of states of mind. It is somewhat too brash for a great many others, and modern attempts to extend it unduly would probably be questioned for decorum by any Elizabethan or Jacobean. As the uses of the figure by Metaphysicals generally evince a very just notion of its function, they are generally quite decorous—though startling—and in the end more striking for their subtlety than for their puzzle value.

It is obvious that all these types of dark figure are useful in satirical or wittily persuasive writing. Their politer and more serious analogue is *allegoria*, which is similarly praised for the

---

[19] Of course this distinction will not be clear if such images are seen in isolation from the poems they help to complete.

intellectual delight given by covert expression of meaning. The following example is from Bishop King; I quote another from Lord Herbert in a note.[20] The literal use of language natural to *allegoria* (examined above) can be noted, as well as the base in conventional symbol:

> Thou hast benighted me, thy set
> This Eve of blackness did beget,
> Who was't my day, ...
>   By thy cleer Sun
> My life and fortune first did run;
> But thou wilt never more appear
> Folded within my Hemisphear,
> Since both thy light and motion
> Like a fled Star is fall'n and gon. . . . .
>
>   ('The Exequy,' p. 38; in HH, p. 639)

Metaphysical poets did not like to give up any obtainable logical pleasures; there is a double metaphor in the homely pun of *folded*. Perhaps it could be matched for 'dissonant' quality by the sunburn that accompanies the same conceit in sonnets by Barnes and Tofte, or by the sweating palfreys of the sun in Drayton.[21] The grave and lovely sweetness of the King is in great part a metrical achievement. But there is much of the delight which traditional theory taught poets to achieve with *allegoria:* the tenuous but firm and pursuable connections between the multiplied terms of a continued metaphor, traceable like veins under the smooth surface of an ostensible concrete structure of meaning.

All dark figures that delight by intellectual subtlety are use-

[20] 'Having interr'd her Infant-birth, / The watry ground that late did mourn, / Was strew'd with flow'rs for the return / Of the wish'd Bridegroom of the earth' ('An Ode upon a Question moved,' in HH, p. 555). Metaphysical poets use the figure where they are not overanxious to argue a position; dialectical impatience will turn it into its overt form—a continued *similitude*, with terms stated (this is one variant of what modern criticism calls an 'expanded image').

[21] *Elizabethan Sonnets*, ed. Sir S. Lee (London, 1904), I, 182 (Barnes [1593]); II, 370 (Tofte [1597]); the Drayton sonnet, No. 47 in 1594, was cut in 1599. King's image is more than matched for cosmological detail by the Antipodes of Constable (Lee, II, 85 [before 1594]) or the zodiacal signs of Drayton. Many such anomalies with respect to the use of homely or learned language, supposedly typical of the later poets, come to the surface in a reading of L. C. John's *Elizabethan Sonnet Sequences* (New York, 1938), which traces the vicissitudes of some of these Petrarchan conceits. Isolation of the sonnet form has kept us from noticing the extent of their use by later poets.

ful 'variations' in writing that must cut with a concealed edge. The traditional and baffling use of *allegoria* for satire we all know to our confusion. But even lesser covert figures were early seized on for their usefulness in deriding or mocking, and Puttenham's various flouts, nips, and frumps all utilize dark or 'strange' conveyance.[22] Day remarks of a *metalepsis* that, instead of calling out upon the 'accursed soil that bred my cause of woe,' one might quite as well call out upon the party himself (p. 79 [1595]), but Fabri advocates the figure for revealing a bad thing under cover (I, 157 [1521]). It is properly far-fetched, that being the cause of its delightfulness. It is normal that a good Spenserian example should come from his sonnets (*Amor.*, xlviii). He is amplifying the strength and permanence of his love for his ungrateful lady, but to draw in a shadow of a mock he addresses rather the letter she burnt. 'Innocent paper!' says he, 'Well worthy thou to have found better hyre / Then so bad end for hereticks ordayned.' Peacham comments with considerable enthusiasm on this figure's power of teaching the understanding to dive down to the bottom of the sense and of instructing the eye of the wit to discern a meaning far off. Like a high prospect, it presents 'to the viewe of the beholder an obiect far distant, by leading the eye from one marke to another by a lineall direction, till it discerneth the thing that is looked for' (p. 24 [1593]).

Such delight in what is fetched from afar, and in an attendant 'obscurity,' is perfectly traditional. Peacham's comparison reminds one of E. K.'s passage in the Epistle to Spenser's *Shepheardes Calender*, with its discussion of the value of 'rough and harsh termes' in poetry; E. K. compares them to discords in music, or to the 'naturall rudenesse' of thickets and craggy clifts in pictures wherein 'the daintie lineaments of beautye' are blazed and portrayed.[23] The delight of the mind in what he calls 'disorderly order' was of course no discovery of the *seventeenth*

[22] *Ironia*, a major figure, I shall treat later (chap. ix, sec. 2); it is not generally praised as a means of delightful 'varying.'

[23] Some citations of interest, showing that the statement had more novel implications when applied to painting, are given by F. Hard, 'E. K.'s Reference to Painting: Some Seventeenth-Century Adaptations,' *ELH*, VII (1940), 121–29 .

century. If we think of it as baroque, or as characteristic of poets in rebellion against earlier fear of dissonance, we shall have to push back the rebellion—back quite out of sight of the Metaphysicals, for example.

The relation of all these covert or subtle or far-fetched figures to 'Metaphysical obscurity' is so close that I must at least mention here that famous cloud, though it will loom up again.[24] The traditional expectation is that such figures will bring delight because they force one to an intellectually athletic (but clear) apprehending of tenuous relationships, to 'a deeper consideration,' and thus 'minister a pleasure to' the wit (Peacham, pp. 18, 13). This seems to me just the expectation which lies behind increased use of such figures in the later period, as genres and subject matters shifted, and as favored forms and typical poetic intentions were narrowed. Added logical difficulty, pleasurable darkness, 'strange' heightening, were traditionally recognized as instruments for achieving *clarté* with greater delightfulness. There is not even a paradox here once we recognize the connection of clearness with light-in-the-mind rather than with the oversimplifications of prosaic noonday. The figures above are a mere few of those recommended by established rhetorical theory as more delightful *because* they were figures of deep obscurity, like a dark night with the stars hidden, or like a mine, the obtaining of whose metal required deep digging. These phrases happen to be taken from Peacham's praise of *aenigma* (p. 29), but the figures had been shaped to provide exactly these delights for centuries before he wrote the phrases. The ellipses and learned allusions, the dark or subtle tropes, the far-fetched figures that attempted to describe states of mind, seem to me traditional in form and normally related to poetic intention,

[24] This has been so much discussed of late years that specific references would have to include most of the contemporary items in the Bibliography in T. Spencer and M. Van Doren, *Studies in Metaphysical Poetry* (New York, 1939). Because my discussion sometimes shows specific disagreement with his analysis, I should perhaps mention R. L. Sharp's articles, and book (*op. cit.*, in chap. ii, n. 9, above). I have not space for the documentation due him if I were to take open issue on points such as the interpretation of *clarté* or the differentiation between the obscurity of Spenser's too well-cloaked symbolism and seventeenth-century obscurity. He isolates as a reference to metaphysical aesthetic the distinction he quotes (p. 45) from Benlowes— between the masculine pleasures of the Understanding and the feminine and sensual pleasures of the eye. It is a traditional rhetorical distinction, considered in sec. 2 below.

whether they occur in sixteenth-century or in Metaphysical writers; a quantitative increase in the use of them by certain later poets is due to various complicated causes of which 'a new sensibility' does not appear to me to have been one. Certain forms of sensibility had always been communicated to readers by such types of image.

As expectations of what such images should accomplish remained constant, so too the old methods of framing them and the old safeguards on their use remained. Intention determines form, and the real difference in poetic method is to come when poets no longer expect to make the subject perspicuous, no longer expect their dark figures to open with a logical key and shed light in the mind. The intellectual subtlety of Metaphysical covert figures differentiates the obscurity they provide from certain added types of obscurity we have had with us since the nineteenth century became interested in the subconscious as no earlier century had been. When obscurity in a poem will become *illustratio* by dint of the reader's hard thinking, that is traditional obscurity. It has received considerable praise in all periods.[25]

Renaissance critics pronounce various caveats about far-fetched figures or about making allegories or metonymies understandable rather than absurd or 'peevish.' One trouble with interpreting these warnings is that modern yardsticks for measuring the distance of the 'fetching' are inadequate; there is every chance of going wrong, and little to check by, when we make up lists of the kind of images the authors of the warnings must have considered reprehensible. Since the kind of obscurity we find in the poetry was persistently recommended, we can only

[25] It was traditional long before and long after Boccaccio's defense of 'The obscurity of poetry' in the *De genealogia*, XIV, xii (Augustine and Petrarch are cited as authorities). Nor is there anything new about the simultaneous inclusion of praise of clarity and praise of obscurity in Renaissance criticism; since the days of the Provençal *trobar clar* and *trobar clus* the idea of fitting this quality of 'strangeness,' like others, to the nature of the subject and intention, had been familiar in medieval poetic.

I add to this note (perhaps not with strictest relevance) a reference to an article which appeared after this book was completed and out of my hands: A. Stein, 'Donne's Obscurity and the Elizabethan Tradition,' *ELH*, XIII (1946), 98–118; that its author and I have independently hit upon certain similar emphases may help to argue the validity of attempting to read these poets in the light of theories contemporary with them.

recognize that the authors of these caveats were simply attempting to hold the balance between what is 'strange' and
what is too dark to be seen through. This is a permanent critical
activity, and in no period has there been perfect agreement on
where the line was to be drawn—nor will there ever be, so long
as poetic communication is an affair of two different minds
seeing, not one. 'Strangeness' was in high repute, and willingly
pursued, throughout all the period here treated, and delightfulness attendant on that pursuit was a consistently recognized
criterion for images.

This excursus on obscurity in one particular period where it
happens to have caused much modern discussion should not be
allowed to separate off dark or subtle figures too markedly.
They are very much like other figures—satisfy similar criteria,
originate similarly, are a normal and necessary element in poetic
method. There is so much of similarity in the ends posed for
ready, copious, and rich imagery and for subtly ingenious imagery, and so much of similarity in the safeguards attached to
both, that it does not seem to me just to erect them into two
'kinds.'

It seems indubitable that the praise of 'delightful varying'
cannot be equated with praise of *copie* defined as facility.
Exuberance without point is not called delightful; ingeniousness without clear significancy is not called delightful. Carefully varied patterning of language, richness gained through
metaphor, subtlety gained through 'strangeness' in the figures,
call for elements in imagery which go far beyond the mere piling-
up of intrinsically delightful particulars. The kinds of delight
asked for are not so simple. Imagery shows certain resultant
characteristics, which become more dominant or less as the
years pass, without causing fundamental changes in its nature
or use.

2. *The Criterion of Delightfulness: 'Beautifying'*

But if 'varying' did mean something other than mere multiplication, what, if not love of superficial 'graces,' are we to
make of the constant and suspicious recommendations of tropes

and figures 'for ornament,' 'to beautify,' to utter the mind aptly, distinctly, 'and ornately'?

Just here we are simply asking whether 'beautifying' in its least profound sense encouraged pretty decorations of style. The rhetoricians are usually thought of as the likeliest exponents of such an understanding. If we look in their treatises for the greatest danger point, the place of all places where decorative graces would be encouraged, we shall find it among figures which provide varied patterns of words—where most later critics have found it. These are the figures frequently distinguished as 'feminine,' or thought to give elegance and gracefulness as over against pith or depth of conceit.

The innumerable and far from meaningless variations between authors as to classification do not destroy certain large general distinctions between figures approved for grace and exquisiteness and figures approved for force and dignity. The notion that the faculty called judgment or understanding is masculine is, of course, time-honored. Cicero's division between masculine and feminine beauty[26] finds a parallel or an application in the division between figures of words, which are effeminate and musical, and figures of thought or sentence, which are manly and martial. These are Peacham's adjectives (p. 61 [1593]). Schemes or arrangements that please the ear (like Puttenham's *auricular* figures) would especially lend grace and harmony; devices that concern the very structure in which the thought is embodied (like distribution of circumstances, or gnome, or apostrophe) would especially lend convincingness or majesty. Peacham says that the first sort are as the color and beauty of a style, the second as its life and affection. The Ramist Talaeus draws the comparison as between *color et sanguis* and *nerui thorique* (chap. 28).[27] Abraham Fraunce's

[26] See K. Gilbert and H. Kuhn, *History of Esthetics* (New York, 1939), p. 103. References to Cicero are to *De offic.* i. i. 36 and *De orat.* 3. 25. See above, chap. v, n. 31, for rhetorical terms used in these paragraphs, and chap. iv, on 'style as a garment,' for discussions in which 'beautifying' is seen in relation to more general points like the separation of content and form.

[27] I have used Omer Talon's *Rhetorica* (1567) but little in Part I because his position as the exponent of Ramist rhetoric complicates matters; see below, Part II, chap. xii, for the wide influence of his rhetoric as a constant accompaniment of Ramus' dialectic.

Ramistic *Arcadian Rhetorike* (1588) similarly thinks of figures of sentence as more forcible and apt to persuade, and of figures of words as more pleasant and fit to delight (chap. 26).

Such divisions were a clarifying device used to help organize practical counsels on the relation of formal elements to tone. These classifications and characterizings of figures do not disturb major underlying assumptions—that *all* these admirable qualities characterize good writing, that Eloquence and Wisdom are not to be severed, that decorum determines choice. Other more important distinctions cut across this one between gracefulness and force, and it is lost in a larger unit like any whole actual poem, for many sententious figures involve 'delightful' word-patterning, while many melodious or repetitive figures are moving or persuasive. All figures of thought (all that have come down to us in the poets, at any rate) contain figures of words. And no poem could possibly be constructed out of the latter alone. No rhetorician thought so, or tried it.

All rhetorics list large numbers of these figures which peculiarly assist grace and harmony. Many of them are outside the province of this discussion, for they do not produce imagery but have to do chiefly with the music of verse. Many of them merely isolate and name the almost innumerable methods by which patterns of sound may modify and enforce sense; they are part of the poet's 'right artificiality,' and have the aims examined above in our discussion of that first level of artistic Imitation. Many of them cannot but move the affections; these are used to modify the forms taken by some images in order that they may better satisfy a criterion of efficacy examined in chapter viii below. Some induce imagery, although the framing of them looks chiefly to melodiousness or emphasis, like the dozens of figures utilizing some type of repetition. The number and ingenious variety of these last indicates very great willingness to pursue the relation which passionate or emphatic or attention-rousing speech has to states of mind. Hoskins states the matter succinctly: 'And as no man is sick in thought upon one thing but for some vehemency or distress, so in speech there is no repetition without importance' (p. 12, speaking of *anadiplosis*). It is

to be remarked that this comment on the psychological importance of formal variations occurs in connection with the most
seemingly mechanical order of figures used to beautify—and
that its author is not scorning the ancient method but advising
mastery of it.

Indeed, it is difficult to see even feminine figures as pretty
decorations unless one is wilfully thinking of bad examples of
them. The difference between recognizing the importance of
figures lending grace and harmony—as every rhetoric does—
and recognizing pretty elaboration as a desideratum, can perhaps be shown only through examples. If one would see how
feminine figures do actually operate to enhance ornately, Herrick's line in the 'Silvia' poem quoted in section 1 is a good example: 'Which renders that quite tarnisht, which was green'; /
And Price*less* now, what Peer*less* once had been.' The last two
feminine figures control the rhythm, enhance the antithesis,
and wake the attention to the possible pun. If we are unwilling
to call these effects 'grace and harmony,' obtained as they are
strictly according to orthodox advice, we simply decide arbi-
trarily that the givers of the advice did not themselves understand it but that Herrick luckily did. There is at least a possibility that the soft, vapid, or verbose poems written in the
name of harmony and sweetness were produced by the bad students, and that the attention which the Renaissance gave to the
minutiae of beautifying through figures is not unconnected with
the extraordinary number of Elizabethan and seventeenth-
century poets who show delicate control of tone.

Or, to keep to authors who we think deliberately avoided
beautifying with ornaments, we may exemplify from Donne
that figure which Puttenham calls 'the Gorgious'—*expolitio*—
and to which he devotes a chapter alone (III, xx). His praise of
its luster and polish, its 'varietie of sentences all running upon
one point & to one inte*n*t,' its 'masse of many figurative
speaches, applied to the bewtifying of our tale or argume*n*t,'
makes it sound very florid. The poem by Queen Elizabeth with
which he illustrates it has the kind of floweriness we choose to
call flowery. But if we are to blame the use of *flores rhetorici* for

this, then it is confusing to find that the first two stanzas of
Donne's 'The Canonization' (p. 14) well exemplify Puttenham's description of *expolitio* and well satisfy Elizabethan understandings of 'lustre' and 'polish.' It would take two pages to
elucidate the nine kinds of 'feminine' figures, by quick count,
which Donne uses (quite as advised) to emphasize meanings
which are also assisted by his several 'manlier' figures. There
are assuredly great differences between his stanzas and that one
from *FQ* (III, iv, 38) with which H. D. Rix exemplifies *expolitio*
in Spenser.[28] We could find others more like, but this would
only confuse the issue. For the point is that we have not isolated the factor of difference when we call the earlier of these
two styles 'more ornamental.' To explain the differences between two poems by assuming that different definitions of
ornament lie behind them is unhelpful when both use the same
decorative devices. If we find Spenser overdecorative and
Donne 'strong,' we must credit the difference to something other
than Spenser's fondness for a type of rhetorical decoration
which no one mastered better than Donne himself.

The complicated answers to this problem do not belong in
this section.[29] However, the principle which helped men decide
just how to 'beautify delightfully' should be indicated. The concept which regulated satisfaction of this criterion is that which
regulated satisfaction of the others—Decorum. Peacham warns
apropos of this same figure *expolitio* (p. 196) that a poet must
not use such ornament except for causes of some weight, nor
leave his conclusion 'in the wildernesse God knoweth where.'
Many lesser poets did both. It would be simple if one could attribute this to rhetoric's attempts to implement the ideas of
poetic with learnable techniques. I do not think that it would be
just. Theory reminded poets constantly that decorum involved
not only restraint in the use of figures but a wise choice *between*

[28] *Op. cit.*, p. 46; in chap. ii, n. 12, above.

[29] This book should, in sum, give an answer to the modern reader who asks 'But why
do the earlier poets seem so florid, then?' A part of the answer lies in the fact that, when
we ask this, we have frequently not asked ourselves two other questions: am I thinking
of the major poets or the indifferent and poor ones? am I as convinced of the importance
of the poetic subjects treated, as the authors were? See above, pp. 48–49; chap. iv, n. 5;
p. 91.

figures and a fit choice of *where* to use them. Insistence on this principle would lead one to believe that Elizabethan rhetoric and poetic meant by beautifying much what Jonson meant by it in a famous passage: the variety of flowers *in a meadow* 'heighten and *beautifie*' it above mere grass and greenness; but ornaments should 'grow to our style' as those flowers do, rather than be gathered to straw houses with or to make garlands (*Discoveries*, p. 99). In other words, the flowers of rhetoric which beautified the subject were supposed to be an organic and natural part of the thing beautified.

It is also significant that the word 'beautifying' (and others like it, sharing its now pejorative implications) is a general term of praise, used in commending all types of ornament. The Renaissance evidently did not think of the term as chiefly applicable to the more decorative or elaborate figures, though I have here emphasized those types, as most suspect. We have seen that some subjects demand ornament that is dark and subtle rather than elaborate. This, too, was thought to beautify the subject. A great many figures other than those I have examined were thought beautiful for their lack of elaboration.[30] Such figures were neither more nor less 'ornaments' of a poem than were the obvious or the detailed figures, and all found their chief beauty in their suitableness. I quote three lines from Yeats, chiefly to underline this difference in critical vocabulary, with which we must reckon; it would seem to us a misuse of language to comment on Yeats's 'beautifying of his subject, through the figure *aenigma*,' yet this is a normal Elizabethan commendation of just such uses of just such figures.

Three Movements

Shakespearean fish swam the sea, far away from land;
Romantic fish swam in nets coming to the hand; ·
What are all those fish that lie gasping on the strand?

(p. 277 [1933])

---

[30] *Syllogismus*, or *noema*, or what Hoskins calls *intimatio*, if anyone is interested to look them up. Or 'conjecture'—as when one indicates a giant's size only by his use of a pine tree for a staff. Donne's 'Thine eyes, and not thy noise wak'd mee' (p. 37) is this figure—used to 'amplify' his lady's luminous beauty.

This tripartite image would have been called *aenigma* by the slower-minded and *allegoria* by the quick. If anyone doubts that it 'beautifies the subject,' let him try to state Yeats's idea without it.

I should be quite willing to grant that we simply cannot tell from the definitions whether or not Renaissance rhetoricians would have thought the Donne and the Spenser and the Yeats examples all equally beautiful examples of ornamental figures. There is frequently no way to tell how they would have rated different individual images all of which satisfy their definitions and observe their safeguards. But, considering their own uses of the words, I am quite as unwilling to believe that they used 'delightful beautifying' as a password to admit what we should admit under it—useless but pretty images. This is simply to slip criteria which they do not even speak of into their poetic.

CHAPTER VII

THE CRITERION OF SIGNIFICANCY

I HAVE tried to ask of Renaissance poetic and practice two seemingly simple questions: was imagery asked to be representationally and sensuously accurate? was the criterion of delightfulness largely thought of as a requirement for decorative imagery? The answers have led time and again to a third criterion for an image: is it a 'significant' image? I am sorry for this; it makes my discussion irretrievably untidy. But it seems to be true, if confusing, that the requirements which come closest to assigning imagery a primarily sensuous function in poetry do not quite stand on their own feet. They are, in certain well-defined literary circumstances or situations, necessary criteria for admirable imagery; but they are not sufficient criteria.

These demands for sensuous vividness and for delightfulness are fairly closely connected with the formal excellence of poems. On this level the maker of a poem was not conceived as a representational painter, but as the maker of an 'artificial' construct that achieved beauty of formal design by imaginative but controlled use of formal means. Of these means the image was one. Accompanying the most technical advice on these means, however, and interwoven in the poets' uses of the techniques, there lies evidence for a further demand made of each image: that it must assist in conveying the poet's interpretative ordering of nature. In turning to direct consideration of this criterion of significancy, we deal directly also with conceptions of Imitation on the more complicated levels, of 'coherent pattern' and of 'truth.'

The inquiry into what was included under this *significancy* asked of images is a complex one. A fair number of ancient monsters are bound to be encountered very soon—among them the

concept of embellished Nature and its relation to the modern
accusation that the orthodox Elizabethans sugar-coated the
'real.' Closely related to these matters are two opposing accusations—that poetry was turned into sweet medicine or disguised
moralistic propaganda and that poetry was escapist. These will
be better met if they are not met head on. I shall pitch camp
upon a good many islands that turn out to be one of these
leviathans or another; the reader will see whether he can be
comfortable under these circumstances if little is said about the
terrain. One frequently seems to have the experience of finding
images pleasant for reasons that turn out to involve critical
positions from which most of us are in headlong flight. Many
commonplaces of Renaissance theory are involved, especially
those which we have treated for some years with that light disbelief judged fitting to commonplaces. I am no more certain
than another that they are 'true.' I do think that they explain
Elizabethan and Jacobean imagery. I shall not even quote the
general positions that everyone knows. Obviously, Sidney's
voice will be heard without my mentioning him; and Tasso's,
and Ronsard's, and the Platonists', and the Aristotelians'. I
shall try to keep to what can be turned to immediate account in
judging the application of these familiar large ideas to small
units like the image.

1. *Significancy, Amplification, and Universals*

A passage in Puttenham will block out two large ways in
which images were asked to be 'significant.'[1] His concern here
is the relation of art to nature; this controls, of course, the relation of images to reality. The passages need careful reading.

> In some cases we say arte is an ayde and coadiutor to nature, and a
> *furtherer of her actions* to good effect, or peradventure a meane to supply her
> wants, by *renforcing the causes wherein shee is impotent and defective,* as doth
> the arte of phisicke, by helping the naturall *concoction, retention, distribution,*
> *expulsion, and other vertues,* in a weake and unhealthie bodie. Or as the good
> gar- / diner seasons his soyle by sundrie sorts of compost: as mucke or marle,
> . . . . : and waters his plants [and weeds, and prunes, and unleaves his boughs
> to let in the sun, etc.] and so makes that never, or *very seldome any of them mis-*

---

[1] All of III, xxv, is pertinent, as well as conventional.

carry, but bring foorth their flours and fruites in season. And in both these cases it is no smal praise for the Phisition & Gardiner to be called *good and cunning artificers.*

In other words artifice within images, or whole images, may simply by selection or emphasis or other 'renforcing' help to state that which the subject already says or means the moment we have a clear view of it. Some descriptive detail is of this nature, many schematic figures, and even possibly some tropes; the poet need only point to the uglinesses that make the ugly woman ugly, or name the effects that show his love to be fervent, or supply nature's want by turning into articulate praise or dispraise the dumb sense he has of his lady's beauty or his critic's stupidity. The poet as gardener assisting nature has but to make her intentions clearer and her fruits more sure. The 'vertues' are in the body, have but to be aided by the physician.[2]

But the authors of the following images were doing more than this. These particulars have another relation to particulars in nature.

> Whiter than be the flocks that straggling feed,
> When washed by Arethusa faint they lie,
> >   Is fair Samela.
> > (Robert Greene, from *Menaphon* [1589]; HH, p. 150)

> Upon Julia's Voice.
> So smooth, so sweet, so silv'ry is thy voice,
> As, could they hear, the Damn'd would make no noise;
> But listen to thee, (walking in thy chamber)
> Melting melodious words to Lutes of Amber.
> > (Herrick, No. 67)

> Weighing the stedfastness and state
> Of some mean things which here below reside,

___

[2] This old simile is used with various implications during the period. The aspect pertinent to the next few paragraphs is that poets, like physicians, are co-operators with nature, yet accomplish what would, without art, be left undone. The notion of the poet as *physician to his reader* is not infrequent; the idea that he can establish a sounder mental order in a reader through his presentation of a wiser understanding of nature and man seems to state a simple fact that every reader has experienced, rather than a theory of poetry, though in this period it is a natural and accepted part of the didactic theory. The notion of the poet as *physician to himself* is also found in Elizabethan theory and is treated in a later section.

    Where birds like watchful Clocks the noiseless date
      And Intercourse of times divide,
    Where Bees at night get home and hive, and flowrs
             Early, aswel as late,
    Rise with the Sun, and set in the same bowrs;

      I would (said I) my God would give
    The staidness of these things to man!
              (Vaughan, 'Man,' in HH, p. 789)

These authors are doing what Puttenham goes on to commend:

> In another respect arte is not only an aide and coadiutor to nature in all her actions, but an alterer of them, and in some sort a surmounter of her skill, so as by meanes of it *her owne effects shall appeare more beautifull or straunge and miraculous.* . . . . The Phisition . . . . shall be able not onely to restore the decayed spirites of man . . . . but also to prolong the terme of his life many yeares over and above the stint of his first and naturall constitution. And the Gardiner by his arte will not onely make an herbe, or flowr, or fruite, come forth in his season without impediment, but also *will embellish the same in vertue, shape,* odour and taste, *that nature of her selfe woulde never have done:* as to make the single gillifloure, or marigold, or daisie, double: . . . . any of *which things nature could not doe without mans help and arte.* These actions also are most singular, when they be most artificiall.

The images in the three poems just quoted are all embellishments of nature (and I do not mean hyperbolical notions of ladies and of stability) to make her own effects appear more strange and miraculous. They make our apprehension of lovely whiteness or of the sweetness of Julia's voice or of desirable stableness include more of meaning than nature 'could doe without mans help and arte.'[3] They all fulfil the same criterion of significancy; they are particulars that wear universals in their faces. The first two images amplify perceptual universals; their character responds to this function. The emotive associations that such universals have are especially emphasized by the

---

[3] I hasten to extricate Puttenham from a position no Elizabethan could take:

    God could only make a tree,
    But poems are made by Poets. Like me.

This capacity in the poet to create meaningful order is also attributed by Puttenham to the operations of 'Nature'—in the poet. Our maker or Poet, in his excellent *invention*, 'holpen by a cleare and bright phantasie and imagination,' is not as the painter counterfeiting, or as the gardener aiding nature, or as the carpenter working effects utterly unlike nature's, 'but *even as nature her selfe working* by her owne peculiar vertue and proper instinct' (p. 307). The linkage of thought which is important in early theory is not between creativeness and self-expression but between creativeness and ordering.

nature of Herrick's hyperbole. Vaughan's birds and bees here illustrate (make more luminously manifest) a conceptual universal, also, of course, possessing such associations.

That universals are made manifest through the particulars
composing poetic images is a fact which one may refer to the
nature of language, or as the Elizabethans did to the nature of
reality and of man's mind, or both. At any rate, earlier poetic
was so aware of this power in images that almost all advice
about them concerns the various ways one may utilize this
capacity they have of figuring-forth more than the particulars
out of which they are shaped.

This embellishing of nature (especially in *vertue*, power
working toward an end, orderly meaning) does not lead to
prettified details. But it does shear off naturalistic observation.
It does not ban the inelegant, if that be pertinent to the aspect
one has chosen to amplify; what it bans is the in-significant.
Either the paltry, that is, or the truly exceptional. That peculiarly useful (because succinct) critical remark, Donne's reported answer to Jonson's criticism of his *Anniversary*, is based
on this understanding. He 'described the Idea of a Woman and
not as she was.'[4] Jonson mistook his amplification of a universal
for a description of an exception. This 'shee, shee' who is dead is
neither the Virgin Mary nor Elizabeth Drury nor any particular woman as nature has made her. Renaissance images of this
hyperbolical sort do not ask us to swallow some almost incredibly exceptional particular; they ask us to look, through particulars, at the blinding light of significances or essences. Even
Julia's voice is not just melodious beyond the common; it is the
distilled quintessence of sweetness. Most readers feel the excite-

---

[4] I make several uses of this remark because it sums up an attitude of orthodox
poetic in smaller compass than any I know, apropos of a poem currently well known and
sympathetically appreciated; it is so well borne out by the nature of the poem that we
may remember without undue nervousness that it has only come to us through Drummond (*Conversations*, in Herford and Simpson, *Ben Jonson* [Oxford, 1925], I, 133). My
somewhat dogmatic interchange of Platonic and Aristotelian terms is also motivated by
the need for compression and clarity; quite aside from the fact that the Renaissance read
its Aristotle in the light of medieval (often Platonized) interpretations, the relevant
possible disagreements do not affect this point about images, though philosophers will
be troubled by my ignoring of an important quarrel. .

ment of this far-reaching 'meaning' in the image, even when they feel nervous about conceding that Julia is anything more than Julia-by-the-river's-brim.

This embellishment through 'artificial' pointing-up of significances must not be confused, then, with a dishonest embellishment of reality intended to cover up flaws. Discussions of hyperbole do not fall into confusing even it with blind praise. For one thing, it may point either way ('augendi atque minuendi,' says Quintilian [viii. vi. 68]). For another, we give our belief to the significance conveyed, while disbelieving the 'facts' used in its conveyance—disbelieving, for instance, Julia's power to silence the lamenting damned. For in Hoskins' words, flat impossibilities are used that rather we may conceive the 'unspeakableness' than the untruth (p. 29); we are to be aware that hyperbole is a device to point at a significancy beyond speech. Tropes, pre-eminently, go beyond speech, not only pointing to universals but relating disparate things on the basis of a universal common to both. The authors of the three poems quoted above do all the things Pontano says poets do to excite wonder: they shade truth with fictions and mythical inventions, even at variance with it and with the nature of things; they add sublimity and ornament through their inventions; and they add digressions or hyperboles (see chap. v, n. 14). Yet this has no necessary connection with presentation of reality as pleasanter than it is. The only flaw in reality which this conception of significancy in images does not tolerate, and assist men to perceive, is—a contradiction in terms—the 'flaw' of meaninglessness.

We do happen to be asked to wonder at something approvable in the three examples given. But Donne's 'Curse' (or Lear's) is equally an embellishment, this time of evil as we meet it in nature: 'The venom of all stepdames, gamsters gall, ... What Plants, Mynes, Beasts, Foule, Fish, / Can contribute, all ill which all / Prophets, or Poets spake; And all which shall / Be annex'd in schedules unto this by mee, / Fall on that man' (p. 42). This bears the same relation to evils as we commonly meet them that some hyperbolical sonneteer's description bears to the goods—isolating *ill* in all these particulars, it excites wonder by 'going nature one better'; it seems thus to exhibit to us ill in its quintessential form. The relation of Donne's wished evils to those which are actually to be met with is the same as the relation of Drayton's grove to one we might find; his is a bower in which a human being is to be allied with divinity:

> Upon this Mount there stood a stately Grove, ...
> Of tufted Cedars, and the branching Pine, ...
> Imbraudring these in curious trailes along,
> The clustred Grapes, the golden Citrons hung,
> More glorious then the precious fruite were these,
> Kept by the Dragon in *Hesperides;* . . . .
>   (*Endimion and Phoebe*, vss. 23, 39) (Author's italics)

Both leave out all extenuating or compromising accidents. Donne's faithfulness to the real no more requires him to interpolate at this point that not all stepdames are evil than Drayton's requires him to note that some groves harbor the Japanese beetle.

This makes both images in a sense unnatural. But to what extent does it make either of them 'untrue'? Every reader answers this for himself, and according to his own philosophical postulates. I am only concerned to point out that Renaissance poets, as aware as we are that neither evil nor opulent splendor occurs in the world of fact in quite such pure and rarefied form, yet endeavor constantly—with images—to make such 'things in their essence' real to us.[5]

It is by no accident that Sidney himself points out that particulars are not just useful, rather that they are required, to indicate such significances. It is not because they help tie us down to what are called the real facts that they are indispensable. Their contribution is not primarily descriptive; Donne

[5] In the notion that the poet's ordering is an order of the real, rather than the apparent or the accidental, lay the basis for the comparison of him to the great Artificer Himself (see Scaliger, *Poet.*, i, 1: *sed velut alter deus condere*). For some convenient references to this ancient idea, see K. Gilbert and H. Kuhn, *op. cit.* (above, chap. ii, n. 5), pp. 183, 158 (Plotinus and Augustine). Cf. p. 135, Augustine on the world as God's poem ('arranged, as it were, by an eloquence not of words, but of things,' *City of God*, xi, chap. 18). Such of my readers as are familiar with the Royal Society scientists' fondness for this last distinction should savor it in Augustine with especial relish.

is tracing out 'the exact curve of his feeling'[6] with that string of particulars *only in the same sense* that Drayton is tracing out Endimion's with the embroidered grapes and citrons. Neither, without his concretions, could point at a significancy in the situation which defies more overt statement. And if this significancy were more complex or profound, tropical language would have been seized upon for its greater assistance.

There is a structure of meaning. But that structure includes something which the power of images can best convey: it includes 'the perfection and excellence of the subject.' This is Fracastoro's phrase for what is made manifest by ornament and constitutes his defense against the claim that ornament is extraneous. Ornament is not *extra rem* when *res* is so defined.[7] 'Perfectio et decor' are a real part of the things nature produces, so also of the things art produces; take them away, and 'you have somehow taken away life itself' (pp. 68–70 [1555]). In both the Donne and the Drayton images one could easily demonstrate the part played by even the minor ornaments (Donne's are the more rhetorically ingenious) in making manifest 'the perfection' of the subject ('perfectionem & nobilitatem reru*m*'). Such a demonstration would, however, require an analysis of the poetic subject in each of the two whole poems.

Such, then, was the nature of the significancy which Renaissance poets might expect readers to look for in their images. In judging the satisfactoriness with which single images met the criterion, the critical reader must (as with other criteria) have recourse to those larger principles which governed all use of ornament. As usual, it is an aspect of the concept of decorum which helped the critic to make fair judgments. Fracastoro's

---

[6] See above, chap. v, n. 27; Hulme's phrase.

[7] Discussing what it is to 'consider objects [*res*] as they should be, and look for perfection,' Fracastoro speaks of columns, peristyles, etc., 'added' to houses: 'extra rem no*n* erunt, sed essentialia & necessaria.' Navagero answers his interlocutor's comparison of 'Virgil and the others' to painters who surround a central subject (a man, for example) with lakes and groves *ad ornamentum*; 'quare quae & pictores & poetae rebus addunt ad perfectione*m*, non extra rem sunt, *si rem consideres non nudam* (ut plebei artifices . . . . faciunt) *sed perfectam & animatam:*' (fols. 162^{r-v}, trans., p. 69).

statement is conveniently short: 'everything that is added to the particular subject *is drawn from the nature of the subject*, either *by metaphor, or epithet, or the other means* that are *inherent in nature* itself.' Poets who do this are not *mendaces*, but *perfectores*. Only an image not truly drawn from this inner core of meaning, and necessary to the manifesting of it, lacked integrity.

I reserve for chapter ix ('The Criterion of Decorum') the precise application of such interpretations to single images. But we shall not fully understand the exact meaning of significancy as a criterion for images unless we notice one implication these interpretations carry; failure to notice it has made for some confusion in modern criticism of Renaissance ornament which attempted to meet this criterion.

These ideas seem innocuous enough; we have heard them so often. Actually applied to actual images, they redirect our attention to a question very uncongenial to the modern mind—to the *truth* of the artist's vision of his subject.

No modern likes to find himself looking openly at such a private and relative matter, and although many modern complaints are really masked appearances of a discontent that the poet has not treated a subject under some aspect that seems truer to the critic, modern accusations are commonly made in terms of faulty technique—'diffuseness' or 'conventional rhetoric' or 'prettiness of detail.' This form of critical self-deception is prevented in the Renaissance. A poet's artifices must (for this principle is universally accepted and demonstrated) be 'according' to his subject—so that the uncontented critic either finds this not the case,[8] or, in quarreling with the manner, thereby quarrels with the matter too. The poet's artifices are a telescope through which, aside from these two considerations, one must be willing to look.

According to such a poetic, Spenser's rhetorical patterns in his portrayal of stubborn and wilful-passionate grief in the *Daphnaida* have precisely the same justification as King's use of

[8] Inconsistent images may show a poet wobbling between two poetic subjects, or contradicting what he has clearly shown to be the subject he wishes to shadow forth.

image after expanded image in the *Exequy*—both are used to draw forth by art the living significance of the subject. Spenser uses intricately patterned verbal music, resoundingly expanded declamatory figures, and the riddle of the Lioness; King uses one after another of the conventional similitudes, heightened and made 'strange' by an extreme expansion: 'my West of life,' nearer by eight hours' sail than before sleep breathed his drowsy gale; the martial image, with the soft drum of the pulse and the slow marches; or his meditation on 'the book, / The library whereon I look / Though almost blind' (p. 38; in HH, p. 639). The two poems use very different ornament;[9] any complaints about the nature of it must be made in terms of the cause of it.

That cause, according to Renaissance principles, is the true and essential nature of the subject. We may if we like complain that Spenser's manner is less decorous, less fitting to his subject, or we may complain that he does not speak the truth; but we may not complain about the intrinsic nature of his ornamentation. Nor indeed praise it either. It merely helps us to see exactly what he is writing about, and exactly why he thought that important. All decisions on the aesthetically successful significancy of images therefore involve most careful answers to these two questions—no simple task, since poet's subject implies not mere subject matter but the meaningful order he has imposed upon subject matter.

Of course, finding new labels for what ornament helps to accomplish in a poem, or rather pointing to the old labels, does not make any magical elucidation of its modes of operation.

---

[9] It is not beside the point perhaps to remark that the last image from King, half-quoted, contains *epizeuxis*, *correctio* involving *asyndeton*, and, of course, *exclamatio*, apostrophe, and metaphor. Attention is so overpowered in reading the Spenser by Alcyon's beating and wilful iterations of his grief that certain images in a different tone do not stand out; I will list some: the sharp resentful reducing of the whole world to a senseless millwheel (428); the Ralegh-like 'pointed' concentration of 'My bread shall be the anguish of my mind' (375); the psychological accuracy through which we find embedded in the irrationally violent series of 'hates' the straightforward tenderness of 'I hate the day, because it lendeth light / To see all things, and not my love to see'; the radical images, like the 'speedie post' (407; translated into twentieth-century terms, the comparison would be to the unregarding rush through the station of the nonstop express).

Nor should similarities seen obliterate differences. I do not believe, however, that there was much relaxation of the criterion of significancy for images during this entire period, nor much change in the definition of it; great changes have come since. Images that satisfied it might yet be very different. One large ground of difference lay in the differences between the things one was asked to wonder at or believe. Another lay in the difference between being asked to wonder with delight, or with scorn. These are not so simple as they sound; they involve the poet's conception of truth. Imagery expressing conceptual universals with special directness took on characteristics that must be considered in Part Two. And variations within functions made other important modifications. But, even so, very few images (if any, ultimately; I am not sure) were exempt from a criterion which necessarily meant that they directed the imagination to a supersensible world.

2. *Significancy and the Supersensible World*

Both in criticism and in rhetorical theory it is an accepted commonplace that the abstract and intangible requires the 'helpe of earthly images' (Peacham, of metaphor, p. 12).[10] The necessity of metaphor is as frequently noted as the grace and beauty of it. Much of this beauty, indeed, consists in its ability to transcend the limitations of language. The impressive heading of this section merely indicates a function of images which, although not until now seen in proper focus, has already received abundant illustration—in the discussions of *chiarezza*, of amplification, of prosopopoeia, of the nature of tropes. Hence I shall here consider the border-line possibilities rather than the clear and obvious use of imagery with this intention. The former have proved most capable of leading modern criticism into strange generalizations concerning sixteenth-century imagery.

It is not always remembered that, with metaphor and related

---

[10] I shall seem to some readers to make great ado over uncovering attributes that are self-evident in all poetry. However, I am discussing the critical positions on grounds of which the attributes were acclaimed; of these positions there is not one which has not been used, especially by recent criticism, as a touchstone to discover characteristics seen as flaws, or used to set off seventeenth-century poets from poets earlier and later. Imagery is the poetic element which figures most largely in such criticism.

tropes, relation to a supersensible world is inescapable. This is true of the simpler ones as well as of the profound ones. Even 'The coming musk-rose, full of dewy wine' had to go through the world of abstractions to be born. This is simple because Keats is pointing to a quality perceived by our senses, through reminding us of similar qualities, similarly perceived. Metaphors vary in difficulty according to the tenuousness of the relation indicated, and in depth according to the nature of what they say about the subject they illuminate. They do not vary with respect to the relation which they bear to the process of abstracting; but the universals which they point to or illuminate vary infinitely.

Peacham instances as metaphors serving to perspicuity 'a greene head,' 'a leaden wit' (9). Marvell's 'a green thought in a green shade' is not different from these by virtue of a different activity asked of the mind, nor by virtue of a 'more abstract' subject than Peacham's 'immaturity' or 'mental heaviness.' Marvell has built up a greater number of significances for *green*, some of them of extreme logical subtlety; but it is the concept which the metaphor helps to make manifest which has the vastness and the metaphysical reach—moreover, that concept is one of such surpassing metaphysical importance. Ontological and metaphysical problems in poetry need metaphor. Especially where they are still our problems, and ours in fairly similar terms, the metaphor will be peculiarly compelling.

It is unfortunate that we cannot explain the greater profundity of some verse by the simple statement that some poets use metaphor to introduce abstractions and some do not. All do. Abstract notions of some degree of profundity enter whenever the language is truly metaphorical, or whenever we can or must read the poem on a figurative rather than a literal level. The increased tendency of modern readers to see images as making a sensuous contribution to a poem has meant the obscuring (in reading) of the 'significant' function of metaphor, unless it is made fairly explicit; this in turn has caused some inaccurate differentiations to be made between earlier and later imagery in the Renaissance. For earlier Elizabethan poetry is more de-

ceptive in this respect. It frequently seems to admit of either a
simpler reading which all but keeps it in the world of concretions
or of story, or a reading in which the further significance of these
concretions brings in a play of concepts or a discussion of metaphysical problems. I think that Elizabethan readers were more
habituated to the second sort. In later poems, such discussions
are likely to be both more obviously intended and more compressed. Such differences demand adjustments in our own
habits of reading.

All this will be best demonstrated if I emphasize somewhat
problematical examples. It is not always easy to be sure of the
extent to which certain types of images had come to be read as
profound tropes by the ordinary Elizabethan. This is especially
the case with images using myth or classical allusion.[11]

We can read the following images from *Hero and Leander* as
though they were literal description of Neptune's actions, a
kind of inspired fanciful toying with ancient story. Remembering that the substitution of *the physical ocean* for *Neptune* was as
natural as breathing to any Elizabethan, we can re-read the
images as convincing and accurate description of the caressing
flow of the water:

> And looking back, saw Neptune follow him; . . . .
> The god put Helle's bracelet on his arm,
> And swore the sea should never do him harm. . . . .
> He watch'd his arms, and as they open'd wide,
> At every stroke, betwixt them would he slide,
> And steal a kiss, and then run out and dance,
> And as he turn'd, cast many a lustful glance,
> And throw him gaudy toys to please his eye,
> And dive into the water, and there pry
> Upon his breast, his thighs, and every limb,
> And up again, and close beside him swim,
> And talk of love. . . . .   (ii, 176)

[11] Genre is a factor; it is less difficult to watch an author's intended introduction
of concepts in reflective genres. Quickly and without second thought we interpret 'I
never dranke of *Aganippe* well' as an author's disclaimer of poetic skill (Sidney, *A. and
S.*, lxxiv). Yet it takes a process of 'translation' for us to see 'Where *Cupid* is sworne
page to Chastitie' as a description of a specific attitude of mind, in Stella (xxxv). This in
spite of the fact that *Cupid* is perhaps the only case in which concretion or personification conveys the abstraction, love, almost as quickly to us as to Sidney's contemporaries.
The first image is a simpler ornament than metaphor—*pronominatio* (*autonomasia*, a
substitute name).

This is all part of the concentrated, almost overpowering, amorousness which pervades the poem; Neptune is but one element
in the impression we are given that all things, all natural powers,
conspire to flatter Leander toward success. The mood, with few
exceptions, is that induced by the seductive and opulent charm
of the underworld palace:

> Leander striv'd, the waves about him wound,
> And pull'd him to the bottom, where the ground
> Was strew'd with pearl, and in low coral groves
> Sweet singing mermaids sported with their loves
> On heaps of heavy gold, and took great pleasure
> To spurn in careless sort the shipwrack treasure.
>
> (ii, 159)

One exception to this pervasive mood is Leander's long and
cunning argument with Hero. Another exception, indifferently
successful, is the hint of Leander's inevitable failure, as Marlowe
tells of Love's request to the Fates, when

> Threat'ning a thousand deaths at every glance,
> They answered Love, nor would vouchsafe so much
> As one poor word, their hate to him was such.
>
> (i, 382)

Marlowe sees this enmity as so important that it is worth the
long explanation given in the inserted fable of Mercury's
treachery. Nevertheless, the amorous mood so predominates
in this, too, that we read it rather as a digressive parallel of
the main amorous tale than as ominous forewarning.

There is considerable weight of evidence from the rest of the
poem against the notion that Marlowe's subject is simply the
love of Leander and Hero. It is not possible to be sure of the subject of an unfinished poem. But there looms large in it the problem of the validity of man's 'natural' desires, including that of
the warrant he finds in nature to support them, the success or
failure which await his wilful pursuit of them. Perhaps the most
insistent problem of Elizabethan drama, it is also that of Marlowe's major plays. This has not ceased to be our problem, but
no modern (perhaps even no Metaphysical) would consider
these the most powerful terms in which to present it. The terms
of myth have lost their seriousness for us. They have lost their

power to portray forcefully the conflicts between love and destiny, the sport of eternal forces with mortal man, the ironic injustice of the jest by which man's aspiring nature out-tops his little strength.

But at Marlowe's and Chapman's date such terms could still convey such ideas with power. Not necessarily with solemnity or awe, but with potency—for they could lend what is now called 'aesthetic distance,' and indeed a certain flippancy is an instrumental part of some poets' use of such terms. If we can momentarily read *as though* myth could be believed, and in the same moment take seriously (as something not yet solved) Marlowe's persistent rebellious concern with the disproportions between man's limited power and his nature, *then* other significances flicker through the images. The way all physical things conspire to make 'natural' amorous desire the only reality, the flattery with which the headstrong human being is courted by the sea (set against our knowledge of the piteous irony of Leander's death), the careless disregard of the mermaids for the symbols of human wealth and disappointment—all these have still their descriptive vividness, but they also help to weight the poem as a whole with meanings which are not irrelevant to Leander's long and sophistic argument that the authority of nature is behind man's wilful desires.

It is not that these meanings are indisputably 'in' each of these and similar images. Such extra significances will even flash out upon us in one reading and not be there in the next. My point is that metaphor has this power, of making the conceptual meanings of whole pieces present to us even in 'sensuous' images. *If* images are metaphors, this is their action. We are unwise if we make too easy decisions upon when an Elizabethan is writing tropes intended to be read as such. It is as dangerous to give too literal a reading to the Fates and Joves and Cupids and Endimions of the Renaissance as it is to read a medieval image involving Saturn and allow impatience with astrology to subtract all the heavy weight of conceptual meaning which was gathered around that planet.

Many images, of course, show us perfectly overtly that they

were intended to be read with the full force of the metaphorical meaning of their terms. Such a one would be Chapman's conclusion to the long and piteous passage in which 'kinde *Neptune*' 'kild as he embraste':

> O theevish Fates, to let Blood, Flesh, and Sence,
> Build two fayre Temples for their Excellence,
> To rob it with a poysoned influence.
> Though soules gifts starve, the bodies are held dear
> In ugliest things; Sence-sport preserves a Beare.
> But here nought serves our turnes; O heaven & earth,
> How most most wretched is our humane birth?

(H. and L., vi, 234)

We may not expect in narrative poetry, however, that the indication of general meanings should always be so straightforward; a mere shift of tone may constitute such an indication. In passages in Marlowe's portion (as in ii, 215 ff.) where the author seems to disturb the tone with witty *sententiae* about love being too credulous, or about illiterate hinds having hard hearts, our surprise is partly due to the fact that overliteral reading led us not to expect general concepts to be introduced.

In Renaissance poetry as in all poetry, the clearness, frequency, and devices with which general meanings are indicated vary greatly. Like other elements in poetic technique, this varies in different genres, in the different 'characters of style,' in different authors with different purposes, and in different poems by the same poet. Many Elizabethan poems would yield much more striking examples of a play of concepts introduced in the play of images. The example which would occur to every one is Spenser's Mutability cantos, where every image and epithet, every speech and gesture, is heightened by the constant presence in our minds of the nature of the philosophical problem presented.

I have wilfully taken examples in which I think it difficult to determine the extent to which serious problems confronted in the whole poem reach down into the smallest units within it. I have wished to take them from a poem which no one would claim to be allegorical in method. For the play of double meanings in Elizabethan image-writing is not restricted to allegory proper. The minds of both writers and readers had long been accustomed to seeing a network of analogies in the world of external nature. Also they had long been accustomed to 'allegorizing' myth, that is, to seeing ancient myths neither as toys nor as part of history, but as sets of symbols embodying universally meaningful notions.[12] Myth used as metaphor is not at all confined to any genre or special type of poetic purpose. Minds so habituated were also trained to the double sight of very many other types of particulars. The transitory rose, the triumphant worm in the grave, the seasons, the elements, shepherd's pipe, king's crown, sun, moon, and nightingale—the 'particulars' in Elizabethan poems turn into metaphors at a touch. This is not entirely due to the fact that many of them had had a long history of metaphorical use. It is to be related to rooted habits of thought.

We are kept from sure and immediate response to Renaissance images of some types not alone by our natural lack of skill in responding to their conventions. Especially touching uses of mythological framework, Petrarchan sonnet conceits, and the pastoral, a kind of crude biological or genetic fallacy sometimes enters into our judgments of uses of their conventions by Elizabethans—as though they were somehow younger, merrier, more naïve and less experienced than men who lived later. Some ascriptions, to the Elizabethan poet, of naïve motivations for using pastoral or myth deserve Boccaccio's explosion as an answer: 'No man in his right mind will agree that these were his final object.'[13] In pastoral, a double level of meaning is,

---

[12] Of course, this could be documented up to the hilt from recent scholarship on the mythographers like Natalis Comes. A first necessity to the consideration of all these matters, giving a far more complete view than can my suggestions, is Douglas Bush's *Mythology and the Renaissance Tradition in English Poetry* (Minneapolis and London, 1932).

[13] The question which provokes it in Boccaccio's discussion is one which men surely asked with equal pertinence of Spenser's *Shepheardes Calender* and Marvell's pastoral dialogues, and its answer served for both: 'I say, would he have taken such pains merely to represent Gallus begging Tyrrhenus for his reeds, or Pamphilus and Mitio in a squabble, or other like pastoral nonsense?' (*De gen. deorum*, XIV, x, trans. Osgood, p. 53).

That the Renaissance conceived of *the reading* of poetry as involving the expectation of many and profound meanings is obvious throughout the whole body of early and later Renaissance poetic. A reading of Boccaccio's chapters ix and x is as swift a

of course, recognized by all contemporary theory; but with myth, too, the realm of second meanings is never far distant. Those who find it impossible to read the Marlowe in any but the simpler way will yet recognize the fact that dozens of Elizabethan poems use ancient myth metaphorically in order to discuss not the affairs of dead deities but certain living and troublesome ideas. Too willing, in general, to reduce earlier Elizabethan poems to a trivial or a superficial level of meaning, we miss the play of double significance in particular images.

A double veil is drawn across the significancy of many Elizabethan images by the fact that we often take both problems and method as chiefly historically interesting. A modern reader does not commonly share in—seriously, and for himself—that debate over the place of man's arrogant will in the structure of the moral universe which is only shadowed in this particular unfinished work of Marlowe's, but is clear enough in the plays. Our pre-decisions on questions that agitated Marlowe and Chapman and their contemporaries combine with our 'historical' attitude toward myth to make us read the images of such poems as though they were unconcerned with that dialectical strife between concepts which characterizes later poetry. The riddles and the dilemmas have to be propounded in some other way if we are to attend. As often in Spenser, a kind of illiteracy operates to encourage us in our unwillingness to go to the heart of the problems posed, and to prevent us from making the connection between images from an outlived mythology and ideas in a form in which they still pierce through to bother us.

The clear statement of the discordance between man's nature and his effort to find his place in the moral world, in Marvell's 'Dialogue between the Soul and Body,' reaches us more easily; this aspect of man's limitations causes even modern man a certain discomfort, while the terms of the images need for

---

way as any of recalling the typical grounds for that conception; they could be fully annotated from Gregory Smith's *Elizabethan Critical Essays*, and the authorities cited (Macrobius, Augustine, Cicero, etc.) had the same prestige to men of later date. There is a useful note, giving references, on the commonness of the expectation that poetry is to be allegorically interpreted, in W. Ringler's commentary to W. Allen's translation of John Rainolds' *Oratio in Laudem Artis Poeticae* (Princeton, 1940), p. 74.

their apprehension only an active mind, not necessarily a mind willing also to conform momentarily to Elizabethan habits of thought.

> O who shall me deliver whole,
> From bonds of this Tyrannic Soul?
> Which, stretcht upright, impales me so,
> That mine own Precipice I go; . . . .
> What but a Soul could have the wit
> To build me up for Sin so fit?
>
> (p. 21; in HH, p. 861)

I make no equation, either in thought or in method, between this poem and Marlowe's. Yet the same relation between concretion and abstraction is shown in this 'impaling' which allows the Body to blame the Soul for its own self-caused 'falls,' as in a Neptune who is but a green wave and who somehow also represents those forces which flatter the human being in his arrogant sense of his own 'natural' power. An interaction between concepts is secured by the use of metaphor. We must know certain myths about human Falls to understand either image, but in the Marvell there is no temptation to stop at the halfway place offered by a simpler meaning.

In earlier poems, instead of the single metaphor, sharp and direct, we often find a diffusion of the metaphorical sense throughout a long unit, so that in single-image units we now catch it, now lose it, as we do the two colors in old-fashioned changeable silk. Wide differences in the nature of the thought and the kind of concretion chosen need not obscure the fact that a play of concepts is intended, and that very different types of images, all of them meeting the criterion of significancy, stood with one foot in the world of intangible meanings.

We are quite within our rights, of course, if we prefer the type of image through which conceptual dialectic enters a seventeenth-century short reflective poem, to the earlier type I have discussed. I find it difficult, however, to see in such differences in kind of artifice a difference in *poetic*. It is equally difficult to see in them a contrast between a new and ruthless fidelity to psychological reality, and an earlier forsaking of the real for the charmingly fanciful. Mere possession of such or such intrinsic qualities is not what weighs in any argument regarding the integrity of images. The grounds for any quarrel that Renaissance poetic would allow us to have with the poet, regarding his integrity and profundity, lie elsewhere.

3. *Significancy, Ancient and Modern*

The grounds for such a quarrel lie in the poet's possible incoherency or his possible untruth. For though this poetic gives the poet wide liberty to use any kind of image that is coherent with his set of significances, it pulls him up short just where we should leave him freest—in that it conceives pretty generally of coherence as rational and conscious, and of truth as disturbingly unrelativistic. The criterion of significancy is uncomfortable to a modern mind in that it pushes the ultimate test of the poet's imagery onto the level where what we must judge is the poet's coherent (logically coherent is generally implied) ordering of nature, and even onto the level where we must judge of his imitation as truth or untruth.

This discomfort would be lessened if the criterion of significancy would admit of a modern definition: 'the image must be significant of the poet's perception of the quality of his experience.' We are quite accustomed to asking for coherency and for truth in poems, in senses that could be translated in ways such as these: 'Do these images accurately convey how it actually seemed to have such a mental experience? Is the feeling engendered such that these disparate images cohere? Were all these images honestly a part of this mental experience? Are they an honestly complete record of it?' These defining questions adequately describe widely accepted modern notions of the function of Metaphysical imagery; also, many aspersions have been cast upon sixteenth-century imagery for failing to meet the criterion of significancy so defined.[14]

[14] This restricted definition is so familiar to anyone who has read the criticism of the last fifteen years that it would be absurd to give specific references; it is rooted, of course, in nineteenth-century criticism, but applications to the Metaphysicals have been more recent. It is either stated or used as a premise by great numbers of critics who currently write on Metaphysical poetry in its 'modern' aspects—examples are T. S. Eliot, F. R. Leavis, Allen Tate, Cleanth Brooks, C. Day Lewis, F. O. Matthiessen, Theodore Spencer, Herbert Read, George Williamson.

So far as I can interpret them, Renaissance theoretical treatments all seem to go beyond these understandings, but it might yet be true that poets anticipated modern aims by using images with no further responsibilities than these. Although evidence lies in whole poems, not in isolated images, I should like at least to pose through typical examples the question of whether poets in the period do seem content to use imagery with this restricted significancy, assisting coherency and truth thus less ambitiously defined. In much modern criticism which assumes that Metaphysical images are intended to direct our attention to the quality rather than to the meaning of experience— especially to any generalized 'truth'—there is considerable emphasis upon images as being conditioned not by the poet's logic but by his sensibility. I shall assume at the outset that these two are never really divorced in any poem, that no poem has ever been born out of logic by immaculate conception, and that, alternatively, no poem ever entirely lacks logical meaning. I shall thus avoid inserting constant reminders that the Elizabethans (and even myself) have no notion that 'poem' and 'logical discourse' are to be identified, even though they do not set the two in opposition.

Of course, all images *do* convey the poet's perception of the quality of his experience. All poetic with which I am acquainted accepts this, as a given; the task here is to look for some indications that the early seventeenth century erected it into a sufficient criterion. Much modern criticism does; modern poems which do are rather harder to find.

T. S. Eliot's fairly careful statements have been greatly extended. Metaphysical poets are increasingly seen as sharing with moderns the 'quality' he says the former have, 'of transmuting ideas into sensations, of transforming an observation into a state of mind.'[15] Their images are presumably a major instru-

---

[15] This and the five following quotations come from Eliot's essay on 'The Metaphysical Poets,' *Selected Essays* (New York, 1932), pp. 241 ff. The whole of it is pertinent; it has had an influence upon modern criticism of the early seventeenth century which is quite incalculable, though many extensions of Eliot's positions, by others, go far beyond the inferences that could be drawn from this or others of his various essays on poets of the period.

ment in their 'task of trying to find the verbal equivalent for states of mind and feeling.' Images more than any other stylistic element should demonstrate in action their 'direct sensuous apprehension of thought, or a recreation of thought into feeling.' If they 'feel their thought as immediately as the odour of a rose,' transmuting their ideas into sensations, their images will not support or illustrate or elucidate, but somehow rather be, thoughts ('the idea and the simile become one'). 'A thought to Donne was an experience; it modified his sensibility.' If a poem consists of the conveyance of that experience (as certain modern poems clearly do), then it begins to look as if the experience of having them was what chiefly interested Metaphysical poets about their thoughts, and as if this is what is chiefly to interest us also.

All rhetorical theory attempts to study the conveyance of thoughts precisely on the ground that they must and will modify the sensibility of readers. Also, it accepts as a premise that this relationship between thought and sensibility characterizes the author's state of mind as well, though any such pigeonholing is post-seventeenth-century.[16] Much of the discussion in preceding sections has been a demonstration of Elizabethan (and traditional) acceptance of the fact that most metaphor, much imagery, helps us to apprehend thought with immediacy, presents thoughts ready for grasping and holding. But, especially as these modern ideas have come to be developed and applied, something further seems to be in question: in that what is praiseworthy is a relation between percept and 'felt thought' which is nothing less than identity, and in that what is especially interesting about a thought is that it was experienced (cf. 'is true'), was amalgamated without a 'dissociation of

[16] No Elizabethan would have considered that his senses could do more than modestly assist in the *apprehension* of *thought*, yet he would not have compartmentalized the various faculties to the extent implied in the statements above (see chap. xiv below). Many distinctions and separations which now seem rigid and unreal were carefully made and tenaciously held—regarding the nature of intellection, the cognition of particulars through sense, the apprehension of universals as an act of discursive thought, etc. But they were not distinctions of this sort, separating whole mental processes one from another as by a difference in kind and mode of operation (as implied, e.g., in the phrase 'a recreation of thought into feeling').

sensibility,' stands in an interesting relation to the unification of the author's sensibility.

The poetic process envisaged, and accordingly the end desired and the technique devised or utilized, seems to be that familiarly commented on in connection with modern poems; I choose from among many Edmund Wilson's description in treating of Eliot—a 'new technique at once laconic, quick and precise' for representing the 'interplay of perception and reflection,' cutting corners, moving not by logical stages but as live thoughts move in live brains.[17] Or (in treating of Yeats's 'Among School Children') a process resulting in a poem that is a 'moment of human life, masterfully seized and made permanent.' Almost any person in our century would take for granted that these are commendations. One reason why so many similar praises have been attempted for Metaphysical poetry is that we admire this accurate recording of what goes on in a poet's consciousness (especially if it represents a unification of sensibility, which we find difficult), regard it as a sufficient 'cause' for a poem, and would generously like to see it as the cause of earlier poems which attract us.

I shall try to apply these familiar modern interpretations of the functioning of poetic imagery, choosing first one of Daniel's sonnets that everyone has by heart—'Care-charmer sleep.'[18] It cannot be denied that such a typical pre-Metaphysical poem does very clearly and stubbornly resist any attempt to *account for its images* by the interpretations of the last few paragraphs. They will fit, after a fashion, but what shall one do with the extreme logical carefulness of the images and the purposes thereby served? To say nothing of the thoughts, even the sensations are not felt primarily as sensations (*sable* night, rising sun, *embracing clouds* in vain) but clearly support an evaluation of an experience, even assist in the statement of general ideas.

[17] *Axel's Castle* (New York, 1932), pp. 107, 62–63.

[18] It is quoted in the Appendix, Note I. As with many points in this discussion, an earlier source for certain phrases would make no difference to the argument. But in this case, as in others, the possibility that borrowings revealed by source study might affect the point being made about the image has been considered (here, see J. G. Scott, *Les sonnets élisabethains* [Paris, 1929], p. 125).

'Brother to death, in silent darknes borne' assists us to seize a notion about sleep, but the notion is quite distinct from the perceiving of how sleep steals upon one. Some images in themselves indicate judgments—the *shipwreck* of my *ill-adventured* youth; as in several others, the words that most clarify the state of mind retreat markedly from the sensuous, requiring in the reader's mind a process of abstracting from long experience— the day's *disdain*, the images of *day-desires*, the torment of the *night's untruth*. The discipline of the logical structure is tautly held step by step through the quatrains, allowing none of the irrelevant dartings of thoughts in live brains. The turn at the beginning of the sestet leads to the wish that is the logical conclusion of two concepts about sleep (the first, touching oblivion, 'illustrated' by percepts; the second, touching dreams, stated outright with the faint help of *model forth*), and two concepts about day. One's pleasure in the surprise of the adjuration to sleep that *it* should *restore the light* depends upon a simultaneous apprehension (not possible sensuously but only logically) that *darkness* is a *quality* of night and *lightness* is an *attribute* of care-lessness.

It somehow will not explain the power of these images to say that they are significant of the poet's perception of the quality of his experience. The conveying of that is left away behind as a complete intention for the poem, and there are so many indications of logical control in it that it is difficult to see its coherence as other than rational by conscious design. I have tried to take a clear and simple early (1592) example, written in the Petrarchan tradition, by a man who espoused the traditional tenets of Elizabethan poetic in a later prose treatise (?1603). We should expect it not to show the Metaphysical-modern characteristics.

If, on the other hand, one looks at Donne's 'The broken heart' (p. 48), with its rapid glancing from image to image, it seems possible that here is, indeed, an actual identification of sensuous perception with reflection. That Donne has transmuted for us the *idea* (of *why* it is stark mad to say one's been in love an hour) into the *sensation* (of seeing a flash of powder unable to burn a day).[19] It seems possible that the very mixture of metaphors results from the fact that the thought 'I can love no more' has been transmuted into a sensation of being a broken mirror, some rags of heart.[20]

But the trouble is that the images are not really written so. The flash of powder, like the plague, is introduced as an analogy following a clear general statement about love's power of rapid destruction. The chained shot and tyrant Pike 'illustrate' (in the traditional sense) the second of Donne's general statements (vss. 4, 9–12) about the nature of love, both made in clear conceptual language. The glasses and rags do not actually mix the metaphor, for we are intended to make the logical abstraction 'attribute of things in pieces: capable of only a part of what the whole could do.' I shall not outline the logical structure, but it is entirely controlled and clear.[21] If I restrict the significance of the images to signifying the quality of experience in a seized moment of human life (even if the experience is 'having this thought about love'), I am at a loss to account for the type of coherence which obtains in the structure, for large areas of the poem given a generalizing force, and for the extremely numerous evaluative shadows upon the diction of the images.

I try to take images which have been praised here or there in modern criticism as evidences of the 'new' Jacobean sensibility, or of the Metaphysical poet's prime interest in the exploration

[19] Of course, the use of metaphorical language, as I have tried to analyze it in earlier sections, does 'transmute' this causal notion in one sense. Not into sensation, however, as can be seen both from the total inability of the mentioned sensations to convey this idea of cause and from the red-herring action of the sensations the moment we attend to them as such. It is not the sensation part of a metaphor that does the transmuting. In this image an idea we may not grasp is put into analogical relation with another *idea* we probably will grasp, because of the simplicity and familiarity of the concrete situation from which we should deduce it. This is the usual, ordinary, immemorial mystery of metaphor, perfectly traditional and perfectly astounding. It is also, as I have tried to point out, traditionally recognized. That there are logically subtler forms of *translatio* than analogy was also recognized.

[20] Though stanza 4 says more than this, it closes:
'And now as broken glasses show
A hundred lesser faces, so
    My ragges of heart can like, wish, and adore,
    But after one such love, can love no more.'

[21] It is free of irrelevancies, from the amplification of love's power in stanza 1 to the end of the specific application illuminating the conclusion, in stanzas 3 and 4.

of his own psychological states; perhaps the following from 'The Will' is a better example (p. 57; 'Thou Love' is addressed throughout the poem):

> Therefore I'll give no more; But I'll undoe
> The world by dying; because love dies too.
> Then all your beauties will bee no more worth
> Then gold in Mines, where none doth draw it forth;
> And all your graces no more use shall have
>   Then a Sun dyall in a grave.
> Thou Love taughtst mee. . . . .

The flow of the argument provides the last image, with perfect directness; the moment Donne has told Love that he will outwit him by dying and thus put him too into a grave, the analogies that confirm Love's uselessness are likely to come from underground. The first image is simple and well worn; the second has great logical subtlety because Donne has seized upon something that is useless in the sense that what made it function cannot get at it, and the parallel with what he can do to love is very accurate. It is a subtlety scarcely to be referred first and foremost to the sensibility. Nor does a lover's revenge upon love represent a new range of feelings, a hitherto concealed area discovered by a highly susceptible consciousness. However, the well-known feelings and ideas assuredly are conveyed with far more than usual bite and force. Because the image is logically so relevant and natural, the suggestions in it, which are controlled with great delicacy, have been prepared for by the logical structure which governs the whole poem. One could hardly read a poem in the framework of the medieval 'testament-formula' without expecting a passing-bell and a grave; but neither do we fail to expect a satirical use of them, after five stanzas in carefully parallel structure, each with its general indictment climaxing the repeated knife slashes of accusatory concrete examples. The sharp thrust of these is lost if we leave it to our senses to apprehend them; none of Donne's five, however sharp, could have found these tenuous analogies. The poem is, of course, famous for its logical coherency, stanza by stanza; each goes beyond the quality of experience to the meaning of it, conveying evaluations conceptually stated, and the whole poem goes quite beyond the single psychological situation in subject.

I keep the Metaphysical examples to love poems and elegy because these belong to genres treated by Elizabethan theory itself with emphases most nearly approaching modern emphases; as, for example, in what Puttenham says of these kinds. A long list of the modifications of sensibility which the poet as lover intends 'throughly to be discovered' explains why love requires

a *forme* of Poesie variable, inconstant, affected, *curious and most witty* of any others . . . . with a thousand delicate devises, odes, songs, elegies . . . . *mooving one way and another to great compassion* [I, xxii, p. 45].

The usual connections between such kinds and either 'praises and dispraises' or 'persuasions,' show up in the slant of the language; nevertheless, the emphasis on states of feeling actually experienced is certainly present.[22]

The emphasis on solace through utterance is greater with poetical lamentations, for there the poet, like a physician—not Galenist but Paracelsian—makes 'the very greef it selfe (in part) cure of the disease.' It is worth note that Puttenham declares against escapism, and the self-pity which his references to pouring out inward sorrows might suggest, taken alone (I, xxiv). No song need be ordered to sorrow over such griefs as could be better cured by 'well doings'; and sentimental laments over misguidings for which we have only ourselves to blame are disparaged by Puttenham with the curt phrase 'voluntary detriment.' But many human predicaments

carry a *reasonable* pretext of *iust* sorrow. . . . . Therefore of death and burials, of th'adversities by warres, and of true love lost or ill bestowed, are th'onely sorrowes that the noble Poets sought *by their arte to remove or appease* . . . . making one dolour to expell another. . . . .

Sidney also reserves his approval for '*iust* causes of lamentation' (in Gregory Smith, p. 176). Donne makes a firmer if equally conventional statement on the solace to be expected,

[22] Love, being the first founder of all good affections, should be 'uttered *in good forme and order* as other laudable things are'; since it is of all affections most puissant and general, none could truly brag of any exemption from its 'moodes and pangs,' and 'the poore soules' have found out therefore especially 'many *formes*' in this general kind, to suit with their praying, praising, railing, rejoicing.

not through utterance, but through the art of it, in 'The triple Foole.'[23] The rest of the poem makes gay application of a notion which is clearly the ancient one of control through disciplined ordering, not the sentimentalist's escape through talk.[24]

These Renaissance statements, though chosen for their 'modernity,' go beyond the modern ones as regards the ultimate end of writing about these emotional situations; nevertheless, they, too, give much room to the *portrayal* of states of feeling. It is important to discover whether or not there is any difference between this and what Wilson says Valéry does—an achievement we recognize and value in many modern poems besides Valéry's: 'Valéry presents, even more completely than Yeats in . . . . "Among School Children," *the emotion merged with the idea* and both *embedded in the scene* where they have occurred' (p. 76). If this is what the Metaphysicals too were trying to do, the nature of the images will show it.

A poem like Donne's 'The Flea'[25] will startle one with a sudden sensuous detail, seemingly admitted to the poem only because it helps to 'embed the emotion in the scene':

> Cruell and sodaine, hast thou since
> *Purpled thy naile*, in blood of innocence?

[23] 'Then as th'earths inward narrow crooked lanes / Do purge sea waters fretfull salt away, / I thought, if I could draw my paines, / Through Rimes vexation, I should them allay, / Griefe brought to numbers cannot be so fierce, / For, he tames it, that fetters it in verse' (p. 16).

[24] Of recent years, what seems to me overreading of Donne's interest in his own psychological complexities has pushed him unjustly toward the latter position. The distinction, as Renaissance writing observes it, is pretty much that made by Yvor Winters in *Primitivism and Decadence* (New York, 1937), p. 5. The chief misinterpretation involved in turning Donne into a 'tortured' psychological sentimentalist seems to me an initial misreading of his subjects—as largely self-revelatory. Elizabethan *reasons* for self-revelation in poetry are (like those just touched upon) equally far either from the self-importance of romantic melancholy or the self-justification of romantic irony—so often recently fastened upon Donne on grounds of the 'dissonance' of his images, skeptically indicating possible flaws in his beliefs before anyone else does. Against the background of practically contemporary attitudes so sane and humorous as Puttenham's (or see Sidney's self-dialogue, *A. and S.*, xxxiv), it seems all the more necessary to consider whether Donne really was the tormented examiner of his own states of mind he is now so commonly thought to have been. The nature of the images is proper evidence and has been used by all those who write upon these matters.

[25] P. 40; the erotic significance which is probably responsible for the choice of the flea does not, I think, affect the points to be made.

Certainly one sees the flea, and the site of the murder. But as soon as a re-reading of the poem has reminded one of the place of this death in the argument (for not a flea dies in Donne but for a cause), the image ceases to seem primarily motivated by the more modern reason for sensuous particularity. At any rate, the detail serves a stout purpose, the better seen if we do not 'merge' idea and emotion; and its vividness illuminates the idea just as in any traditional amplification: this peculiarly bloody death transpires openly on the stage in order to make both a Herod and a self-murderer out of the lady, and thence (by an ironic contrast with this amplified hyperbolical sin) to laugh her into a parallel loss of her honor. The false analogy of the last two lines, that draw the parallel, is a more delectable example than could be found in any logic textbook of the hackneyed warning that 'every likeness hobbles.' The poem as a whole, like the others examined, uses what Puttenham calls 'curious and most witty form,' bringing a single situation to bear upon one of the usual aims for poems of this genre—to persuade, to move, to 'discover throughly' and note the significance of, to reorder, to praise, dispraise, condemn, or otherwise evaluate.

This is continually one's experience with the poems of Donne's that ought by modern interpretations to be satisfied with conveying the quality of an experience, or with conveying the mental experience of 'feeling his thought.' One looks at an image alone, and it seems strictly comparable to modern sensuous imagery with this especial function; one looks at the image in its indicated relation to the poem's whole meaning, and the comparableness melts. In 'A nocturnall upon S. Lucies day' (p. 44), the alchemical images, the life-sap of earth shrunk to the beds-feet, seem like daring contortions if we focus our attention upon psychological realism as the sufficient end of each image. If we are willing to apprehend them in their logical relation to the structure of the poem, they are seen to be excellently accurate clarifications of the poet's distinctions.[26]

[26] See the different judgment expressed by R. L. Sharp, *op. cit.*, p. 12 (chap. ii, n. 9, above; cf. also p. 24 on the sundial-in-the-grave image). Too much quotation would be required in a proper demonstration of the traditional functioning of Donne's 'significant' imagery, and only a few much-discussed examples may be touched upon; see the Appendix, Note J, for one other

Interest and skill in psychological realism is necessary to any poet and found in all poetries; modern exaltation of it into a primary and sufficient end seems to me to deny place to some of the intentions of earlier poets, as one may judge these *from their images*. I even find it not impossible to believe that Donne intended to convey some of the concepts about the nature of love which are the ostensible subject, and ostensibly produce the images, of a poem like 'Loves growth' (p. 33).

We accept this intention, in a poem like Lodge's 'Sonnet' (based on Desportes) from *Scilla's Metamorphosis*, which has the simplicity that the nineteenth century taught us to associate with meaning what one says. At first blush, Donne's imagery seems very different in function (as it is very different in logical complexity) from Lodge's plain contrasts—'The earth, late choked with showers, / Is now arrayed in green,' the woods are decked out, whereas I go in black; the thrushes seek out shade, I my grave; they have their flight to heaven, I my walk on earth (HH, p. 156). All these are differences to support 'They free, I thrall,' and are part of a comment on the power of love; though it is a far from solemn one we yet recognize in it an intended meaning beyond the description of an isolated situation.

Donne, too, seizes on parallels and contrasts with natural phenomena, but the similarities and differences between what spring does to him and to the rest of the world are far more complicated, requiring images whose intellectual difficulty causes us to attend more to their nature than to their function. For example, 'And yet no greater, but more eminent, / Love by the spring is growne,' requires three similitudes, each throwing its significant light on the meaning. His concluding concept on the power of love is a good deal more daring than any Lodge arrived at: 'No winter shall abate the springs encrease.' His images (like that of love's 'being elemented too') help him to make certain reservations, to which we must attend. But the conclusion that he therefore intended the focus of our attention to be the accurate description of his process of mind, rather than the general concepts he discusses, is not borne out by his manner of utilizing his images. Though they accomplish

much else, Donne's images are for one thing a series of strenu-
ous attempts to make us put our feet in exactly the path that
will lead us through an inquiry; unexplained qualities of the
images stick out awkwardly on all sides, if we try to cover them
with the aim now oftenest assigned him, faithful description of
his processes of mind.

One does not therefore need to vulgarize and oversimplify
his meanings. A man may intend us to read his poems as in-
quiries into the real nature or the truth of something without
solemn pontificating. Elizabethan poetic would have seen the
inquiry, however daringly contorted it was, and regardless of
whether or not it resulted in conventionally accepted conclusions, as a valid poetic end; the description, not. Early poetic
makes so little ado about a poet's mental biography that one
cannot but conclude that descriptions of events in it were seen
as insufficiently significant poetic subjects, like other sorts of
history. True, this poetic is uncomfortably serious about a
poet's ideas. A corresponding seriousness in the poet is only uncomfortable if his ideas are vapid or puerile ones. Donne's seldom compromise his dignity, or even ours. At least, interpretation of Donne by earlier poetic would have the advantage of re-
moving from that keen critical mind the stifling seriousness
about the experiences of his own consciousness with which much
modern comment has cloaked it. There is no poet of any stature,
carefully read, who does not reveal such experiences; the Metaphysicals do not stand alone but with their great predecessors in
this. I believe that they also stood with their predecessors in
using images whose significancy committed them to generalized
interpretations of experience or to evaluations with general
implications.

4. *Significancy and 'Statement'*

When one adopts Renaissance poetic as a background for the
poetry written throughout the entire period, one other feature
of that poetry, mentioned in the introductory examination of
problems, falls into place as explicable. This feature is the
willingness to include overt statement of meanings, and to sup-

ply clear directive phrases articulating the images with the rest of the structure. If the subject of a poem is 'thus and thus felt I,' images will carry it; if it is rather 'this and this I conclude, by way of this experience, to be true,' the conveyance is not likely to be trusted solely to images. The more compressed the form, and the more logically pertinent and complex the images, the shorter usually the conceptual statements, and the more a method of overt statement will give way to the mere use of articulating links. The latter method is equally clear and direct, and equally orthodox, if less immediately noticeable.

Not much illustration of this is required for the earlier poets of the period, whose unabashed outright statement of concepts is now frequently pointed to as a fault. It does certainly go beyond modern taste, which for many reasons prefers ellipsis, indirection, and, if possible, a spice of doubt. Later Renaissance poets show a fondness for genres traditionally favoring these last-named qualities (like satire), or for short kinds favoring great concentration; they characteristically point up the significance of groups of images in advance, or they use sharp epigrammatic summary statements at the close of a formally separate section. All poets make some use of all these methods, of course, and the intent in all is similar—to clarify that rationally coherent framework from within which the images reach out with all their suggestions and implied meanings.

To re-read King's 'Exequy' or Donne's 'Anniversaries' with this in mind is to be amazed at the willingness with which each poet indicates the force of images, usually before they appear. We think of 'The Exequy' as a tissue of images, indirect in its method, avoiding the statement of any of the obvious concepts —about immortality, or the finality of death, for example. True, the stages of meditative grief, of hopelessness, and of hope, traditional in elegy, are only *realized* for us by the images—and could by Elizabethan theory not otherwise be made evident and 'luminous.' They are, however, introduced by clear direct statement.[27] It is through that sailing image which embodies the un-

[27] 'My task hath been to meditate . . . .'; 'But thou wilt never more appear . . . .'; 'then we shall rise . . . . in that calm Region, where. . . . .'

obstructed swiftness with which man approaches death that the meaning seizes hold; we are scarcely even aware that King has preceded it with 'And follow thee *with all the speed* / *Desire can make, or sorrows breed.*' Each image is introduced meaning-end-first, as it were. It is done with consummate skill, but it is not left undone, nor left to us to do.

I cannot quote all of Yeats's 'Easter, 1916.'[28] But the function of Yeats's's image of the stone is very similar to the function of some of King's images as both poets meditate the unsevered relations of the dead to the living, and the meaning and nature of the loss:

> Hearts with one purpose alone
> Through summer and winter seem
> Enchanted to a stone
> To trouble the living stream. . . . .
> A shadow of cloud on the stream
> Changes minute by minute;
> A horse-hoof slides on the brim,
> And a horse plashes within it;
> The long-legged moor-hens dive,
> And hens to moor-cocks call;
> Minute by minute they live:
> The stone's in the midst of all.[29]

The pertinent difference here is the greater readiness of the earlier poet to prepare his reader by expository phrases for the exact significance of his images. Both poets use imagery with far-echoing suggestions, exquisitely controlled. In a poem by

[28] Yeats's images are often more traditional than other modern poets' in method, as though in spite of his Symbolist alignments he felt the need of pointing a reader toward the significance 'meant to be seen'—but few modern poets quite like to do this. This is one reason why there are few difficult images in Yeats in which the syntax does not repay study; syntax is the most unobtrusive of all methods of clarification, the closest one can come to the paradox of saying something tacitly.

[29] P. 208 (1916). The function (not the meaning) of the image is similar, for example, to King's 'eclipse' image (vs. 37). Function conditions method. King, like Yeats, seeks the help of a traditional symbol; like Yeats, he enriches meaning by the device of a vehicle which has reference to more than one tenor (though he makes our understanding of the double meaning of 'An earth now interposed is' more sure; cf. 'the living stream'). The image is simple when first introduced (vs. 21) and gradually grows in complexity. With either of these poems, comment roughens and distorts the meanings.

King, however, we should have caught sight of the significance of the cloud-shadows and the moor-hens' calls before they entered the poem; in Yeats we are rather asked to enter and sit down within a mind and presently understand. All understanding of another mind is partial and fallible, but earlier poets show a certain determination that a minimum of common ground be shared, writing their images with an eye to making the common ground as large as possible. Donne is especially careful to indicate how we are to conceive the relation of smaller units to the structure of a whole.[30] Such writing utilizes rather than avoids generalized conceptual language.

I can see nothing either more or less 'poetic' about either the Renaissance care to show where the poem is going or the modern habit of leaving the direction of images to be puzzled out. I do see a different attitude toward that person of whom the Renaissance writer is always conscious—the reader. An intimate connection between poetry and rhetoric is not the sole cause for this, although the connection did certainly exalt the importance of that shadowy, demanding, explanation-needing Reader whose affections must be moved and whose reason must be assailed by sensible approaches.

We have preserved to modern times a much more nearly parallel conception of the responsibility of the poet toward reality than of the responsibility of the poet toward his reader. On the responsibility of the poet to himself, earlier poetic is silent. To judge by the poetry that was written, I do not think that the period found this question especially interesting. Donne's statement at the close of the 'Second Anniversary' manifests the traditional understanding of the relation of poetic subject to purpose, the accepted conception of the way

---

[30] Any passage will illustrate his normal manner—the lines from 205 on in 'The second Anniversary,' for example. The speed of her soul's passage is first stated (188, 205), then illustrated with the image of the stars strung like beads, and another direct statement closes the image, clarifying an added element it had introduced (213); heaven's closeness to her is stated, then illuminated by the image of the bringing-in of tapers; the general application is made, in the direct form of an adjuration with several members; 'wee understood / Her by her sight' *precedes* the image of the blood speaking in her cheeks; 'as we were . . . . Oppress'd with ignorance' *precedes* the string of particular ways we are ignorant—etc.

poetry was related to rhetorical persuasion, and the conventional attitude toward the poet:

> Since [God's] will is, that to posteritie,
> Thou should'st for life, and death, a patterne bee,
> And that the world should notice have of this,
> The purpose, and th'authoritie is his;
> Thou art the Proclamation; and I am
> The Trumpet, at whose voyce the people came.

I do not read this as irony. It has none of the earmarks which Donne meticulously gives to his ironic statements. Like most Elizabethan comment, it asks us to read poems as though language were not a tool for announcing facts about a particular *thou* or *I* in their character of particular phenomena, but a medium for intimating and ordering significances which particulars shadow forth. That is why it needs three metaphors, and is a humble rather than an arrogant statement, and receives our 'belief,' independently of our concurrence in certain special tenets of seventeenth-century Platonized Christianity.

CHAPTER VIII

THE CRITERION OF RHETORICAL EFFICACY

CONSTANT adjustment to some hypothetical reader is responsible for much advice in Renaissance poetic, and poets' practice shows the advice willingly taken. This meant that the poetic image was almost universally expected to meet a criterion of 'efficacy.'

The final determination of efficacy—efficacy upon the affections, as generally understood—depended upon many factors which did not reside in the poem at all but in the mind which was to read it. The nature of that mind, its approachability, its needs—these are constant concerns of the Renaissance theorist and poet. The latter does not appear to have rebelled against this aspect of his problem; grumbles are scarce. Diatribes against particular audiences are legion; there are plenty of home thrusts at stupid critics, and complaints against ladies who do not respond to a good sonnet when they are sent one, but the poets simply declare for another audience or for silence, and no one seems to hit on the solution of thinking of poems independently of readers.

The inclusion of poets among persons who have out-and-out plans to affect readers causes discomfort, again, to a modern mind. It brings up suggestions of dogmatism or immature arrogance and seems to open the way to a confusion between perfection of technical skill and shrewd employment of neat trickery, or, worse still, to a confusion between poet and preacher. I push aside these difficulties for the moment, though they are far from chimerical, to distinguish certain emphases which this criterion brought into criticism and certain qualities which it underlined in images.

Images are often brought forward in the critical writings

to demonstrate and fortify the accepted tenet that poetry should, or rather necessarily will, move the affections of a reader and hence persuade him. Among other kinds of form-determining ornament, they exemplify the poet's power to do what Puttenham calls 'inveigle and appassionate the mind,' like 'a pleader' rather than a judge.[1] The 'moving' power of poetry is everywhere noted, often in comments which stress the middle term in the commonplace *docendi, movendi, de-lectandi*, which (though dependent on Cicero and Quintilian) was applied to both poetry and rhetoric. The notion is implicit or stated in dozens of writers[2] and in chance comment on poems or poets; and acceptance of it clearly shows through discussions of 'delight' or 'teaching,' or of the nature and power of figures.

The criterion of efficacy was interpreted in close relation to the poet's special problems, yet statements of it show, too, how close his problems were to those of the *rhetor*. These typical passages, from DuBellay and Peacham, point to an oratorical power in the poet and yet especially recall notions earlier examined of imagery's power to 'amplify,' to endow matters with importance or with 'evident' immediacy:

... saiches, Lecteur, que celuy sera veritablement le poëte que je cherche en nostre langue, qui me fera indigner, apayser, ejouyr, douloir, aymer, hayr, admirer, etonner, bref, qui me tiendra la bride de mes affections, me tournant ça et la à son plaisir [ii, chap. 11 (1549)].

[The author, especially through amplification] may prevaile much in drawing the mindes of his hearers to his owne will and affection: he may winde them from their former opinions, ... may move them to be of his side, ... to mourne or to marvel, to love or to hate, to be pleased or .... angry, ... to de-

---

[1] III, vii, p. 154. For more emphasis on 'persuading copiously and vehemently,' see, e.g., p. 196, entreating the poet to 'play also the Orator ...., to pleade, or to praise, or to advise.' See above, chap. v, n.14, n.9, or see references cited in W. Ringler's note to Rainolds' statement of the idea (*op. cit.*, in chap.vii, n.13, above). Relations between the disciplines are more carefully examined in Part II below. Obviously, no criterion for imagery can ignore poetry's *capacity* to move the affections, but this one makes specific demands.

[2] This tenet is so universally propounded that I make no attempt to cite the passages concerning it which everyone familiar with Renaissance poetic will recall—in Sidney, Minturno, Boccaccio, Tasso, Pontano, Mazzoni, DuBellay, Scaliger, Daniel, Jonson, Carew, and others.

sire or to be satisfied . . . . to envy, to abhorre . . . . to be subiect to the power of his speech whither soever it tendeth [p. 121 (1593)].

It was as obvious to the Renaissance as to us that such powers as these in a poet find their parallel in powers ascribed to the orator by Cicero, Quintilian, and many others. This relation was accepted without cavil. The element that was seen as rhetorical in poetry was this conscious *penetration* into men's faculties with such power that they could not choose but be moved. 'How wonderfully shall . . . . his wordes pearce into their inward partes,' says Peacham (sig. A iii [1577]). It would be easy to annotate this understanding by quoting from the poets themselves—Drayton, King, Daniel.[3] This power which critics and poets pluck out as the distinguishing characteristic of rhetoric is a power to which poetry would be unwilling to relinquish its claim. These persuasions felt in the heart and felt along the blood are not to be confined to the sister-discipline.

However, conceptions like these involve certain differences between Renaissance and modern ways of thinking about poetry. In earlier thinking the unity of the process *moving:persuading* is not disturbed. Even a modern reader, if not forewarned, is likely to testify that both together are 'what actually happens' in reading a poem (in however small a degree). So, too, early theorists do not share the uneasiness of the modern poet who is unwilling to do the second and yet aware that poetry is bound to do the first. Moreover, until long after the Elizabethans, the reader is thought of as not merely the spectator of the great 'motion of mind' of the poet. Although it is accepted that a vehement 'inward stir' will characterize the poet's sensibilities as well, discussions are little preoccupied with his feelings, greatly preoccupied with those he will evoke. The critical question of 'sincerity' is neglected in favor of the poetic problem of efficacy through credibility.[4] The truth of the affections was a serious matter, but it stood to be answered less

[3] See the Appendix, Note K, for typical characterizations of 'rhetoric' by poets; the idea furnishes the basis for a favorite image.

[4] Sincerity is sometimes commented on, by both theorists and poets, as a prerequisite for writing credibly; Sidney's 'look in thy heart and write' is a statement on method and is so presented.

in terms of the question 'did the poet feel it?' than 'will the reader feel it and why should he?' Nor do men of the Renaissance expect poetry to achieve this moving power simply as a by-product of the excited state of the author's sensibilities. The line the earlier period ignores is the line nervously drawn by modern poetic between *a poet himself moved* and a poet *persuading or convincing*. If the Renaissance had tried to stay to one side of this line, we should probably have lost Donne, who explodes the meaning straight out of Yeats's famous distinction: 'We make out of the quarrel with others, rhetoric, but of the quarrel with ourselves, poetry.'

All this does not convict Elizabethans of thinking up ways to work on readers' 'emotions.' I have used various Elizabethan circumlocutions rather than the word 'emotions,' since the true meaning of their tenets would be belied by introducing terms that carry our sharper distinction between feelings and thoughts. Several of the faculties are concerned, in both parties to the communication. Images have efficacy to move a reader's affections, to quite properly affect his judgments; they move him to feel intensely, to will, to act, to understand, to believe, to change his mind.

Though poetry and rhetoric share the power of moving readers, and although to a Renaissance man this included persuading them to certain mental acts, methods of doing so may, of course, differ.[5] Yet many methods are shared, and these touch imagery nearly. Though Sidney says he deserves 'to be pounded for straying' from Poetry to Oratory, he thinks nevertheless that 'both have such an affinity in this wordish consideration' that his digression but assists his meaning. Moreover, one of the few actual statements on imagery as such, in Sidney, is his comment here on the similitude—one of the devices of rhetorical

---

[5] Tasso, Castelvetro, Mazzoni, Sidney, and others, of course, have well-known passages in which distinctions between the disciplines are stated or implied. The important ones may be conveniently turned up through the index in A. H. Gilbert (see Bibliography). They are usually very general, and most points which affect imagery have already been drawn into this discussion (like Mazzoni's 'the credible as credible is the subject of rhetoric and the credible as marvelous is the subject of poetry,' in Gilbert, p. 370; the relation to discussions of amplification, hyperbole, and trope is clear).

persuasion of which poetry makes most use.[6] But special cases need not be adduced; a large amount of common ground is accepted by poets of every stripe throughout the period. Especially the tropes and figured patterns of language which rhetoric had set down as bound to move the affections of men were regarded as common property. This is not so extraordinary, and is still true; all poetry, like other impassioned speech, makes use of the methods which the rhetorician lists. But the Renaissance poet did so consciously, very willingly, and with keener realization of purposes shared with other disciplines.

His willingness to move readers by these means has already been demonstrated time and again. With clear intent to persuade readers to share their ideas of the value of something, the poets use figure after figure chiefly praised by rhetoricians for this special power. I exemplify with a handful only: *aetiologia* or the *tellcause*, to 'fortifie our allegations' (Puttenham, p. 228; this is the form of some of the most beautiful images in Elizabethan poetry and is a favorite with the Metaphysicals); similitudes;[7] *ironia*, to reprove by derision and illusion; *sarcasmus*, like bitter corrections in physic; proverbs, strong to confirm and piercing to imprint; *congeries* or the heaping figure, like the violent strokes of battle; *micterismus* (Puttenham's *fleering frumpe*, p. 191), to reprove and jest subtly, like a black frost that will nip a man's nose before he sees it.

[6] Sidney is reminding writers that the 'force' of a similitude is not 'to proove anything to a contrary Disputer but onely to explane to a willing hearer,' so that *a surfeit* of them is absurd, no 'whit informing the iudgement, already eyther satisfied, or by similitudes not to be satisfied' (in Gregory Smith, I, 203; he is criticizing euphuistic writing). This antipathy to overuse of the similitude is based not on a distinction between poetry and rhetoric but on the new Ramistic definitions of the dialectic proper to all three disciplines (see below, chap. xii). The point to be noticed here is that Sidney is not concerned to make any such distinction as Yeats makes, though he, too, sees contentious 'proving' as out of place. What Yeats really objects to is what sixteenth and seventeenth century alike condemned—false or sophistical rhetoric. His remark is from 'Anima Hominis,' dated 1917; that he uses the word with its usual (and uninformed) nineteenth-century connotations is clear from the closely related poem which precedes these meditations in prose ('Ego Dominus Tuus,' dated 1915; see *Essays*, Vol. IV of the *Complete Works* [New York, 1924], pp. 492, 482).

[7] Which, of course, 'confirm'—and 'to the short form of similitude pertains the metaphor' (Milton, *Art of Logic*, I, xxi). The unattributed characterizations following are from Peacham.

I have overweighted this list with satirical figures partly because they grew in favor as poets later in the period grew fonder
of satire's backhanded form of persuasion and partly because
much admirably subtle modern use of these same figures has
somewhat extended or changed them. *Ironia* is the most important of these. The figure has no trace of the modern meaning frequently termed romantic irony; and this fact is symptomatic of the earlier period's extreme concern with the reader
and his understanding of the subject, and small concern with the
author save as artist. *Ironia* is praised as one of the most moving and subtle of 'dark' tropes; by it one says more forcefully
what one means by saying what one does not mean. It has no
tinge of self-protectiveness; it is not thought of (and so far as I
can see is not used in the poetry) as a device by which the poet
may forestall the objections of those who might suggest he had
not seen all around his subject. He may through it forestall objections which he does not share; but I find no sure cases of
what Eliot, for example, can do with such uncanny deftness—
suggest sometimes what he dares not mean, sometimes what he
hopes is not true. The Renaissance expectation is that the reader
is more likely to be *moved* if, with delight at an added logical
subtlety, he apprehends the author's true evaluation under a
mask. Whether some darling conventionality is being 'derided'
or only some bizarre unconventionality, the reader's assent is
equally the poet's concern, and it is understood that the reader
will give it on grounds of some subtlety in the argument, not
some sophistication in the arguer. *Ironia* is used generally when
the poet is also to some degree persuader; it is used not as a
shield to ward off accusations of semi-blindness or sentimentality, but to help wind him better into the heart of his subject.

Concern with moving the affections had other immediate effects upon imagery besides a very conscious use of figures, but
many of them have already been mentioned. A chief effect is
increased emphasis upon imagery as functional. Given the general principle that ornament functions to move the affections,
poets had yet to solve problems of choice—through processes
which probably have not changed much, though sterner and

more settled requisites gave more help. Donne chose patternings
of repetition in the first of the two images below, intellectually
pleasing subtleties in the second. Such of his reasons as we may
follow lie in differences of genre, 'cause,' mood (inseparable
from subject), affections and faculties addressed in the reader—
all the considerations regulated by that decorum which must
become second nature to a poet.

> When thou sigh'st, thou sigh'st not winde,
>   But sigh'st my soule away,
> When thou weep'st, unkindly kinde,
>   My lifes blood doth decay.
>
> ('Song,' p. 19)

> . . . . Preachers which are
> Seas of Wit and Arts, you can, then dare,
> Drowne the sinnes of this place, for, for mee
> Which am but a scarce brooke, it enough shall bee
> To wash the staines away. . . . .
>
> ('Satyre IIII,' 237, p. 167)

Both kinds of ornament 'pierce into man's inward parts,' either
the *copie* that makes the first ebb and flow and breathe itself
away, or the brevity of the ironic challenge in the second, en-
forced by the harsh wrenching of the rhythm and the homely
mocking contrast in the double similitude. The criterion of
efficacy does not determine what kind of ornament a poet must
use; it merely reminds him that an image powerful perhaps to
him but powerless to move another fails in one of its purposes.

Such reminders strengthened the element of sensuousness in
images, for 'the minde is not assailable unless it be by sensible
approches' (Puttenham, III, xix, p. 197). Delighting the ear
received the most attention, so that poetic elements especially
affected are those of tone and of music—not melodiousness
alone, but everything in which verse resembles music: phrasing,
pauses, repetitive structures, pitch variations, accelerated and
retarded tempo, etc. Such considerations modified the nature of
images so greatly (as, of course, they still do) that it is generally
very misleading to judge any image without reference to the
design of sounds of which it forms a part.

Vividness and concreteness in the image are also affected—

not always, however, increased. The sensuousness is likely to be truly an 'approach,' to be perceived and as quickly dropped by the reader. Marston's first image below would be the opposite of efficacious if the *gulf* remained long enough to swallow up the *cormorant:*

To everlasting *Oblivion*

Thou mighty gulfe, insatiat cormorant,
  Deride me not, though I seeme petulant
  To fall into thy chops. . . . .
But as for mee, hungry *Oblivion*
Devoure me quick, accept my orizon:
  My earnest prayers, which doe importune thee,
  With gloomy shade of thy still Emperie,
  To vaile both me and my rude poesie. . . . .

(*Scourge of Villanie*, ed. Harrison, p. 119;
in HH, p. 368) (Author's italics)

The vaguely sensuous epithet for *gulf* allows it, too, to have *chops.* Similarly *gloomy shade*, etc., needs the modulation through three general phrases before *hungry* Oblivion can come to possess the motionless silent power of a still empery that can veil (vail?) one. A poet's skill in muting his images must equal his skill in producing them, if the appeal to a reader's affections is to be at all a controlled one. Donne has so marvelous a power in this respect that one all but resents his dominion over one's eyes and ears. But, of course, there is scarce a poem without an example of it. It could not but receive special attention in an era when the tenets of poetic constantly reminded poets that the kind and amount of sensuousness in an image must be fitted to the way the receiving mind would work.

These conscious designs upon a reader may seem to us to give the 'art' of poetry a disreputable slot-machine quality: press a button, and a spark will ignite the reader's affections. The safeguard lay in unrelaxed attention to the principle of decorum (for one aspect or another of this principle safeguards each criterion for imagery). The poet was a trumpet to make manifest the perfection of the subject; he was in part creator of that subject, but, nevertheless, its manifested perfection was what exerted its legitimate power over the reader. The poet's responsibility not to abuse this trust is not forgotten even in speaking of the humblest kind of rhetorical figure. Images must be *both* efficacious and proportionate to the nature of what they help to express.

Comments on single figures ring all manner of changes on this double tune of fitness and efficacy (no wonder, since the two are assumed to be causally connected). *Epizeuxis* (as in 'O Absalom, my son, my son') suits the vehement expression of any affection—for pleasant ones, it is like a quaver in music; for sorrow, like a double sigh of the heart; for anger, like a double stab (Peacham, p. 47); it is not to be used but in passion, says Hoskins (p. 12). *Articulus* (*cutted comma*), if used in causes of perturbation and haste, can be a thick and thundering peal of ordnance (Peacham, p. 57). *Traductio* (like Donne's *unkindly kinde* above) may be used with or without passion, 'but so as the use of it come from some choice and not from barrenness' (Hoskins, p. 17). Puttenham rejects some examples of repetitive figures, saying they are 'not figurative but phantastical, for a figure is ever used to a purpose'; one he disdains because it neither urges affection, nor beautifies or enforces the sense, nor has any other subtlety in it, 'and therefore is a very foolish impertinency of speech, and not a figure' (III, xix, p. 202).

Figures of larger scope, and more likely to produce as well as to modify images, receive similar comment. *Congeries,* a multiplication of words 'beatyng in all one thing' (Sherry, fol. 50ᵛ) will be used especially in summing up, being earnest and hasty, and good to enforce the cause and renew the hearer's memory (Puttenham, p. 237). *Incrementum,* the scaling ladder, which climbs to the top of high comparison, requires worthy matter; like fire it can go as high as the matter can carry it.[8] *Exclamation* is not lawful but in extremity of 'motion'; *interrogation* 'is but a warm proposition' and serves where bare affirmation would be too gentle and harmless a speech (Hoskins, pp. 33, 32). One

[8] Peacham, p. 169; cf. also *auxesis,* Puttenham's *avancer,* p. 218. A particular kind of *copie* is commended by Hoskins—dividing and making instances—but commended *when* the subject, if 'generally spoken,' would seem but a flourish, and when one must give more especial note of that which 'universally' could not be conceived without confusion and dulness (p. 24).

might continue this for some hours. All such advices concern the responsibility which the writer has toward his subject. All these means of expressing subjects are treated with strict attention to suitability as well as to power.

Concepts to which I have called attention in this chapter show, naturally, differences in emphasis rather than absolute differences from modern ideas of poetry. Earlier theory reads as if poetry were conceived of as a relation established between a subject and a reader, though only establishable by a poet. The emphasis on poetry as interesting evidence of the relation between a subject and a particular poet is an emphasis we have learned since, and one which seems the least helpful of any to the understanding of earlier poetry. The earlier kind of polarity, with 'a reader to be affected' as one of the poles, did mean that poets are likely to plead, or complain, or exhort, or argue, much too openly for modern taste, and that we can often easily detect that they intend to 'breede no little alteration in man.' 'For to say truely,' says Puttenham, in discussing the sententious or rhetorical figures, 'what els is man but his minde? . . . . He therefore that hath vanquished the minde of man, hath made the greatest and most glorious conquest' (III, xix, p. 197). Modern thinking finds such emphasis upon a poet's power over readers both arrogant and aesthetically improper.

However, the oscillations toward the pole of 'affecting a reader' were counteracted by the equal strength of the other pole, 'the poem's true vision of the subject.' This latter responsibility, which earlier writers felt themselves able to meet as we do not, kept serious poets from self-righteous preaching, and honest poets from technically shrewd trickery. We will style their writings exalted propaganda if we think of all ideas as postulates and all defense of the validity of any idea as hawking for one's own postulates. But the Elizabethan and seventeenth-century poet did not think thus. Consequently, he did not take ironically the responsibility of 'truth to the subject'—though he took it very gaily, and the notion that he should gain credence only for what is true did not prevent him from piling Pelion on Ossa to demonstrate the real shape of a molehill.

This tension maintained between the requirements of subject and of reader is often neglected in modern discussions of the relevance of poetic ornament to a core of conceptual meaning. Quite aside from the Renaissance poet's sterner idea of the logical control which a whole should exhibit in all its parts, he would, I think, have seen even seemingly irrelevant richness of texture as having the relevance of instrument—it is instrumental to the establishing of a right relation between reader and subject, and the medium (language) through which he must establish this relation does inescapably thus function. The modern has difficulty answering the question, '*Why* add the ornament characteristic of poetic discourse, when the idea can be more clearly and economically stated otherwise?' The Elizabethan, I think, would have simply answered 'Because it would not be heard.' His answer *would have included* the other important assumption, that to 'hear it' without the strength and delicacy of poetry's form of statement was to give not that subject, but some other, a hearing.

Despite this last, there is nothing gained by denying the fact that the Elizabethan thought of the poet's function as close to that of any other thinker—philosophers, preachers, and orators included. He did see the world as a world in which the ideas of human beings were paramount realities[9]—and images convey a man's ideas movingly to others. Yet in the world of 1580 or 1630 this rhetorical aim for imagery did not so much arrogantly place man in the center of the universe, as admit sensibly that, since men were going to read the poetry, it would have to be written to men's eyes, ears, and minds, and written to the scale of human importances. Elizabethan poetry is centered in man's moral, intellectual, and affective impulses and needs, but in much the same way that a modern scholar has remarked that even Copernican astronomy is geocentric: the observations can be made only from where the observer himself is located, and are stated in terms relative to the earth.[10] Like medieval poets,

[9] See Appendix, Note L, for a fuller admission of the unmodern character of Renaissance poetry in this respect.

[10] See Francis R. Johnson, *Astronomical Thought in Renaissance England* (Baltimore, 1937), p. 117.

Elizabethan and seventeenth-century poets frequently suggested the insufficiency of this world-view. But meanwhile, however willingly the insignificancy of man is admitted, there is willing acceptance of the nature of man's mind as a condition for poetry. Even the hard conditions imposed by the nature of a reader's mind are accepted, and images take their form in obedience to the necessity of speaking to the affections, the understanding, the powers of evaluation of the only readers a poet has—other men.

CHAPTER IX

THE CRITERION OF DECORUM

THE question 'Is it decorous?' is not like the other questions present in the mind of the Renaissance reader, judging the excellence of an image, or of the poet as self-critic, deciding whether to omit or to change an image. For this is the question which helped to determine his answer to all the others. Propriety or decorum was the basic criterion in terms of which all the others were understood.

Suitability or proportion is, of course, equivocal as a criterion until it is defined in relation to all the many factors, in a given particular poem, with which the images are supposed to suit. This is accepted by the theorists, who seldom attempt more than a general statement of principle,[1] but who as they proceed call to account every element in poetic technique, however tiny, on these grounds of 'aptness,' 'decency,' 'seemliness.' Discussions take cognizance of the various bases for decorum familiar from classical theory—decorum in respect to the person who speaks, to whom he speaks, of whom or what, in respect to the time, the place, the purpose. But for practical purposes, in its effect upon imagery, these more or less fell together into the general notion that the poet's images must suit the 'cause and purpose he hath in hand'—the poetic subject, be it high invention or lightly considered trifle, commendatory or satirical in intent, grave or fanciful in nature.

Refinements which helped to define the general idea were of considerable practical assistance. Notions of what was fitting to the three styles, fairly loosely distinguished in poetic writing, consistently affected images; the same poet will admit very dif-

---

[1] Puttenham's general chapter 'of that which the Latines call Decorum' (III, xxiii) is as useful as any for one who is trying to interpret the principle as it must have affected images.

ferent images as decorous when he writes a narrative in the grand style, a verse-letter in the expository mean style, or a satire in the base or humble style. Habitual interpretations of decorum in the various genres consistently affected images. These refinements operated to make enjoyment of the propriety of images a peculiarly delicate and subtle element in poetic pleasure. They also operated to make it quite fruitless for us to compare, without the proper reservations, an image from one of Donne's deliberative lyrics, in the mean style and intended as a dispraise, with an image from the *Faerie Queene*, or from *Hero and Leander*, or from an eclogue by Drayton, or Herrick's 'To Anthea,' or *Comus*, or Daniel's 'Complaint of Rosamond,' or Jonson's 'Drink to me only with thine eyes.'

But even when we understand the major outlines of the conception of decorum and habitually take cognizance of its workings where imagery was concerned, there yet remain a number of questions that should be considered. Chiefly these are questions about what was thought to constitute an *in*decorous image. Are some images simply not suitable to poetry at all? Does Metaphysical imagery fly in the face of orthodox definitions of the decorous image? Are there any positive precepts which maintain and mark out the extent of a poet's freedom in this matter, or was the principle of decorum fundamentally an influence toward circumscription and rigidity?

Each of these questions represents a familiar stereotype of criticism. In so far as it has seriously considered the matter of decorum at all, post-Romantic and modern criticism has tended to link it with 'poetic diction' of the sterile kind, to think of Jacobean poets as rebels against the decorous in imagery, to consider decorum as a matter of barren rule. Since these seem to me to be the important danger points at which misinterpretation of large areas of sixteenth- and seventeenth-century poetry can enter, I shall try to see if there is any answer to these questions by discussing, against the background of accepted theory, the decorousness of images from various genres, decades, schools, subject matters, and levels of style. Such a discussion cannot 'prove'; it can only indicate ways of looking at the poetic suitability of images. But at least they were accepted ways of looking at it in the century when the images were written.

1. *Decorum and 'Literary' Diction*

There is little evidence that, to either the sixteenth or the seventeenth century, poetic decorum involved cutting out some images because they were not suitable 'to poetry,' or putting in others because of some intrinsic 'literary' elegance or charm. When a mere handbook-writer like Sherry gives a list of 'ungarnished' figures, and we look at them expecting to find ways of using language that are too commonplace for literature, we find them distinguished as indecorous not because they are insufficiently high-flown, but because words and subject are unsuited. *Bomphiologia* uses gay and blazing words for a light matter; *asiatismus* is a kind of inditing full of figures but lacking in matter; there are various other classifications of language too much befigured and begayed (fols. ix ff. [1555]).[2] Or, as in the vices of incongruity distinguished by Fabri (1521), the fault is sometimes lack of economy or significancy.[2] Puttenham mocks at one of these, in an image; quoting six lines on spring, complete with Dan Phoebus' rays and Aries' horned head, he remarks that 'the whole matter is not worth all this solemne circumstance to describe the tenth day of March.'

These exemplify the common position on 'poetic diction.' Precisely what is damned is (1) the gaudy and (2) the inane. The principle invoked to damn them is that of decorum. Quite probably we should not admire certain single examples of decorously elaborate figures which these gentlemen would have considered properly outside the nets they spread for the indecorous. But at all events what their definitions of decorum attempt is to snare the very creature sometimes thought of as encouraged to enter under that heading—'literary' elegance. Writers in this era do

---

[2] *Pleonasmus* and *macrologia* add superfluous words, *perittologia* uses words without pith, *periergia* uses many words for a small matter. Puttenham names the last 'overlabour' 'for his overmuch curiositie and studie to shew himself fine in a light matter,' and exemplifies it (p. 258) as below. Day (1595), treating such figures, implies that if seeming superfluity increases our reasons (i.e., underscores our intentions), it is permissible.

not talk about a style suitable to poetry; they talk about many poetic styles suitable to many poetic subjects. The emphasis is consistently that in Fracastoro's unequivocal statement concerning the language of the poet, who alone speaks *simpliciter:*

> But when I speak of simply beautiful language I wish to be understood in this way: that this beauty harmonizes with the subject under discussion and is appropriate to it and its different attributes, and is not merely beautiful in and for itself [*Naugerius*, p. 64, trans. of fol. 160ʳ (1555)].

As a robe of gold does not dignify a peasant, he says, so heroic dignity given to a light subject is unseemly. Perhaps one of our real quarrels with the Renaissance lies in our evaluation of peasants and of heroic dignity; perhaps new judgments as to which *are* weighty matters and which inconsequential, were forming even as early as the sixteenth century. This is not primarily a difference in poetic.

When we examine actual examples of phrases condemned by sixteenth-century writers as indecorous, we do frequently find that their preferred phrases seem like 'poetic diction' to us on just this score—that we are quite willing to lower some subject which they thought fit to heighten. Puttenham objects to a translation of Virgil which says that Aeneas was fain to *trudge* out of Troy; this were better spoken of a beggar, a rogue, or a lackey; 'for so wee use to say to such maner of people, be trudging hence' (III, xxiii, p. 273). A historiographer does not write of a king or emperor that he took to his heels and ran out of the field, though of a mean soldier or captain this 'were not undecently spoken.' Juno must not *tug* at Aeneas; it is a carter's word and connotes the pulling of oxen and horses, or boys tugging each other by the ear.

Perhaps we forget that usages or 'decencies' which happen to fit within our own sense of values do not, like these, seem like arbitrary elevation of language, but like what these really are— an attempt to fit the word to the idea we have of the object. Daily readers of the *New York Times* would expect it to say that John L. Lewis *ramped* up and down the room, that his beetle-brows pushed his two small sharp eyes together like a greedy mole's—but not to say the same of Einstein. The latter image might conceivably be used to mark an ironic contrast between Einstein's outer man and his meaning to the world of thought; but, if so, heightened language would inescapably accompany the exalting *of the latter*. We, too, do what Peacham says is decent and due—bow the knee of our speech and light up the eye of our phrase to the bright beams of earthly glory (p. 23). When Puttenham boggles at a translator's calling Aeneas a *fugitive*, seeing in this 'a notable indignity offred to that princely person,' his *grounds* are impeccable: first, that the connotations of words are important and powerful and, second, that it is 'not to the Authours intent,' *he meant not to make him a fugitive*.

The grounds for Elizabethan insistence upon decorum have often been assumed, rather, to be a certain reverence for poetic etiquette, trivially defined, and for 'literary' diction, in and for itself. This sort of mistranslation of the underlying motive of various critical strictures has had unfortunate effects in the history of criticism.

2. *Decorum and the Lowering of Style*

Even more important misinterpretations of the concept of decorum have resulted from another habitual oversight, still very common. Most examples above happen to be instances of decorum working toward elevation of style. This is only half the story. Decorum worked quite as consistently toward lowering the style to suit the author's subject and intent. Modern remarks about decorum seldom show an appreciation of this side of the matter. There is plenty of room in orthodox theory for what we like to think of as audacious images, or for the poem which uses images as one of the most economical of all elements in poetic technique for deflating rather than inflating the importance, value, or prestige of something.

Puttenham happens to exemplify outright this double operation of decorum by an image which is indecorous used for one subject, decorous when used for another, precisely because it has this deflating effect, in the second instance desirable. The word used, *pelf*, has by now all but lost its metaphorical sense, so that to us the question is not one of imagery; to Puttenham *pelf* is still 'properly the scrappes or shreds of taylors and of skinners, which are accompted of so vile price as they be commonly cast out of dores' (III, xxiii, p. 274). He reprimands a poet for saying, in a verse in dispraise of a rich man: *thou hast a princes pelfe.* This, he says, is 'a lewde terme to be spoken of a princes treasure.'[3] But what is interesting is his defense of the decorum of the belittling image 'pelf' in *case* the poetic subject requires this diminution. In the image condemned, this metaphor

carrieth not the like reason or decencie, as when we say in reproch of a niggard or userer . . . . that he setteth more by *a little pelfe* of the world, than by his credit or health, or conscience. For in comparison of these treasours, all the gold or silver in the world may by a skornefull terme be called pelfe, *& so ye see that the reason of the decencie holdeth not alike in both cases.*

This is sound poetic, and a clear and plain exemplification of the tenet that decorum *demands in the proper situations* homely, displeasing, harsh images—which are poetic, not 'unpoetic,' *because* they have that character. Incidentally, it illuminates very considerably the reasons for the use of such images by the Metaphysicals.

It can properly be claimed for the Metaphysical poets, I think, that exactly this kind of keeping poetic decorum, when 'abbasing a matter,' is responsible for most of their rough or homely images—ironic and self-depreciating, unpleasing, or just surprisingly down-to-earth. They may make unorthodox evaluations of men and things; I find little that is unorthodox in this respect about their images or their poetic. At least I can find few if any 'low' images which can be questioned as out of line with the accepted requirements of decorum, in Donne, King, Carew, Suckling, Marvell, the Herberts.[4] Certainly not in the mystical

[3] Of course, this notion is easier to smile at now than in 1589. It is only fair to quote from Puttenham's earlier chapter: 'for neither is all that may be written of Kings and Princes such as ought to keepe a high stile, nor all that may be written upon a shepheard to keepe the low, but according to the matter reported' (chap. v).

[4] The demonstrations of decorous single images which follow are all subject to revision when we shall have new knowledge about the exact connotations of particular words to Elizabethans and Jacobeans. Much of the required knowledge is forever inaccessible to us. The type of linguistic research necessary before we shall be able to pronounce with real sureness on what was 'indecorous' in specific images is exemplified in A. H. King's *Language of Satirical Characters in 'Poetaster'* (London, 1941).

poets, for their type of subject and intention had required from time, immemorial this magnification of the *in*significance of things which other men accepted as significant and desirable (this is what the 'pelf' image does to the gold and silver).

I find, of course, a great many contributory reasons for the *predominance* of 'deflating' images in the verse of these poets: the genres in which their best work was done (an extremely narrow list compared with that of the 1590's); the development of reflective 'lyric' forms written in the base or middle styles; changed intentions attendant on the separation of some forms from music; the growing importance of prose as a vehicle for graver matters which in previous centuries had been treated in verse (as Suckling and Lord Herbert, for example, left us treatises rather than poems 'of religion' and 'of truth'); many factors affecting single poets—such as the fact that many of these poets have left us little work done in their mature years, or the fact that if the Donne who wrote the sermons had put all his ideas into poems he might have had a somewhat different set of advocates in the 1930's. In general, reasons underlying what we like to think of as the peculiar character of Metaphysical imagery are far too complicated to obey our desire to force them into some simple generalization about pessimism or psychological conflict.[5] It is tempting but inaccurate to see in these poets a reflection of our own need to defy hierarchical principles like that of fitness and proportion.

Donne is peculiarly sensitive to what the keeping of decorum required of his imagery. The exact propriety of his images is perhaps the largest factor in the vigor and acuteness of his style, for the poet has no sharper instrument than this, especially if he be in other ways a deft logician. Of all elements in poetic technique it is most economical, and relative brevity was required in all the kinds Donne chose to write in. Unless he chooses to have his images convey two evaluations at once (which he can do

---

[5] I should not myself add to this list of reasons 'the disturbed *Weltanschauung* which accompanied the acceptance of the Copernican world-picture.' This idea is frequently bound up with some form of the notion that 'scientific' images involve some disturbance of poetic decorum. See the Appendix, Note M.

with unambiguous skill, generally subscribing to but one), he is particularly adept at seizing on images in which the thrust is lightning-quick and unmistakable in direction.

With short images, this is often because they are familiar or make use of some known convention. If Donne wishes to shrink up the world and its sun into nothing, beside the marvelous greatness of God brought to the incredible paradox of a human death, then we have:

> What a death were it then to see God dye? . . . .
> It made his footstoole crack, and the Sunne winke.
>
> ('Goodfriday, 1613,' p. 336)

Both of these last are unassailably decorous images. Their fitness is traditional; men had not waited for the Copernican theory to point—at the moment of the Crucifixion—to the inglorious littleness of man's world. The rhetoric of the whole passage, with its interwoven echoes of *death-die-life*, and the rush of the repeated grammatical structures, helps to give the images their effect of shocking disintegration. If Donne wishes rather to stretch the world's diameter out to unimaginable distances, then we have, instead of this cracked stool,

> At the round earths imagin'd corners, blow
> Your trumpets, Angells, and arise, arise. . . . .
>
> (*Holy Sonnets*, vii; p. 325)

It is not possible to separate the images from the metrical pattern in which they inhere, and the bold sponde and triumphant upspringing rhythm underline the extension of earth's limits rapidly denoted through the remaking of the doubly familiar image (*round, corners*).

Donne is already on his way to another amplification: 'arise, arise / From death, you numberlesse infinities / Of soules. . . . .' A very different crowd, though it is precisely the same one, from that in the resurrection-image of 'The Relique,' where his intention is rather to diminish the importance of these innumerable millions. There, he is amplifying instead a love which outlasts all earthly events, and to which even the Day of Resurrection offers pre-eminently a last lovers' meeting:

> Who thought that this device might be some way
> To make their soules, at the last busie day,
> Meet at this grave, and make a little stay. . . . .
>
> (p. 62)

The indecorous and truly dissonant image would put this busy rush of other souls intent on their own destinations into the serious grandeur of the sonnet; or put the trumpeting Gabriel up onto the mere footstool; or point to the world's splendor and the sun's unceasing march in lines on the death of that Son who begot for men a different kind of endless day.[6]

It is necessary, if we would stay with orthodox theory, to rid ourselves of the notion that some images are inherently decorous, likewise of the notion that the 'trivial' or superficially inelegant image is indecorous. Like Puttenham, we must examine the final purport of the image in connection with the poem's 'cause.'[7] In poems where Donne scoffs at the notion that "Tis not the bodies marry, but the mindes,' he is ready to swear that women 'are but *Mummy*, possest' ('Loves Alchymie, p. 39); in poems arguing that 'Chang'd loves are but chang'd sorts of meat' he will conclude: 'And when hee hath the kernell eate, / Who doth not fling away the shell?' ('Communitie,' p. 32). These diminishings, or bitter reductions into low and common terms, are entirely decorous for a poet with such a subject and purpose in hand. They would not be decorous, and do not appear, in poems whose subject is the parting of lovers 'Inter-assured of the mind,' or which treat 'Loves mysteries [which] in soules doe

---

[6] Donne can amplify what is conventionally amplified when he chooses. The sun may be used to signify might and power, or may find its traditional use to figure forth the greatness of a king: 'The Sun it selfe, *which makes times*, as they passe' ('The Anniversarie,' p. 24); 'A Taper of his Torch, a copie writ / From his Originall, and a faire beame / Of the same warme, and dazeling Sun . . . . ('To Sir H. W. at his going Ambassador to Venice,' p. 214). But naturally this is not what he does when he wishes rather to amplify the power of something beside which the sun's greatness becomes a mere external irrelevance: '*Busie old foole*, unruly Sunne, ... Thy beames, so reverend, and strong / Why shouldst thou think? / I could eclipse and cloud them with a winke, / But that I would not lose her sight so long' ('The Sunne Rising,' p. 11).

[7] See above, chap. i, n. 7, on this term.

grow.' Then we have rather love's enduring strength *amplified* through 'Like gold to ayery thinnesse beate,' or exposition of the relation between body and essential self through an elevated cosmological similitude.[8]

All these differences are simply examples of what Puttenham is driving at when he points out 'that the reason of the decencie holdeth not alike in both cases.'

There are occasional examples of violent diminishing figures which I at least am unable to defend on grounds of decorum, and it might be useful to point out one or two. In the 'Elegie on M[ris] Boulstred' (p. 282), Donne's first two lines show how consciously he used language to amplify or diminish[9] a subject:

> Death I recant, and say, unsaid by mee
> What ere hath slip'd, that *might diminish thee.*

Two lines later he begins a long amplification of Death's power, harshly reducing the earth and all things on it to the miserable dimensions they take on in respect of this power: 'Th' earths face is but thy Table; there are set / Plants, cattell, men, dishes for Death to eate. / In a rude hunger now hee millions drawes / Into his bloody, or plaguy, or sterv'd jawes.' These images, for twenty lines, are violent and horrible—but a heightened awareness of Death's power is scarcely an indecorum in an elegy (first section). The image that seems to me indecorous by the poetic of the time occurs as Donne proceeds to claim that M[ris] Boulstred is one of those few who are but made God's own by dying, Death's blow being so ineffective:

> She was more stories high: hopeless to come
> To her Soule, thou 'hast offer'd at her lower roome.

[8] E.g., 'Our bodies why doe wee forbeare? / They are ours, though they are not wee, Wee are / The intelligences, they the spheare' ('The Extasie,' vs. 50; p. 51). I do not disregard claims that the subject of this poem is almost opposite to that I have stated (in the semiquotation from vss. 71–72), but consider these claims to have been sufficiently answered. For the controversy, see G. R. Potter, 'Donne's "Extasie," Contra Legouis,' *PQ*, XV (1936), 247–53, and references. The other poem used above is 'A Valediction: forbidding mourning,' p. 49.

[9] I use 'amplify' somewhat inaccurately and untechnically here; all diminishing is a form of amplification—magnifying the lack of power, dignity, or value of something. I should also remark that in a swift review of many images it is not possible to state subjects of poems with anything like a proper subtlety or inclusiveness. That is done by the poem.

The wrench by which we are made to conceive of the relation between soul-and-body, higher-and-lower, in purely spatial terms, seems to me out of keeping with what the rest of the poem tries to say about that relationship. It is not the vehicle used in the comparison which makes it disproportionate; a following image is decorous enough:

> As houses fall not, though the King remove,
> Bodies of Saints rest for their soules above.

The flaw seems to be in the logic; a frivolous *libertin* poem might expound through images the subject 'our souls are just our top stories,' but this poem gives no other indication of such an intention.

I relegate a second example to the notes,[10] but in both, and contrary to his usual practice, Donne seems to do what we expect of Symbolist poets—admit as an image a kind of isolated fancy which arose, largely by association, out of his original notion ('overthrowing' in the first, 'death th' Ocean' in the second). But, in any case, the first poem especially runs from interest to interest somewhat too gaspingly.

It is natural enough that these examples come from Donne's *Epicedes* and *Obsequies*. Their images have come in for much abuse, frequently from objectors who take for granted a connection between intellectual ingenuity and insincerity. Defenders of Donne deny the connection, but frequently by providing us with a substitute scapegoat—other poets' rhetorical ingenuity, seen as a vice. Decorum as understood in this period bars out neither kind of ingenuity in poems of deep feeling. Possession

---

[10] Cf. the 'Elegie on the Lady Marckham,' p. 279, vs. 17: 'In her this sea of death hath made no breach, / But as the tide doth wash the slimie beach, / And leaves embroder'd workes upon the sand, / So is her flesh refin'd by deaths cold hand.' *Slimie* is a fairly usual word for the body, not too harsh to be decorous, for instance, in Spenser's Castle of Alma, where a paradoxical contrast *is* pointed at, between the substantial impermanence and goodly workmanship of man's body (*FQ*, II, ix, 21). But here it magnifies disproportionately (for me) the lowness of flesh which in a line or so is said to have been 'Diamonds, Rubies, Saphires, Pearles,' especially when an image denoting change (not decoration) of substance was really wanted. That the image seems both trivial and violent may be because I cannot abstract as quickly as Donne's contemporaries could, and have less interest in what happens to my flesh after death.

of either may no more be our touchstone for the integrity of images than may the use of inelegant or unpleasant vehicles of comparison. All the epicedes miss the sweeping power and profundity of the *Anniversaries*. Yet the images in these last are certainly no less ingenious.[11] The first, the *Anatomie*, is occupied with one long metaphor used to diminish, a method quite in accord with the poem's stated subject—'the frailty and the decay of this whole World.' The violent single examples of diminishing —the world a carcass, a cripple, a wan ghost, a dry cinder—are strictly proportioned to the nature of the subject.

I have used Donne to exemplify normal and accepted ways in which decorum operated to lower rather than to elevate a subject through images, because it was expedient to use the work of a single poet and because so much has been made of his harsh, violent, or displeasing images. It seems to me an error to call these images dissonant or audaciously discordant. They are not inharmonious with the subjects he chose, nor do I think that his half-century saw them so; they are sometimes inharmonious with a given reader's preconceived notion of what kind of subject the contemplation of 'Love' or 'Woman' or 'The Soul' *ought to* lead one to propound. Donne's subjects are audacious and so is his unabashed importation of the strictness of logic into the poetic genres he preferred. But we use amplifying images to commend, diminishing images to condemn, every day of our lives; such a use of imagery implies no daring new tenet in the poetic of its user. These ugly or homely images are for the most part simply the ordinary rhetorical figure meiosis, recommended by the orthodox rhetorician for just the purposes for which the Metaphysical poets (and the others) used it.

Puttenham calls this figure the Disabler. It may be used 'in derision and for a kind of contempt,' as in some of the examples above from Donne: the used woman a shell to fling away, the

---

[11] If one of the longest of the epicedes be, as Grierson calls it, an 'ingenious, tasteless poem' (II, 206; that on Lord Harrington), I cannot find that the images make it so, though the first epithet may be justly applied to them. It contains some of the most dangerous and striking of Donne's 'radical' images, but they uphold a subject of more real unity and more range of application than some of the obsequies concern themselves with.

sun eclipsed with a wink, men as mere dishes for Death.[12] It comes into play 'if you diminish and abbase a thing by way of spight or malice, as it were to deprave it,' as in 'A heavy burthen perdy, as a pound of fethers' (Puttenham, p. 185). The figure meiosis is not new to our discussion; it is simply the type of amplification which is decorous if one intends appraisal which lessens rather than magnifies. Hoskins says that *diminution* differs from amplification 'no otherwise than up-hill and down-hill' (pp. 35–36; see pp. 85, 91). One may make impressive the smallness of a man's wisdom by saying, *he is not the wisest man that ever I saw.* In one of its meanings it is thus simply litotes. And, as Hoskins remarks, 'why should I give examples of the most usual phrases in the English tongue?'

However, in this form of litotes and in certain others it takes, meiosis happens to be peculiarly useful for poets when they wish—often because they are condemning or complaining—by indirection to seek direction out. There are certain innocent-looking uses of the figure 'by way of pleasant familiaritie'—as Puttenham says, he may call his Muse *my moppe*, 'a litle prety Lady, or tender young thing.' Such uses, however, may range from endearing diminutives[13] to more serious and dignified diminutions which get a troublesome thing into manageable dimensions, seen as its true ones. This sort occurs in Herrick's remark to his tiresome conscience: 'Can I not sin, but thou wilt be / My private Protonotarie?' (*Noble Numbers*, No. 72). Or in Herbert's, to his: 'Peace pratler, do not lowre' (p. 105). Or in Southwell's advice to lovers to leave off the idle pain of serving love 'delightful in the rind, / Corrupted in the core' ('Love's servile lot' [HH, p. 236]). These simpler diminutions, which enable a poet to indicate by an image his sense of the true proportions of a thing, are to be distinguished from disabling-images which carry a faint tinge of the author's disbelief that these are necessarily the true dimensions of the thing. The simpler use

[12] It is used to make a thing appear small (Peacham, p. 168—as when one calls a learned doctor a 'prettie scholler'). Puttenham's chief treatment of it is in III, xix, pp. 219–21.

[13] See Appendix, Note N, for 'duck' in I. A. Richards.

does not have, for example, the disappointed bitterness of Donne's 'women . . . . are but *Mummy*, possest' (i.e., would they *were* thus easily dismissed, once had). Or the sardonic tone of Eliot's 'Am an attendant lord, one that will do / To swell a progress, start a scene or two' ('Prufrock,' p. 16).

The difference lies in the presence or absence of *ironia*, a figure frequently accompanying or superimposed upon meiosis. If it is present, the author does not wholeheartedly subscribe to the diminishing. We can judge of irony only in a context, as we must depend upon inferences regarding the poet's other and real meaning. For example, we could not tell except for Puttenham's *comment* whether the line calling a burden no heavier than a pound of feathers was said by a man cheering the bearer up ('heavy, but you can take it') or seeing truth under appearance ('nonsense, mere feathers'). *Ironia* is not present in the second.

It should be clear, then, that 'diminishing' may be either ironic or not ironic. The irony may be slight, a mere denying of the contrary (litotes). Then, as Hoskins says, this figure 'sometimes in *ironious sort goes for amplification'—we may mean that a personage is great and call him 'no mean man.' We simply intend to be taken as saying a mere modicum of what we mean. The irony may be simple, a mere affirming of the contrary, when we quite clearly do not mean what we say. Thus Donne will say that he does not believe it possible to find a woman both true and fair, by telling us to effect a string of impossibilities which he does not mean us even to attempt. That a hypothetical such she might last until we write our letter is not litotes; it is overstatement. All such images are meiosis using irony of a fairly simple sort.

The irony may be more complicated. The poet may mean not so much what he appears to say as something else, unmentioned. Hoskins gives as examples of diminutions, from Sidney:

Those fantastical-minded people which children and musicians call lovers.
This color of mine, which she in the deceivable style of affection would entitle beautiful.

The first is not the considered opinion even of Musidorus; he yet means enough of it to intend it as a dash of the cold water of fact upon Pyrocles' flame. Meiosis has commonly this tempering or astringent effect. When a poet himself dashes cold water on his own fervency, or fervency he thinks others may attribute to him, then we have the kind of irony which has in recent years all but usurped the entire definition of the term. There is an element of this self-conscious and somewhat youthful self-protectiveness in the second example. 'Do not think I do not correctly estimate my own limitations,' says Pyrocles' meiosis in the second quotation. When the ironic reservation is a more important one, or is maturely seen and faced as one of those tormenting doubts which universally prick men's confidence in the validity of cherished truths, then the irony appears rather as a courageous and thoughtful willingness to see all aspects of reality.[14]

Both in its derisive and in its ironic form, meiosis is obviously a figure of marked usefulness in all writing with a satiric intent and is therein particularly pleasing for its decorousness. It is also naturally useful in reflective poetry, the more as this is argumentative in tone or approaches dialectic in method and intention. The form in which irony embodies an 'objection foreseen' is peculiarly natural to the method of dialectic, since a first requirement of the method is that the contrary of a position, later refuted, must be stated with authoritative power, or, in poetry, with utmost vividness. A powerful ironic figure of extreme logical subtlety will in effect convey the two contradictory positions on some question which it is the business of the whole poem's dialectic to resolve.

More frequently, figures are flatly opposed to each other in

---

[14] The difference could be exemplified by two of Donne's uses of meiosis to make ironic reference to a problem. In the somewhat youthfully self-concerned 'Loves Alchymie'' (p. 39), the question of where love's 'centrique happinesse doth lie' receives vivid metaphorical statement, and the diminishing figures are harsh and contemptuous, although I believe also ironic, e.g.: 'Our ease, our thrift, our honor, and our day, / Shall we, for *this vaine Bubles shadow* pay?' In 'The Canonization' (p. 14) there is more of cogent argument, and instead of begging the question he moves from the meiosis in the line '*Call* her one, mee another *flye*,' to the sequent amplifications which lead him into the center of his subject: 'We 'are Tapers *too* .... And wee in us finde *the'Eagle and the Dove*. / The *Phoenix* ridle hath more wit / By us.....' The figure quoted from 'Prufrock' a few paragraphs above ('Am an attendant lord ....') is this last type of rather complicated ironic meiosis.

the manner of the *débat*. It is revealing to see Marvell break down a problem into opposed but still ironic figures in debates like those between soul and body or soul and pleasure, with the help of the prosopopoeia he has chosen as a structure. He will counter one meiosis with another, and in each case the nature of this figure operates as a criticism of the opposing position, so that we obtain from the whole the impression of a peculiarly honest and inclusive consideration. Again, this is not new. The dialogue of Daniel's *Musophilus* exemplifies the same process, though the wit of the radical or homely figures impresses less because of differences in length and in metrical form and skill. Ironic and superficially 'indecorous' images in Spenser's Mutability Cantos are evidence of a similar intention; despite the necessities imposed by the epic form (on tempo and pace especially), the rough insolence of some of the images and the insinuating quality of others reveal the normal effect of meiosis, in this earliest important attempt to state seriously in poetry the accusations later so common in *libertin* thought.

But it is wiser to exemplify from shorter poems. We detect (through the violence of the paradox) that Marvell does not entirely assent to the enslaved Soul's 'diminishings' of those capabilities which make the body 'for sin so fit':

> Here blinded with an Eye; and there
> Deaf with the drumming of an Ear.
> A Soul hung up, as 'twere, in Chains
> Of Nerves, and Arteries, and Veins.
>
> ('A Dialogue between the Soul and Body,'
> p. 20; in HH, p. 860)

Yet, also, in the Body's remarks about 'this ill Spirit,' the tyrannic Soul, we feel the poet's own ironic qualifications—a dry reminder, in the figure's hyperbolical inconsequence, that only the Body would think being upright is responsible for falling:

> Which, stretcht upright, impales me so,
> That mine own Precipice I go;
> And warms and moves this needless Frame;
> (A Fever could but do the same.)

In this poem Marvell introduces no 'Chorus' to indicate his resolution of the question, and I do not think that it is possible to know the extent of the irony in the concluding figure:

> What but a Soul could have the wit
> To build me up for Sin so fit?
> So Architects do square and hew,
> Green Trees that in the Forest grew.

Throughout the poem the Body rebels against capacities which it has by virtue of being informed with Soul; the architect-image would thence presumably be read as another of the Body's impatient objections to the discipline of Form. If one wishes to erect it into something more than this (into a statement of Marvell's rebellious preference for the 'natural' and unspoiled, for example), one must do it upon indecisive grounds like the poet's other uses of the connotations of *green;* or one may be tempted by 'The Mower against Gardens' to apply Rousseauistic notions in interpreting the images of an era which in general quite approved of what the art of the architect necessitated doing to the green trees.[15] The Body stands by its own answer convicted of a sophistry if we weight the irony heavily, that is, if we think of Marvell as taking a critical rather than a naïve attitude toward the logical flaw in the Body's argument. A readiness to listen to the notion that 'he who perfects trees into buildings is part author of the ill uses they are put to' characterizes a later era than Marvell's; perhaps the ambiguity is not so much in the poem as imposed by understandings we bring to it. But this is to some extent unavoidable with tropes, and the images remain partially ambiguous, much as though Marvell had juxtaposed in a single dialectical poem the values emphasized in 'The Garden' and in 'To his Coy Mistress.' Ironic figures demand more frequently than any others this admission that we cannot be sure, from the images alone, what the poet meant.

[15] The complex of ideas is a very different one in 'The Mower,' where man's arrogant seizing of an illegitimate sovereignty over Nature is in question (see above, chap. ii, n. 15). As usual in the Renaissance, the art-ificial is not condemned in itself but with respect to its motivation; artifice is 'allow'd' to 'Man, that sov'raign thing,' but not perverted artifice, dealing in 'Forbidden mixtures' (p. 40).

The Metaphysical poets knew this as well as or better than we; hence they commonly buttress such figures with statement.

It is perhaps worth while to distinguish one other function of meiosis, not usually ironic, which is more common in hortatory writing and in lyrics which persuade, plead, or justify. Putten- ham says that the figure can be used as a 'kind of Extenuation when we take in hand to comfort or cheare any perillous enter- prise, making a great matter seem small, and of litle difficultie' (p. 220). Since, as Peacham says (p. 168), it often serves to plant hope or to excuse, all writers of love poems (including the Metaphysicals) find use for it in complaints or protestations. Suckling cheers himself as the sonnet-writers had done with calling attention to 'how unregarded now / That *piece of* beauty passes' (in HH, p. 705). Carew in 'Eternity of love protested' puts lesser lovers into the low category of 'paper set on fire' (in HH, p. 680). Obviously, such figures are useful only in certain types of poetic situation; neither the poets nor we ourselves reach out for belittling images when our design is to praise, a fact which may be swiftly substantiated in Herrick, Shake- speare, Donne, Spenser, or Yeats. A lover protesting against ill usage, however, is likely to put proud ladies in their place with a meiosis. One who is justifying an uncomplimentary estimate will make the matter small with a violent diminution:

> As a bathtub lined with white porcelain,
> When the hot water gives out or goes tepid,
> So is the slow cooling of our chivalrous passion,
> O my much praised but-not-altogether-satisfactory lady.
>
> (Ezra Pound, 'The Bath Tub,' from *Lustra* [1915];
> in *Selected Poems*, p. 80)

This is a common type of image in daily speech, falls in with the simple derisive use of meiosis to undervalue that which no longer seems desirable, and is everywhere met with. Drayton tells 'His Rivall' that 'she to thee / Reades *but old Lessons over*' (II, 369); Daniel reminds his lady that 'Men doe not weigh *the stalke* for that it was, / When once they finde her flowre, her glory passe' (*Delia*, xxxii; in HH, p. 244). Lodge tells his that though her skin is soft like wool of wethers, she exhibits 'Solemn vows, but sorry thinking'; and, since 'Others warm them *at my fuel*,' he concludes by advising himself: 'Change *thy pasture*, take thy pleasure' (HH, p. 162). Lodge's *fuel* diminishes the fire of love into a sort of stolen household coal; Donne can amplify it by the use of the very same noun:

> Make her for love fit fewell. . . . .
> So may shee faire, rich, glad, and in nothing lame,
> *To day put on perfection, and a womans name.*
> > ('Epithal. made at Lincolnes Inne,' p. 141)
> > (Author's italics)

These are *not* 'the same image'; they differ because purpose and surroundings change the way words are understood, change our evaluation of what they refer to. To call both 'radical images' points to a characteristic, but not a distinguishing characteristic. Neither is more or less decorous, more or less daring, more or less dissonant, than the other.

All these images are decorous. They suit the cause and purpose that the author has in hand. A disbeliever in love should speak like a disbeliever in love; there is a reason in Nature for it. It is true that we feel a twinge of rebellion when Whetstone comes out flat with 'grave olde men should instruct,' 'Clownes should speake disorderlye.' But he places his reason squarely in the nature of things, and we are forced to agree that in so far as they *are* grave or clownish, so they will speak, and that this is truly what enables a writer to 'worke a Comedie *kindly*'—according to men's natures (Dedication to *Promos and Cassandra* [1578]; in Gregory Smith, I, 60). We read poetry on the understanding that a poet will not 'use one order of speach for all persons'—e.g., for those different persons: himself as sardonic commentator, himself as serious reasoner, himself as ardent lover. When poets do, and we protest that their poems are vapid in tone, insensitive and undiscriminating in the use of images, pretentious and unreal in their attempt to convey thoughts and emotions, our protest is really Whetstone's own—that they have committed 'a grose *Indecorum*, for a Crowe wyll yll counterfet the Nightingale's sweete voice.' Many a Whetstone remained for all his pains a crow, yet the fault lay not in the notion of what should be done but in the difficulty of the doing.

Similarly, warnings against indecorous diction or imagery which may seem to us rigid curbs on the poet's freedom are seldom truly such because they do not ignore or deny this fundamental conception of the relation of imagery to purpose.[16] Hoskins merely states a law of communication to which most poets try to conform, and the workings of which all readers experience daily, when he warns: 'But ever (*unless your purpose be to disgrace*) let the word be taken from a thing of equal or greater dignity' (p. 9). There are nevertheless infinite variations within this purpose of 'disgracing,' and, moreover, the poet's skill in part controls the 'dignity' of the things (as in Donne's *fit fewell*).

Except for this warning that words are headstrong, that their connotations may throttle one's intentions in a poem, the principle of decorum calls little attention to the area whence content of comparisons is drawn. Attention is centered on the cogency and illuminating power of the relation between two terms; if this outshines the stubborn irrelevancies present *in every comparison*, then the image is decorous. On such considerations depend the defenses which we find of the radical and the far-fetched image. They are praised because they surprise the attention into alertness and because they give a more vigorous intellectual pleasure—both modern grounds as well. They are not defended on the modern ground that, when one of the terms is of a low imaginative value, the achievement of the poet in making such links gives the verse higher imaginative intensity. In earlier theory attention is directed toward the intrinsic imaginative value of the terms only in so far as a habitual value may play havoc with, or enhance, their relatableness. The poet's task is to bring out those possibilities of relation which are pertinent to his purpose and veil those which are not. In this he is not merely the user, but the creator, of language.

Suggestions, like denotative meanings, are judged pleasing for their fit relation rather than assumed to be pleasant for some imaginative quality they inherently possess. Connotations

---

[16] Even when Hoskins warns against using metaphors that are 'too base' (e.g., *shoulders of friendship*, or *a red herring is a shoeing-horn to a pot of ale*), he yet concludes, 'But they that speak of a scornful thing *speak* grossly.'

which have nothing to do with the poem seem not to be prized whether they are 'imaginative' or not—that is, suggestion is thought of as controlled, whether tending toward amplification or diminution, and strictures such as those I have quoted warn the poet that there are cases where words can escape his control. Hence Puttenham refers the determination of decorum to the *judgment*.[17] He finds an infinite variety of reasons why poets will find infinitely varied images to be fitting, but he leaves no doubt as to which faculty must finally help the poet to decide whether they are so:

it resteth in the discerning part of the minde, so as he who can make the best and most differences of things by reasonable and wittie distinction is to be the fittest iudge or sentencer of [*decencie*] [III, xxiii, p. 263]. [Author's italics.]

The poet is thus given great freedom, though subject always to the discipline of his own alert judgment. He may seize his comparable terms from wherever he wishes, provided he can wittily detect, and make impressive, similitudes missed by others, with that peculiar acuteness for seeing relations which Aristotle praises in the *Poetics*. What he must not do is to blunder into connotations which are unwanted: 'if ye abase your thing or matter by ignorance or errour in the choise of your word,' you have not the subtle ironic reservation or controlled suggestion of meiosis, but the vice of tapinosis (Puttenham, p. 185).[18] *Bomphiologia*, the opposite vice, is just as bad. A radical, homely image is a tapinosis if its diminishing connotations are unwanted, confusing, or unmanageable; a pleasingly decorative image is a *bomphiologia* if it distorts. Otherwise one type of image is as decorous as the other.

Modern criticism of Elizabethan and Metaphysical writing neither recognizes that the radical image was orthodox in early literary theory nor admits the necessity of this degree of rational control.

[17] Although he admits the complexity and variety of judgments on whether this or that speech 'be decent or indecent' and notes the importance of much observation and experience of how language works as a social phenomenon.

[18] Peacham exemplifies it (p. 168); if you want dignity, do not call the Thames a *brook*, or a 'foughten field' a *fray*. *Bomphiologia*, conversely, gives high praises to small deserts.

Unlike a modern post-Symbolist critic, when Hoskins expressly praises the radical image, he praises not the poet's awareness and reconciliation of diversities but his perception of a forceful similarity; the diversities in the terms, far from being pleasurable for introducing subtle overtones of meaning, are neglected, meant not to obtrude themselves. The entire emphasis is upon the agreements which the poet reveals—once the wit of the comparison has achieved that initial surprise which makes the 'amplification' more 'forcible' (the *amplification*, not the possible ironic qualifications of it). These agreements truly exist, to be seen by any discerning mind; they obtain logically, are discovered, not conjectured, are pleasing because they are so apt, not because they are so wrenched.[19] It seems to me that such an understanding of the witty forcefulness of the radical image should be urged as the typical Metaphysical understanding of it. Better than the modern understanding (which is bent on revealing a kind of tortured confusion in these poets), it fits the rest of what they put in their poems, the matrix in which such images are imbedded.

Donne particularly shows as a surer artist and a clearer and more mature thinker if we read his innumerable vivid diminishing images and subtle but firm ironic figures by the light of these traditional understandings. One cannot but perceive the delicacy and needle-like acuteness with which he can convey overtones in cases where the rest of the poem shows that he clearly intended to do so. Hence it seems to me illegitimate to fit out his poems with overtones which diverge ambiguously from his apparent meaning and which are only to be traced in the connotations of his image-terms. This method of attributing meanings to Metaphysical poems should be restricted to those whose knowledge of Elizabethan linguistic habits far outshines

---

[19] Of course, Renaissance theory has room also for the profound symbol (not usually 'far-fetched') of wider and deeper import. But concerning the type here discussed, see Hoskins' paragraph on 'Policy is like the sea'; also his praise of 'great affinity' if 'different' things are compared (p. 20). The sixteenth century was entirely aware of what Dr. Johnson was to notice; 'And you shall most of all profit by inventing [finding] matter of agreement in things most unlike, as London and a tennis court: for *in both all the gain goes to the hazard*' (p. 18). (Author's italics.)

that of a mere *NED*. It seems illegitimate, for example, to conjecture that Donne's choice of a compass (in order to illuminate how 'our two soules' be one) has some equivocal force used of lovers, or was meant to cast an obscure ironic shadow. It is to us rather than to Donne that compasses are part of the commonplace paraphernalia of high-school mathematics.[20] Donne is so adept at conveying intended ironic reservations that I find it more reasonable to believe that he did not intend us, for example, to attend to suggestions of the numerous ridiculous differences between souls and bullets, while he wittily distinguishes (in *the trajectory of* the two) three quite dignified logical likenesses:

> And so my soule more earnestly releas'd,
> Will outstrip hers; As bullets flowen before
> A latter bullet may o'rtake, the pouder being more.
>
> ('The Dissolution,' p. 65)

Much of the supposed rebellious 'indecorum' of homely or radical Metaphysical images disappears when we thus observe every caution not to read what was not written. Reading what the poet did not write is, of course, entirely allowable as a way of enjoying poems (is even inevitable because of the nature of tropes, but there are safeguards). It is only that findings resulting from this pursuit should not creep into our critical judgments of a poet's aims or a period's character. Such findings are part of literary history—but of the history of the *critic's* period.

3. Decorum and the Mixture of Styles

These matters are obviously related to the comparison so frequently drawn in modern criticism between the Metaphysicals and Symbolist or modern poets on the ground that both, in rebellion against accepted poetic decorum in their eras, exhibit a

[20] At all events, in 1608 the court audience could be trusted to interpret both the zodiac and the compass as 'known ensignes of *perfection*'; see Jonson's *Masque of Beautie* (gloss; author's italics), and on the whole approach to imagery here exemplified see the book on *The Symbolic Persons in the Masques of Jonson* by A. H. Gilbert, to whom I owe this reference (Durham, N.C., forthcoming). See Pl. 36*f*, in D. J. Gordon, 'The Imagery of Ben Jonson's *The Masque of Blacknesse* and *The Masque of Beautie*,' *Journal of Warburg and Cortauld Institutes*, VI (1943), 122–41.

combination of the grand with the prosaic, 'a constant alternation of the magniloquent and the colloquial.'[21] The comparison
becomes somewhat less forceful if large numbers of the homely
prosaic images of the Metaphysical poets belong to a type of
image sanctioned as quite dignified by orthodox rhetoric and
poetic of the fifty years preceding them, and indeed by much
earlier theory. Moreover, there is only an adventitious similarity between images of a content which might have homely or
sordid associations, used for the orthodox reasons exemplified
above, and images used with deliberate exploitation of such associations in order to portray the sensibility of the poet in all
its rich confusion and with all its unresolved ironies. Unconventional imagery used as a sharp tool to explore the rationally apprehensible relations of things is not the same as unconventional
imagery admitted in order to reflect as honestly as possible the
movements of a consciousness, including its irrational movements. The latter is frequently the reason for post-Symbolist
combination of the grand and the prosaic. An examination of
early seventeenth-century unconventional images in their contexts does not reveal it.

All writing with an overt or hidden satirical purpose does, of
course, juxtapose the grand and the trivial in order to bring out
the triviality of the trivial. When they share such purposes,
moderns resemble Metaphysicals just as both resemble classical
or medieval writers of satire. An image using the figure meiosis
momentarily allows the entrance into any poem of the purposes
which in satire characterize the whole piece. This juxtaposition
is not a combination of the grand or lovely with the trivial or
sordid; it is a contrast between them. The use of the method in
satire is one of the reasons why that genre has always been
recognized as 'rough.' Many more Metaphysical 'lyrics' and
other short forms belong to this kind than have generally been
recognized; adding some of the 'demonstrative' purposes and
methods of satire (a dispraise), they are a normal development
from the 'deliberative' short piece which in earlier times took

[21] The quotation comes from C. Day Lewis, *A Hope for Poetry* (Oxford, 1935), p. 60;
the point has been ceaselessly reiterated in modern appreciations of Metaphysical poets.

such forms as Chaucer's *Fortune* or *Lenvoy a Bukton*. They decorously exhibit the argumentative and diminishing images
proper to these kinds.

Again, one must emphasize the general caveat that it is difficult to tell when we have a combination of the magniloquent
with the colloquial, outside our own era. When Davies, in his
Orchestra, compares all earth's rivers to blue veins that through
her body spread, and the great hills to 'The Earth's great duggs;
for every wight is fed / With sweet fresh moisture from them
issuing,' is this a deliberate alternation of the grand with the
trivial?[22] Do we term it such when Marlowe's Hero cries, and
'Forth from those two tralucent cisterns brake / A stream of
liquid pearl, which down her face / Made milk-white paths'
(i, 296)? Were *dugs* any more colloquial than veins, or how shall
we know the extent to which *cisterns* have changed their status,
or who can decide whether *milk-white* is literary because of the
ballad, folk diction for the same reason, or prosaic because of
the pail in the offing? The most ineffably complex *NED* could
not answer these questions. Surely the way out of this critical
difficulty is the practicing Renaissance poet's way out of it: (1)
there are obstreperous words or images whose unmanageable
connotations a writer will avoid if they endanger his communication; (2) outside these limits (obviously not strictly definable), the poet's control of the meaning of word or image
through its relation to others and to the purpose of the whole
must *make* it grand or prosaic, 'poetic' or 'unpoetic.' There are
surer guides to a poet's intentions than our own connotations;
Marlowe, for example, obliterates a possible barnyard cow with
his next phrase, for his own connotation is that of the Milky
Way. No guide is entirely sure, but if these examples are to be
termed a combination of the magniloquent and the colloquial,
then all poets commonly combine them; and if they are not,

[22] Stanza 52. I select quite usual images from poets seldom if ever put forth as showing the intensity supposed to result from such combination. Davies' 'inferiority' (and
that of 'the whole Spenserian school') is attributed to 'the lack of tension in his style,'
by Allen Tate, commenting on the 'ornamental decoration of image' in Spenser and
Davies (*Reactionary Essays* [New York, 1936], p. 74). On this image cf. Ripa's *Icono-
logia* ('Natura') (Rome, 1603; many eds.).

then neither are Donne's sour prentices and busy-foolish suns, his heart in rags and his dead earth sunk to the bed's-feet.

In one type of radical image much used by certain Metaphysical poets and not so common in the poetry of forty years before, it is possible to see a more deliberate relating of the grand or the transcendental to the simple or homely. This is the kind of image used by the mystical poets to make the ineffable more nearly tangible, or the paradoxical image used by any poet striving to bring out simultaneously man's insignificance and his high significance as God's creature. Here it becomes even more apparent that the area whence the vehicle of the comparison has been taken does not determine the decorum of the image.[23]

As the extreme of a thing often reveals its true nature most clearly, the short religious or mystical poem of the first half of the seventeenth century shows earlier Elizabethan understandings of the functioning of images especially saliently. The decorum of the images is also easier to discuss for the simple reason that the poems are shorter. When a Spenser treated the problem of man's paradoxical grandeur and smallness, he took a whole epic to do it, while a Davies wrote in the genre later almost engulfed by prose—the long philosophical poem. Other poets—Marlowe, Chapman—handled this subject in the dramatic form's dialectic-at-one-remove; since we must be chary of giving any disputer the rubric of *auctor*, discussion of the decorum of any image involves deciding the extremely difficult question of what conclusion is reached through the dialectic (i.e., the play's *real subject*). Though all these are metaphysical poets, among the greater early figures only Ralegh, and occasionally Sidney and Chapman, chose to write metaphysical poetry within the short compass favored by later poets. I shall therefore examine later and shorter poems, but with the reser-

[23] The unimportance of Marvell's 'Drop of Dew' no more comes in question than the commonness of Crashaw's *bowls* of fierce desire, or of Herbert's *glass* of blessings with Rest in the bottom. It will appear that 'charming' qualities in image-vehicles are equally impertinent. We are compelled in poems with such subjects to a greater than usual willingness to obey the poet's directive toward the possibilities of relation which the object offers rather than toward the object.

vation that characteristics pointed out are affected by the factor of date largely by way of the factors of length or of genre.
Three points, though not the only ones, are interesting as confirmation and clarification of points made earlier.

In the first place, the simple nature of many images in such
writing is notable. Because of the transcendental nature of subjects treated, images in mystical or related types of writing have
from time immemorial been chosen on the ground of perceived
relations which are easy to grasp and almost universally apprehensible. This is partly because such writing is admittedly
didactic. The significancy of the images being of prime importance, the comparableness for which the poet chooses the image
must be of such a nature that every man's experience enables
him to see it, and must yet allow of applications which are profound, sure, and powerful.

Hence the images themselves are likely to be perspicuous, in
this type of Metaphysical poem, are likely to have the simplicity of Spenser's larger tropes (the wandering of Phaedria's boat,
the connection of Una with sunlight, Talus' iron mold). Crashaw need not pause to explain the twofold applicability of
each phrase when he says, in the Nativity Hymn, 'Where he
mean't *frost*, he scatter'd *flowrs*' (769)[24] or 'Hath mett love's
Noon in Nature's *night*' (768). Vaughan says ''Twas but Just
now *my bleak leaves* hopeles hung' (802), and Herbert, 'And now
in age *I bud again*' (748); we 'see' neither man as a Fradubio,
and accept without pausing the transferred epithet *bleak* as
psychological description.[25] For with images of this kind we

[24] In these next few paragraphs I wish to use so many short references to images from
many poems that I have regretfully confined examples to those which appear in Hebel
and Hudson (*op. cit.*, see my Foreword) and have simply appended page reference without title. The burden of citation would otherwise cloud entirely the points made.
The images are all from familiar poems; used (unidentified) in this paragraph and its
note are: Vaughan's *Unprofitablenes, Idle Verse, Man;* Herbert's *The Flower;* Traherne's *Wonder.* Italics used to signalize the images are mine, throughout; as usual, I
follow the text of standard scholarly editions of the several poets.

[25] Vaughan needs only the bare indicator of 'Go, go, queint *folies*' to make 'I will no
longer *Cobwebs* spin' (783) carry what it must of impermanence, and of curious if
slightly sinister fragility. Nor are we troubled by his quick shift from the images of the
line before—'*sugred* sin,/*Shadow* no more my *door*,' for we abstract the comparable element in each image so obediently that irrelevancies have no chance to obtrude and
'mix' the two metaphors.

rather see immediately with the eye of the conceiving mind, to which these things are, for the moment, their meanings— through long usage and through the special simplicity of the logical process required of us. Traherne says he 'within did flow / With *seas* of life *like wine*' (804); Vaughan says man 'knows he *hath a home*, but scarce knows where, ... *knocks at all doors*, strays and roams' (790). We are conscious of no process of 'seeing the significance'; we apprehend abstractions as if they were these concretions.

This is nothing but the secret operation of all metaphor, at a level where it is peculiarly easy to watch.[26] Especially applicable, the reader will observe, is all that has been said of allegory and the reasons for its need of simple particulars and logically uncomplicated figures. Writing which conveys the mystic's apprehension of the world invades, though it is not coincident with, the territory of allegory. Poems of both kinds have a fundamental metaphorical base. A mystical poem sees all sensible phenomena as metaphor; an allegorical poem is, formally and structurally, metaphor. Both are written in the language of correspondences; neither requires intellectually ingenious tropical figures. Both demand of a reader that he read whole poetic units as great tropes, alert to what Puttenham sees as the basis of decorum, 'this lovely conformitie, or proportion, or conveniencie betweene the sence and the sensible' (III, xxiii, p. 262).

A second Elizabethan habit in the use of imagery, related to the care for perspicuity which characterized poems of this nature, is the use of public and conventional figures which have come to have almost the force of symbols. Vaughan's 'dark *contest of waves and winde*' (786) and his '*surly winds* / Blasted my infant buds' (794), or Herbert's 'That I am he / On whom *thy*

---

[26] All the important general observations made earlier apply to the images now being examined, as could be demonstrated if it were not so time-taking: the reasons for the luminousness, the fundamental nature of tropes and the relation they exhibit between significancy and sensuousness, the artifice which illuminates universals in the author's ordering of embellished nature, the avoidance of obscurity through the interpenetration of statement with image, the economy and necessity of figurative language, the preservation of decorum through the firm focusing of attention upon relation of functional ornament to the poetic subject.

tempests fell all night' (748), need no gloss. A connection that has been learned rather than experienced is frequently the important element in such figures; inland readers do not stumble over symbolic uses of *sea*. The image of thirst (of love, or for death) has the power of a long history of use; Crashaw has but to modify, not to invent, in 'dares *drink up*,/A thousand cold deaths *in one cup*' (775), or 'By thy larg draughts of intellectuall day' (780). Similar facts of linguistic history explain why the usual surprise accompanying radical images is tempered, in many cases, in religious poems. In Vaughan's 'The Water-fall,' 'My sacred *wash and cleanser* here' (788) surely carried no unsuitable reverberations conveying irony; the figure simply counts upon readers acquainted with the notion of purification, though the seventeenth century, too, had its 'beauticians.' Marvell quite naturally and normally uses both these ancient images (of thirst and cleansing) in a context which utilizes the old pastoral convention of Christ as Pan. In such a context it is entirely fitting and unastounding to ask of fountains 'Might a Soul *bath there* and be clean, / Or slake its *Drought?*' (858).[27]

As allegory is metaphor continued, so symbol is most frequently synecdoche become fixed. Hence a kind of literacy is necessary, or the reader will not know the rest of that whole which gives the part its profound significance or catch the reverberating meanings awakened by its use. In this one respect the kind of obscurity these poets show is precisely comparable to that of certain modern poets, notably Yeats. A young undergraduate with no knowledge of liturgy or Catholic thought, reading Crashaw, one with no knowledge of classical myth, reading Spenser, finds exactly similar blocks to comprehension of the images that he and other persons find in reading such a volume as Yeats's *Winding Stair* (1933). Vaughan's synecdochic reduction of the heavenly vision to 'That shady City of Palme trees' (796), Herbert's 'milk and sweetnesses' (734), Una's lamb, the Last Judgment in Donne's 'Death be not proud,' the

---

[27] This paragraph uses images from Vaughan's *Quickness, Regeneration, The Waterfall*; Herbert's *The Flower*; Crashaw's *Hymne to St. Teresa, The Flaming Heart*; Marvell's *Clorinda and Damon*. The next paragraph, from Vaughan's *The Retreate*, Herbert's *Affliction(i)*.

Gardin of Adonis—all these need annotation precisely as do Yeats's blood and mire, sun and moon. The difference is that what used to be an 'ordinary' knowledge of Christian and pagan myth and history is sufficient to give the earlier poets *a* meaning, if not the full and moving meaning they intended.[28]

The use of known and conceptually weighted symbols to form powerful images is habitual throughout the entire period. It can be as well illustrated earlier as later. I know none more daring than Spenser's use of the Communion in the insidiously flippant scene of Hellenore's seduction by Paridell; the whole weight of his meaning (concerning the lustful perversion of Love) is concentrated in the symbolic act of Paridell as he spills his wine and as Hellenore replies by allowing hers to be 'shed' into her lap:

> And by the dauncing bubbles did divine,
> Or therein write *to let his love be showne;*
> Which well she red . . . .
> *A sacrament prophane* in mistery of wine.

                                        (*FQ*, III, ix, 30)

The contrast between the lewd meaning of the act and the meaning of the shed blood of the Communion, openly manifesting Heavenly Love in Christ's blood shed anew, conveys without comment and almost without words the shocking blasphemy of man's perversion of a heavenly Passion into self-seeking lust; the image contains within itself the theme of all this part of the poem. From such use of the echoing significances of 'public' figures depends much of the grave and piercing sweetness of Marvell's 'The Coronet.' As eclectic as Spenser, he interweaves three such figures (the crown of thorns, the serpent old, the heavenly crown) and one from pastoral tradition, into a de-

---

[28] There is no doubt, however, that even the 'educated' modern reader is unable to give these knowledge-demanding figures the reading which contemporaries gave them; nor can he adequately judge their decorum, being unable to experience their functioning as he was meant to. Most of us are inadequate to judge the moving fitness even of the innumerable biblical figures, only sometimes synecdochic, only sometimes used as symbols. Many of the images termed 'learned' in Donne receive that epithet only by virtue of our ignorance, those using scholastic commonplaces, for instance. If our university training had become unclassical as early as it became Protestant, much of the earlier-Elizabethan 'pagan' imagery would similarly have been classified as 'learned,' rather than as 'conventional.'

liberative lyric of strange and passionate beauty. Secular Elizabethan and Jacobean verse counts upon the known history of its
symbolic images in a similar but less obvious fashion.

This might seem to be the place to draw the line distinguishing metaphor or synecdoche from 'symbol,' in the Renaissance.
I do not think that the line can be tightly drawn, certainly not
for an era whose linguistic habits and shared connotations we
know but imperfectly. It is certain, at any rate, that metaphors
(or other figures) become symbols when writers can be entirely
sure that readers will take one thing as truly *presenting* another
—usually a concretion as standing for an abstraction. Since a
symbol is frequently a traditional synecdoche, the connection
(between particular and meaning) will be strictly logical only as
part-to-whole is a logical relation, or the connection may be that
between details and whole import of a story or situation (as the
nail-pierced hands were part of Christ's suffering, but the gifts
of the Wise Men became symbols too). Metaphors which became symbols (flower as transient loveliness, love as a flame)
more frequently have a strictly logical base, like shared properties; often it is 'extra' knowledge, of immemorial usage or even
locus classicus, which tells us which property to attend to.[29]
Imprese, banners, emblems, heraldic symbols, exhibit all these
types of connection. The connection is always intelligible;[30] but
only for some symbols do we know enough to realize what the logic
of connections is. Some antedate any critical or speculative
thought. And few of us know the trains of events and thoughts
which provide each person with sets of symbols peculiar to him.

An Elizabethan or Jacobean poet desiring to use one of the
latter type will make clear what a thing symbolizes to him by

[29] *Man:grass of the field* says transience to us, but it might symbolize ever-springing-
ness to a Druid or rare and miraculous life to a desert people. Survival of remnants of
social mores preserved in symbols is not essential to their life; *the potter and the clay*
convey their meanings to men of a machine age. Yet certainly those symbols are stronger, surer, and more moving which use connections so basic to human existence (like
love:fire) that they 'speak' at the most elementary level of experience.

[30] Because it is usually reasonable; we 'understand' it. That which is too deep and
complex to be spoken, evades conceptual formulation, is so many-faceted and so
deeply moving that it seems to escape the 'understanding,' is not the connection but
that which we seek to present through the symbol utilizing the connection.

his manner of using it; a Symbolist poet does not do so. I am quite sure that an earlier poet would see this use of obscure symbols as a fault of *decorum*—hence the pertinence of this discussion here. The decorum of symbols is determined upon precisely the same considerations as determine the decorum of other images. As is especially clear from images in mystical poems, the vehicle of the comparison may be of almost any character, provided the apt relation is such that the image suitably illuminates the poetic subject. The reader cannot appreciate this fitness unless he can follow the poet's mind along the connecting link which makes one thing truly *present* another (it is understood, of course, that this 'meaning' resists literal or complete statement, for otherwise neither earlier nor later poet would need symbols). For example: earlier theory would have no quarrel with Yeats for introducing 'those horrible green birds' into his poem 'On a Picture of a Black Centaur'[31] or for introducing them rather than some conceptual statement of his 'meaning'; if these swinging parrots symbolize the ingenious and morbid fancies in the wood of magical or false magnificence, then earlier theory would find indecorum in the fact that Yeats does not discover to us the links which made the symbol a fit one to him and can enable us to accompany him in the final leap of the thought.

The earlier poets crowd their verses with unexplained symbols, without the least offense against decorum, though the image-terms are often either so homely or so far-fetched as to border upon the ridiculous. But either the images are of extreme logical simplicity or they are based upon connections made clear through usage and a heritage of meanings shared with readers. The Symbolist poet counts usually upon other channels by which individuals come to share meanings, upon subconscious or physiologically primitive likenesses between persons. The Elizabethan or Jacobean poet willingly makes use of such channels to deepen his meaning, but he does not trust

[31] Pp. 248–49; from *The Tower* (1928). The interpretation of the image is taken from J. C. Ransom, 'The Irish, the Gaelic, the Byzantine,' *Southern Review*, VII (1941), 517–46 (W. B. Yeats Memorial Issue).

his communication solely or chiefly to them. At the same time, I think that all metaphor, and perhaps other tropes, had then more of the character we should now call symbolic. It is difficult and probably fruitless to draw the line more exactly, between metaphor and symbol, where we think the sixteenth and seventeenth centuries would have drawn it, given changes in the very tissue of thought since that time.[32] It would be drawn in precisely the same place only by persons whose ontological presuppositions were precisely similar.

The third observation regarding the images of religious and mystical poetry is, like the others, not peculiar to these alone. I would merely remark on the tissue of meiosis and hyperbole which they present. A great number of the radical images, like the 'toylsom Mole' or the foil of Vaughan's 'Quickness' (786), are diminutions which result from the contrast posed in all mystical poetry between the false and the real life. The corresponding amplifications necessarily use hyperbole and symbol.[33] Some hyperbolical amplifications are borrowed from other 'public' systems of conventions.[34]

[32] I refer to such differentiations as are made, e.g., by P. O. Kristeller, *Philosophy of Marsilio Ficino* (New York, 1943); to such points as the modern tendency to consider truth as an attribute of propositions rather than primarily of things (see chap. iv), or the modern retreat from a consideration of reality as directed toward principles or causes (see chap. vi). Anyone who has read many Renaissance Platonists' treatments of Plato's ideas, or many Christian Aristotelians' discussions of Aristotle's universals, will recognize the fact that it is very difficult to judge of the extent to which the many metaphors concerning (for example) Christ as Wisdom, God as Light, *are* 'merely' metaphorical. Various ways of conceiving of reality as formal coincide in thinking that the rose *is* Transient Loveliness as really as it *is* a flower of a certain shape and odor. To separate off symbols as a distinguishable type of image is hence very difficult.

[33] In the images of 'The World,' one may notice a similar obedience to the nature of the poetic subject; cf. symbol and hyperbole in the bridegroom's ring, the 'way where you might *tread the Sun*'—with meiosis like the digging, clutching mole, the statesman moving 'Like a thick midnight-fog' (799). Or cf. the untainted ever flowing spring, which 'though here born, yet is acquainted / Elsewhere,' with the dead puddle-water of corrupt security, in 'The Dawning' (798).

[34] The paradoxes of dying to find life, of a love that is consumed by what it feeds upon, of unity in difference, are, as is usual and necessary, framed in the language of earthly love. They use the artifices and the weighted or symbolic language which had evolved as conventions during the long history of the courtly love tradition. Familiar examples are the fire, the eyes as suns, the rhetorically emphasized paradoxes, of Crashaw's 'A song' (780); or the dart, arrow and quiver, siege and fort, thawing heart, wounds and long war, in the persuasion of Lady Denbigh (767).

In Herbert, who shows chiefly just those elements of mysticism which in some degree pervade all Christian devotional poetry, the juxtaposition of meiosis and amplification generally results from the paradox of man's insignificance and his greatness as child and heir of God. Man's worth is amplified with 'The starres have us to bed' (733), or with the old image of 'Man is one world, and hath / Another to attend him.' Seemingly diminished by 'He is a tree,' 'A beast,' his worth is as quickly amplified by the immediate addition of 'yet bears more fruit,' 'yet is, or should be more.'[35] Man is 'a brittle crazie glasse,' yet a window through which God's light gloriously shines (743); he is a vessel in which venomous suggestions 'fume and work,' yet he is God's stronghold (736). He is a 'blunted knife,' is restive under a collar, brought to God only by a pulley, but he is also the one for whom the whole banquet of heavenly Love is spread. He can be haled with a metaphor from the mean to the transcendent and back again within the frame of a single short poem, without the slightest offense to decorum; this contrast is part of Herbert's subject, and his images properly obey it.

This is no new combination of the grand and the prosaic. Both this contrast and its effect upon a poet's images are very old and very natural. The foreshortening which occurs when these ancient ideas are crowded into the short scope of the devotional lyric—frequently read rather than sung, a reflection rather than a prayer or hymn—makes for a certain seeming-new sharpness and terse precision. The Despair canto of Book I of the *Faerie Queene* (to go no further back) is one long meiosis revealing man's insufficiency, but it takes the form of a long psychological drama, though it, too, is set within the mind of man. Slowly constructing the larger unit of meaning in which these metaphors sharply oppose each other, it moves with pitiful in-

[35] I follow Hutchinson's 'more fruit' rather than the 'yet bears *no fruit*' which Hebel and Hudson print from the edition of 1633. Upon this difference between *no* and *more* depends the function (diminishing or amplifying) and hence the essential nature and proper classification of the image—a neat example of the falsities inevitable should one classify images by content. See the Appendix, Note O, for further comment, especially upon the common habit of deciding such textual puzzles by finding 'similar' images in other works of a poet. Poems of Herbert's quoted in this paragraph are: *Man, The Windows, Nature, Affliction*(i).

evitability through spare and nervous argument, seductive languors, cutting and insidious irony. It is answered with the triumphant amplifications of following cantos. The paradox of weakness and magnificence is here also powerfully communicated; the harmony of diminution and amplification is similarly woven, but the pace proper to such a form is very different.

The mystical and religious poems of the Metaphysicals do thus offer one type of 'alternation' of the magniloquent and the trivial, and assuredly they make large use of radical or homely images. Yet their imagery appears to me both decorous and in conformity with traditional understandings of the structure and function of images.

4. *Decorum and Revolt*

So far as images are concerned, the more one looks at contemporary or earlier theory, the more difficult does it become to see the Metaphysicals as boldly tearing out their thoughts and emotions without regard for the rules of decorum. It is so hard to find in the theory those principles they are supposed to have been rebelling against, and so equally hard to find opposed principles in them.[36] They may have misinterpreted the principles and hence have fought some straw man whose features we can only dimly conjecture. Or certain vapid and tasteless poets, now chiefly forgotten, against whose manner of writing they doubtless did rebel, may have misinterpreted the principles first. In either case, it is highly inaccurate to affirm and reaffirm, as our handbooks have done for years, that important differences in poetic separated Spenserians from Metaphysicals. If the latter were exploring new and unattempted regions of the sensibility, I cannot find that they had to wave the red flag against established principles of poetic and rhetoric to do it. In large numbers of cases they seem to me to have explored rather

[36] Just as it is difficult to find a new anti-Petrarchan revolt in poets who are following a convention half-a-century old in decrying the extravagant aspects of Petrarchan love-poetry. These poets, like the protesters who preceded them, continue to base figures upon Petrarchan conceits; we read *over* numerous examples (e.g., in Carew, Donne, King). See the Appendix, Note P, for further discussion of this handbook generalization about the Metaphysical 'revolt.'

the possibilities of the short reflective lyric, and pressed them to their limits. They did this along lines of development implicit in the earlier tradition in that form, using established poetic techniques (including imagery) to limn out their particular purposes—never quite the same as the last poet's purposes, as no good poet's ever are, fully defined.

It is difficult also to think of the Metaphysicals as departing from poetic decorum in order to bring a greater sensuous freedom and range into their images. This is supposed by many critics to result *from* new and subtler responses to the world of the senses in all its rich complexity and to result *in* language whose connotative power outweighed its denotative clearness. The supposed cause has been conjectured from the supposed result. Both fitly describe the Symbolist poet and his language; neither seems to me to indicate distinguishing characteristics of the poetry of the Metaphysicals.[37]

I am not sure that a distinction between connotative and denotative language has much meaning in the context of early or late Renaissance understandings of the functioning of words and images.[38] Remarks about the power of tropes or about amplification unself-consciously take 'suggestions' for granted, as inescapably part of the meaning a word will have in a poem; suggestiveness in words is simply accepted as an attribute of the medium. Both earlier and later poets utilize suggestions and denotative meanings of words for harmonious, not contrasting, purposes in their poems, and both control suggestions and denotative meanings in accordance with the same criterion— the needs of the poetic subject. The point at which a difference might come, and by now has come, is not exemplified in the Metaphysical poets—at least I do not find in them exploitation

---

[37] These modern desiderata would involve indecorum according to earlier poetic because the fit relation between subject and medium is disturbed by exploitation of the medium for its own sake or for the sake of implying interesting things about the poet (e.g., about his capacity for responsive awareness).

[38] The most critically acute statement of the seventeenth century's greater interest in connotative language is chap. ii of F. W. Bateson's *English Poetry and the English Language* (Oxford, 1934). To look at his examples in the light of certain principles I have mentioned would result in a different set of conclusions; I exemplify in the Appendix, Note Q, for readers who know his chapter.

of connotation as a thing in itself, somehow outside the ostensible purpose of a poem. They did define the purposes of poems with extreme and deliberate subtlety. So did earlier poets.

Traditional conceptions of the functioning of words and images cut across this whole question in a different way. Traditionally conceived, the balance any poet holds between the simpler use of language and a more profound and 'suggestive' significancy is largely a function of the different operation of nontropical and tropical language. The more complicated relation between strict sense and 'significance' which characterizes tropical language characterizes much Metaphysical writing; these poets' choices of subject, of genre, of formal unit, are such as to indorse plentiful use of tropes. The most orthodox advice would have impelled them toward such a stylistic choice. It is hard to see in this formal difference an argument for attributing to Metaphysical poets that modern desideratum: the use of connotative language to express economically a sensuously rich 'awareness' which all but displaces the ostensible subject.[39] Less complete control of connotations enters with the use of trope, and every rhetorician and poet knew it. It is unsafe to erect theories about changed intentions of poets upon what that linguistic fact allows us to make of their poems.

Perhaps the most usual among current generalizations about rebellious indecorum in the Metaphysical poets is the notion that their writing is obscure rather than perspicuous because they flouted the polite rules of more decorous writers. True, theorists condemn obscurity in connection with decorum. But, again, it is the kind of obscurity which representative Metaphysical poets do not show. Indecorous obscurity is the kind which prefers rich confusion to illuminating a meaning, prefers

[39] In fact, the poet who springs to mind as a possible example is one whom I have never seen ranged among the rebels against decorum—Herrick, not Donne. Herrick's language is delicately rich where Donne's is ideationally acute, yet, despite Herrick's subtler notations of sensuous experience, moderns find it embarrassing to attribute a modern 'awareness' to any poet who makes such untortured comments on the world he sees. It may be that we should understand Donne more truly if we did not try to postulate for him a more 'modern' relation between informing concept and possible connotations, between the poet commenting on the world of sense and the importunities of that world.

intricacy (whether of syntax or of ornament) to clear formal relations. In our times, honestly more aware of confusion than sure of meanings, this no longer constitutes dispraise of a poem's images. But in the Renaissance 'darkness' was respected on quite other grounds, and praised in the same breath with condemnation of indecorous obscurity. We have no warrant for interpreting their dark figures according to our poetic rather than their own unless their poetry inescapably demands it.

If we are determined to fasten upon the Metaphysicals the kind of obscurity their own century condemned, we can do so only by a set of arbitrary judgments about the 'real' meanings of their poems. We must maintain (as certain modern critics have) that their elliptically compressed figures were meant to suggest that clarity would be an oversimplification—when, meanwhile, orthodox poetic of their day praises brevity as leading to a more sharply lit clarity, and when that is what poets praise each other for attaining (Carew's Elegy on Donne, vss. 15–21). We must maintain that their figures, being dark, could not have been intended to carry a sure significance—when, meanwhile, orthodox poetic of their day praises figures of deep reach on grounds of this very quality of acute and profound significancy. Such conclusions on our part are scarcely warranted even if Jonson did remark in conversation that John Donne would perish because he was too hard to understand. He did not because he was not; and Ben Jonson was not 'neoclassical' but mistaken—in a judgment regarding readers. Jonson merely mistook the amount of difficulty which is consonant with survival; his statement is not evidence for a notion that Donne headed an opposing school of poets who had given up the idea that poetry is to be understood.

In sum, careful considerations of the actual workings of the principle of decorum in its application to images seem to point to the wisdom of attempting to see seventeenth-century poets in their relation to the great poetic developments of the era to which they belonged—the late Renaissance. These developments show profundity of thought and feeling in both provinces, the practice and the theory of poetry; our tendency to see a gap between the two may result from our own ignorance or narrow interpretation. Whatever mistakes have been made in the application of tenets as I have made them, some points at least are beyond question. The principle of decorum is the most important regulatory principle determining the nature of images. When Milton called it the grand masterpiece to observe, he made no simple requirement of poets. No part of a poet's task demands more exquisite fineness of sensibility or more penetrating acuteness of judgment. The conceptions which this principle represents deserve our thoughtful respect. They are neither naïve nor bigoted. It may be that more careful study of these conceptions, under the presumption that poets of the greatest originality and profoundest feeling still found them valid, may serve to deepen our understanding and enjoyment of both later and earlier poetry of the period.

5. *Decorum and the 'Three Styles'*

One radical obstacle to a just understanding of Renaissance applications of decorum lies in our having interpreted a flexible stricture regarding *proportion* in style as if it were a rigid rule regarding the *nature* of style. This principle marks out for the poet a very wide degree of freedom. He is expected to use it responsibly, and there is general acceptance of the notion that the demands of the poetic subject are paramount and supersede the capricious and momentary demands of his fancy. But this is not necessarily inimical to his freedom of choice. Statements regarding decorum are often bare and difficult to apply, for adjurations to preserve 'apt proportion' are necessarily equivocal, like adjurations to keep to the middle way between two undefinable extremes.[40] They invite misinterpretation. But this is precisely the difficulty of a flexible rule. It was the de-

---

[40] Puttenham remarks amusingly upon this difficulty. After listing the six points set down by 'our learned forefathers' for maintaining beauty and good grace of utterance without error or difficulty, he comments, 'But sir, all this being by them very well conceived, there remayned a greater difficultie to know what this proportion, volubilitie, good construction, & the rest *were*' (III, viii). Hence his lengthy attempts to define decorum.

mand that decorum be observed which was inflexible, not the definition of decorum.

Puttenham both notes the flexibility and admits the justice of the principle: 'the matter *resteth much in the definition* and acceptance of this word [*decorum*] for whatsoever is so, *cannot iustly be misliked*' (III, vii). Nevertheless, like all men of this century, he is aware that though 'the election is the writers, the iudgement is the worlds, as theirs to whom the reading apperteineth' (III, xxiii, p. 263). The poet calls the tune, right enough, and the nature of the poetic subject he himself chooses determines how he does it, but no Renaissance poet forgot that he wanted his music to reach the hearts of others.

Long-proved ways of maintaining this proportion made for a common ground between poet and public. One simplest way was the preservation of the differences between the three levels of style. Poets knew, and readers expected, that writing in the highest or grand style would maintain a different tension from that which characterized the middle or the base styles. The determinant is the familiar one: 'it behooveth the maker or Poet to follow the nature of his subiect' in choosing between these three levels (Puttenham, III, v).

This is so commonplace and so familiar from classical and medieval theory that it is perhaps idle to quote from among the dozens of statements. Discussions are likely to turn immediately to practical helps. For the division into characters of style led to most usable and definite advice regarding the use of ornament. The rhetoricians' 'mere lists of figures' have come in for much derisive comment; but the Renaissance user of these lists of practical aids had been taught to see very specific meanings in the general caveats which precede them—underscoring the concept of proportion-to-the-subject as the governing principle in the use of all figures. The lists in these technical manuals were meant to assist two groups: the writer who has to define the general rule of 'proportion' in concrete poetic situations, and the reader who will enjoy suitable ornament more immediately and more intelligently if he perceives its nature and form.

Wilson's popular *Arte of Rhetorique* (1560) has a typical short statement of the relation of the fundamental threefold division to 'exornation':

There are three maner of stiles or inditings, the great or mightie kinde, when we use great wordes, or vehement figures.

The small kinde, when wee moderate our heate by meaner wordes, and use not the most stirring sentences.

The lawe kinde, when we use no *Metaphores* nor translated words, nor yet use any amplifications, but goe plainly to worke, and speake altogether in common wordes [p. 169]. [Author's italics.]

Applied to poetry as well as oratory, these three divisions marked out rather three stylistic tendencies than three separate boxes to put poems in. Even a critic of lesser insight like Webbe shows that he does not conceive of monotonously maintained levels of style befitting rigidly separated types of subject. He rather points out, whether he speaks of the majesty of Virgil's heroical verse or of the ruder eclogue like the *Shepheardes Calender*, that in a good author that which a modern critic would call 'tone' will vary 'agreeably to' the differing emotions being portrayed and evoked.[41] That he conceives this to be a function of form is clear, but his comments concern metrics and diction rather than imagery. Of course, it takes no ghost come from the grave to tell us this—but the sensible purport of the principle of decorum has more than once been turned by historians of criticism into admonitions no respectable ghost would repeat. Some advisers, like Puttenham, go on, as Wilson does, to consider the various figures. Some, like Scaliger, try to assist discretion by noticing the qualities one may expect to achieve on the three different levels of intensity.[42]

[41] *A Discourse of English Poetrie* (1586); see, e.g. (in Gregory Smith), I, 256 ff. The various meters in *S.C.* are commended for being decorously 'agreeable to such affections' as their subjects call forth. See also the steady emphasis upon decorum throughout the portion of George Fabricius' *De Re Poetica* (1560) which Webbe translates (pp. 290 ff., Latin original pp. 417 ff.). These emphases are entirely typical and familiar. Jonson's numerous remarks about the decorum of the various styles and the various genres (in the *Discoveries*) are especially suggestive and well balanced.

[42] In the grand style one looks to find *dignitas, sonus,* and on occasion *gravitas, vehementia;* in the base style, always *tenuitas,* occasionally *simplicitas, securitas;* in the moderate style, *rotunditas, volubilitas.* These last tags remind us that such were the qualities to which Bacon objected in a famous passage in the *Advancement of Learning,* and that he and other anti-Ciceronians attempted to substitute the *genus humile* for other styles, in prose. Common to all three are *perspicuitas, venustas, proprietas,* and, as occasion demands, *mollitia, incitatio, puritas* (*Poet.* iv. 2).

Naturally, there were disagreements as to the suitability of such single qualities to the subjects and purposes of a given work in a given style; naturally, there were disagreements as to whether large use of such or such figures gave poems this character or that. Campion's attack on rhyme in his *Observations* (1602) is simply such a disagreement. He thinks that proportion is disturbed by the exaltation of this one rhetorical figure, which is a mere scheme—the *figura verbi* called *similiter desinentia*. 'The world is made by Simmetry and proportion,' and who can see proportion in treating high and grave subjects with the ornaments that suit ballating and song? (In Gregory Smith, II, 329–32.) Campion, of course, has not the slightest notion of resigning this high territory to *prose;* he simply sees indecorum in the overuse of one of the colors of rhetoric.

Daniel answers him on his own ground, seeing the charge of disproportion disproved by the achievements of 'the best of this Age.' He finds 'not Ryme but our ydle Arguments' the cause why men have come to question poetry's capacity to deal with matters of grave import. Daniel's curious gift for standing outside his own era and watching times as they pass gives a strange poignancy to his meditative divining of the judgments posterity may set upon his age, the same poignancy we feel in the soberly beautiful end of his treatise, or in his confidence that men to come cannot but see fitness in a form of poetry wherein 'so many honourable spirits' have built, showing in rhyme 'by what divine influence they have beene moved, and under what starres they lived.' It is because they have reared it so high, and bestowed their understanding to furnish it, that rhymed verse can be embraced 'as the fittest dwelling for our invention'; England need see no unfitness in 'her native ornaments,' for great poetry has established their decorum.

In point of fact, this is precisely what happened. It will always happen, for standards of what is fitly proportioned are continually being set in new places by poets who cannot say what they have to say without creating unfamiliar kinds of harmony between poetic subject and form. Although this happens constantly, it is also true that there are points of culmination, when

great and influential choices are made. The disagreement between Campion and Daniel points up one tiny facet of such a
choice. For the great revolutionary achievement of the earlier
Renaissance poets with respect to the decorum of styles, subjects, and kinds is one which prepared the way for the minor
variations of decorum introduced by the Metaphysical poets, no
less than it prepared the way for Milton. The choice made by
English Renaissance writers has an air of paradox; what they
really chose was not to give up the Middle Ages. Instead, they
pushed the concept of 'suitability' to limits never foreseen by
its ancient originators. Instead of breaking with the forms,
habitual modes of ornamentation, 'causes' and purposes for
poems, which had been familiar for hundreds of years in the
vernacular literature of medieval Europe, poets and critics
through two generations gradually integrated these imaginative
discoveries with classical purposes, forms, theoretical principles.
True, they merely married two traditions that had lived together for centuries, and there is even something incestuous
about my figure. Nevertheless, the fact that the best gains of
medieval poetic practice in the vernaculars were henceforth
firmly denizened in the province of classical poetics made for a
synthesis which remained fruitful at least until the late nineteenth century.

No comparable turning-point came for three centuries, although Romantic thought blocked a few exits and obscured a
few 'Danger' signs. The most truly revolutionary change with
respect to decorum in poetry must come when men are no
longer able to accept the principle upon which it is erected, a
principle which underlies both classical poetic and medieval cul-
ture. When the notion of a hierarchy of values becomes suspect,
the principle of decorum simply ceases to operate.

Modern critical thinking cannot but see hierarchical divisions
like that into the three styles as distasteful and even somewhat
ridiculous. Nevertheless, and unhappily, the whole matter is
intimately connected with the very possibility of communication in poems. Language as a poetic instrument is built upon
shared ideas of what is 'greater' or 'lesser,' common to writer

and reader—all power of figures to move without accompanying explanation, all amplification, comparison, diminution, counts upon this. As that common ground shrinks, the communication of the writer's own set of significances to a reader becomes increasingly difficult. This is responsible for much of the necessary obscurity of modern imagery—for this kind of obscurity is not under modern conditions of thought an avoidable fault of the poet's; it is an inevitable difficulty, harder on him than on readers. The Elizabethan writer, on the other hand, could communicate part of his intention to his reader by the mere choice of his form, enlarge their common meeting-ground before he had advanced beyond his title-page.

It is, of course, true that all the greater modern poets make as much use as they honestly can of these very conventions, whether or no the substructure on which they were erected be in danger of collapse. One of the few who venture upon the high style, Yeats maintains the ancient distinctions in his images with such exquisite tact that it is a pleasure to read through the volume of collected verse solely to watch him do so.[43] A decorous division between high, middle, and low styles is in fact more nicely preserved by some moderns than by Romantic or Victorian poets. Men who are not secure walk more carefully in dangerous places then those who are merely not safe. Eliot is a master of the base style, used for satire. Surer, in that genre,

[43] One could not find better Elizabethan examples of decorum justly and delicately maintained in the character of images, and governing: absence or presence of tropes; their complexity, logical tautness, or emotional reach; amplifying or diminishing suggestions through epithet or detail; brevity or expansion; amount and character of rhetorical ornament; all adjusted, by syntactical or metrical means, to tone. Turn, for example, from 'Byzantium' or 'Leda and the Swan' (pp. 285, 247) to the short reflective lyric ('Stream and Sun at Glendalough,' p. 293) or the much-favored short deliberative piece in the middle style, meditative or conversational like the old poetic epistle ('Coole and Ballylee, 1931,' 'The People,' pp. 280, 171); thence to the compact satirical quatrains or epigrams ('Spilt Milk,' 'The Nineteenth Century and After,' 'Three Movements,' pp. 276–77; or 'The Witch,' p. 137, an image that must have roused the envy of more than one Elizabethan ghost). On the other hand, decorum of genre is sometimes not observed; a sixteenth- or seventeenth-century poet would either not have written 'Leda' as a sonnet, and 'Two Songs from a Play' (p. 246) as songs, or else would have deliberately lowered the tension of the style. Yeats's earlier poems, like the younger work of many Elizabethan poets, show far less mastery of the numerous aspects of decorum.

of their subjects, many moderns handle it with orthodox competence. This partial survival of decorum as a regulatory principle is not an anomaly. It seems to me to result largely from the fact that poets (like reading publics) have stubbornly persisted in refusing complete assent to a notion fairly common among critics—that the subject of a poem does not really matter very much.

Even so, the distance we have traveled in this respect from a point of view common to Campion and Daniel, to Donne and Spenser, will be apparent if I quote a statement of Daniel's in which none of these other three would have seen cause for discontent. As a defense of poetry, it shocks a modern ear, though I am not sure that there is any honest poet who does not try to be worth such defense.

> But when after-times shall make a quest of inquirie, to examine the best of this Age, *peradventure there will be found* in the now contemned recordes of Ryme *matter not unfitting the gravest Divine and severest Lawyer* in this kingdome [in Gregory Smith, II, 380 (1603)].

Peradventure there has been. Daniel could not foresee what a disadvantage their high matter would prove to some of the best of that age. For men of all schools were agreed that 'elevation' of subject made a difference, and that poetry could be of all discourse the most serious. So far as I can discover, the modern antididactic complaint of 'purposes better suited to prose' is a complaint never uttered by a late Elizabethan about an early one.[44]

Careful maintaining of the decorum of the middle or the base style by Metaphysical poets is sometimes mistaken by moderns

[44] One cannot but recall Drayton's comment in his verse-letter to Reynolds, that contemporaries found Daniel 'too much *Historian* in verse.' One glance at Drayton's own subjects is enough to remind one that this does not raise an objection to Daniel's choice of historical subject matters but is probably to be understood in terms of the familiar restatements (like Sidney's) of Aristotle's distinction. I.e., that Daniel was too *un*philosophical, too content with the historian's 'bare *Was*' instead of dealing as poetry should 'with the universall consideration' (see Sidney, in Gregory Smith, I, 167 ff.). When Drayton said that Daniel's *manner* better fitted prose, he probably meant just that. It is an objection on grounds of decorum, and Jonson's curt 'Daniel . . . . no poet' in the conversations with Drummond is probably such another. It would certainly be a falsification of the poetic theory of both these critics if we were to align them with moderns who criticize Daniel for his didacticism.

for a new (and more modern) attitude toward grave and high matter for poetry. But if Donne, the 'severest Lawyer' we have in English rhymed verse, had not stood upon Daniel's position, even in his amorous verses, he would never have received from Dryden that famous censure which fixed upon the Metaphysicals their name. In Dryden's comment we see a certain ossifying of the more flexible earlier notions of decorum; he does not think Donne's nice speculations of philosophy are suited to love poems. Yet the modern willingness to turn over these speculations, one of the most ancient of poetry's provinces, to prose, might have shocked even Dryden; certainly it would have disconcerted any Elizabethan or Jacobean.

6. *Decorum and the 'Kinds'*

The loosely applied division into three levels of style, according with purpose, regularized what long experience had found to characterize communication on different levels of intensity and elaboration. So the further division into genres was similarly held to work toward effective and beautiful harmony, inasmuch as it was thought to assist poets to maintain, and readers to enjoy, proportion or conformity between subject and form.

Again, distinctions did not hold like the teeth of a vice, and no two lists of kinds show exactly the same inclusions or classification. We should be put to it to set down opposite all the titles in an anthology of Elizabethan literature the separate kind to which each piece must be assigned. Such a procedure would have brought out disagreements among the Elizabethans themselves, I am sure. But this does not alter the fact that certain important differences affecting images were accepted, as a given, by both writer and public. Once more, the matter is too much a commonplace to need support by quotations.[45] For anyone attempting a better understanding of Renaissance images, the distinctions between genres are chiefly important and helpful

[45] In English, Puttenham's discussions in Book I, *passim*, and in the first six and the last three chapters of Book III, are most interesting because he is fertile in exemplification and because he does not allow so much to go by implication as do others. In this section, in order to use contemporary wordings without interlarding the text with references, I shall use Puttenham's phraseology and merely append the chapter number from Book III. His notions are the typical ones.

in so far as they provide certain large general caveats. This is what I think the distinctions provided for the writers of those images.

Theories of epic poetry received, of course, enormous elaboration. We need remember principally that the great or weighty 'causes' of epic and related genres brought in their train lofty amplifications, leisurely rather than dialectical expansion of similes, many majestically eloquent figures as against fewer pointedly eloquent ones. When we understand that 'all *hymnes* .... were written in the high stile' (vi), we shall not look in Spenser's *Fowre Hymnes* for images with the jabbing brevity or retorted wit of those in Donne's verse-letters or argumentative satirical short poems, or images with the grave and moving straightforwardness of those in some of King's elegies. All these, like the 'common Poesies of loves', are kinds written in the middle or in the base style.

Everyone knows that this was a period of fertile experimentation with the genres. If in thinking of smaller matters like imagery as well as larger ones like epic structure we remember that men were experimenting with the current generalization that 'histories' were best written in the high style, we shall not think that Marlowe is chiefly indulging in 'youthful' 'Elizabethan' exuberance when he reports:

> Now had the Morn espied her lover's steeds;
> Whereat she starts, puts on her purple weeds. . . . .
>
> (*H. and L.*, ii, 87)

Except for one lyric in the pastoral convention, Marlowe simply did not write any poems in which we can look for descriptive images to compare with those we find, say, in Herrick's short 'demonstrative' lyrics.[46] Still less do we dare compare the

[46] The universally apparent attempt, by Elizabethan poets, to satisfy the requirement of decorum according to genre is a factor which must be regarded in any use of imagery to determine authorship. For example, unless we have comic scenes which are surely from Marlowe's hand, we have no norm by which to determine whether or not he wrote the images in other comic scenes of doubtful authorship; such a norm is not provided by the imagery Marlowe uses in tragedies. A first principle of scientific investigation is the isolation of factors; some of the factors which influenced a dramatist *writing* images and which we neglect at our peril in *reading* them are: general purpose (e.g., satire; cf. philosophical reflection), immediate purpose, subject matter, character

magnificent amplifications in *Hero and Leander* or in Drayton's early narrative verse with images in short *deliberative* pieces— Marvell's 'On a Drop of Dew,' Herbert's 'Man,' Carew's 'My Mistress commanding me to return her letters.' Moreover, we oversimplify matters if we think of Drayton as out of the main line of development when, between *Mortimeriados* and the *Barons Warres*, between 1596 and 1603, we find him *heightening* his style. The changes toward elevation and dignity in the latter piece[47] belong to the very years during which Drayton was revising his sonnets in the direction of witty terseness and frankly bold irony. He has not changed his poetic creed; the orthodox one fits both types of change, in the two different kinds.

Perhaps we are more accustomed, however, to discounting for the additional elevation in images found in kinds generally related to the high style than to noticing the effects of genre upon images from the other kinds. It is equally important to be aware of these effects in writing that belongs to genres to which the base and middle styles were appropriate.

The chief representatives of the base style are eclogues and pastoral poems, and satire—including, of course, many types of short poems we might include in collections of 'lyrics' but which shared the purposes of these kinds. Poetic subjects of the sort found in pastoral are 'to be holden with-/in their teder, by a

---

speaking, source, type of scene, audience, type of company, stage conditions, pace or tempo of scene. Nothing could be more natural than that Marion B. Smith should find that 'most of these un-Marlowe-like images are found in the comic scenes' of *The Jew of Malta* (*Marlowe's Imagery and the Marlowe Canon* [Philadelphia, 1940], p. 119). Our notions of Marlowe-like images have necessarily been formed upon images which obey different necessities. To arrive at scientifically valid criteria for assigning authorship would seem to me almost insuperably difficult.

[47] Once he had decided that the subject's dignity (as he says) required careful avoidance of ignoble suggestions in certain areas, it is quite natural that we should find him turning night 'Powting' 'in mistie rugge' to night lowering under 'blacke Curtaine'; or taking out stars prying like *thieves*, or 'for his crowne must *scuffle*.' It is also reasonable that he does not mind keeping, in a descriptive detail, the ugly realism of 'Ones feet intangled in anothers guts,' while at the same time he removes a comparable trope— which could operate to 'abbase' his subject (shores *like a slaughter-house*). These may be found in the Hebel edition of *Mortim.* (1596) and *BW* (1603), as follows: *M.* 694 (cf. *BW* iii, st. 17); *M.* 702; *M.* 220; *M.* 427 (kept in *BW* ii, 40); *M.* 441. Actually I quote from Hebel's 1619 text, but the Variant Readings show here only immaterial changes since 1603. (See Vol. V of the Hebel edition, ed. K. Tillotson and B. Newdigate, which opens up materials invaluable for study of ideas of poetics during these years.)

low, myld, and simple maner of utterance, creeping rather then clyming, & marching rather then mounting upwardes' (v). Hence Googe is not guilty of indecorum—whatever one may think of his metrical ineptitude—in such an image as this in his *Egloga tertia* (p. 40):

> And yet, they dare account them selves
> to be of Noble bludde.
> But Fisshe bred up, in durtye Pooles,
> wyll ever stynke of mudde.

Nor are these indecorously harsh or rough images, from Donne's 'Ecclogue' (p. 131):

> What delicacie can in fields appeare,
>   Whil'st Flora 'herselfe doth a freeze jerkin weare?
> Whil'st windes do all the trees and hedges strip
>   Of leafes, to furnish roddes enough to whip
> Thy madnesse from thee. . . . .

Many later images in the same poem exemplify the terse sharpness and pointed, argumentative sententiousness which characterize the base style used for purposes of satire, in or out of the pastoral framework. The *tour de force* by which Donne remakes 'Come live with me, and be my love' (p. 46) into a piscatory eclogue of witty, satirical, and probably ironic intent, with its colloquial syntax and 'rough' detail, shows how adept were these poets in transposing themes from key to key, with corresponding shifts in tone and in what one might term the pitch of the images.

The ordinary Renaissance acceptance of 'decorum according to subject and genre' is exemplified in E. K.'s glosses to the October eclogue of the *Shepheardes Calender*, that on the poet and poetry. It is difficult for a modern reader to accustom himself to the way in which this concept reached down into the poet's decisions on the smallest points of diction and imagery.[48]

---

[48] It is a shock, but possible, to think that practicing poets (including other Metaphysicals, if they had written epics) might simply see their own daily experience in composing and revising, in a remark like Cowley's 'And *Spouse* is not an *Heroical Word*' (ed. Grosart, II, 82). We have little way of knowing. It is hard to detect by internal evidence where the gradual rigidifying of notions of decorum began, since the

Spenser's use of rustic archaisms in the *Calender* is, of course, a famous example of an experiment in suiting language to genre. As everyone knows, Sidney found it too daring. Spenser used archaisms with very different intention and effect in the *Faerie Queene*. There we do not find them used because they are pithy, 'darke and unaccustomed wordes, or rusticall and homely' (vi, of the base style). There, archaisms are rather used for richness in the emotional tone, for stately and antiquated majesty, for imaginative reach into a subject matter with the most fitting connotations. Or, we may detect frequent cases in which an archaism avoids choppiness or extra syllables destroying the force or music of the line, or in which it recalls by its sound a related word which will strengthen and intensify an effect.[49] These uses, in turn, are primarily devices for heightening and would not have suited the nature of the *Calender*. Praised though they are by such writers as Minturno and Du Bellay, they are not praised as proper to the low style.

Of mean (middle) matters, as in nonsatirical 'common Poesies of loves' (vi) or the types loosely gathered under the term *elegy*, one normally writes with 'wordes and speaches of smothnesse and pleasant moderation' (v). The verse-letter or the longish reflective poem are likely to show less rough and violent figures than satire proper, though the sharp diminishings proper to some subjects approach this character. They are almost certain to show less stirring or vehement or elaborately eloquent figures than those poems which, treating matters stately and high, required words and figures 'magnifik in proportion' (v). Yet these kinds written in the middle style may find need for, and always permit, a considerable use of tropes of varying degrees of imaginative profundity. Thus, within a few lines of each other, in Daniel's *Musophilus*, we may find figures very different in

---

dignity of any given word in a given decade is a matter for such meticulous linguistic research. We are on slightly surer ground with respect to images, as the several factors producing elevation can point all in one direction and corroborate our inferences.

[49] These generalizations are based upon a survey and partial tabulation of the uses of archaisms in four cantos in each of three books (earlier and later) of *FQ*. B. R. Mc-Elderry's distinctions between different degrees of 'archaism' were used (see 'Archaism and Innovation in Spenser's Poetic Diction,' *PMLA*, XLVII [1932], 144–70).

construction and effect. We find brief tropes with Miltonic largeness of suggestion:

> That all this little All, might not descend
> Into the darke a universall pray.
>
> (v. 37; in HH, p. 267)

And yet, within the next few lines given to the same speaker, such a radical, discursive image as the comparison between the intellectual yes-man and the compass foot:

> The vulgar foote: that never takes his wayes
> By reason, but by imitation;
> Rowling on with the rest, and never way's
> The course which he should go, but what is gone.

And in complaints like that of Daniel's Rosamond, colloquial locutions, briefly significant figures, and fairly elevated amplifications are all decorous. The proportion in which these are found will vary with author's intention, and with the formal differences which the latter also induces (e.g., length, verse form). A moment's thought will remind one that practically all those Metaphysical poems with which current criticism is most occupied belong to types normally using the mean style or by the intrusion of satire or dialectic pushed toward the use of base-style conventions.

Probably the slow establishment of a reading rather than a listening public, during a hundred years of printing, had something to do with the increasing number of short poems which were not 'short sung poems' or lyrics proper. As in the prose of the anti-Ciceronians there was a gradual development toward establishing the philosophical (as cf. the oratorical) style as the norm,[50] so in poetry many of the smaller kinds which had previously been more carefully distinguished moved toward a central type. Satire, with its rougher and harsher tone, remained fairly distinguishable. Lyly and Campion wrote songs; Marvell and Lord Herbert wrote short poems rather deliberative than

---

[50] See M. W. Croll, 'Attic Prose in the Seventeenth Century,' *SP*, XVIII (1921), 79-128. For prose, Croll distinguishes between two kinds (oratorical *genus grande*, philosophical *genus humile*), the third character found in all Latin criticism being recognized as somewhat of a makeshift.

demonstrative. The *Faerie Queene* and *Hero and Leander* embrace satirical incidents (Braggadochio, Malbecco) or passages of persuasive argument (Leander's with Hero); Drayton's later sonnets and Donne's 'sonets' and elegies are many of them virtually short satires, combining the conventions of philosophical dialectic (*genus humile*) with the *energia* and diminishing figures of rhetoric's demonstrative 'dispraise,' and both with the conventionally harsh tone of satire.[51] A Carew or a King writes many more poems in the mean style than a Marlowe or a Spenser, a Herbert more than any of these; and Donne and all the Metaphysicals write many poems in which base-style conventions have been assimilated into kinds previously characterized by the 'smoother' moderation proper to typical earlier poetic subjects. For such facts as these there are many and complicated reasons. Perhaps it is sufficient here merely to recognize that such choices by poets are but ill explained by the easy reasons based on 'personality factors' and 'intellectual climate' which our overpsychologized and oversociologized century so readily spins out.

All the examples and explanations in this chapter are the merest fraction of the innumerable and subtle gradations with which the poet's task of decorously suiting his style to his subject and purpose was limned out in theory, and demonstrated in practice, in the sixteenth and seventeenth centuries. Whether by studied care or by a second nature that was the product of long training and discreet taste, he must confront and decide no small number of most slippery questions. To observe with what mastery a poet handled these was part of a reader's pleasure. This does not quarrel with the fact that the reader's first pleasure, then as now, was to be moved by that mastery.

[51] In other words, and as noted above in other connections, many appearances of rugged, homely, harsh, or violent qualities in the diction of Metaphysical poems are to be referred not to changed theories of poetry but to the conventional theories concerning the 'low' style proper to poems in the satirical kinds. This especially touches Donne, who likes even in songs to take satirical shots at those who disagree with what he praises or dispraises. The same obtains for his use of certain conventions—monologue, or inserted dramatic incident almost in dialogue, disclaimers of Petrarchan hyperboles, etc. For convenient quotation of several statements of such conventions see O. J. Campbell, *Comicall Satyre and Shakespeare's 'Troilus and Cressida'* (San Marino, Calif., 1938), chap. ii.

7. Decorum 'According to the Speaker'

Although the principle of decorum gave the writer great freedom, it is not the sort of freedom which suits with certain modern notions of the nature and function of creative writing. The
Renaissance poet is in command certainly, but he is master
rather than center of his work. For there is one other aspect of
decorum to which Renaissance writers give little explicit attention. When the poetry spoken of is not dramatic, but written
in the poet's own voice, 'decorum according to the speaker'
does not appear to concern either theorist or artist overmuch.
Style is to be suitable to a number of things, but that it should
be first and foremost a suitable expression of the nature of the
man writing does not emerge as an operative criterion.

Upholders of decorum freely recognize as valid and admirable
a great variety of 'humours' of style—'the plaine and obscure,
the rough and smoth, the facill and hard, the plentifull and
barraine, the rude and eloquent, the strong and feeble, the
vehement and cold stiles,' as Puttenham reels them off (III, v).
But it does not seem to occur to this unromantic generation to
assume that these qualities are to be regarded as inescapable
results of 'the personality of the author.'[52] Puttenham remarks
that 'men doo chuse their subiects according to the mettal of
their minds, & therefore a high minded man chuseth him high &
lofty matter to write of,' and others otherwise. But he has no
sooner remarked that 'if the minde be haughtie and hoate, the
speech and stile is also vehement and stirring' than he corrects it
with 'And yet peradventure *not altogether so*, but that *every mans
stile is for the most part according to the matter and subiect of the
writer*, or so ought to be.'

This is perhaps a radical difference between sixteenth- and
seventeenth-century poetic and modern poetic. When Leavis
says that we must 'invent techniques . . . . adequate to the
ways of feeling, or modes of experience, of adult, sensitive
moderns,' he seems to define decorum in poetry according to the

[52] In extremely rare cases the latter seems to be recognized as a factor; Sherry, for
example, remarks that the vice *cacozelia* comes from 'a pevishe desyre to folowe suche a
kynde of wrytyng as thou arte not mete for' (fol. x^r [1555]). This may have merely
Puttenham's meaning, when he calls the vice 'Fonde affectation,' regarding it as the
common fault of the untrained and immature (III, xxii).

nature and emotional possibilities of the man who writes it; if the reader can momentarily at least be the same kind of man, he will properly apprehend the poetry. The poet of the Renaissance was certainly interested in ways of feeling and modes of experience. But he does not determine the validity and importance of those ways and modes, as poetic subjects, in quite the modern fashion. It would be hard to find an Elizabethan or Jacobean defense of certain feelings and experiences as subjects on the ground that some sensitive Elizabethan or Jacobean had them. Accordingly, these earlier poets tried to invent techniques adequate to yet more ambitious ends than these.

It is possible to disagree with Sparrow's contention that the poetry of the Symbolists is egoistically concerned to 'vindicate the importance of the individual' and that much of such poetry is necessarily unintelligible because images which embody associations personal to the writer thus received sanction.[53] But whether or not this is a just characterization of motive, and an accurate judgment of result, it is certainly true that the sixteenth and seventeenth centuries had a very different conception than have we of the extent to which the poet's nature and idiosyncracies do govern or should govern the nature of his images. Seventeenth-century poets still chose to write in images whose significance can be grasped without knowledge of a set of associations peculiar to the writer's experience. The chief reason why they chose to do this lies, I think, in their acceptance of the tenet that poetry, not being history, transcends the particular, the local, the individual, a single isolated experience, a feeling as felt by one man, however sensitive.

It seems to me that we must admit that a radical difference in philosophical outlook stands behind and is even responsible for a radical difference between the imagery of these earlier poets and much poetic imagery in our own day. The difference came slowly and obtains but partially. Much modern imagery is decorous in precisely the ways I have suggested or demonstrated. But much is not, for the principle of 'decorum according to the

---

[53] John Sparrow, *Sense and Poetry* (New Haven, 1934), Intro., p. xvi. The quotation from F. R. Leavis comes from *New Bearings in English Poetry* (London, 1932), but may also be found in Sparrow (p. x).

subject' cannot operate under any other conception of poetic truth than the ancient one that poetry deals with things 'in their universal consideration.' To the poet who does not believe this possible (or interesting), the rule of decorum cannot make sense. The historian's conception of truth does not allow him to choose details for their 'suitability'; the concept is irrelevant. His particulars are 'true' if they occurred, credible if they could have occurred (for 'story' as such is history, as the Renaissance well knew). The writer who presents the 'particulars' or 'individuals' of his physical or mental world does not choose his images on the ground that they fitly assist him to make manifest what he conceives to be the true significance of experiences and feelings; he has relinquished his claim to that subject.

This relinquishment came not in the seventeenth century but in the nineteenth. From the simple demonstrative 'praise' of beauty in a woman to the complex Donnean examination of the nature of love or of transiency, the poems which the earlier century has left us include elements whose presence we cannot explain except by seeing the poems as evaluative in purpose. Occasional *libertin* poems in the seventeenth century attack certain values. We cannot read the body of work of any seventeenth-century poet and find that there emerges from it a serious and consistent *disbelief in the existence of any basis for concepts of value which is not relative to the observer*. Much modern poetry has had to be written by men to whom such disbelief was an initial assumption. Decorum 'according to the subject' has little meaning under such circumstances. Except perhaps in the sense that the nature and exact experience of the poet becomes the only subject—and to this the typical Symbolist image, and many images in Yeats and Eliot, are very accurately suited. But the seventeenth-century poet did not yet find himself out on that limb; the most we can discover is, in poems here and there, his bravado or his dismay at finding himself less sure than his predecessors of the exact nature of truth and of how man is to come at it.

The inability of the modern thinker to believe that poetry can be an instrument with which to pursue and make manifest 'the true' meanings which inform the world of appearances is the real reason for such indecorum as an earlier theorist would find in modern imagery; the fact that nevertheless modern poets frequently do go straight on to 'pursue and make manifest' in the time-honored way is the reason why much modern imagery is still decorous. The fact that modern images (in poems which do not presume to embark on that pursuit) often possess qualities which characterize seventeenth-century images, should not blind us to the fact that a radical difference is often to be observed if we look at what the later poet omits—from his poem as a whole. For it is not the qualities of images which make them truly and essentially similar; it is the function they serve in the integrated artistic unit.

Neither a modern nor a seventeenth-century image is to be judged indecorous by virtue of its being unconventional. I hope that I have shown that imagery can be entirely in line with orthodox pronouncements on decorum even though it be unconventional, homely, rough, difficult to understand. It can be decorous though it be used to abase rather than amplify a matter, though it be ironic, an understatement, vitriolic in its satirical force. It can be decorous when it surprisingly juxtaposes the grand and the colloquial, and whether it takes the shape of elaborate hyperbole, of briefly witty analogy, or of dark and profound symbol. It has to meet but one criterion—that it suit with the true 'height' of the cause which the poet has in hand. This is precisely where the modern poet cannot entirely follow his predecessors. He can no longer range subjects in an order of elevation or importance, certainly not in an order of importance for which he would dare claim a validity defined by reference to the nature of things, rather than by reference to himself as honest observer of appearances. The seventeenth-century poet could still suit his style to the 'essential' or true 'greatness' of his subject. That in many poems he set himself to quarrel with old 'truths,' to readjust the hierarchical order of values as he found it, is nothing to the purpose. He had not been forced to resign the ancient endeavor. That he might pursue it with strength and power, he 'kept decorum.'

PART II
THE LOGICAL FUNCTIONS OF IMAGERY

CHAPTER X

IMAGES LOGICALLY DEFINED

THE break between Parts I and II of this book has no virtue whatsoever save pure expository convenience; in the consideration of any given poem the separation it appears to indicate would be a fictitious, and probably in every case a falsifying, separation.

It is obvious from the reading of any sixteenth- or seventeenth-century poem using figures of even a minor degree of complication that to discuss the significancy of images and stop short of their possible logical function in a poem is an impossibility. The endeavor has not been mistaken, merely incomplete. I do not thereby imply that what remains to be discussed is climactic, in a study of images. Nor may related intentions and meanings which we might term 'imaginative' be forgotten, for no opposition whatsoever was posed in the era here treated between logical and other functions for images. The fact that such oppositions have since been posed means that this part must concern itself more strictly with the images of the earlier period, for only certain ones of the generalizations made will apply to the images of our own day.

The general principles outlined earlier form the background for this portion of the discussion as well. Decorum regulates all images of whatever function; in fact, it determines and defines function. The type of images here treated will be seen to fall into place under the conceptions of Imitation initially sketched out. Images functioning logically have no quarrel with conceptions like *ut pictura poesis* or with style as the clothing and embodiment of thought. Images which amplify or illustrate are not *il*logical images, and, though they might be sensuously full and rich, I doubt whether an Elizabethan could have thought of them even as *a*logical. Nevertheless, certain other functions which images have in poems bear a clearer and more direct relation to logic, and to logic as it was taught in the sixteenth and seventeenth centuries—functions, for example, of definition, of discrimination or careful drawing of distinctions, of support through analogy.

Purposes like these result in images of a special and distinguishable character. The ease and orderliness with which such images fall into relation with the teachings of logic, as this period conceived of that discipline, make it very hard to believe that poets nourished on the discipline did not intend to maintain the relation. It would be equally hard to believe that the Ramistic reorganization of logic did not press writers toward a more conscious attempt to relate poetry to dialectic. It is the business of Part II to examine these possibilities.

I do not think that it is possible to separate the historical part of the problem—the relations of the images of a particular era to logic as it was then studied—from the more general considerations which make the problem a part of poetics. Many of my observations about the nature of images functioning logically hold equally well for the poetic imagery of other eras, or for the images used in daily conversation, or in prose. I shall notice some of these general implications. On the whole, however, I consider the points in this part to be more limited in their applicability, and my primary concern—once the possible relationships of images to logic are clearly defined—is to examine the *nature* of images serving predominantly logical functions, in poets from Sidney to Marvell, and the *modifications* of that nature resulting from varying definitions of these functions.[1]

1. *The Logical Base of an Image*

It is only now, after long consideration of the many different contributions which differing images may make, that we can usefully consider what is the *basic element by which* the nature of

[1] The major ideas in this second part were summarily presented in an article, 'Imagery and Logic: Ramus and Metaphysical Poetics,' *JHI*, III (1942), 365–400, and had been presented at the Modern Language Association meeting of 1940 in a paper based on work done from 1934 to 1939. I trust that this will make any relation my discussion shows to kindred work done recently by others more clear; and I should like to thank the editors of the *Journal of the History of Ideas* for permission to use again here certain materials in altered form.

an image may be defined, especially in case it uses tropical language. The chief reason for wanting an answer to such a question is that we have otherwise no basis on which all readers are bound to agree, for comparing one image with another—in another poem by the same poet, in another poet, or in another literary period. I think that such comparisons should be made on grounds of the function served. But there is still a difficulty. Especially with tropes, which usually have a multiple function, involving delicate questions of the complete meaning of whole poems, one frequently seems to be in the situation described by the famous elephant story—*what* the image is depends so much upon which functioning part of it is seized upon that one can only explain its nature to those who already agree. Lacking even a terminology with which to discriminate formally between different examples of the same type of trope, one is frequently at a loss in explaining one's perception of either the nature or the functions of a particular image.

Rhetorical schemes offer less difficulty; they are defined by their form. A type of systematic repetition, or a syntactical pattern, has no chamelion propensities; an epizeuxis is an epizeuxis to the end of time. Its nature agreed upon, the figure's effect and its purpose may be profitably discussed. Certain large divisions between tropes we have noted; about most of them there is some uncertainty, so that one must frequently say of a given image 'probably *ironia*,' or, 'as I read it, *allegoria*.' With this type of indefiniteness I am in sympathy; I do not see anything but critical impoverishment to be gained by ruling out differences of interpretation of the author's possible meanings. What one wishes to avoid is rather the fruitless critical argument which results from haphazard characterizations of the nature of given images. On grounds of what element may we say, beyond cavil, 'this metaphor is formally *comparable* to this other,' 'this image has a different structure, another shape, hence possibly another intention, another kind of inner power'?

It will be simplest to let the only answer I have found to this appear by demonstration.

Perhaps the only moderately long sixteenth-century poem

well known in its details is *Hero and Leander*. I shall use it as a finding-ground, making comparisons, whenever they are useful, to images from Carew.[2] The disadvantage of using Marlowe is that we cannot make definitive judgments of the ultimate functions of any image in an unfinished poem. There are, however, advantages. I have wished to search out the logical basis which offers a formal differentia between metaphor and metaphor, in images from a poem that is as sensuous, as 'pagan,' as far from the 'didactic' as any we might choose. Certain points of view will thus be introduced in as unfriendly an atmosphere as possible. This way of looking at imagery minimizes the importance of 'personality' factors; it is useful to do this also in connection with a poet whose style many persons interpret as almost autobiographically revealing.

I should perhaps confess at the outset that the basis upon which images are now most frequently differentiated and classified—i.e., the area from whence comparisons are drawn, because of personal predilections of the author—seems to me an unfirm basis, if not indeed an aesthetically irrelevant consideration. It is all but useless in the determination of the nature of an image using trope.[3] It is possible that the question, 'What characterizes the imagery of a man like Marlowe?' is not a reasonable question.

Everyone would agree that the two following images differ greatly. The first is part of the description of Hero's effect upon the standers-by:

> Even as, when gaudy nymphs pursue the chase,
> Wretched Ixion's shaggy-footed race,
> Incens'd with savage heat, gallop amain
> From steep pine-bearing mountains to the plain,
> So ran the people forth to gaze upon her. . . . .
>
> (*Hero and Leander*, i, 113)

[2] The latter has been chosen at random; awkwardness of reference may be avoided by using only two authors. I might quite as well have chosen early Drayton and Marvell, or have turned the dates around and found comparable and noncomparable images in Donne and in Spenser.

[3] What seem to me the scientific unreliability and aesthetic helplessness of this approach to imagery are more fiercely commented on in the Appendix, Note R. The pioneering study using this basis of classification was C. F. E. Spurgeon's *Shakespeare's Imagery* (Cambridge, 1925).

This is pictorial, energetic, ornate, or at least not concise; its effectiveness depends upon our ability to transfer quickly, to the people running to catch sight of Hero, the speed and ardor which push the centaurs down the precipitous descent of the lines. The following figures have none of these characteristics; they come from the persuasive argument Leander addresses to Hero:

> Like untun'd golden strings all women are,
> Which long time lie untouch'd, will harshly jar.
> Vessels of brass oft handled, brightly shine;
> What difference betwixt the richest mine
> And basest mould, but use? . . . .
>
> (i, 229)

Here realization of sensuous qualities is not pertinent to the effect of the figures; no situation is clearly visualized; a woman is a musical string, a brass vessel, rich mine, base mold, in quick succession, and she is all of them with reference to but one characteristic which all share—of no worth if unused. Syntactical and rhetorical differences from the other image are obvious.

The intent of the first image is not so much sensuous as dramatic; we are to re-create with the help of a simile not only a sight but a situation. The intent of the second is to assist Leander to carry his point 'like to a bold sharp sophister' (197), with witty, seeming-logical acuteness. I would suggest that this difference in function and effect is first indicated to us by a marked difference in formal nature, and that this constitutes the basis upon which the two images, and any two similarly constructed, may be said to differ.

The first simply compares two actions on the basis of that Aristotelian predicament known as 'manner of doing.' This is the basis of innumerable logically simple images, especially useful in narrative and in demonstrative, unargumentative lyrics. However ornate or spare in detail, they are *always* like each each other. And they are *never* like images of the brass-vessels type, which is a similitude with the usual four terms,[4] a com-

---

[4] The most easily accessible description of this type of image, traditionally described in logic textbooks, is Milton's in his *Art of Logic*, I, xxi; touching the present point, it is entirely orthodox and typical. And, like theorists of the generations preceding him,

mon logical argument in which things are found to be like on the basis of certain common 'places' of logic (here, common 'manner of suffering' or action received, and common 'effect': both women and brass vessels being oft handled shine the brighter).

These two images are much less comparable to each other than each would be to an image similarly formed but written by a different poet and at a different date. Carew's 'Good Counsel to a Young Maid' begins with an image based like Marlowe's first on 'manner of doing,' in which the pursuing lover is compared to a hot traveler seeking to quench his thirst:

> When you the sun-burnt pilgrim see
>   Fainting with thirst, haste to the springs;
> Mark how at first with bended knee
>   He courts the crystal nymphs, and flings
> His body to the earth, where he
>   Prostrate adores the flowing deity.

Again the visualizing of action is important, concision is not allowed to rule out epithet and detail, and the effectiveness of the image depends on our ability to transfer the vehemence of the thirsty pilgrim to the ardent lover. Hidden within the traditional metaphors of which Carew is making use, however, are certain further logical bases for a similitude. And, after a stanza in which the situation is further pictorialized (with a double meaning, of course), we arrive at an image in which the terms of the similitude are drawn together with the same witty sharpness which characterized the second Marlowe image. Like Leander, Carew is now making a persuasive point, in which a conclusion is argued on the ground of similarities based on certain logical 'positions.' These happen to be again 'manner of suffering' and effect, and, although the image is more complicated, the same brevity, acuteness, and concealed syllogistic skeleton characterize the figure (p. 33):

> So shalt thou be despised, fair maid,
>   When, by the sated lover tasted,

---

and like all school- or college-trained writers, Milton is aware that 'the metaphor is a similitude contracted to one word without signs.' 'As the rhetoricians teach,' he says— a statement which may be corroborated if one wishes, for example in the first popular rhetoric in English, Wilson's *Arte of Rhetorique*, p. 171.

What first he did with tears invade
Shall afterwards with scorn be wasted. . . . .

If we want an image which *contrasts* with Marlowe's brass-
vessels argument, in tone, tempo, kind of concreteness, we had
better turn rather to one in Marlowe's own poem in which his
purpose is not persuasion but praise:

She ware no gloves, for neither sun nor wind
Would burn or parch her hands, but to her mind
Or warm or cool them, for they took delight
To play upon those hands, they were so white.

(i, 27)

Rhetorically, this amplifies a lovely quality in the lady by
means of a personification which allows a hyperbolical effect to
be mentioned; that is to say—logically, it is 'invented' or found
from the common place, effect, linked to the quality thus
praised, as cause. As rhetoricians and logicians note, and as
anyone knows from daily speech, 'effect' is one of the fruitfullest
places used in praising. Images so framed abound in every
author who sets about such a purpose. This or any other image
similarly constructed in Marlowe is bound to contrast with his
brass-vessels image and resemble rather Carew's

If when the sun at noon displays
            His brighter rays,
        Thou but appear,
He then, all pale with shame and fear,
        Quencheth his light. . . . .

('Song: A Beautiful Mistress,' p. 7)

As Carew's image is continued in the rest of the song, its
climax bears an even stricter formal resemblance to another
image of Marlowe's, when Hero rises blushing

And from her countenance behold ye might
A kind of twilight break, which through the hair,
As from an orient cloud, glimps'd here and there;
And round about the chamber this false morn
Brought forth the day before the day was born.

(ii, 318)[5]

[5] The greater element of comparableness with Carew's image (which continues
'If thou but show thy face . . . . light is hurl'd / Round about the silent world') lies in
the fact that the quality praised is, unlike the whiteness of Hero's hands, figuratively

The deliberate complicating of the image by a further circumstance or 'adjunct' of dawn (the orient clouds of hair) adds another formal element; Carew may choose to do the same, and, as
Celia's sweet singing dies away, may direct us to unveil our
eyes and behold where that voice dwells,

> . . . . and, as we know
> When the *cocks crow*,
> We freely may
> Gaze on the day,
> So may you, when the music's done,
> Awake and *see the rising sun*.
>
> ('Song: Celia Singing,' p. 54)

The same little rush of quick wit accompanies the same junc-
ture of figurative and literal 'sun.' That cocks and clouds are far
asunder does not put these two images into different categories;
and we should still have a firm basis for accurate comparison of
their nature *and poetic effect* if in one of them the lady were a
polestar, the quality 'guiding-influence,' the effect worshipful
dependence, and the reality-enforcing added circumstance an
actual boat tacking about in a disturbed sea.

It seems to me that we cannot make just comparison of the
power and beauty of different images unless we can thus determine when we are dealing with truly comparable figures and
can watch the similar poetic working of images framed similarly, though by different men at different dates. It is equally
clarifying if we can detect fundamental differences, and watch
the same poet use them to poetic advantage. Both the last-
quoted images differ in their logical base from this one, part of
Leander's comparison between Venus and Hero:

> Why should you worship her? her you surpass
> As much as sparkling diamonds flaring glass.
>
> (i, 213)

This makes use of qualities, in the flattering epithets, but the
logical base is the first of the usual series of predicaments—

---

rather than literally attributed (the brightness of beauty's shining is metaphorical).
This permits, and gives a certain witty energy to, the paradox of Marlowe's last line,
contrasting figurative and literal dawn.

substance; and this is a 'figure of difference.' Carew makes the
same type of swift discrimination, arguing with 'A. D., Unrea-
sonable, Distrustful of her own Beauty' (p. 119):

> . . . . thou shalt not say
> That is but brittle glass, which I have found
> By strict enquiry a firm diamond.

The similarity is, of course, emphasized by the use of similar
substances, but the properties signalized differ, and the real
similarity which sets off these two images in a different class
from the others quoted is their use of the predicament *substance*
as a distinction-making tool in an argument.

Such images, though simple, must be distinguished from
equally simple images differently framed. An enormous majority of images of all times, places, purposes, and types of writing
make use of the predicament 'quality.' They are easily distinguishable from those I have just quoted and are not ordinarily similar in tone. For example, Hero enchanted the gazer's
mind,

> For like sea-nymphs' inveigling harmony,
> So was her beauty to the standers by. . . . .
>
> (i, 105)

The sensuous response is strong, but the intent is not descriptive. One cannot *hear* the kind of beauty 'gazers' apprehend.
We seize from the sirens' harmony 'mind-enchanting power
thereof' and transpose this into praise of Hero's beauty, which
acts upon another sense, but moves the affections similarly, by
a shared attribute which can *only* be stated abstractly. There is
no irrelevancy in this little excursion; the enrichment it provides cannot be separated from Marlowe's purposes, and the
Elizabethan term for such heightening is amplification.

Carew does not find a great deal of use for simple images
of quality, though one might quote:

> You're fresh as April, sweet as May,
> Bright as is the morning star. . . . .

The crucial importance of logical function served, in determining the tone of an image, will be apparent if I complete this quotation:

> Think not, 'cause men flattering say
> You're fresh as April, sweet as May,
> Bright as is the morning star,
> That you are so; . . . .

('To A. L.: Persuasions to Love,' p. 2)

This is not, after all, like Marlowe's, an image based on quality and constituting a praise of the thing thus defined; it is a negative argument found from the common place *cause* and supporting the notion attributed-qualities-need-not-be-real-qualities, which is part of Carew's 'Persuasion.' Carew's image changed into an *ironia* under our eyes, but the *only factor* differentiating the two *different* images in the two quotations is their different logical structure. This is the determining element in terms of which we define the different nature of these two images, and I do not well see how there could be any other, all remarks about stars and months of the year being helpless to assist us in defining this difference.

This is not to say that the nature of the vehicle (April, morning star) has nothing to do with the effect of an image. Far from it. This character, like the qualities of anything else we meet in nature, is our first help in apprehending what the thing is. But an image is more than a plenum of qualities; it is an operative unit in an artistic structure. It is because a poem like any other work of art exists as a formal unit that we shall come closest to the secret working power of an image if we can define it by its 'formal cause.' But *to this* the nature of the vehicle is not always irrelevant; if Carew were to say 'You're fresh as spoiled fish, sweet as swill,' the contradictions would immediately warn us to be aware of a different formal cause. The addition of yet another logical complication turns the image into satire. One should add that the rhetorical cacophony would not be irrelevant either.

Most images utilize more than one of the predicaments or places. It is not always possible to detect certainly where the author's emphasis lay, nor is it to be expected that readers can always agree. This mode of knowing what an image is and means is no more perfect than knowledge usually is. When Marlowe describes the throngs of lovely women in the streets of Sestos (i, 97) with an image based upon the predicaments of quality and quantity-or-number, we do not know which of these impressed him most:

> For every street like to a firmament
> Glistered with breathing stars. . . . .

'Innumerableness' strikes me most forcibly here; I should not dare pronounce for another reader. Yet when Carew uses an image based on the same two predicaments, I should realize that he chose Alps pre-eminently for their 'quantity,' even though meanwhile the properties of Alps crowd the lines with (to me) more powerful suggestions:

> Nor can your snow, *though* you should take
> *Alps* into your bosom, slake
> The heat of my enamour'd heart.
>   ('Song: To my Mistress, I burning in love,' p. 46)

Determining the logical base thus gives us no mechanically sure key to an image's full meaning. I should only insist, and feel that this image's logical structure gave me a right to insist, that no historian of taste should use it to mark the early entrance of an interest in mountains into the seventeenth-century sensibility, and that no returned tourist should be launched by it into remarks upon the still and snowy majesty of the Simplon. To define this image by its formal cause is to realize that all we know from it is that Carew picked up somewhere that Alps were large, numerous, and snowy. I carry the example *ad absurdum*, but a great deal of criticism of imagery takes either one or the other of these paths; either it discovers psychosociological attitudes or it comments impressionistically on connotations. I do not think that the only alternative is a formalistic and dogmatic interpretation of images; it must be conceded at once that the full meaning of any image, to its creator, cannot be surely and completely defined. Poets differ widely and interestingly with respect to the firmness and delicacy of the logical indications which assist us to such definition.

Poets also differ widely in the proportionate number of images of different formal types which their works exhibit; that is to say, differing purposes, subjects, and genres impel them quite decorously toward the use of more or fewer images of this or that logical structure. This should not prevent us from noticing that most poets use most kinds, and that their passage from one kind to another is accompanied by an undeniable and locatable difference in style. Only a very insensitive reader would lump together Marlowe's sea-nymphs and starry-firmament images with this one:

> Like as the sun in a diameter
> Fires and inflames objects removed far,
> And heateth kindly, shining lat'rally;
> So beauty sweetly quickens when 'tis nigh,
> But being separated and removed,
> Burns where it cherish'd, murders where it loved.
>
> (ii, 123)

This concerns Leander, is in Marlowe's own voice, and is a psychological explanation. Resembling the similitudes quoted earlier, in form, but used in exposition rather than in argument, it lacks the triumphant concluding term of the analogy used to argue; if Marlowe had so completed it (by implication or statement) and had used it as part of a speech by Leander persuading Hero to come save him from scorching, the tone of the image would have changed with the form. But Marlowe is not here interested to persuade by contending that if-x-and-y-are-true-then-z-must-follow; he goes impassively on to explain that this is how Leander's father knew where he had been, his look being the index to his heated mind.

This last image, like most which form part of an exposition of a state of mind rather than a mere description or indication of one, is built upon several logical bases simultaneously (it is a figure of difference using manner of doing, spatial relation, proportion or degree of relation, cause and effect, implied properties). Distinction-making figures must frequently exhibit such a character; Carew's do too. In 'Boldness in Love,' as he contrasts the courting of the amorous marigold by the 'bashful morn' and by the bold planet of the day, setting a failure over against a success, we are meant to see the whole as advice to the lover; every detail has its metaphorical counterpart, based on this or that predicament—the 'sighing blasts,' 'weeping rain,' the refusal to 'unfold,' the 'powerful ray,' making her 'receive / His warmer beams into her virgin leaves' (p. 59).

Marlowe did not write that portion of the story of Hero and Leander which has most need of the exposition of complicated states of mind, which delineates the tragic conflict when motives and events collide; that task fell to Chapman. In his powerful and swift-rising action, Marlowe found use for logically acute figures chiefly in Leander's persuasive speech. They are often sharp rather than complicated; even those based on the logical place *cause* (which can produce very tenuous and hair-splitting figures) are sometimes simple—

> Who builds a palace and rams up the gate,
> Shall see it ruinous and desolate. . . . .
>
> (i, 239)

When this leads to 'Lone women like to empty houses perish,' we are reminded that Marlowe is writing sophistic, as he himself said; it is adroit but specious, and readers are not meant to miss the rash weakness of these image-arguments, though many seem as untroubled by it as Hero. The very numerousness here of arguments which are similitude-images is a comment of Marlowe's to the reader: men doing wishful thinking forget the common warning of the schools—*omne simile claudicat.* Perhaps the most delightful example is Leander's wine-and-water argument for the superiority of marriage to virginity (i, 259)—

> Wild savages, that drink of running springs
> Think water far excels all earthly things:
> But they, that daily taste neat wine, despise it. . . . .

Some, of course, prize even virginity. But had Hero 'tried them both,' she would find that marriage

> Differs as much as wine and water doth.

As much as could scarcely be bettered, if one has a fondness for red herrings; and the difficulties of achieving a free choice after experimentation are left excellently vague. But the similitude is neatly found, and the cunning avoidance of an argument from common effect, the fake suggested cause in the opposition of primitive to sophisticated, the argument 'from privation' (how can a blind man judge color)—all these are as deliberate and as witty as in most images based on multiple logical parallels.

For I would suggest that an image based simultaneously on a number of predicaments or common places in logic has a particular character which is formally distinguishable, is naturally allied to certain types of function (often closely resembling those of dialectic), and is stylistically very striking. I would suggest that a 'metaphysical conceit' is just such an image, framed with especial subtlety. Indeed the formal defining element in any conceit, Elizabethan or medieval or Metaphysical, in any poet or in any language, seems to me to be this use of *multiple logical bases*, upon all of which the comparison obtains.

No strict lines can be drawn separating all conceits from all other figures, for they are entirely similar in manner of formation and find their origin in a similar psychological process. Moreover, a sort of compensation operates, by which a single but more tenuous logical link takes the place of two simpler logical relationships; the image embodying only one of the former will yet be the more logically complicated, and 'conceited.' This, too, is formally distinguishable.[6] Numerous and delicate differences in function cause equally numerous and delicate differences between the poetic effect of this conceit or that; minute formal variations are accompanied by very real stylistic differences.

In this section, however, I am not concerned to notice the factors which operate in this endless variety of interrelationships between function, form, and effect. But it is perhaps wise not to leave this bare explanation of the logical base of images without some exemplification from other poets, and it might be useful to test whether such a method of comparing images enables us to make some statements which are at least verifiable

[6] An image based on three simpler links, on *substance*, *quantity*, and *quality*, for example, will ordinarily be less 'conceited' than one based on *quality* and on the place *cause and effect*, which was commonly used to dispose concepts in an orderly manner. Later sections take up the 'places of Invention' as well as the other predicaments.

regarding the very different poetic effect of Chapman's continuation of Marlowe's poem. Although I do not believe that
differences in imagery are the major reason for this difference
in effect, probably everyone would agree that they contribute
to it. The question of what the differences are has received
more impressionistic comment—sometimes unfair—than careful analysis.

A fair number of Chapman's images would not surprise us if
we found them in Marlowe's portion. These are a few such:

> [a maid's state] without love is rude, disconsolate,
> And wants loves fire to make it milde and bright,
> Til when, maids are but Torches wanting light. (vi, 73)

> Love is a golden bubble full of dreames,
> That waking breakes, and fils us with extreames. (iii, 231)

> It [her garment] was as blew as the most freezing skies,
> Neere the Seas hew, for thence her Goddesse came: (iv, 35)

> Enioyes a beautie richer than the skie,
> Through whose white skin, softer then soundest sleep,
> With damaske eyes, the rubie blood doth peep,
> And runs in branches through her azure vaines. . . . . (iii, 38)

> Whose disposition silken is and kinde (iii, 45)

> [Leander, coming out of the sea, ran along the shore]
> Sprinkling the earth, that to their tombs tooke in
> Streames dead for love, to leave his ivorie skin, ...
> [and from their foam] did the first white Roses spring,
> (For love is sweet and faire in every thing)
> And all the sweetned shore as he did goe,
> Was crowned with odrous roses white as snow. (iii, 75)

There are three types of images here. The first two are *sententiae*
(I omit the signalizing by italics, a not uncommon practice); they
are concise and swift 'bare similitudes' based, like those I quoted
from Marlowe, on common properties, manner of doing, or
effect. The next three are amplifying images, partially descriptive in purpose, embodying comparisons and metaphors which
are sensuously or connotatively potent, but logically simple; as
we should expect, they are based on quality, or manner of doing.
The images in the last passage are little 'fictions' which allow

hyperbolical praises to be paid, as do Marlowe's fancies of the bees which return to Hero's breath, or the obsequious sun and wind. They fake a cause-and-effect in order to use the predicament 'quality' for special effects; they not only amplify but contribute generously to the setting of mood.

All these images accomplish purposes that are closely related to tasks which Marlowe also had to accomplish with his images, things which have to be done especially in the early portion of most narratives—they describe or amplify personages, establish tone or set a mood, realize a situation, point up the significance of an event, or indicate swiftly the author's attitude toward the action.

But I have not in every case given the whole of each image. The metaphor of maids as torches is part of a passage some fifty lines long which is smuggled in apropos of Hero's lighting of her torch to guide Leander. This flare is first used to light up the general proposition, 'What man does good, but he consumes thereby?' (vi, 61). Hero must needs make her torch of precious substances, she grieves to see it waste, would grieve more if it did not, since 'what made it nothing, gave it all the prize'; it is thus a 'true Glasse of our societie.' This is followed by a figure of difference which gives Chapman a chance to comment on how poor virtue is now but 'obscur'd, held low.' He proceeds to claim that 'When Bees makes waxe, Nature doth not intend / It shall be made a torch: but we that *know* / *The proper vertue* of it make it so, / And when t'is made we light it'; this last is the setting for the maids-as-torches metaphor. Even so each creature strives to make '*by her soule* the best of her free state'; *soule* and *proper vertue* are evidently set in relation.[7] The conclusion adds other twists to the argument, and the passage closes at line 89 with 'Her Torch and *Hero*, figure shew and vertue.'

I have not interrupted this paraphrase to indicate the logical

[7] The image is thus clearly removed from the category of Marlowe's used-vessels-shining-brighter (unloved maids being unlit torches) *by the addition of* certain further logical links, indicating (as always) conceptual additions. E.g.: formal 'cause' or 'vertue,' i.e., primary or essential capacity not quality or accident, final cause, manner of doing as well as receiving action.

positions which Chapman utilizes; it would take too long and introduce too many Elizabethan terms demanding explanation. It is obvious that these 'places' are numerous and varied, ranging in intellectual complexity from mere quality to double contrasted causes and effects; and the progression is swift. Chapman gives us expositions of certain elements in the state of mind of Hero; he also uses these as springboards (not always quite strong enough for a successful dive) to discuss more than one of the philosophical problems with which we know he was preoccupied. It would be an oversimplification to say 'the above image is typical of Chapman'; like other poets, he frames certain ones of his images so in certain literary situations.

I think that it would be just to say that he is fond of introducing an unexpected logical complication into an image. Sometimes this is because he is really pursuing a philosophical or psychological element in the situation which we had not realized was in it. But not always. In the omitted portion of the last passage of the group above, he adds to the description of the water flowing from Leander's limbs onto the shore the accurate observation that it leaves a snowy foam as it sinks rapidly in; but he also adds that this foam is 'As soule to the dead water that did love.' The notions (of the nature of souls and of bodies) upon which this comparison is based are complicated, and the formal cause of the image is abruptly changed by this addition. Chapman is free with intellectual gratuities; he does not always deny himself the luxury of giving them when the reader already has all he can spend. This is a large element in his obscurity.

I think that the logical structure of his images is evidence against the idea that Chapman framed his images as some modern poets do, deliberately giving them a base the logic of which is obscure even to the writer. Chapman's sometimes bear a superficial resemblance to such modern images, resembling them more, indeed, than do those of later Metaphysicals whose logic was sterner.[8] Chapman says of Hero, throwing herself on the

[8] In the second image of the quoted group, for example, I doubt if a poet of Donne's logical acuteness and hence linguistic tact would have allowed Love's golden bubble full of dreams to *wake*, break, and fill us with extremes, in quite so swiftly unbroken a progression. The visual image of *breaks*, being so exactly what actual bubbles primarily

bed where Leander had lain, 'And all this while the red sea of her blood / Ebd with *Leander*'—a striking but quite traditionally formed image. He continues, however, with a long passage investigating the exact nature of the conflict between her passion and understanding, of which I quote the beginning (iii, 323):

> And all her fleete of sprites came swelling in
> With childe of saile, and did hot fight begin
> With those severe conceits, she too much markt,
> And here *Leanders* beauties were imbarkt.
> He came in swimming painted all with ioyes,
> Such as might sweeten hell: his thought destroyes
> All her destroying thoughts: . . . .

With childe of saile is the only simple image here. And at first it looks as if Chapman meant this image to have the abrupt inconsequence of dream, and meant us to read it so—not sure whether the sea is her blood or her mind, not sure what form Leander has, of ship embarked in this embattled fleet, of man swimming the actual Hellespont, not sure whether he is a thought or a creature of sense. But this is probably just unadvised reading. Chapman expected from his readers an amount of information about Elizabethan notions of psychology considerably larger than the amount we possess. For a few of the conceptions which furnish the ground of this image and hence would allow us to understand it, we have only to turn to Chapman's uses of *spirit* in *Ovids Banquet of Sence*, stanzas 17–36. Hidden technicalities cause the obscurity—to us—of a fair number of Chapman's images. Others simply demand an alert reading, with full willingness to allow images to state abstract notions as dialectic does, precisely and acutely, inviting a generalized conclusion.

All these images, though some of them are 'Metaphysical,' seem to me quite as different as are Marlowe's from images in

---

do, makes our minds predicate the *waking* too of the literal rather than the figurative bubble; this prevents the meaning of the image from deepening and spreading. Unlike Chapman, Donne to my observation always makes seemingly illegitimate syntax serve the logic of his poem's meaning. When Chapman's images resist our thought, it is not because their nature is such as to incur an imaginative loss had he taken pains to think them really through; his loose ends would *gain* by articulation. Either of these poets would have more poetic sense than to turn this image into a 'clear' one the easy way— i.e., *waking*-a-man-in-love-breaks-the-golden-bubble-of-his-dreams.

modern poets writing under the influence of Symbolist poetic, and they seem to me to differ by formal definition. I shall exemplify merely with a few images from Yeats, confining myself to 'The Tower' (p. 224 [1926]).[9]

Yeats's poem begins and ends with images traditionally framed, serving a quite simple logical function.[10] The two tropes with which the poem ends are highly connotative. Now will he 'make his soul' (an Irish locution), compelling it to study till the wreck of body, the slow decay of blood

> Seem but the clouds of the sky
> When the horizon fades;
> Or a bird's sleepy cry
> Among the deepening shades.

As tropes must, these allow many reverberations of meaning (most readers habitually *ad lib.* from the predicament *quality*). But the logical base in which they probably had their spring and upon which readers can agree is that these are 'adjuncts' ('circumstances') of evening, the conventional metaphor *evening:end of life* being understood. The first image in the poem is one of those sharp, hard-edged, or logically single-barreled images whose use frequently gives incisiveness to Yeats's style—

> this absurdity . . . .
> Decrepit age that has been tied to me
> As to a dog's tail . . . .
> A sort of battered kettle at the heel.

The complication all lies in the reasons why he feels 'derided' by age; the image itself is based on the simple common *effect*, ridiculousness, and the parallel between *battered* and the transferred

---

[9] Eliot's *Waste Land* or *Ash Wednesday* might serve even better, except that there are fewer traditional images to point the contrast; and length of poems so complicates analysis that I have in general had to forego choosing images from these poems.

[10] Although one must admit that the repeated experience of discovering further significance for Yeats's *terms*, through his other works, makes one chary of claiming non-symbolic functions for any given image. This is simply an exaggeration of the ordinary difficulty which, as I have conceded, obtains for all images—we can never properly define the full meaning of an image to its creator. The exaggeration comes through the fact that Symbolist poetic sanctions the use of images as symbols whether or not there exists some prior agreement as to their meaning, in the cultural, religious, or social group. Such an agreement is merely an extreme form of the shared significancy of terms which all trope counts upon in some degree.

epithet or metonymy *decrepit* makes 'tied to me' melt immediately into place. All these, as I have said, are traditional images.

But that of the daws' nest in Section III seems to me differently formed. Yeats merely juxtaposes it beside his list of the learned Italian things, the Grecian stones, the poet's imaginings and the memories, out of which 'Man makes a superhuman / Mirror-resembling dream,' just as the twigs of the nest are dropped layer upon layer. This last is one of the logical indications which helps us, and as a likeness is clear enough; yet it leads us only dimly to the more obscure relation between man and

> The mother bird [who] will rest
> On their hollow top,
> And so warm her wild nest.

Most readers will play the mind over all the overt and suggested details of such an image, making their own logical connections between this wild nest and man's predicament in the world, between the whole passage and the previous declaration that man 'made up the whole, / Made lock, stock and barrel / Out of his bitter soul.' But few readers would dare claim that they surely read what Yeats surely wrote; more than that, these connections are seldom the same in two consecutive readings by the same reader. A great many connections are possible, and not any are surely indicated. Readers who may agree upon the bravery and the pity which underlie the passage may disagree violently as to whence these arise, and upon another reading it may seem to carry rather defiance and irony. The image will be differently read according as readers sympathize more or less with Yeats's conception of 'pride'—a conception which resembles in many ways what the Renaissance called *sprezzatura*, and which provides the beautiful series of images beginning 'Pride, like that of the morn, / When the headlong light is loose.' These images may be interpreted as logically simple *or* complicated, and there is no sure indication in the formal cause of any of this group of tropes to insure our giving them Yeats's own reading.

Similar comments could be made upon the symbolic images of moonlight and daylight which culminate in 'O may the moon and sunlight seem / One inextricable beam, / For if I triumph I must make men mad.' Here, of course, we can make use of the aid of Yeats's *The Vision*, and his 'phases' of sun and moon have been better explained than I could do here.[11] But another difficulty not characteristic of traditional use of symbols appears: we do not know and cannot tell when the terms are *not* meant as symbols; for example, I do not know any way of telling whether or not Yeats meant me to take all the further meanings of primary and antithetical, etc., in a use of the declining light of day four stanzas earlier.[12] Certainly, at any rate, the final effect of the image-technique when we read the poem as a whole is such that we come away feeling that there is but one image which is surely and entirely simple—the 'Tree, like a sooty finger,' starting from the earth. It is worth mentioning that this image occurs in precisely the same form in *The Wanderings of Oisin* (i.e., *in 1889*; p. 330).

These differences in the formal nature of modern images are not adventitious, nor are they to be carelessly attributed to an unhappy confusion of mind, or a lack of logical training, or a pigheaded refusal to be 'clear,' on the part of modern poets. There has been a real development in conceptions of the function of images in poetry, and a real departure from traditional conceptions. To examine these developments is not a proper part of my subject, certainly not here. I am not sure that it can be done as yet. The structure and functions of images as Elizabethans and Jacobeans saw them are suited to notions of

[11] The most forthright, and the most illuminating, treatment that I know is that by Cleanth Brooks in chap. viii of *Modern Poetry and the Tradition* (Chapel Hill, 1939).

[12] Or in the shadowed close of the poem, traditionally 'clear' though it be. So, too, in the several short 'fictions,' of Mrs. French, Red Hanrahan, the peasant girl celebrated in the song, we cannot but feel a further purpose than Yeats indicates—that he would question all, come who can. The imagery of descriptive detail which they embrace is strictly similar in type to that which orthodox earlier writers use in schemes with the function Yeats indicates (e.g., the *clarté* of exact detail in the 'little covered dish' in which the ears were brought, the sconces lighting up the dark mahogany, the amplifying praise 'by effect' in the farmers jostling at the fair, etc.). An Elizabethan who meant us to see these as *allegoria* or 'continued metaphor' would have seen to it that we did so.

the mind-processes as the faculty psychology conceived of them; when modern psychology has provided us with terms and methods of description as clear and as universally accepted as those developed during the centuries between Aristotle and Sir John Davies, we may be able to delineate as clearly the formal and final causes of modern images. The old categories do not suffice to distinguish and describe new elements in the structure and functioning of imagery which result from modern attempts to bring nonrational levels of consciousness into poems through images. These levels 'got into poetry,' and that long before the Elizabethan period. But the deliberate use of images with that primary function is a different thing.

2. *The Relation of Image-Functions to Formal Character*

It has not been possible to discuss logical base as the defining element of an image without touching also on logical functions. These are two separate matters, however. Or rather, though not separable in composition, they are separate for criticism. For only the analyzing critic need be deliberately conscious of the first; indeed, it is frequently only after some examination that we realize that an image has been found from such and such predicaments and places of logic. Like many other subtle motions of the mind, the effects can be sure, though the process is not realized either by the originator or by the receiver. But of the second matter—the logical functioning of images in a whole unit—every comprehending reader is conscious. We tend to think that we 'respond to' images without 'thinking' about them. I am not sure that this is true; yet, of course, taking part in the process is the important thing, not labeling it. At any rate, however, the moment we enter upon the critical activities of comparison and evaluation, it is well to be as precise as possible about relations between the nature and the function of images.

All subtle and probing comment upon the exact logical function which an author may have intended an image to serve must be set in the historical framework of the logical training and habits of his day. Before we embark on that, it might be

wise to give a swift review of the variety of logical functions
served in a single poem, so as to demonstrate the ease and
unself-consciousness with which images obey the shifting winds
of those numerous tiny purposes exhibited during the progress
of any piece of communication. This is a kind of inner decorum
maintained by images, of which neither writer nor reader is entirely conscious. It is not studiously planned, or generally
applauded. It happens. Time and quotations will be saved if
we watch this process in the first sestiad of Marlowe's poem.

The intentions distinguished above—to re-create situations,
to argue a position or note a distinction, to move to acceptance
of a hyperbolical value placed upon something—are only a few
of those which Marlowe necessarily shows in so long a poem. As
he moves from these to others and back again, the images shift
and change in method, terms, and tone with an almost uncanny
sureness. To go through the poem is to see the images range in
character from ornate to homely, from simple to complex, from
a sensuousness almost like direct experience to the dryness of
dialectic. This is not at all extraordinary. The range of Drayton's imagery, for example, is much wider; the reasons for this
lie outside the strict limits of the problem of imagery as such.

One perhaps thinks of Marlowe as willing to lavish words
upon physical description. Actually the fact that he is not writing in the allegorical mode (like Spenser) releases him from this
necessity, and most of his description turns out to be amplification—hence its exuberant quality. To the first placing of his tale
he gives but one image.[13] The group of details descriptive of
Hero's clothing helps to set the tone of opulent splendor: her
garments of lawn, the purple silk lining with gilt stars drawn,
the border pictured with Venus and Adonis (here amplification
enters), the buskins with their sparrows (doubtless symbolically
amorous, like ivy). One notes that the method is the simplest

---

[13] 'Two cities . . . . Sea-borderers, disjoin'd by Neptune's might' (i, 2). I do not
think that this is an ironic reference to the outcome of his plot; were this allegory, it
would be. Images are commented upon in order as they occur in the first sestiad; hence
I shall give line numbers only when I skip to passages at some distance from each other.
That some of Marlowe's images show the influence of images he had read elsewhere
(see Martin's notes) does not affect the points made here or earlier.

enumeration of detail. The moment a further purpose obtrudes —to persuade us of Hero's amazing loveliness—the concrete recedes, the images demand a response which calls on the judging faculty. In terms of sensuous experience, a kirtle stained 'with the blood of wretched lovers' would be, we must grant, an unattractive garment; to the senses, the blood of lovers is singularly like the blood of slain lawyers or slain grocerymen. But not to the judging intelligence, which ranges those unfortunate witnesses to Hero's or Love's power with the others—Apollo, Cupid, the bees. This is rhetorical rather than dialectical persuasion, but any shadow of a more strictly conceptual function will bring with it images whose 'logic' can be formally distinguished. Trope is not needed as yet; and the logical means of the amplification is that used by any reporter of a large fire or a campaign speech: effect upon the bystanders.

There is no occult reason why the bees, the sun and wind, nature herself, are personified to bear witness thus; Marlowe has simply chosen less easily convinced witnesses, as is proper to hyperbole. Every day shows us ill-judging men enslaved to women of most indifferent beauty, but few ladies are so sweet of breath that they make conquest even of bees, expert in honey. These are the animistic figures of which H. W. Wells makes mention in his discussion of 'The Exuberant Image,'[14] so many examples of which he takes from Marlowe. I do not think we shall find Marlowe using them when his purpose shifts away from hyperbolical praise or dispraise—and this is the purpose for which all poets use them. The images in this general

[14] These figures show the first type of 'animism' discussed on p. 200 (*Poetic Imagery* [New York, 1924]). Figures entirely comparable in form, and only differing in acceptability, are discussed as 'Decorative' images on p. 47, and as 'Violent Images or Fustian' on p. 106; this is a demonstration of the difficulties involved when the criteria used to define the nature of images regard chiefly the effect of their terms upon a (necessarily single) reader.

All these supposedly differing images have similar purposes and are similarly framed. Our judgment of their artistic fitness does depend on whether the things they magnify seem to us (in the context) *over*praised or *over*condemned by such images, and there is nothing gained by evading this facet of the fundamental subjectivity of criticism. But neither is anything gained by obtruding it into our very classifications. The supposedly useless distinctions *in form* for which the 'pedantic' rhetoricians are so ridiculed allow in the end of far subtler discrimination between aesthetic effects.

class will differ in tone precisely to the extent that some purpose
beyond that of simple praise enters to complicate them, as in

> . . . . Nature wept, thinking she was undone,
> Because she took more from her than she left,
> And of such wondrous beauty her bereft:
> Therefore, in sign her treasure suffer'd wrack,
> Since Hero's time hath half the world been black.

This, like the *description* of Cupid's behavior when he mistook
Hero for Venus, is in praise of Hero's beauty; but here the purpose of *explaining* Nature's behavior brings in a further logical
complication, and we have the effect (Negroes) of an effect
(resentment at her treasure's wrack) of the effect of Hero's
beauty (it robbed her treasure).[15]

Nevertheless, these are still just examples of the small rhetorical *fictio* used to praise. Being so, they are bound to differ in
structure and thence in tone from some image about the
Goddess Natura in Spenser's Mutability cantos—where he
would need a trope or *allegoria* stating part of a philosophical
argument, or from some astronomical image in one of Donne's
deliberative lyrics—where the moon in her sphere (cf. Cynthia
in the note below) would be a dialectical counter in a war of
wits.

The images which impress us with Leander's beauty are similarly constructed and similar in tone.[16] Then comes a passage,
the description of Venus' temple, in which the images approach
the very nearly nonlogical functions of a rhetorical *descriptio*.
Accordingly, their terms are at first richly sensuous, coming as
close as Elizabethan writers come to sensuous precision (the
terms are still amplifications). As Marlowe approaches the first
small climax in his narrative—Leander's falling in love at first

---

[15] Any other image which not only praises but explains will show similar developments; the concision of expository writing sharpens this image, written of Leander:
'Fair Cynthia wish'd his arms might be her sphere; / Grief makes her pale, because she
moves not there.'

[16] A similar series of hyperbolical imagined effects brings in a similar series of witnesses to his beauty's potency—wild Hippolytus, the barbarous Thracian soldier.
Marlowe is still occupied with fairly simple narrative tasks, and the only image approaching witty concision is the comparison of Hero's victims to the soldiers in a battle,
which he uses to sum up the whole dramatic situation with some rapidity. General
terms, balanced clauses, and an epigram result.

sight—the images take on a further function; they begin to show in their form the character of images used to set a special emotional pitch. This shift is not necessarily highly deliberate; if it were, perhaps it would not show up with such consistency in so many authors of different eras and habits of mind. The heavy, full series of the voluptuous encounters of the gods (i, 143–56) has an effect chiefly upon mood, blotting out other aspects of reality with a recurrent drumbeat of amorousness, much as a tone-poem swathes hearers in a single mood. For the swiftly connotative allusions serve a function frequently served by images in modern poetry, approximating the effect of insistently repeated motifs in certain types of music (usually program music). It will be noticed, however, that the Elizabethan poet feels it necessary to give them an intelligible place in the narrative structure; they are in form simply an actual part of the setting for an action and, as such, were a recognized part of current theory for narrative, part of the duty of an author achieving an 'imitation' that should point up the full significance of what was about to happen. Lyrical poetry of the period uses such images far less.

By virtue of their intent, all these images share certain characteristics: indefiniteness of outline ('such towns' as Troy), combined with a sort of flash-picture technique (Danae's *brazen* tower, Jove *slyly* stealing, bellowing for Europa, tumbling with the rainbow in a cloud); the use of literal language; the dependence upon epithet (blood-quaffing Mars, limping Vulcan); the use of insinuating effects of sound to increase the image-bearing quality of the words. Logically they are extremely simple; 'quality' and 'manner of doing' are noted but are not used here to form even simple tropes. A masterly example of an image also functioning to objectify the significance of a narrative situation is that used at the moment when 'dumb signs their yielding hearts entangled':

> The air with sparks of living fire was spangled;
> And Night, deep-drench'd in misty Acheron,
> Heav'd up her head, and half the world upon
> Breath'd darkness forth (dark night is Cupid's day).
>
> (i, 188; labeled 'A periphrasis of night')

When Leander begins to 'display Love's holy fire' with words
and sighs, the conventional nature of the metaphor enables us
to apprehend it almost by a reflex action of the mind, and we do
not pause to decide whether the air was spangled with the last
red flecks of the sun or with these metaphorical equivalents. His
fiery words enter Hero's ears 'like sweet music'; but this is
simple comparison—both so enter. This dramatic moment is no
time for Marlowe to halt us with a metaphysical conceit turning
love's fire into music that breaks the silent dark; if this were a
Donnean discourse upon the nature of the passion of love, he
might have done so. It could be done with no change whatsoever in the terms of the image—merely by the addition of a
group of complicating logical links.

Only once so far has Marlowe broken off to elucidate or comment directly upon the action. His reason was the logical one of
forestalling an objection that would destroy the credibility of
his story; and the images which accomplish this are totally different in character. He is supporting what we must here believe,
that, though no man knows the reason, what we behold is
censured by our eyes, that none ever loved who loved not at
first sight. His analogies are brief, the sensuous element is unimportant, the patness of the logical connections furnishes the
pleasure:

> When two are stript, long ere the course begin,
> We wish that one should lose, the other win;
> And one especially do we affect
> Of two gold ingots, like in each respect.
>
> (i, 169)

The logic is obvious, not subtle, but the comparison holds in at
least three points, and the tone of this whole passage, functioning to convince, differs sharply from the tone of surrounding
passages.

When Leander leaves off sighs and tears to try his luck with
bold argument, not one but all of the images which crowd his
hundred lines differ markedly from any and all of the images so
far, with the sole exception of these last-quoted argumentative
images. The impact is like that of a sudden drenching; nor is

this any haphazard shower, for the stream is controlled, purposeful, and accurately aimed. It is directed straight at Hero's judgment, and the images are all different in the same way. They are curt, acute, denuded of sensuous appeal; they demand and get intellectual participation from the reader, their chief stylistic quality concision, their chief effect a delight in appropriate arguments wittily put—and just sufficiently unsound. The reason for this abrupt turn in image-technique[17] lies in Marlowe's own summary of Leander's speeches, 'These *arguments* he us'd, and many more' (i, 329). When images have the dialectical function of convincing us of the reasonableness of a position, they take on the usual characteristics of writing in that discipline.

Images can assist such an endeavor in a good many ways; Marlowe's are not so varied as some more accomplished logician's might be—Sidney's, or Donne's. A number of them take the form of an implied syllogism. Another group argues by making a distinction; the force of an argument 'from difference' lies, of course, in the fact that a dissimilarity in one logical 'place' holds *within* similarities in other predicaments. So in the contrast between Hero's sin of frugality and that of the rich man who starves himself to save his treasure (i, 247); his gold remains and can be bequeathed, but her virginity, a fair gem

> . . . . sweet in the loss alone,
> When you fleet hence, can be bequeath'd to none.

Another group of figures may be loosely classified as what Puttenham calls 'the Reason rendrer or the Tell cause.' These may vary in logical complexity.[18] Still others assist in a process of definition, the language frequently becoming so abstract that what perhaps began as an image develops into a statement in

---

[17] It would not be wise to account for it by concluding that Marlowe sat one day to his desk in a different humor, unless we conclude also that he changed it just long enough to interpolate the tears-as-liquid-pearl image which separates two parts of Leander's speech, or to write into Hero's answer the enchanted suggestions which are evoked by her famous description of her turret.

[18] 'The richest corn dies, if it be not reapt' uses one more logical place, and is correspondingly sharper, than 'Be not unkind and fair; misshapen stuff / Are of behaviour boisterous and rough' (i, 203; cf. 327). For this figure, *aetiologia*, see Puttenham, III, xix, p. 228.

purely conceptual terms—for example, Leander's defining the
'idol' of Virginity as no thing, according to regular places used
in definition.[19] Images which elucidate or clarify, those which assist for instance in an exposition of the precise nature of a state
of mind, share some but not necessarily all of the characteristics
of images which argue. As in this (i, 361):

> And, like a planet moving several ways
> At one self instant, she poor soul assays,
> Loving, not to love at all, and every part
> Strove to resist the motions of her heart.

It is obvious that images which function thus will frequently
be 'dissonant,' 'radical,' or 'conical'; their terms are chosen on
different grounds from those of amplifying images, and a relation between vehicle and tenor frequently holds by but one
subtle and tenuous link. A reader is likely to be more conscious
of the more complicated logical processes involved, so that he is
likely to term such images 'intellectual' and to note more readily their clearly 'functional' character. They frequently show
interrelation between concepts, utilize general notions or abstractions rather than objects. Since this is sophistical argument, large mountains of concepts are often used to bring forth
small mice of conclusions with witty effect—as in 'As heaven
preserves all things, so save thou one' (i.e., save *me;* i, 224). The
fact that syntax is affected by the simplicity or complexity of
the formal cause of an image plays in with other factors to give
a markedly different tone to poems or passages which use such
images generously. They make frequent use of *sententia,* of
paradox, of witty turns, of 'points,' of puns, of double meanings.
The last is exemplified in Leander's argument against hoarding
'treasure,' ostensibly applied only to the kind which misers keep
too jealously:

> . . . . being put to loan,
> In time it will return us two for one.

> (i, 235)

[19] Substance, qualities, place where, material cause, formal cause. 'This idol which
you term Virginity, / Is neither essence subject to the eye, / No, nor to any one exterior
sense, / Nor hath it any place of residence, / Nor is't of earth or mould celestial, / Or
capable of any form at all . . . . Things that are not at all are never lost' (i, 269).

As is quite usual in images with such functions, terms are home-ly; the possibly ironic effect of dissonant connotations is often disregarded. Unlike meiosis, which uses homely terms with malice aforethought, the unrelated aspects of the terms are far more nearly indifferent to the effect of the figure than in any other type of image.

All these characteristics are characteristics generally at-tributed to images favored by the Metaphysical poets. I would suggest that they characterize the imagery of any poet whose poetic purposes put him in need of images which serve func-tions of the sort just described. If 'epoch' and 'personality' are factors, then they are factors in that they affect the types of subject and intention which poets choose. Genre is certainly a factor. We could not expect to find in Marlowe's 'high' narrative so large a variety of logical functions of the subtlest kind as we might find in shorter forms whose different purposes led to different applications of the principle of decorum. Other forms would not have room, for example, for the hundred-line *aetiologia* in the form of a fable, which concludes the sestiad— Marlowe's explanation of the reasons why Cupid's suit no better sped, when he hied him to the Destinies to plead for these lovers' success. I do not analyze its figures; although there are some interesting differences in tone, not a great deal would be added to this rapid survey of the way in which function operates to govern the formal nature and hence the stylistic character of images.

CHAPTER XI

RENAISSANCE LOGIC AND THE FRAMING
OF RENAISSANCE IMAGES

THE universality and importance of logical training in the Renaissance has been made clear by recent studies.[1] No modern way of training the mind is comparable to this training, either for universal diffusion in educational systems over the various areas of the Western world, and length of time spent, or for stubborn adherence to a time-honored body of content and method. It was a training which touched the poet as educated man, rather than the poet as learned man, in an era in which many poets were the second, and practically all were the first. During many years of school and university study, and even in its most technical aspects as an art, logic was the concern not of specialized students but of all students; familiarity with its terms and its methods of arranging concepts was shared by the poet with all the more important members of the group of readers he most tried to please. Nor was logic the temporary concern of a few student years, nor had it been dropped behind as academic baggage by men of affairs. As with rhetoric, its prestige as a tool in governing and persuading men—especially in those areas of religious and political thought wherein lay the dearest objects of so many Elizabethans—was still unquestioned. The Ramistic reorganization of logic, far from questioning this prestige, enormously strengthened it. During the late

[1] Proper documentation of this point would simply result in a bibliography of Renaissance education; instead I refer to the long and excellent one by Adamson in the *Cambridge Bibliography*, I, 364-80. Ample specific support for generalizations regarding the Renaissance veneration of logic has been provided through work done on school and university curricula and textbooks, by Leach, Foster Watson, Mullinger, and others during the last half-century, and recently especially by T. W. Baldwin (see below, Appendix, Note B). Good short statements regarding the Ramistic strengthening of logic's position are in Hardin Craig, *The Enchanted Glass* (New York, 1936), chap. vi; Baldwin, chap. xxxi; Perry Miller, *The New England Mind: The Seventeenth Century* (New York, 1939), chap. v.

sixteenth and early seventeenth centuries, this new organization reshaped the peripatetic logic in which men had been
trained generation after generation, and changed the look of
logic textbooks. But this only served to make logical method a
burning question during the period we are examining. The
volume and the bitterness of the controversies raised by Ramus'
reorganization are evidence of the widespread concern and the
crucial importance which educated men assigned to problems
touching this basic discipline of thought. One English poet
after another—Sidney, Marlowe, Milton—has left clear evidence of his individual concern with the problems so raised.

This is not merely because Renaissance poets were men of
catholic intellectual interests, and hence able and ready like
Shakespeare to turn logical terms to humorous uses, or like
Lord Herbert to call attention to the precise logical base of an
image being used. There is a more profound reason, important
to the historical study of poetics, why poets of this era concerned themselves with technical developments in the discipline
of logic and took knowledge of it for granted in their readers.

The three learnings of rhetoric, poetry, and logic, far from
being considered enemies, were still so interlocked on the basis
of certain common aims that all of them were still thought to
be the concern of a proponent of any one of the three. The relations of poetry with rhetoric have been demonstrated at some
length. The accepted interdependence of rhetoric and logic is
clear in book after book.[2] The connections of poetry with logic,
though less apparent, held with equal firmness and unself-
consciousness. The subtlest methods of dialectic were not denied to poetry as an art of persuasion if the latter's own peculiar
conditions could also be met. But poetry was chiefly considered
to be 'grounded in' logic in that it was thought of as reasonable

---

[2] In, for example (to keep roughly to the period), Fabri (1521); Cox (1524)
(dependent on Melanchthon [1521]); both of Wilson's handbooks (on logic and on rhetoric) (1551, 1553); Rainolde (1563); Fenner (1584); Sherry's two manuals (1550, 1555);
Peacham's two (1577, 1593). The connection between the three learnings is drawn yet
more closely in all Ramist books and in all rhetorics influenced by Ramus' disciple,
Talaeus. The question of relations between the disciplines in the Renaissance, of
course, cannot be separated from the same question as medieval thinkers discussed it
(see R. McKeon, 'Rhetoric in the Middle Ages,' *Speculum*, XVII [1942], 1–32).

discourse, arranging thought in an orderly manner. The laws of logic were the laws of thought, and the poet must know and use them; he will not otherwise be able to approach truth or direct the mind of man toward it. This last appears to me to be the basic Renaissance understanding of the didactic function of poetry. In that it was thought to affect the minds of men through the judging intelligence, poetry resembled these other similarly directed disciplines;[3] in that some of its methods and approaches differed from theirs it is frequently differentiated from them in Renaissance criticism.

For poetry is certainly not thought of as a part of the discipline of logic, nor as subordinated to it, nor as identical with it in method. The methods overlap because all three disciplines have some part in the final aim of the communication of truth from one human mind to another; hence, the freedom with which poetry may combine methods developed in the other two disciplines, with its own, is complete. But differences between poet and logician are, of course, indicated, and admired. The chief strengths and special procedures of poetry are differentiated from those of logic; but the first was no less concerned to speak to men's rational faculties than the second, and we find no trace in the different learnings of differing conceptions of how the mind is made, or of differing conceptions of its relations to the rest of the total personality. Poetry's share in the common aim of establishing an active relation between the whole man and the living truth is accepted not with rebellion but with enthusiasm, is considered not as a restriction upon poetry but as an enhancement of its dignity.

In sum, such interrelationships and general conceptions could not but affect the practice of poets. One route by which this background of ideas came to affect poetic imagery is especially related to the actual logical training which poets of the period received. A large number of the processes taught in the study of logic naturally produce images. Since there were no bars hin-

[3] Such statements as these are dangerously liable to oversimplified interpretation, since all the words available for making them have undergone subtle changes in import as a result of developments and quarrels during the three centuries since the Renaissance. All these matters are treated with more care in chap. xiv.

dering close co-operation between the two learnings, habits formed in the years of practice given to these processes also came to characterize the framing of poetic images, when poets moved from the province of logic to that of poetic. The fact that many of these procedures were taught or consciously employed in rhetoric must also be kept in mind. I think that Renaissance poets were more conscious than are we of the exact nature of the logical processes they utilized in their poems. However, the specific relation with images is chiefly a matter of the transference of habitual modes of thought which had been engrained by years of familiarity, of practice, of analysis. The best way to show how this would work in practice is to consider here the major divisions of logic as it was taught to sixteenth- and seventeenth-century writers, attending almost entirely to those processes which naturally produce images. I shall illustrate all important processes, in which students were given much practice, with images from poems of the period, choosing images which precisely resemble those we should frame were we simply trying to demonstrate the processes of thought taught in an ordinary study of logic.[4]

1. *The Predicaments as Springs of Imagery*

If one were an ordinary educated person in the Renaissance, one was taught from adolescence that the first step in disciplined thinking was to know what a thing is by reference to or application of the ten Aristotelian categories or predicaments. According to Wilson's popular handbook, *The Rule of Reason*,[5]

[4] Differences in emphasis and attitude which were to occur as Ramistic ideas penetrated the teaching (or individual study) of logic in England will be regarded. I start out by using peripatetic logic as a groundwork, since this process of penetration took some time, since even the student taught by a thoroughgoing Ramist could not avoid learning much of what I shall use in his study of rhetoric, and since Ramistic teaching did not go in a different direction but rather got into the same vehicle and went farther in a shorter time.

[5] The texts from which I shall quote may be found in the Bibliography. I quote English rather than Latin handbooks for convenience. No special importance attaches to the 'author' of a quotation; I follow them in their similarities and not in their differences. The latter are few and unimportant. Similarly, date of text quoted almost never affects points being illustrated; when I give dates, as pegs to hold the discussion

these 'name the very Nature of thynges,' declaring 'what thei are in very deede' (fol. 8ʳ). Blundeville's manual, also popular (1599, and later editions), refers 'all things that be in the world' to definition according to these categories; Du Moulin (trans. De-Lawne [1624]) says that there is nothing 'done either by Nature, or by Art, by Councell or Chance' which may not be referred to these categories.⁶ The predicaments as usually listed are: substance, quantity, quality, relation, manner of doing, manner of suffering, when, where, *situs*, and *habitus*. The familiar list occurs in the first few pages of any orthodox Renaissance logic;⁷ some writers devote a chapter to each, giving numerous examples.

Such examples are, of course, frequently simply images; for it is clear that 'thinking from' certain ones of the predicaments will immediately produce images—as the reader will notice if he attempts, for example, to consider anything he chooses from the viewpoint of its qualities or of its manner of action. The practice which students were given in defining or characterizing things on the basis of the predicaments, or in analyzing or noting how other writers had done so, thus turned out to be practice in the framing of images or in noticing the process by which others had framed them. One may frame images without realizing the na-

---

in a chronological frame, it has seemed sensible to give the date of first appearance. Wilson's handbook, for example, came out in 1551 and had several later editions and reprintings; of many which I have seen, I quote from that of 1580. Blundeville's handbook (1599; I cite the more accessible 1619) was popular enough so that the *Epistola Dedicatoria* to Granger's treatise of 1620 claims 'That heer's all Blundevile, and somewhat more.' The fact that Ramist influence crept into manuals early in the century has been regarded in any generalizations made.

⁶ P. 5. Evans notes a frequently mentioned commodity of the predicaments, that they enable one not to confound substance with accidents; Lever (p. 47 [1573]) notes another, that they serve to amplify and set forth a matter at large.

⁷ The most immediately noticeable difference in a Ramist text is the absence of this list of categories at the beginning of the discussion, since Ramus rather taught them in connection with the framing of arguments from the various places. Hence when the Ramist *uses* the predicaments, adducing examples which we should term images, these are complicated by the simultaneous use of more logical processes than this simplest one. I should hesitate to press this more complicated kind of training (producing more complicated images) as a primary causal factor in the decreasing use of simpler images; too many other factors were operating (such as genre, subjects favored). I should yet be surprised if there were no connection whatsoever between these parallel trends in training and in poetic habits and taste.

ture of this logical process; but the Renaissance student was forced to be conscious of it and to do a good deal of it.

Like all good peripatetics, Wilson tells the student that if he would know the 'proper nature' of anything, he 'must needes have these Predicamentes ready, that . . . . [he] maie come to this store house, and take stuffe at will'; if you would know what virtue is, what is the nature of a father, think with the help of this and that category. The stage of composition at which they are helpful, in other words, is that of Invention. The process in which they assist a thinker and writer is that of penetrating into the reaches of his subject, and images that occur to him as that process goes on are part of 'the invention of his matter.' A well-invented figure did not only mean an ingenious or intellectually cunning figure; it meant a suitable and penetrating figure, one which went to the heart of the true nature of the matter.

The number of images in English poetry whose function is to assist in 'finding' the true nature of something is quite incalculable. Not all of them result from this simple process of playing the mind about something by considering it in various predicaments; this is only one step in uncovering the exact nature of something. But it is the only step which a great many images take, especially those which we find in descriptive detail not using trope. *Quality* is, of course, by far the most fruitful spring of images which assist in getting at the nature of something; *manner of doing* runs it a close second. An epithet is nothing but the 'applying' of the predicament *quality;* if the epithet is metaphorical, the author of the image has seen two things as comparable on the basis of *quality.* In fact, the majority of images using trope would be covered formally by the definition: two things seen to be in parallel predicaments or 'places.' Multiple parallels in predicaments or places result in more and more complicated images.

It should be mentioned at once that the fact that an image is based upon one or more of the predicaments does not determine the *terms* of the image; it does have a marked effect upon the basic structure of that image, and it acts as a limitation upon the nature of the terms chosen. This has poetic consequences to which I shall return; my concern here is simply to demonstrate what seems to me a fact—that training year after year in certain processes of thinking which naturally produce images could not but affect a poet's conscious attempts to frame images effectively in other types of composing as well. Such training could not but make a writer both more conscious of the structural nature of his images and more purposeful in the use of them for particular functions.

If one has given considerable time to exercises using the predicament *quantity*, and to inventing comparisons based on numerousness or size—the giant's staff was great as a Norway pine, his reasons were as plentiful as beggars, as blackberries—then one is not likely to be unaware that an image can accomplish precisely this function, and to select one's terms accordingly. Or, rather, one is likely to pare down or phrase one's image accordingly, or to select on this basis between two that spring to mind. When Sir John Davies says that the castle of Penelope shone with a thousand lamps, that 'Not *Iove's* blew tent . . . . Is seene to sparkle with more twinckling fires' (*Orch.*, st. 8), he is not likely to include in his image some epithet designed to reproduce for us the precise effect of a star upon a beholder. And if he decides against his stars-image for some reason, he is likely to fall upon the grasses of the field or the sands of the sea or something equally commonly thought of as innumerable. Certain reproaches cast upon images because they do not possess this or that quality—sensuous richness, or surprise, or complexity—would obviously have to be withheld if we as critics confined our animadversions to how such an image served its purpose as an image of quantity. It is to be *expected* that Daniel makes no attempt to introduce subtle figures conveying precisely how he felt when he sighed, if he is occupied in telling Delia that he has cast the accounts of all his care, summed up his sighs, totaled up the 'deere expences' of his youth, and decided to 'crosse' his cares ere greater sums arise (sonnet i).

The predicament *quantity* requires so simple an act of relating that it rarely occurs alone in poetic imagery. The pursuit through various ramifications of an argument or image so invented results often in witty conceit, perhaps because it introduces a kind of fanciful arithmetic into matters usually thought of as not quantitative. Lord Herbert in his 'Ditty,' 'If you refuse me once,' builds three stanzas (4–6) on requests for 'so much love' as will make the lovers blind to all but the light of their own fires, so much 'that we may move / Like starrs of love, / And glad and happy times to Lovers bring,' and so on.[8] Spenser pursues through various logical refinements the two-to-one odds under which Britomart and Scudamour suffered when set upon by four knights; the important part of the image is not the difference in numbers which caused it to be invented but the usurer-figure based on similar *action*, similar *effect*, and *final cause:*

> Foure charged two, and two surcharged one;
> Yet did those two themselves so bravely beare,
> That the other litle gained by the lone,
> But with their owne repayed duely weare,
> And usury withall: such gaine was gotten deare.

(IV, ix, 30)

The joke in the author's ironical comment is based on the fact that the four knights mixed their final causes; the end of usurious transactions is gain—they got it.

A student looking for applications of the predicament *substance* would also turn up a good many images. Unless they were very simple *descriptio* or lyrical 'amplifications,' he would generally find that they also illustrated the use of other predicaments and places. *Relation* is often a take-off for further developments in an image; even cliché uses of it are dear to writers of the whole period. Perhaps the concision of figures based on relation was pleasing; Daniel need only call himself 'Th' Orphan of fortune' (*Delia*, xxiii), Sidney in 'Invention Natures

---

[8] It will be noted that Daniel's image serves but to elaborate upon one aspect of his passion, its expensiveness; Herbert's argues for an action on certain grounds. He argues from *cause* to effect, using also *quality* (love:fire; fire:light) and the *relation* of mover to moved. These are not the three stanzas attributed to Suckling (see Moore Smith's notes to p. 31 of his edition).

childe, fledde Stepdames studies blowes' can convey several notions about a mental situation through a figure of difference based on contrasted relations (*A. and S.*, i).[9]

Readers well schooled in illustrating or in watching for uses of the predicaments were quite aware that metaphors or other figures were not 'mixed' as long as all were found from the same position, however some irrelevant connotations might clash. Sidney, addressing his ruler Vertue, can pursue the relation between governor and governed through a string of figures using scepters and 'olde Catoes,' enthronement in church and school, and can end up 'My mouth too tender is for thy hard bit' (*A. and S.*, iv). On the other hand, real logical inconsistencies within figures are infrequent—the kind of thing which provokes us, for example, when in Wordsworth's *Ode* we seem forced to make the relationship of master to slave include brooding like the day over one's varlet. Elizabethan images stand up to severe logical examination; both writers and readers were trained to it.

Far and away the most important of the predicaments in exercising the imaging faculty is that of *quality*.

Its importance is generally remarked upon both by rhetoricians and by logicians in treating the 'similitude.' The poet borrows this tool of logic when he needs it; he also uses similitudes for less strictly ratiocinative ends. Even as rhetorician, Wilson is quite conscious of these other effects; having defined a similitude as 'a likenesse when two thinges, or moe then two, are so compared and resembled together, that they both *in some one propertie* seeme like,' he goes on to show its usefulness 'to beautifie [a matter], to delite the hearers, to make the matter plaine, and to shewe a certaine maiestie.'[10] He concludes by refer-

[9] Sir John Davies makes a distinction by a figure of the same form; he tells us we 'thinke amis' if we think Time and Dancing both one, 'But if you iudge them twins, together got, / And Time first borne, your iudgement erreth not' (*Orch.*, st. 23). Figures introducing various particulars of the relation between king and subjects, conqueror and conquered, or even longer examples of the favored father-mother-brother figures, are likely to be thought of as exemplifying primarily the logical process of 'distribution by adjuncts' or circumstances (see below, sec. 3).

[10] *Arte of Rhetorique*, pp. 188–90 of the reprint of the 1560 edition, considerably altered from that of 1553. I shall distinguish my few quotations from *The Arte* by appending abbreviated title, since I refer fairly frequently to 'Wilson' as author of his logic, *The Rule of Reason*.

ring the reader to his treatment of the similitude in his book on logic. The fact that the 'pleasantness' and usefulness of the similitude was recognized in all three disciplines served to increase the consciously functional use of it by poets. Poetic similitudes are not in practice confined to agreements in quality or property. The poet also uses the predicament *quality* in framing very many other types of images.

If we wish proof that poets were conscious of this logical process, we may find it in their own words. Lord Herbert writes a short poem 'In a Glass-Window for Inconstancy' (p. 21):

> Love, of this clearest, frailest Glass,
> Divide the properties, so as
> In the division may appear
> Clearness for me, frailty for her.

Donne writes, with 'A Ieat Ring sent' (p. 65):

> Thou art not so black, as my heart,
> Nor halfe so brittle, as her heart, thou art;
> What would'st thou say? shall *both our properties* by thee *be spoke*,
> Nothing more *endlesse*, nothing *sooner broke?*

These images were obviously not found by a process of free association—even had Donne not complicated his last line by a pun contrasting seemingly contradictory qualities (though endlessness understood as circularness is not incompatible with brittleness). His words *say* and *spoke* interestingly bear witness to what seems to me the characteristic Elizabethan conception of the very working of imagery, an attitude made still more habitual by this consciousness of logical process. Concretions (like the black jet) 'say' abstractions; particulars 'speak,' or make articulate, universals. This easy interchange between things and the meanings of things is subtly different from modern notions of the way images work; 'objective correlative' does not quite suit the Elizabethan habit of mind. One might phrase it carelessly and say that Elizabethans write and read images not like nominalists but like realists. But, however that may be, we are here bound to notice only the awareness these poets show of the logical base and the process through which their images are 'found' (invented).

Anyone who practices defining from the predicament *quality* will find that he produces images as fast as he can write. Even tropes so framed seem simple, and poets show strings of them—as in Daniel's sonnet vi: her eyes are sunny, her smile lightning, her disdains gall, her favors honey. Even a Donne image, so framed, will strike us as Marlovian:

> Your gown going off, such beautious state reveals,
> As when from flowry meads th' hills shadow steales.
>
> ('Elegie XIX,' p. 120)

Marlowe makes much use of images which praise or amplify on the basis of *quality*, choosing splendid or powerful natural phenomena[11] for simple but magnificent comparisons; poets who have in hand such tasks as he chose generally show comparable images.

There is no poet but shows many simple images of quality. They are used on the way to more complicated purposes, even in discursive poems like epistles—as Donne, in his to Goodyere, calls the life of a man who spends each day like the last 'but like a paire of beads' (p. 183). Such images find a natural place in poems which, like so many lyrics, praise by defining the nature of the thing praised. When late or 'obscure' poets choose to do this, their images, too, show characteristics which critics have preferred to think of as 'early.'[12] Or Donne can make a

[11] When Elizabeth Holmes notes that Marlowe 'loves to measure one beauty or marvel by another,' her phrase simply defines a type of what the Elizabethans called rhetorical amplification. See p. 21 of her *Aspects of Elizabethan Imagery* (Oxford, 1929), an observant study which nevertheless does not help us greatly toward making serviceable distinctions; e.g., most of her generalizations upon the 'metaphysical' imagination, poetry, or style, fit all good poetry—but nevertheless this author usefully emphasizes a continuity where less well-read modern critics have imposed a discontinuity.

[12] This from Lord Herbert's 'To Mrs. Diana Cecyl'' (p. 34) is an example: '. . . . that rare beauty thou dost show / Is not of Milk, or Snow, / Or such as pale and whitely things do ow. / But an illustrious Oriental Bright, / Like to the Diamonds refracted light. . . . .' Five of Ramus' books were in that portion of Lord Herbert's library which he gave to Jesus College, Oxford; see C. J. Fordyce and T. M. Knox, 'The Library of Jesus College, Oxford,' *Oxford Bibliographical Society, Proceedings and Papers*, V (1936–39), 75 ff.

mocking use of the image from *quality* by employing it to diminish instead of magnify:[13]

> Thou art not soft, and cleare, and strait, and faire,
> As *Down*, as *Stars*, *Cedars*, and *Lillies* are,
> But thy right hand, and cheek, and eye, only
> Are like thy other hand, and cheek, and eye.

Only the rhetorical patterning here is complicated; logically the image is extremely simple. If it sounds especially Donne-like to us, we shall have to grant that it is the sentiment rather than the character of the image which gives us this impression. The image is very conventional.

Complications enter the image based on *quality* in various ways, all of which would soon be met by anyone who set himself to define or invent from this predicament. A metaphor so based may be 'continued' into an *allegoria*, or a conventional such metaphor enlivened by extending the number of parallels. The connection which produced so many images like 'green youth' and 'salad days' may emerge as 'my blooming yeares' and lead to the mention of various 'circumstances' ('My flowre untimely's withred,' 'winter woes'; *Delia*, xxi). 'Honey speech' for sweet, often untrustworthy, discourse could be given a dozen exemplifications besides those with which the *Variorum Spenser* illustrates it, used of Despair:

> His subtill tongue, like dropping honny, mealt'th
> Into the hart, and searcheth every vaine,
> That ere one be aware, by secret stealth
> His powre is reft, and weaknesse doth remaine.

> (I, ix, 31)

This uses other predicaments too; a familiar metaphor based on properties has led to the admirably just comparisons between the way despair enters the human heart and honey's secret stealing movement, pressing down the veins to melt into and fuse with the blood stream. *Tongue* has a shadow of its unmetaphorical sense.

---

[13] Using also the quadruple-parallel rhetorical scheme which amused many poets; see *Delia*, xiv, for an extreme example. The italics (not mine) in the Donne image show the unwillingness to let any possibly inattentive reader miss the trick; it comes from 'Sapho to Philaenis,' p. 124.

This image offers a good example of the way Elizabethans always manage to indicate the fact to readers, in case they intend to pull into an image many connoted qualities; one's unexpected experiences with the deceptive mobility of honey are not here irrelevant, and *mealt'th, secret, stealth* awaken remembered perceptions. 'Summer's honey breath' shows no such intention, or Shakespeare could never have gone straight on to the wrackful siege of battering days. Less well trained logically than the Elizabethan reader, the modern commentator on images using *quality* is likely to overread them unless he observes the limits set by the image's logic quite as sensitively as he notes the connotations evoked by its terms.[14]

The greater likelihood of sensuous precision resulting from the very nature of this category allowed poets to use images of quality for very different effects in different poetic situations. Either luxuriant, florid imagery or sharp surprise may result. A student's logical or rhetorical exercise or *descriptio* would demonstrate the first of these results as well as do narrative poems of the period. The second may need illustration. When Donne, with purposes far from those of narrative or description, announces that he can love both the tearful kind 'And her who is dry corke,' we have the minute shock which results when a simple image of quality intrudes in argumentative discourse

[14] The capacity to 'mute' images before they become mixed, a type of logical alertness, was evidently expected of readers. I cannot believe that many Renaissance readers would have been troubled by the logical task of abstracting 'vastness, recurrence of numberless units' from Hamlet's *a sea of troubles*, quickly enough to get the waves out of the way before 'And by opposing end them' came along. The same quickness would make the logical opposition between *suffering* and *taking arms against* fortune far too impressive to allow the arms to be taken against the *waves*.

Two points in this connection can scarcely be overemphasized: (1) that the way in which things 'stand for' their meanings asks for a reading which is alien to modern habits of mind but typical of the very tissue of Renaissance thought, with its peculiar blend of medievalized 'Platonic' conceptions of reality interbred with Aristotelian notions; (2) that the habit of regarding images as a treasury of 'connotations' is not a Renaissance habit. Intended multiple meanings are one thing; possible connotations another. To shear off the latter except as the poet directs does not make the reading of poetry into a dull logical exercise in which the metaphor is subdued and lost after contributing a conceptual notion. The whole English Renaissance at least seems to me to write images on the understanding that we can apprehend a particular and a universal at one self instant and not lose either; the Ramists flatly say so. They may have been mistaken.

('The Indifferent,' p. 12). When Lord Herbert wants to praise 'The Sun-burn'd Exotique Beauty,' he ends a careful argument for this unpopular and froward preference by telling her that paler ladies will pine to jaundice from envy, and then 'by thy Gold shew like some Copper-mine' (p. 70).[15]

Complication will enter if the image is a trope. The greater the emphasis on the fact that the property obtains only metaphorically of one element in the image, the more likelihood of a sense of logical complication; 'melting ice of vanity' would be simpler than what Daniel chose to say—'Written in yce of melting vanitie' (*Musoph.*, 130). This emphasis is present if the quality (e.g., love as fiery) is pursued through many fanciful elaborations; such a method will produce a conceit, but not a conceit of the truly logically complicated type characteristic, for instance, of Donne.[16] Puzzling differences of effect between 'Elizabethan' and 'Metaphysical' conceits are often explicable as differences between extended pursuit of a simple logical parallel and extended pursuit of a likeness by basing it on several logical parallels.

This last, the addition of parallels in other predicaments, is the commonest way in which complication enters the ordinarily simple image based on common qualities. Lord Herbert notes the *effect* of certain qualities, in his 'Elegy for Doctor Dunn' (p. 58):

> Praises, like Garments, then, if loose and wide,
> Are subject to fall off: if gay and py'd,
> Make men ridiculous. . . . .

Donne in an epistle 'To the Countesse of Bedford' (p. 190) argues that an attribute (her goodness) denied, as heretics deny God's goodness, nevertheless remains predicable of that which truly possesses it, 'For, rockes, which high top'd and deep rooted sticke, / Waves wash, not undermine, nor overthrow.'

---

[15] When Lovelace writes an epistle to Cotton in the form of an *exemplum* and *allegoria* pretending to be about 'The grasshopper,' one is similarly pleased by the tiny quick surprise of 'Poor verdant fool! and now green ice!' (HH, p. 716).

[16] Sidney's fanciful fiction about Love burning himself is an example (*A. and S.*, viii). Note S in the Appendix exemplifies, with conceits based on the testament-formula, in Daniel, Carew, Donne.

This uses another predicament and a 'place' (*manner of suffering*, cause and effect). The epistle was a genre ordinarily thought of as suited to reflective or ratiocinative subjects (whereas the sonnet only gradually developed in that direction). Drayton's or Daniel's epistles demonstrate the way in which this purpose changes the character of a man's imagery. Images obey the demands a poet's purposes make of them with the subtlest possible variations in structure and stylistic character.

Images of quality do not only explain. The argument may be sharp, and Donne will ask Sir Henry Wotton curtly how city or court can be a refuge: 'Can dung and garlike be 'a perfume?' (p. 180). It may occupy a whole song, and Suckling will dilate on the curious fact that 'That piece of beauty' passes unregarded now, though his *qualities* and hers remain as they were ('Sonnet I,' p. 14; in HH, p. 705). Or a poet may merely wish to threaten his lady with the reminder that her beauty is not only sweet and fair but transitory, and so strip her bare with a neat little insult:

> Men doe not weigh *the stalke* for that it was,
> When once they finde her flowre, her glory passe.[17]

The last few examples are all similitudes, and several use the figure meiosis.

These pages will suffice to demonstrate the fact that the processes which the student of logic was asked to master when he studied the predicament *quality*, or the place *similitudo* so frequently based on it, are processes which cannot but result in images such as we find in the poems those students wrote later. That particular poems actually do represent conscious use of such processes is, of course, not capable of proof except in occasional instances. It is too late now to gather the subjective data.

I think that we may note as well, in images of this period, the

---

[17] *Delia*, xxxii. In a more leisurely genre, the long complaint, when Daniel puts the same argument into the mouth of Rosamond's bad counsellor, the old Dame may use smoother speech, but yet 'cunning' and 'subtelised': '. . . . those rayes which all these flames doe nourish, / Canceld with Time, will have their date expyred, / And men will scorne what now is so desired: / Our frailtyes doome is written in the flowers' (vss. 221, 241).

clear-cut sureness with which qualities are predicated of things being defined or being used in advancing the discourse; it is generally difficult *not* to see why a given vehicle has been selected. One must look long for images like that in Eliot's 'Prufrock'—'I should have been a pair of ragged claws / Scuttling across the floors of silent seas' (p. 14). Numerous common qualities are hinted at, but one is free both to conjecture and to choose; different readers, or the same reader at different times, may base the comparisons on what they please. One must be very wilful, and go in blinders, to find these statements to be true of Elizabethan and seventeenth-century images.

Similar points would be noted if we were to look at the hundreds of images which English poets have wittingly or unwittingly based upon the predicament *manner of doing*. These can be of all images the simplest. They occur with great frequency in allegorical writing, and are often simple because they are mere comparisons. Red Crosse's 'hand did quake, / And tremble like a leafe of Aspin greene'; both really shake (I, ix, 51). All narrators use such figures plentifully, a fact one may verify by looking into any novel (any at least which describes actions). In shorter kinds, more ingenious figures based on manner of acting may be expository, as in Lord Herbert's comparison of the lover who speaks after seven years, to the orange-tree which even in England's cold climate finally comes to the point of producing (p. 28). This has a tropical element (*fruits : speech*), and it was probably more consciously found than Spenser's figure. Obviously, many such require no consciously logical process; but, as with the other predicaments, constant analysis made for habits which can be detected in the structural character of images, once we look beyond the very simplest.

This is easier to see in longer examples, where poets have simply done what rhetorical and logical exercises in the multiplication of 'circumstances' based on *manner of doing* would require of them. Donne's long river-image in 'Elegie VI' (p. 88) is an example. His stream chides, swells if any bough dares to stoop and kiss her, gnaws at the banks, roars and braves it, flouts the channel she was wont to flow in. This is imbedded in a kind not usually amenable to such lengthy figures as *icon;* like other kinds of *icon* (in which the element of similitude is usually present), it flourishes a key to its meaning as a sort of conclusion: 'that is shee, and this am I.' The metaphorical element 'continued' makes the figure technically an *allegoria;* though a little outspoken for that figure, it is precisely such a one as many a sonnet-writer made use of (e.g., Drayton's Sea-farer sonnet).

Donne's image is exactly comparable to Daniel's sixteen-line figure of an empty creek which steals into a new way, is seconded by added streams, finally is glutted and leaves this channel for a worse—all finally compared to the way 'this humorous world, ... Rapt with the Current of a present course, / Runs into that which laie contemnd before' (*Musoph.*, 271 ff.). Differences in tone are especially conveyed through syntax and meter; men speak differently in satirical reprehending and in expository reflection; but the *images* are similarly framed.[18] The different effect when this logical base is used for an epic simile (as it very frequently is) may be noted in Spenser's image of the Shannon in IV, iii, 27. It is carefully observed, but logically simple as befits an image describing a battle action—except for a little sting in the last two lines which would pass unobserved by a reader who forgot that this was trope and not mere description.

It will be noticed that this tropical element in an image is that in which the author's own commentary on the action resides or inheres. This is normal and is recognized by rhetoricians, who comment on metaphor as aiding perspicuity, offering 'special lights' to the 'sentence' or thought. Though true of other tropes, it may be usefully exemplified here in tropes based on *manner of doing*. These are almost always simple enough to aid a reader in quick comprehension of an author's attitude. Such helps appear in Eliot's 'Prufrock': 'I have measured out my life with coffee spoons,' 'To have bitten off the matter with a smile,' 'To have squeezed the universe into a ball / To roll it toward . . . .' (pp.

[18] The similarity in the vehicle merely makes the comparableness more obvious; Daniel's extended image of an edifice in the epistle to Lady Cumberland is also comparable, though the tropical element in the image is less consistently sustained (the result, a loss in concentration). In HH, p. 261.

13, 15). Among various images whose logical base is undetermined, these reorient the reader; squeezing into a ball is not a private but a usual 'symbol' of concentration, even if one did not remember Marvell's 'Coy Mistress.' Daniel uses the same method of communicating his own attitude when he supposes that this is love, this painting on floods, and tilling of the sea-shore, this crying to the empty air (*Delia*, ix). All images in this paragraph, like most trope, use more than one predicament. Complication ordinarily enters any image by this door, and I should think no Elizabethan could fail to know it.

For this last reason and for others, images all based on *manner of doing* may yet, of course, impress us differently. Of the numerous possible elements responsible for this, I shall exemplify one other. Donne tells Sir Henry Wotton not to 'sleepe / Upon the waters face' as a cork does, in this world's sea (p. 182). Daniel also discommends a mode of action in 'If this be love, ... The never-resting stone of care to roule' (ix). Daniel's subject is more commonplace, but the chief element in the last which makes it 'sound earlier' in date is the hidden classical allusion. The same effect is visible in an image which is actually wittily persuasive, though only a reader remembering Danae would get any amusement out of the final pun (the figure is one of the arguments of Rosamond's wicked-duenna adviser, vs. 232):

> Doost thou not see how that thy King thy *Iove*,
> Lightens foorth glory on thy darke estate:
> And showres downe golde and treasure from above,
> Whilst thou doost *shutte thy lappe* against thy fate. . . . .[19]

A discussion of the two or three predicaments I have not exemplified would serve merely to underline the points already

[19] Of course, pleasure in this type of allusiveness did not cease entirely to affect images. It is what gives vigor and amplifying 'splendor' to Lovelace's command 'To Amarantha, that she would dishevel her hair' (HH, p. 713):

> 'Do not then wind up that light
> In ribands, and o'er-cloud in night;
>   Like the sun in's early ray,
>   But shake your head and scatter day.'

This figure would be much more poor and thin if the author could not count upon readers to whose minds the picture of many-rayed bright Phoebus could be brought.

made. *Situs* and *habitus* produced images of a type which merged with those a student would produce when he was asked to invent by looking out the 'circumstances' or the 'adjuncts' of any given thing. *Manner of suffering* is frequently found in combination with *manner of doing* or implied in images of the latter type. It is exemplified in Suckling's

> What in our watches, that in us is found;
> So to the height and nick
>   We up be wound,
> No matter by what hand or trick.

('Sonnet II,' p. 15; in HH, p. 706)

Being a less familiar and habitual position in thinking, it may give a subtler cast to a figure.

Not even this last simple image could be framed simply and solely by that motion of the mind which occurs when one sets one's self to think 'how can I uncover the true nature of this thing I am speaking of—noting its manner of suffering some action done to it?' I should not claim that any but the simplest of images could result from this process. No similitude can be framed solely by considering a thing in this or that predicament; the Places of Invention are required for the inventing and disposing of concepts. I believe, however, that early and constant practice in the processes demonstrated above made poets frequently conscious of the precise logical bases of the images they invented—and quite conscious of the logic of images they approved or condemned as critics or self-critics. I do not think that such habitual modes of thinking could fail to come into play in later composing. There is every reason to suppose, from the formal nature of the images in the poems of these writers who were so trained, that what they had learned did become second nature to them and that they were far more aware than are we of the precise character of the logical connection they made when they formed an image.

2. *Definition, Division, and Method*

The orthodox logic handbook ordinarily followed its treatment of the predicaments with sections on *Definition, Division,*

Methodus. These were cant terms; not only every budding schoolman but every youth of parts found himself constrained to learn how to 'define and divide.'[20] The first two were studied again among the 'places of Invention,' as, for example, in Blundeville, in Wilson, in Du Moulin; they were also reconsidered as part of 'method' in the popular manuals of Blundeville and Wilson.

The interrelating of logic and rhetoric as sister-disciplines is especially clear at this point, and their combined influence upon the neighboring art of poetry can be seen in the form of organization of the short poems, and of the long images in longer poems, which have come down to us from this period. Commentary on long images frequently takes the form of noting how the author has 'parted' his matter; 'division' in the rhetorics is represented by important figures—*partitio*, or what Puttenham calls 'the Distributer' (*merismus*), or Peacham's *diaeresis* (p. 123; general into kinds). Wilson, in his *Arte of Rhetorique*, includes both 'definition' and 'parts' in a list of 'The places of Logicke' which are essential to the framing of a praise or dispraise, that is, of any piece of the 'demonstrative' type. The other places listed as useful here are causes, effects, 'things adioyning,' contraries. Giving the usual rhetorical places by which such pieces are organized, Wilson concludes that 'these of *Logicke* must first bee minded, ere the other can well be had' (p. 23).[21] The relation is close, between what poets learned about 'defining' and 'dividing' in logic, and relearned in rhetoric, and what they did in their poems. That they were conscious of this close relation is often perfectly evident from the methods of pro-

---

[20] Such a book as James Cleland's *The Institution of a young noble man* (Oxford, 1607), for example, having given advice on the duty of parents to children, proceeds to discourse upon the duties of a tutor toward his charge. One is to teach him Methods, Definition, and Division (p. 89). Cleland would not descend into every cavil of the commentators, but to leave a youth uninstructed in these methods of thinking would be to overlook Logic's usefulness in other knowledges. He proceeds to duties toward God and parents and to advice on civil conversation and travel.

[21] Vast numbers of sixteenth- and seventeenth-century short poems are, rhetorically speaking, short 'demonstrative orations'; the short 'deliberative' piece was very nearly as common. See above, chap. v, sec. 1, for the influence of these rhetorical divisions upon lyric theory, i.e., upon conceptions of the functions of short pieces.

cedure, the statements of purpose, even the titles, of their poems.

There is a twofold relation between sixteenth- and seventeenth-century imagery and the constant practice in 'defining' which students thus received in several connections in the two traditional disciplines.

Blundeville (for example) says that defining can be by name, by difference from other things, metaphorical by a figure (e.g., adolescence is the flower of man's age), by contrary, by circumlocution, by example, by want or defect, by praise or dispraise, by similitude (e.g., the sun is the eye of the world), by etymology (Book ii, chap. i). In the first place, it is obvious that if I set myself to define the true nature of any subject in which I am interested, by these means, many of my 'definitions' will be nothing more nor less than images. Indeed, students could hardly have been unaware that such a list includes a large number of the most commonly used rhetorical figures—*pronominatio*, *horismos* or the 'figure of difference,' metaphor, simile, and analogy, *periphrasis* of various types, *exemplum* and *parabola*, hyperbole, meiosis. Nothing could be easier than to annotate Blundeville's list from the innumerable images which poets who studied him (or another like him) used in their poems with intent to define or to elucidate the precise nature of something. This point concerns merely the functioning of images as single units.

But in the second place—and this is more difficult of exemplification—there is a relation between this method as studied in logic and the form of organization of many short poems, their nature as structural units and their function as wholes. Many lyrics of this period are just such compositions as this section of a logic handbook asks for: they are definitions by praise and dispraise, definitions by differences, definitions by similitudes. One after another sonnet or lyric on Sleep, or on Death, or on a lady's power, or on a deceased friend's virtues, or on the exact nature of Love, turns out to be a commendation or 'depraving,' or a persuasion, framed by the habitual methods of 'definition.' It is obvious that any such habitual compositional framework could not but affect the character of the images which form an important functional part of it.

It is not possible to demonstrate this properly, since I cannot quote whole poems. But it is not unprofitable to read the sections on 'definition' in a set of popularly used logics, and then to leaf through an anthology of sixteenth- and seventeenth-century verse like that of Hebel and Hudson, and notice the poems which even declare outright that they are 'definitions.' There are, of course, dozens which accomplish this aim in more covert fashion, especially among the sequences of sonnets.[22]

If we keep only to those which overtly declare this purpose, we find, for example, that the long line of definitions of love extends from Ralegh's 'Now what is Love, I praie thee tell'; Greene's 'Ah, what is love?'; Lodge's 'I'll teach thee, lovely Phillis, what love is'; Daniel's 'Love is a sickness full of woes'—down to Marvell's 'The Definition of Love.' Such poems are sometimes signalized by the rhetorical title, so familiar in the margins of longer poems, of *descriptio*—as is Ralegh's, or the 'Ask what love is? It is a passion . . . .' from the *Georgeous Gallery of Gallant Inventions* ('A true description of love'), or the 'plain description of perfect friendship' from the *Forest of Fancy*.[23] The *descriptio* need not try to be pictorial, and is, of course, a time-honored figure; logicians call it an imperfect definition. The *descriptio* of spring so dear to medieval poets did not die out; not only Surrey's (p. 27) but Sir Henry Wotton's (p. 552) follow the ancient pattern. Or Grimald will choose to write a 'Description of virtue' from the places *habitus* and adjuncts; or Wyatt will use the favored riddle-technique in the description of a gun, or piled antithetical similitudes in 'The lover to his bed.' Wyatt also describes 'such a one as he would love'; it is a short unelaborated invention, on a pattern that has

[22] The conventional method of strings of similitudes in sonnets on Sleep will come to anyone's mind, but Surrey's 'The frailty and hurtfulness of beauty' or Constable's 'To live in hell and heaven to behold' are equally 'definitions' invented from the ordinary places (HH, p. 27, p. 230). I here confine illustrations to this anthology for the convenience of the reader who is willing to test out these statements to make sure that I am not just seeing in every bush a thief, in every poet a logician.

[23] These definitions of love and friendship may be found in HH at the following pages: 135, 152 ('The shepherd's wife's song'), 162, 280, 865, 193, 195.

but to be filled out for Crashaw's poem about 'that not impossible she'; the pattern produced a good many in between. Descriptions of 'The man of life upright,' like Campion's, or of the mean estate, or of the contented mind, are about as numerous.[24]

Some defining poems show their rhetorical lineage more clearly than others. Surrey's 'Description and praise of his love Geraldine' (p. 28) follows the usual places for the 'praise or dispraise of persons' in demonstrative orations. A poem 'To Time' will break off to say 'How can I iustly praise thee, or dispraise?' (p. 204). Other poems are closer to the similar methods advised by the logic handbooks—methods such as those discussed by Wilson under *definition* among the *loci* of Invention (kind, property, difference, parts, etc.), or such as those treated by Evans (essential and causal definitions, parts, accidents).

Definition by *cause* is fruitful in producing images; these are frequently of a witty or ingenious character—and indeed the function of defining is likely to influence images in this direction at any date. Definition by *accidents* obviously leads to the multiplication of images; Evans' own example is one: evening the time of long shadows. Even the 'perfect' definition (the 'general' with his 'difference') is not scorned by the poets.[25] Many poets, of course, use 'definition' on their way to something else, as Donne does frequently or as Herbert does in 'Man' (p. 732) or in various poems on this or that abstraction. But many poems are simply praises-or-dispraises-by-a-definition. Definitions 'by differences' are a favorite pattern, as in Herbert's 'Virtue' (p. 748). Vaughan's 'Quickness' is a definition of true 'life' by differences.

I cannot believe that poets, trained as these poets were, were

[24] See the following pages in HH for: Grimald, 50; Wyatt, 17, 16; Crashaw, 763; Campion, 448. The first lines of the Wyatt poems are: 'Vulcane bygat me'; 'The restfull place, revyver of my smarte'; 'A face that shuld content me.'

[25] Still other poems choose to dilate upon some 'special' within a 'general' and conclude by identifying or defining the latter more accurately—as in Campion's 'Young and simple though I am . . . . Venus, grant it be not love' (p. 454); Donne in this way or others defines some aspect of the true nature of the same 'general' in a wide variety of poems on 'Loves growth,' 'Lovers infinitenesse,' 'Negative love,' 'Loves Alchymie,' 'Confined Love.'

unaware of the connections between what they chose to do in
their poems and what was taught in the two disciplines supposed to deal with the problems of organizing and expressing
thought. Lord Herbert at least was not:

> Praises should then like definitions be
> Round, neat, convertible, such as agree
> To persons so, that, were their names conceal'd,
> Must make them known as well as if reveal'd:
> Such as contain the kind and difference,
> And all the properties arising thence.
>
> ('Elegy for Doctor Dunn,' 39 ff.; p. 58)

I shall not pause here to examine the various specific effects
upon temper or tone of a poem, or upon the stylistic characteristics of the figures, when poets use images as functional
parts of a 'definition.' Defining images vary in character with
differing purposes or 'causes,' and with the extent to which
many or subtle logical links have played a part in their 'finding,'
and deserve a section to themselves (chap. xiii, sec. 1). I should
perhaps simply note two facts by a couple of early examples:
that images which define tend to be witty, radical, or homely;
and that the occurrence of a passage which tries to define, in
types of literature with other aims, will result usually in the intrusion of imagery of such a character. Other factors intervene;
Greene's pastoral song may not be expected to resemble in tone
a short deliberative piece in the middle style like Marvell's
'Definition.' And one should remark in passing that these conventions of genre were as comfortable as old shoes to Renaissance poets; they no more had to plan laboriously for them than
an experienced car-driver has to plot out his gear-shifting.

This is the second stanza of the poem 'To Time' mentioned
above; it purports to be a demonstrative lyric:[26]

> Both free and scarce, thou giv'st and tak'st againe,
> Thy wombe that all doth breed, is Tombe to all:
> Whatso by thee hath life, by thee is slaine,
> From thee do all things rise, by thee they fall.
>   Constant, inconstant, mooving, standing still,
>   Was, is, shall bee, do thee both breed and kill.
>
> I loose thee, while I seeke to finde thee out.

[26] In HH, p. 204; by 'A. W.'—perhaps just 'anonymous writer'—in Davison's
Poetical Rhapsody, ed. H. Rollins (Cambridge, Mass., 1931), I, 195.

The imagery in this tissue of general and particular is markedly different from amplifying imagery; and its further function demands greater logical complication. The quite natural result is: double antithesis, apparently contradictory qualities resulting in paradox; personification to state concepts—kept however from sharply pictorial *clarté;* curt simplicity of diction especially in verbs of action; a contrast in tone (syntactical) as the definer introduces time's homeliest relation to us (we waste it). I choose this poem for no peculiar qualities, rather because it is like dozens of passages in poems before and after it.

It is like those *only* which show a similar intent and thence a similar method of framing images; poets of the whole period concerned had been taught that such methods best suited such intentions. When the latter intrude in longer poems, as they do momentarily even in epic, method of framing images shifts, and tone with it. As long as Spenser is describing the arras-hung walls of Castle Joyeous, or amplifying the loveliness of Britomart with a stanza on the moon breaking forth above the discomfited traveler, his intentions prevent (as they should) any images which would puncture with the sharp instrument of logical subtlety the first mood of loose voluptuousness, or the second of amazement at the shining-forth of loveliness. When he turns aside to discriminate somewhat slyly between honest love and loose lust, for the benefit of any stray lady readers 'that to love captived arre,' we are scarcely very alert readers if we do not distinguish a different tone in images which turn to homely comparisons with 'a coale to kindle . . . . Giving the bridle to . . . . treading under foote' (III, i, 50). Then, instead of long descriptive stanzas 'parted' according to 'circumstances,' with an occasional leisurely simile based on *quality* or *effect*, we have three or four different predicaments in three lines, leading to sharp paradox. Spenser still prefers to keep the decorum of heroic poetry rather than to insert a dialectical passage written in the philosophical middle style. Precisely the same conception of poetic virtue is responsible for the fact that we find no stretches written in the grand style in Donne's epistles and satire when descriptive or amplifying intentions momentarily intrude.

'What a *division* is' in a typical logic tells the student to divide according to traditional ways—the whole with its parts, the 'general' with its 'specials,' or the substance with its accidents. All these produce imagery. So, too, of course, do principles of organization as taught to modern students; differences come in the uniformity and pervasiveness of the training and in the more conscious use of well-recognized methods familiar alike to writers and readers.

These ways of dividing became recognized forms of organization for long images, when the figure rather than the piece was thought of as the unit. This probably resulted from the fact that rhetoric here underlined the instructions of logic.[27] Puttenham's three pages on *merismus* or the Distributer are chiefly concerned with dividing the whole into its parts.[28] This simplest division, which we all use constantly, producing imagery in the process, is the base for many examples of *icon* and *allegoria;* like all conventions, it could be neatly mocked, as in Donne's description of Flavia, part by part, in 'Elegie II' (p. 80, *The Anagram*) or in 'Elegie VIII' (p. 90, *The Comparison*). This type of division (and the type of images it produces) is peculiar to no period; it is peculiar to certain intentions which poems have, useless in assisting others.

Obviously, a division 'by whole into parts' is useful for narrative and descriptive poetry and for demonstrative short pieces. One need only look at one of the latter—Ralegh's 'The Lie'—to see that such a division need not be confined to pictorially detailed images (though Spenser, for example, necessarily must

[27] It jogged the student's memory with figures like *distributio, partitio,* and so on; or it gave sections to 'Division,' as Wilson does, *Arte of Rhet.,* pp. 109 ff., stressing the importance of a writer's having 'his *Logique* perfit,' p. 113.

[28] III, xix, 222 ff.; he thinks it a figure very meet for 'eloquent perswaders such as our maker or Poet must in some cases shew him selfe to be'; or one may amplify "peecemeale,' heightening matters (for rhetoricians are quite aware of the evident relation of this formal organization to what we should call emotional effect). This kind of division is recognized as natural to many kinds of discourse other than dialectic; Thomas Granger, in his *Syntagma Logicum* (1620) (designed especially 'for the use of Divines in . . . . preaching') comments that as there is manifold use of this category in every simple exposition or amplification, so the chiefest use of it is in poets, orators, philosophers (p. 180). Logics based on or influenced by Ramus take up *Distribution* among the Places of Invention (as here, or as in Milton's).

make large use of it). Any rhetoric or any logic could furnish Ralegh with the pattern for the series of riveter's blows with which he drives at aspect after aspect of society, first from one logical position and then from another—distinguishing real from apparent properties by a similitude ('Say to the Court it glowes, / and shines like rotten wood'), hammering out series of definitions ('tell skill it is prevention: . . . . tell law it is contention') or series of characterizations by qualities (the stanza 'Tell fortune of her blindnesse'; p. 46, in HH, p. 139). Or, for another example, the old pattern of a catalogue-of-beauties, which is this type of division, has left its mark on the formal structure of Crashaw's 'Wishes. To his (supposed) Mistresse.' I do not think that his readers missed the division of whole into parts, combined, as is frequent and natural, with the place *subjects-adjuncts*, enlarging upon the latter to include joys (smiles, blushes), fears (tears), day, night, life, time, so that the division moves to one of substance and accidents. As with the half-conscious perceiving of the logical base underlying single images, the perception of a familiar structural pattern simply gave trained readers an added pleasure like that felt by a person who listens with different enjoyment to a suite and to a sonata. There is nothing to prevent others from listening without caring to apprehend the formal differences, if they prefer.

The division by 'a general with his specials,' based upon a less simple concept, is likely to produce more arresting results, leading quickly from concretions to abstractions and sometimes giving an effect more logical than poetical. As Constable pursues each special sin in 'Mine eye with all the deadly sins is fraught,' he starts up images which are quite radical and subtle enough for the next century; one simply does not notice this because they are not sufficiently brilliant to outshine certain uses of conventions (HH, p. 229; from *Diana* [1592]). Donne's adjuration to that 'Busie old foole,' the unruly sun, finds its list of slaves-to-time by this division (the schoolboys and the sour prentices, etc.; 'The Sunne Rising,' p. 11). Lists of *exempla* can be presented under this kind of dividing.

Division by substance and accidents, and the kind of analysis and practice which it involved, stands in close relation to a group of logical places of which the most commonly mentioned is *adjuncts*, and both merge with the process of image-finding taught in the rhetorics as invention of 'circumstances'; as far as poetic practice is concerned, it is unprofitable to separate them. These processes of thinking are fruitful springs of imagery. Sometimes poets who do not ordinarily write so are led into markedly sensuous passages by thinking from this pattern; we can hardly believe that Lord Herbert stopped teasing his mind long enough to see the surprisingly fresh landscape in a 'Sonnet, Made upon the Groves near Merlow Castle.' His 'division' (very proper to his subject) gives us its whistling wind and singing birds, and the lovely cool warmth of 'Upon a Greene embroidering through each Glade / An Airy Silver, and a Sunny Gold' (p. 54). The series of images in the first part of Ralegh's 'The Passionate Mans Pilgrimage' is constructed by a division from the familiar adjuncts that spelled *pilgrim* as inescapably as scepter and crown spelled kingship (p. 43; in HH, p. 142).[29] The translation one by one of these physical 'things adjoining' into spiritual terms, which gives the imagery its strange and visionary quality, is a normal image-technique in the poetry of vision, of which allegory is a type. As the rhetoricians note, such *translatio* is merely metaphor continued; this causes us to apprehend physical image and significance, first disparate and then merging, as in a slowed-up film.

Some types of the extended images popular among the Metaphysicals are drawn out on the framework of division by accidents or adjuncts. Frequently their base is some well-worn conventional metaphor—as in Suckling's love-siege, in ''Tis now, since I sat down before / That foolish fort, a heart' (p. 25; in HH, p. 707). The *function* of a division by accidents naturally has much to do with the tone and character of the images it pro-

---

[29] Iconographical 'images' spell out with adjuncts, too. In a *Horae* MS bearing Ralegh's signature (MS Bodleian Add. A 185), the illumination picturing St. James furnishes this palmer par excellence with the *scallop-shell, staff, scrip, gown* of Ralegh's poem. For Ralegh's interest in MSS see the present writer's 'Spenser and Some Pictorial Conventions,' *SP*, XXXVII (1940), 151 n.

duces—they will differ as they suit amplifying description, definition, persuasion.

In many logics a short section on 'Method' led to the important section on Propositions. This study is not concerned with the latter; though it furnished much further training in the proper use of such tools of thought as have been examined, it did not serve directly to inculcate habits of finding and framing images. I need say nothing about *methodus* or the 'readie waie' to 'set forthe any thyng plainly' except to remark that it gave students still further practice in processes which Wilson lists as follows: what a thing is, how defined, how divided, its causes (notably efficient and final), effects or proper working, what agrees with it, what disagrees (contraries), witness or examples (i.e., the argument from testimony or authority, always last and weakest). It should now be sufficiently clear that long-continued training, especially in 'defining' and 'dividing,' induced habits which were bound to affect the framing of poetic images. This conclusion is firmly borne out by the characteristics shown by the images.

3. *The Places of Invention*

The section which generally followed the treatment of Propositions in ordinary peripatetic logics finds such clear illustration in the formal character of Renaissance images that I have not been able to keep it out of the discussion, having chosen to illustrate with actual images from poems rather than with made-up examples. It deals with the Places of Invention. This simultaneous use of processes analyzed in different sections of a logical manual, which characterizes images, characterizes also the way those processes were taught in the discipline of logic itself. These positions or standpoints of thought from which matter for any discourse was 'invented' were again so familiar as to be cant terms,[30] and many of them produce imagery almost inevitably.

[30] I shall not try to treat these either completely or with care to preserve certain distinctions kept by the logicians—such as that between *loci interni* and *externi* (places not in the substance or nature of the thing; see Wilson or Blundeville or Cicero's *Topica*). I do not omit, but I allocate points to such sections or chapters as best allow demonstration of the poetic utilizing of these materials.

In drawing a relation between Invention in logic and the process of poetic invention which produced (among other things) images, I do not wish to imply that there is no difference between these two or that the Elizabethans thought there was none. When a student applies the places *general-and-special*, as Blundeville does (Book iv), and comes out with the argument that, since every virtue is to be desired, justice is to be desired, he is scarcely embarked on the writing of a poem about justice, although indeed many poems about specific lady-loves or some friend's virtues do follow this pattern. What happens rather is that writers trained for years in finding matter for persuasive, demonstrative, expository, or disputative discourse, by the means of playing the mind down certain prescribed paths, do not forget this useful process when they turn to the 'finding' of ways to shape poetic subjects.

Invention, the finding or figuring out of what one was going to say of a subject, was one of the two divisions treated in both logic and rhetoric (*Inventio, Dispositio*). It should be remembered that the invention of proper matter, finding a way to make one's purpose articulate, held a position of high importance in a theory of poetics such as that accepted during this period; indeed, perhaps, 'How did he think of embodying it thus?' will always be the central mystery of any art of expression. Invention was no slave's labor. In both logic and rhetoric this division of *Inventio* was that in which the faculty of imagination was thought to be most active. A writer who was barren in invention produced what we should call an unimaginative treatment of a subject; perhaps the modern cliché would be 'lacking in insight.'

Hence when Wilson remarks that these 'places' be but coverts, where one may find game at pleasure, we may believe that even the aspiring poet did not willingly cast out what he had learned from their use. Certainly he started up innumerable excellently poetic images by thinking from the places *similitudo* and *adjuncts*, whether this was deliberate or not (I believe it to have been so, in a great many cases). The importance to a poet of constant practice (from adolescence) in framing similitudes and their short form metaphor, and of constant practice in observing what things are spoken of by translations (as Wilson directs students to do), is quite obvious. 'Translations' or metaphors come in for mention under other places; Blundeville (Book iv) treats them separately from the comparison and example, and Wilson takes them up under 'Name' of a thing and exemplifies how they can help 'interpret' things by the metaphor *ignis*:*love*. Similitudes proper, or arguments from likeness (usually in property), vary from simple parallels, like that of parson and shepherd, to tightly constructed analogies. Logicians recognize the suitability of this place to other types of discourse than dialectical argument; Du Moulin says (p. 71) that 'Similitudes are rather ornaments of a speech, then any proofes,' and Lever calls it rather 'a kind of reasoning' than a place (p. 195). For more elaborate training in this kind of reasoning a student looked to an adjacent discipline; all rhetorics treat various forms of similitude.

All this co-operative interchange and correlation of emphases upon the primary poetic trope (metaphor and its extensions) must needs give poets a conception of that trope which would differ from prevalent modern conceptions. Writers could scarcely avoid being awake to its possible logical functions and to the nature of the logical process involved in metaphor-making. Nothing in all this was unpalatable to the sixteenth- and seventeenth-century poet; quite the contrary. And it no more turned the making of metaphors into a barren logical exercise than 'art' in poetry turned it into false and hollow formality. Distinctions between false and true art, between stale and lively invention, held here as elsewhere.

It is equally obvious that the place *adjuncts* would produce imagery, and again writers in one discipline comment upon relations to the kind of discourse taught in another. Wilson's logic remarks on the usefulness of this place in praises and dispraises (i.e., demonstrative pieces), and rhetoricians tell those who would amplify by circumstances to recall division as learned in logic. Various related places would give practice in composing images of the same general type; logicians themselves note the similarities,[31] and the distinctions need not be preserved here. When a process of inventing was thus hammered into the student in sundry connections in two disciplines of composition, it would be strange if he did not realize what he was doing when he wrote images that are little else than collections of adjuncts. A very large number of images are found from this place.

Its connection with the sensuously full images treated in an earlier chapter—*icon, descriptio,* etc.—is evident without further remark. Thinking of the adjuncts of something has provided the pattern for innumerable short poems, and for innumerable longish images within poems, whether we think of Campion's 'There is a garden in her face,' or Donne's 'The baite,' or Wyatt's 'Like to these unmesurable montayns.'[32] As is frequent, Wyatt combines adjuncts with the place *similitude;* and the mountains' boisterous winds, feeding cattle, singing birds, etc., each have counterparts in the lover's sad condition. Or, in Campion, 'her eyes' might not have been like angels had the poet not realized what were the proper adjuncts of heavenly gardens. The wit of the last stanza depends on our realizing what cherubim generally do in such places.

Images which originate in the motion of mind indicated by this place need not remain descriptively simple or rhetorically conventional. Especially in reflective poems, poets frequently use adjuncts to define wittily or to argue convincingly. A familiar pattern is the negative use of the place to point out triumphantly that such and such past conduct was far from being that of an insolent lout, or that such and such an action has none of the earmarks of sin. The court nymphs cannot but say of Sidney, 'no I dare sweare, / He cannot love,' noting the

[31] Between adjacents, accidents, things annexed or knit (*connexa*), things chancing (*contingentia;* these last two may be pursued by the curious reader in Wilson). Indeed Blundeville, treating of Adjacents, considers them to be contained either under the place of Property, of Difference, or else of common Accidents, and hence refers us to those other places (Book iv).

[32] For these poems see: HH, p. 454; Donne, p. 46, sts. 1, 5, 6; Wyatt, sonnet 19, p. 31; in HH, p. 13.

absence of that string of familiar circumstances which define a
Lover to the world—treasured locks of hair, groans that punctuate sentences, and so on. Thus may Sidney at one stroke mock
nymphs, depreciate conventional lovers unlike himself, persuade
Stella, and characterize true love (*A. and S.*, liv).

Donne piles up questions using the conventional 'things ad-
joined' to the lover—his sighs, his tears, his coldnesses, his
heats. But since he wishes to use the figure to argue mockingly
against love's unprofitableness, addressing those dolts who
would rather improve their worldly position than be love's
saints, he attaches to each adjunct another subject which
literally is accompanied by strong winds, floods of water, low
temperatures, and fever:

> Alas, alas, who's injur'd by my love?
>   What merchants ships have my sighs drown'd?
> Who saies my teares have overflow'd his ground?
>   When did my colds a forward spring remove?
>   When did the heats which my veines fill
>   Adde one more to the plaguie Bill?
>
> ('The Canonization,' p. 14)

However simply found from the place *adjuncts*, an image which
jokes about its own conventional logical base (*material cause;*
tears and water), uses *manner of doing* and the place *efficient
cause*, a couple of 'feminine' figures and the potent scheme
interrogatio, and also by a division into 'parts' gives the four
elements a push in passing, just for good measure—such an
image cannot remain simple. It has too much to do.

Ordinarily, however, and especially in more spacious forms
than the short deliberative lyric, images invented or extended
by the place *adjuncts* will contribute not sharpness but leisureliness, or richness, or in reflective writing a tone of grave and
sweet reasonableness. Herrick often exemplifies the second of
these effects, Herbert the last (e.g., 'The Flower,' p. 165; in
HH, p. 747). The fairly long reflective disputation, a kind to
which Daniel's *Musophilus* belongs, allows a poet space for

more leisurely images of this type.[33] As in allegory, to which such figures are very close, the leisureliness is often very rewarding. In Daniel's vignette of idle travelers at Stonehenge, made thoughtful against their will by this 'huge domb heap' that figures forth man's inability to defend his own memory against unsparing time, a meditative and grave pathos underlies all the quiet questions and fragmentary thoughts half-caught in a gesture. It is rhetorically parted by 'circumstances'; the slow pace of the figure and its more than dramatic function co-operate to admit the suggestion of greater range and depth in the concepts than their bare statement provides (vss. 331–90). No reader who three hundred years after has re-enacted Daniel's situation, circumstance for circumstance, who has noted the same aspects of the speechless great stones and heard the same huddled questioning of the living dwarfed and drawn together by the dead who baffle them—no such reader would exchange this typical rhetorical *descriptio*, with its amplifications and generalities and half-shadows, for a sharply accurate and 'concrete' delineation of Stonehenge in the 1590's, however such a one maintained the best Imagist tradition of precision and fidelity.

These reservations do not gainsay the fact, however, that images admitting many or vivid adjuncts are likely to be among the more sensuously precise of Renaissance images; and this place is likely to be used where that character is suitable. Frequently in traditional figures one adjunct is sufficient to call up a sharply realized visual image, the more so if there is an iconographical or emblematic tradition (Red Crosse, Una, Charity with her babes, Hercules, Nimrod, Phaedra, are among the dozens of examples in the *Faerie Queene*).

Instead of illustrating anything so universally found, it might

[33] To fortify Musophilus' generalization upon man's wilful zigzagging between extremes, Daniel introduces a dozen lines on one especial institution, Religion: how gorgeously she is sometimes decked, how sweet perfum'd, how shining clear—another time how plain, how threadbare, sitting how poorly without light, disrob'd (295 ff.). These epithets are metaphorical equivalents for adjuncts of a contemporary institution, which every man supplied as he read. Descriptive poetry unconcerned with a conceptual point underlying the whole would have foregone trope for well-realized visual detail.

be more profitable to examine this characteristic together with another in a much-discussed early conceit of Milton's:

> So when the Sun in bed,
> Curtain'd with cloudy red,
>   Pillows his chin upon an Orient wave,
> The flocking shadows pale
> Troop to th' infernal jail. . . . .[34]

The conceited element here does not lie in the chin-pillowing. To contemporaries the single adjunct of the curtaining clouds would recall the whole dignified tradition of awakening Phoebus, and iconographical associations (even if only through astronomical diagrams) with the round and rosy-faced planet would provide an effect markedly different from that which some commentators seem to think Milton intended. There is no flavor of old-Gaffer-Sun-in-his-nightcap, bedtime-story style, in the image itself.

The conceit lies in the parallel between the light-bringer and Christ as *Sun*:*Son*, and in the hyperbolical amplification in the parallel between the fleeing of the dispersed spirits or 'shades' and the sullen flight of the false gods, who are darkness even as Christ is light. These are traditional Christian conceits. The interpretation is supported by an earlier stanza (7). The place of such heightened amplifications in this special type of demonstrative lyric (a praise, but in the form of a hymn) is secure. Such logical complexity as the figure has depends from its use of the place *cause*.

This place can lead the mind to the forming of images which differ noticeably in aesthetic effect. There is a formal difference between this traditional hyperbole and the rather repellent fancifulness of an image, only apparently similar, earlier in the poem (st. 2). The notion of sinful earth hiding her shame in con-

---

[34] *Nat. Hymn*, st. 26. An article by Bonamy Dobrée has led me to fasten upon these examples and the next few following. To have included Milton's imagery in this study would have been to overbalance it; but issues are clarified if I demonstrate ways of looking at imagery by using examples which others have used on their way to different conclusions. Dobrée comments on all these Milton examples except those in *Nat. Hymn*, st. 2, and in *Comus;* he also uses those I introduce presently from Dryden, Marvell and Spenser compared, and Crashaw. See 'Milton and Dryden: A Comparison and Contrast in Poetic Ideas and Poetic Method,' *ELH*, III (1936), 83–100.

fusion with a veil of white snow develops no basic concept lying at the very core of the poem. It is an amplifying image framed like those Marlowe uses to elevate Hero, a little fiction in which a faked cause is assigned to an effect which thus gains inflated significance. That Milton learned to dislike this image-technique for subjects of great spiritual dignity is apparent from his unfinished poem on the Passion; that he continued to use it where it was suitable is apparent in (for example) the two praises of the Lady's song in *Comus*—her song that smoothed the raven down of darkness till it smiled, that made even Silence wish to be never more, still to be so displaced (251, 557). These are among the loveliest of Milton's conceits, examples of a type of image his purposes did not often demand of him. However, he broke off the poem which attempted to amplify the sorrow felt at the spectacle of the Passion through images framed similarly to these, having evidently the good sense to perceive the indecorum of his own style. For the remark he himself appended to the fragment—that the *subject* was 'above the years he had'—goes to the heart of the poem's trouble. The depths of such a 'cause' are unplumbed by such stylistic instruments as Milton had so far learned to handle. It is in 'invention' that the poem falls short; an insight into the true nature of the subject is not conveyed by the ingenious exuberance of these pretended chains of cause and effect, these tears that are so well instructed that they would fall in ordered characters on Christ's tomb, these sorrows which would beget a race of mourners on some pregnant cloud.

It is not their ingeniousness that makes these conceits frigid when used of such a subject; they are indeed too unsubtle logically to carry what they should. They differ *logically* from Donne's vast displacements of natural law in 'Goodfriday, 1613'—'There I should see a Sunne, by rising set, / And by that setting endlesse day beget,' and the others. There is a sense in which these modes of operation, these seemingly unnatural effects from causes, can be truly predicated of Son as Sun, and Donne does not scruple to state his meaning outright: without this rising sun 'Sinne had eternally benighted all' (p. 336). There is no sense in which loud sorrow begets upon a pregnant cloud a race of mourning echoes. Indeed, there is not supposed to be; all we are to take seriously in a figure of hyperbolical effects is the attributed quality, as in fairy tales ('so big his foot would cover this town,' etc.). The core of Milton's fanciful echoes-begetting figure is not a trope, possessing therefore the logical base and the reasonableness of metaphor, the 'truth' of Donne's *benighted*. It is rather just a fanciful imputation.

Such hyperbolical effects from causes convey excited enthusiasm, or the lover's exaggerated sense that the very leaves bow to his lady when she walks in her garden. But they cannot convey the significance of the Passion to the whole world as can Donne's image of 'those hands which . . . . turne all spheares at once, peirc'd with those holes,' which keeps to powers and modes of operation Donne thought were truly predicable of their subjects. Good metaphors do predicate truly and are hence logically stronger and tougher than mere amplifying fancies. There exists a poem in which Donne did treat a subject similar to the Passion ('Resurrection, imperfect,' p. 333) through pretended situations in which he told the sun that it need not rise, since Christ was a more ambitious sun, that Christ outdid him by enlightening hell as well, along with other ingenious magnifications—and that poem was not finished either.

Although these unsuccessful conceits in Milton's Passion fragment were probably thought of from the place *adjuncts* (epitaphs, mourners, etc., one of our most natural and familiar processes of invention), they demonstrate the fact that any use of the place *cause* generally provides images which impress one as conceited and ingenious. This is entirely natural, considering the nature of the process indicated by this place, which involves the ordering of concepts, and considering the subtilizing of the process in the study of dialectic, which directed students into tireless discriminations between material, efficient, formal, and final causes. Some aspect of the notion of causation has assisted the 'invention' of vast numbers of images; as Blundeville says of the place, 'the use thereof is divers and manifold,' since in both deliberative and demonstrative discourse the *end* and *effect* are the most germane questions to consider (pp. 106–7, in 1619). By its very nature, thinking from this place produces images showing the use of multiple predicaments.[35] It is easiest to demonstrate this natural complexity through unsuccessful conceits, where logical flaws act as litmus paper.

In an image which has called forth sundry comments, Dryden says of the smallpox which caused the death of Lord Hastings:

> Blisters with pride swell'd, which th'row's flesh did sprout
> Like Rose-buds, stuck i' th' Lilly-skin about.
> Each little Pimple had a Tear in it,
> To wail the fault its rising did commit:
> Who, Rebel-like, with their own Lord at strife,
> Thus made an Insurrection 'gainst his Life.
>
> ('Upon the Death of the Lord Hastings,' vss. 57 ff.)

The trouble with these images is not that they are overingenious but that they are (1) colossal frauds which (2) work at cross-purposes.

Ordinary hyperbole exaggerates 'that rather you may conceive the unspeakableness than the untruth' of what is being related, as Hoskins says (p. 29); but here it is not possible to discover what Dryden is concerned to amplify—there is surely no conceivable reason for magnifying the grief of the pimples at the fact that they must rise. If there were, Dryden effectively negates it by comparing them to rebels rising in insurrection against their lord; these rebels show arrogance, and grief at their own arrogance, not by turns but in the same instant—so that the psychology of these assigned causes is as weak as the logic. We have no right to object to blisters swelling with pride and becoming rosebuds in the next line, for this is merely the rapid abstraction of parallels[36] by which comparisons work; they never hold throughout and are not meant to, and Dryden does not really stick rosebuds into lilies. But we do have a right to object to his injecting an image whose only purpose can be

---

[35] Effects are generally argued or intimated to be from certain causes on grounds of a parallel in *relation*, or in *quality*, or in both plus several others.

[36] In *cause*, in visible *properties*, in *manner of doing*.

visual realization, in between three explanations of why the blisters rose looking as they did, two of which contradict each other. The tissue of assigned efficient causes and final causes is incredible because it serves no orderly arrangement of believable concepts; Dryden does not get away with that egregious fake of the weeping pimples because no possible purpose is served by our believing them to be heartbroken. The 'tear' was found from material and formal cause, but to extend the parallel to final causes is to use the logic of images without a trace of conscience.

This last is, I think, what happened as the Metaphysical conceit decayed. The real difference between this and a poetically successful conceit *of any date* is not the extent of the ingenuity—which of itself is an indifferent factor *in our aesthetic evaluation* of the figure. The real difference is, rather, this complete irresponsibility with respect to the demands of the subject. The Renaissance called it indecorum.

Unceasing practice in framing arguments from *cause* not only habituated poets to finding single images from this place, probably deliberately,[37] but also to inventing structural frameworks for whole poems which are essentially arguments based on this place. Such poems need not dispute or harangue. Poets with reflective or expository purposes commonly utilized such tools of dialectic, especially as Ramist ideas of the functions of logic became more pervasive.[38] It is the more fitting that I should exemplify poem structures of this type from the sonnets of Sid-

[37] At any rate, poets had been given practice in doing just this, deliberately, elsewhere than in logic. Rhetoric had taught them to make images thus, in, e.g., the figure *aetiologia* (Puttenham's *telcause*), in definitions, in 'confirming' by similitudes, in *metonimia* of the cause, or of the thing caused. A Ramist rhetoric like Fraunce's gives these last a careful treatment, distinguishing also *metonimia* of the subject and of the adjunct; it is interesting that Peacham added this last division when, in 1593, he enlarged by some pages his 1577 treatment of metonymy. We think of 'Death is pale' as a simple figure enough; a user of Peacham (1577) was made to realize that it was a metonymy in which the effect is understood of the efficient cause. Such divisions and awarenesses of process are natural enough to students trained as these were.

[38] Ramists took exception to certain aspects of the orthodox treatment of cause and Ramist textbooks treat this place at considerable length, with separate chapters on matter, form, efficient cause, and end, and further chapters on distribution by causes, by effects.

ney, who is known to have had a lively interest in Ramistic logic—though this interest would affect only attitudes and emphases, not information or basic method.

The structure of sonnet xxvii ('Because I oft in darke abstracted guise')[39] is this: of that and that and that common effect of pride (or adjunct of the proud man), they deem the efficient cause in me to be the foul poison of bubbling pride that makes me fawn on myself and despise others (general effect embracing the specials); yet this is not the cause, for . . . . (and he gives the efficient cause by the figure *aetiologia*). Rather it is ambition which makes me pass my best friends unseen, unheard (effect) *because* my thought bends all its powers to the highest place, Stella's grace. This sonnet uses *cause* to frame what is called in the list of places a *differing* or *dissentany* argument; Sidney uses it in other sonnets with equal skill. Ramist logics give it long and careful consideration; they give as the 'sign' of it *not this* . . . . *but that*, and append poetic examples. When these are short, as in the case of single image-units, they are what rhetoricians call the 'figure of difference' (*horismos*); the example in Wotton's Ramistic logic (1626) is from *FQ*, IV, ii, 42.

No doubt a poet may consistently write in structures of this kind without realizing that he is being a good sixteenth-century logician—though anyone who cares to try will find it oddly difficult to find, in Keats or the Pre-Raphaelites or the moderns, sonnets which might, like this one, be appended to exemplify the discussions in the logics. One has only to open Sidney to find one.

It is necessary to get rid of the modern notion that 'logic' in a poem will make it either coldly unimaginative or pedantically 'abstract,' if one is to notice without prejudice the relations between the poems these men wrote and the training they were given in logical invention. It is well to keep in mind the cooperation between the learnings,[40] the part assigned to fancy or

---

[39] The sonnet is quoted in the Appendix, Note T.

[40] Even Minturno, referring to Cicero's *Topica*, lists places with poetic illustrations in his two works on poetics; many of the illustrations are images (Latin in the *De poeta*, Italian in *L'Arte poetica*). The chief places dealt with are *effects, cause, adjuncts* (said to be especially useful to the poet), *conjugates, genus, similitude, contraries,*

imaginatio in the process of inventing, and the Renaissance respect for—simultaneously—deliberate artistry and lively fresh-
ness. One of Sidney's gayest sonnets is that beginning 'Deere,
why make you more of a dogge than me?' (lix). It is a string of
suggested possible causes; all are thrown out on the ground that
Sidney himself has each of the virtues of this unjustly successful animal. He alights finally upon a conclusion: not-being-
these-it-must-be-*this;* very well-I'll-have-that-too (this is argued
after the fashion of the disjunctive syllogism, exalted by
Ramists in the teeth of peripatetic objections).[41] The pretended
sternness of the dialectic carries the invention into unexpected
corners, turns up particulars else passed by, so that we see Sidney, dog and all, and hear the very tone of voice with which he
demands: whether the cause be the dog's lovingness? alas he
himself burns in love. Whether it be that he waits so well? Sidney 'never thence would move.' Bidden, he fetches a glove?
quite unbidden, here has Sidney fetched his very soul and
presented it. It must be that Stella grants such delight only to
things without wits—there is hope there, for he will soon be
eased of his.

Sidney is fond of arguments from *cause;* they tumble over
each other even in the *Arcadia.* To glance at other sonnets than
his is to see, however, how naturally suited such structures were
to the reflective, persuasive or 'deliberative,' expository, or
argumentative purposes which sonnets share with certain other
short kinds. Donne displays all but innumerable variations on

---

repugnancy, greater, less, equal. The passage occurs between a considerable treatment
of figures and a discussion of decorum (latter part of Book vi in the *De poeta,* pp.
538–46 [1559]; latter part of iv in *L'Arte poetica,* pp. 417–26 in the editions of 1563
[colophon 1564]) and 1725.

[41] Since I think that the influences of logical study upon images were chiefly exerted
through habituation to certain basic processes of invention, I do not take up those
portions of logic in which students learned to *dispose* arguments found by these processes
into propositions or syllogisms. Although syllogistic types of reasoning frequently occur
in Renaissance poems, the effects of such structures upon images would not show us
anything I do not mention. Certain general notions propounded by Ramists about the
very nature of proof, etc., may have affected images, and I shall presently deal briefly
with them. Ramistic emphasis upon the disjunctive syllogism may have been one
such influential general point; for a clear exposition of what this emphasis involved
see Perry Miller, *The New England Mind* (New York, 1939), esp. pp. 136–39.

the general pattern of an argument from *cause*, producing enormous numbers of single images using this logical base; this fact is a commentary on his conception of the uses of poetry and the functions of images. One looks at Drayton's *Idea;* the second sonnet begins with the structure which in logic produced disjunctive syllogisms ('My heart was slaine'; it must have been you or I, it was not I, it must have been you). He cites three effects, as 'evidence,' and concludes, with a logical leap scarcely intended to be innocent, that 'Heav'n will still have Murther out at last.'[42]

In *Delia* (1592; the year after *Astrophel and Stella's* appearance), Daniel's purposes are such as to be better suited by amplifying images of the simpler types; the sonnets are most of them 'demonstrative,' sometimes simple praises, sometimes amplification of his pains and thus pleading but indirectly. This makes the difference in tone the more striking when occasional sonnets move toward the purposes of deliberative pieces—the general development of the sonnet as years went on. Such a one is sonnet xxix, and as the poet inquires 'O why dooth *Delia* credite so her glasse,' it is the invention from the place *cause* which is responsible for the similitude, for the compression of a *mercy-wanting* storm, and for the malicious comparison with Narcissus which allows Daniel to finish, with witty insolence,

> And you are chaung'd, but not t'a Hiacint;
> I feare your eye hath turn'd your hart to flint.

Neither Daniel nor Spenser is such an acute logician as is Sidney, but the frequent examples of a tone of delicate mockery in the *Amoretti* are more than once found to accompany argument or images from the place *cause*. Both tone and image-technique are related to a shift from demonstrative to deliberative intentions, from magnifying commendation to persuasion

---

[42] Sonnet added in 1599. For an example in which a string of possible causes is allowed to remain in generalized language, leading to an either-or conclusion, see 'Is not Love here, as 'tis in other Clymes' (No. 27; new in 1619). For one, pursuing causes, in which an argument 'from differences' entails the use of several rhetorical figures, see the charming 'Deare, why should you command me to my Rest' (No. 37; first appearance 1602).

and laughing disproof. Sonnet xviii ('The rolling wheele that runneth often round') adduces a couple of examples of common-ordinary effects of given actions, which in all conscience ought to support him in thinking that he may soften her hard heart with *enough* dropping tears and sufficiently long-*continued* entreaty. But

> . . . . when I pleade, she bids me 'play my part,'
> and when I weep, she sayes 'teares are but water':
> and when I sigh, she sayes I 'know the art,'
> and when I waile she turnes hir selfe to laughter.[43]

Or, in pursuing the knotty problem of why Nature has given such goodly gifts of beauty to so hard a heart, Spenser remarks on the otherwise reasonable conduct of that benefactress, who 'to all *other* beastes of bloody race' has at least given a dreadful countenance, thus amicably arranging a warning to possible victims (xxxi).

I could spread the net much more widely. If this quick list of sonnets whose structural framework utilizes the place *cause* could rather be a careful examination of all the sonnets of all the poets mentioned, I think we should find that considerations of date and of personality are quite eclipsed by considerations of decorum. That is, we should find ourselves watching not the unconscious betrayal of differences in *psyche*, but the operation of 'laws' of decorum which govern the suitable use by any poet of certain dialectical and poetic tools, in obedience to the nature of the poem's purpose and subject. Nor is this pedantry; it is the secret inner orderliness of artistic form. The unconscious

---

[43] I have signalized the indirect discourse by this unauthorized punctuation because I do not know of any Elizabethan sonnet series which has suffered more than the *Amoretti* by being too solemnly read, though I think that in many others as well criticism has shown itself oblivious to those indications of the *tone of voice* which contemporaries caught immediately because they were trained to perceive an author's purpose through delicate rhetorical variations. I suppose that there have even been critics who have read *Amor.*, xxxii, as though Spenser really intended 'the paynefull smith' to lead him to the serious conclusion 'What then remaines but I to ashes burne?' and as though the rhyme scheme were responsible for the metaphor and pun in the plaints he has *applyde*, and for the lacrimose reflection that this unnatural substance the 'harder growes the harder she is smit.' The lighthearted and entertaining self-criticism (in the implied comparison between the smith's *heavy sledge* and all the poems which Spenser has composed to 'beat on th' andvyle of her stubberne wit') is not noticed in this or other poems by those who are convinced that 'Spenser had no humor.'

betrayals are in the poems, but we have no instrument so delicate that it can measure them, and little right to be pseudo-
scientific about ultimate reasons for things while disregarding
immediate ones.

Some of these examples have pursued efficient causes, some
final cause (like Spenser's remarks upon Nature's arrangements
for a lack of facial charm in bears and tigers, in xxxi, above).
Final cause is not infrequently pursued at some length, resulting
in a structural pattern like that in Sidney's 'Come let me write,
and to what end?' (xxxiv). Self-argument appears in Elizabethan literature not only in the dramatic soliloquy; in this as
in numerous poems (q.v. Donne) a purpose to which methods of
dialectic are suitable has produced a sonnet in dialogue form. It
shows *stichomythia* that must be rapidly spoken, contrasted with
passages in a very different tone. There is a series of neatly compressed arguments; some are similitudes based on parallel final
cause ('Oh, cruell fights well pictured forth doe please'), some
are simply statements of the traditional 'places' in rhetorical
'deliberations' (useful or useless to be done, hard or easy: 'What
idler thing than speake and not be heard?' 'What harder thing
than smart and not to speake?').[44] Sidney neatly turns the
whole to a 'praise' of Stella in his last couplet, finding the
efficient cause of this useless-useful writing of his in '*Stellas*
great power, that so confus'd' his mind.

This 'demonstrative' intention is not infrequent in deliberations of the to-what-end variety; method obeys, the usual
amplifying figures enter, and the tone is accordingly elevated
rather than incisive. Single figures based on final cause, on the
other hand, are likely to serve rather sternly ratiocinative func-

[44] The frequency with which poets use these traditional 'places' may have more to
do with the fact that they are just naturally the positions of persuasion than with the
fact that every poet must have written dozens of exercises based on them (on whether a
thing be honest, profitable, hard or easy, necessary or not, possible, etc.). It probably
pleased readers, in any case, to meet these old faithfuls. I have not tried modern
poems to see whether those untrained in sixteenth-century rhetoric can avoid these
'places,' for I find it more curious than important that even Donne's 'By our first strange
and fatall interview' proceeds: from *profitableness*, to *honesty*, to *possibility*, to *difficulty*,
and finally to the persuasive recommendation of a better course to follow ('Elegy XVI,'
pp. 111–13).

tions. They are frequently sharp and short; in any case, they generally please by witty point.[45] In fact, most images utilizing the place *cause* are persuasions, or support of a position. This appears to be the case regardless of date and regardless of whether the poet is 'Spenserian' or 'Metaphysical.'

Here it is wise not to allow differences in pace or verse form to draw us into false antitheses regarding the nature of *images*. It is easy to note the acuteness, the close relation of the conceit to the conceptual point, in Marvell's

> As Lines so Loves *oblique* may well
> Themselves in every Angle greet:
> But ours so truly *Paralel*,
> Though infinite can never meet.
>
> ('The Definition of Love,' p. 37) (Author's italics)

If we are to perceive that Spenser, too, in the providential-storm image of *Amoretti*, xlvi, is supporting an equally precarious position on arguments from *cause*, and if we are to perceive the resultant effect on the tone of the sonnet as a whole, we shall have to read Spenser's conceit through to its finish.[46] This only begins it:

> When my abodes prefixed time is spent,
>   My cruell fayre streight bids me wend my way:
>   but then from heaven most hideous stormes are sent
>   as willing me against her will to stay.

The dilemma into which this puts a lover is one not unfamiliar to the class (and I suppose the odds are three to one that this cloudburst is *metaphor* for—anything the quick reader has the wit to imagine): whom shall he then, 'or heaven or her' obey? Horrid and dangerous choice. Quite ready to make the pious but ironical assertion that 'the heavens know best what is the best for me,' he escapes on the back of an image—for who can

[45] A longish example is Sidney's comparison of Love's foolishness, in not seeking to get into Stella's very heart, to the naiveté of the child who does not know enough to use a book for *its own proper ends:* 'That like a Childe that some faire booke doth finde / With gilden leaves of colloured Velom, playes; / Or at the most on some faire picture staies, / But never heedes the fruite of Writers minde' (*A. and S.*, xi).

[46] See Dobrée, *op. cit.* (n. 34 above); only the first four lines of Spenser's conceit are used for comparison with Marvell's, which is said to differ by virtue of the fact that it 'involves thought.'

gainsay that the governing force emanates from the nearer spheres? So

> as *she* will, ...
> my *lower* heaven, so it perforce must bee.

Here, too, 'the conceit is itself the idea . . . . when you grasp the conceit you have the idea of the poem; if you do not grasp it, you are lost.'[47] Spenser concludes his sonnet with a sestet in which he suggests with some reserve to 'ye *high* hevens' that, though their power is, to be sure, not up to the lady's, the two of them together are indeed a little more than a man can stand, and some assuagement—from the only quarter whence it can be expected—would be the part of mercy:

> Enough it is for one man to sustaine
> the stormes, which she alone on me doth raine.

This web-thin innuendo which damns with loud praise, a tiger's-paw blow which kills as it caresses, is admittedly different from Marvell's knifelike dialectic. Marvell's poem has little trace of the intention of praise-and-dispraise to which Spenser's at least pretends. The poems differ in many other ways not strictly related to an examination of imagery; line length and other formal-unit differences have subtle effect. The formal patterns which give the two images their character show dissimilarities as well as the single likeness in logical base (*cause*). Spenser uses his antithesis *sotto voce;* Marvell's comes out in the overt form of a figure of difference, a declared similitude. As an element in poetic technique, the images are comparable largely in their functional use to support a position or explain a course of action and in their contribution of witty tenuousness and delicate (or penetrating) compression; both images indicate the

---

[47] Dobrée, p. 86; said of Marvell. I also find difficulty in another familiar differentia for the Metaphysical conceit: 'the unexpected bringing together of ideas that seem to have nothing in common.' It is so hard to know when ideas would seem unrelated, to others, that I find this almost useless as a tool for discriminating between images. On the face of it, one of the lower spheres is no more like a woman than a line is like love. Our reactions really depend on the aptness of the *logical link which relates* the ideas, *for the given image,* and on how cunning the author may be in making us see it. Or, as Aristotle remarked, on how much genius the writer may show in seizing relationships (*Poet.* xxii).

author's own attitude toward his subject with precision and reserve.

These not, after all, inconsiderable similarities would not, I think, be missed—in many other images written by poets commonly set in opposition to each other—were we as alert as their own contemporary readers to the possible logical functions of conceits.[48]

The only other places of Invention that led to kinds of training which affected habits of framing images are the various places concerned with different types or degrees of diversity or 'repugnancy.' Things may differ simply by being placed in diverse predicaments; discordants may be contraries or contradictories; or one's argument may be found 'from relatives' or 'from privation.' All these are clear enough, except perhaps the last. 'Blind youth' is an image based on *privation* (and metaphorical *effect*); Drayton's 'domb heap' of Stonehenge (*Musoph.*, 339) is simple 'translation' or metaphor, for one does not 'deprive' a thing of what it could never have had. 'Blind mouths' is both, combined with the synecdoche which has caused so much trouble. The 'pastors' of this traditional *allegoria*, here reduced to naught but ravening mouths such as they are supposed to guard their flocks against, are blind 'by privation' as well as metaphorically 'by translation.' Most of Milton's contemporary readers were too used to the process of logical abstracting, inherent in metaphor and in these other figures, to be troubled by having three such processes to perform at once.

Many telling single images take their vigor from the fact that they are good short arguments from the place *contraries*. Since

[48] Another conceit differentiated by Dobrée from those in the Metaphysical manner is Crashaw's: 'Eyes are vocall, Tears have Tongues, / And there be words not made with lungs; / Sententious showers, ô let them fall, / Their cadence is Rhetoricall' ('Upon the Death of a Gentleman,' p. 135). Dobrée calls this 'completely rounded, self-sufficing.' Crashaw could not have thought so, for it is part of an eighteen-line passage about the gentleman's being jealously mourned by Eloquence herself, and it seeks to particularize several prior general remarks about no language being more fluent than grief—hence, 'Wee are contented' even though Eloquence denies us all but 'The sad language of our eyes.' This is a favored conceit found from *final cause*, finds its best parallels in Bishop King (see the Appendix, Note K), and commonly makes capital of the paradox germane to the image (furnishing real or near-puns, as here in *cadence*). It is probably the amplifying function which makes this image seem Spenserian to some critics.

this came to be a favorite pattern for organizing short poems or sonnets, a few examples may serve as reminders that we are likely to find, in the train of arguments so invented: paradox, argumentative tone, hyperbolical claims (often ironic), certain syntactical characteristics (balance, interrogation, exclamation), antithetical figures. In a sonnet to *Delia* which differs considerably in tone from those around it, Daniel begins a string of some eleven sundry oppositions with 'What it is to breathe and live without life,' and ends (noting the method by name)—

> This cruell *knowledge of these contraries*,
> Delia my hart hath learnd out of those eies.
>
> (p. 175; not in the edition of 1592)

The use of particulars (like 'How to be bold far off, and bashfull neare') rather than of sensuous images, or trope, is a not infrequent result. So, too, is the dialectically dry and pseudo-precise language of such a sonnet as *Amoretti*, xxx ('My love is lyke to yse, and I to fyre'). Triumphant emergence with a conclusion, all the better sometimes for not being really tenable, is also typical. If the function of the whole piece remains 'amplifying,' tone will be affected by that factor more than by the bare fact that a dialectical tool has been employed.

But any use of oppositions or diversities tends to bring in (naturally enough) sharpness, pugnacious diction in the images, abruptness. Witness *Amoretti*, xliii, based on that extreme form of 'things differing' which Ramists termed *adversatives:* 'Shall I then silent be or shall I speake?' The whole octave has this explosive quality, especially

> that nether I may speake nor thinke at all,
> but like a stupid stock in silence die.

The sestet shows a marked contrast in tone, as Spenser resolves the opposition with a paradox and a couple of far-fetched figures. Sometimes such patterns will induce meiosis, diminishing the lady to the point where 'she is no woman, but a sencelesse stone,' as in *Amor.*, liiii.[49] Or perhaps a tumblingly argu-

---

[49] This final line is climax to a long diminishing similitude which sees the lady as the apathetic spectator in this world's theater, viewing with the same idle calm those comedies and those tragedies which the vexed pageant-playing writer has made out of his very heart's stuff.

mentative flurry of objections, as in the sonnet wherein Sidney takes an informant to task for telling him casually that he left Stella quite-well-thank-you, when the ardent lover would like all the details his own avid eye would have noted. This sonnet, too, is framed as a so-called 'dissentany argument' (I-did-not-want-this-but-that); and elaboration on the least that would have satisfied this lover produces a delightful rush of 'I would know whether shee did sit or walke: / How cloathd : how waited on: sighd shee or smilde: / Whereof: with whome: how often did shee talke: . . . .' (xcii). The places of diversity more than any others give rise to images whose harsh vigor and wrenched rhythms test the rhetorical knowledge and skill of the reader, no less than of the writer.

These pages have been but the barest outline of the processes by which the writers who left us these poems had been taught to invent from the places. It is always more laborious to follow after and see how a thing is done than to do it. Also, it is a good deal more laborious to do a thing for the first time than for the hundredth. If these processes seem *recherché* and alien to the modern reader, he must remember that they were not so to the writers I have quoted. And to what the reader has just given an hour, those writers had given great numbers of hours spread over several years. Moreover, they had given those hours not to a subject which was generally thought to be unrelated to their 'creative' activity, one which was 'merely theoretical' and 'only academically interesting'; they had given them to a subject which was regarded, without cavil, as the substructure of all types of discourse. The training was ubiquitous, uniform as to method, consistent over several years, and high in prestige. The Renaissance had large respect for theory; and the world of the learned, the world of the 'creative writer,' and that of the 'worthy' reader, were not then three worlds. The sixteenth- or the seventeenth-century poet did not object to this state of affairs; it would be hard to name one who does not do his best to maintain it.

However, the processes I have illustrated are scarcely to be thought of as ways in which writers carefully made poetry learned. Such modes of mental operation certainly required no profound calculations or deep-laid planning on the part of the poets whence I have taken my examples, to whom these motions of the mind were as common-ordinary as the multiplication table. These writers emerged from such training not with a grim determination to make poetry logical—but simply with a set of habits. They were regarded as the habits of a gentleman, and many of my quotations have demonstrated that a poet was not loath to point to their appearance in his work.

Men demonstrate every day their ability to frame images without studying sixteenth-century logic. We should have had poems rich with images if the poets had never heard of the 'common places.' The images we should have had might have been even more rich, for I think that they would surely have been less accurately aimed. Careful control toward a realized purpose is the most noticeable characteristic of sixteenth- and seventeenth-century imagery. The purposes were not always sententious—but never were poets less irresponsible. Poetic of the time demanded that poets be responsible and purposeful. That imagery is frequently framed so that it serves with subtle and quiet skill certain logical functions is but one result.

This logically functional use of imagery is evidently quite deliberate, and here the fact of logical training is undeniably pertinent. Renaissance poets knew that they were doing certain things which most of us do in the dark; it is only natural that they do them more neatly. The matter I shall next consider— the nature of Ramistic logic—is not, I think, unconnected with a development in the direction of still greater logical acumen, a development toward wittily apt imagery, increasingly subtle and logically just. What had been only one element in the purposeful control of images—control toward the ends of dialectic— received very considerable impetus from certain general ideas which gained popularity as Ramus' logic received more and more ardent support. There are not new kinds of images; there are better and better images of certain of the old kinds. The development is intensive.

CHAPTER XII

RAMIST LOGIC: CERTAIN GENERAL CON-CEPTIONS AFFECTING IMAGERY

WHEN one picks up a Ramist logic, one's eye is immediately caught by two striking differences from the ordinary peripatetic manual. The book does not begin with a list of the predicaments but embarks immediately upon the Places of Invention. And place after place is illustrated by passages from poems.

These differences are both less remarkable and more important than they look. They are typical of the kind of change which Ramus' reorganization introduced into the ancient discipline. For they are in a sense mere rearrangements and not changes at all, but nevertheless these differences result from and imply general conceptions of the function and workings of logic which were to prove profoundly influential. It is a tribute to their foresight that men of Ramus' own time divided into camps according as they thought him to be a potent danger or an intellectual messiah. That this mere logician should have been killed and cast into the Seine during the massacre of St. Bartholomew's Day was cruel; it was not entirely disproportionate. Ramist logic was firmly built into the substructure of much Protestant disputation. However, despite his great prestige as a martyr, in a Protestant country, English defenses of his logic were still contentious nearly a hundred years after his thesis of 1536 had put to the test of dialectic the statement: *Quaecumque ab Aristotele dicta essent, commentitia esse.*

English interest in the controversy, which was hot during the 1560's and 1570's, did not wait for the publication in 1584 of Sir William Temple's annotated edition of the *Dialecticae libri duo,* or for the work of the influential Cambridge Ramists

Downham of Christ's and Richardson of Queen's, or for the English translations of 1574 and later dates, from which I shall quote for convenience. The important facts for a student of English literature are those which everyone knows: That Cambridge was a Ramist center. That Temple was Sidney's secretary and friend as well as fellow and tutor of King's College. That Harvey's support of the Talaean rhetoric involves support of the reorganization of the disciplines as made by Talaeus' master Ramus. That Abraham Fraunce, who says Sidney interested him in Ramus, brought out two books in English in 1588 illustrating Ramist rhetoric and logic, respectively, with great numbers of passages from Sidney and Spenser. That Marlowe, writing of Ramus' death in the *Massacre at Paris*, must have known at least the major controversial aspects of the man's work. That Milton wrote a recension of Ramus' *Dialecticae*, to which is attached a *praxis analytica* from Downham. That it is not mere chance that the two poets (Sidney and Milton) most indisputably connected with Ramist thought were Puritan in their sympathies.[1]

It is not strictly proper, however, to speak of 'Ramist thought.' There is no body of revolutionary thought which we can ascribe to Ramus. He reorganized a method. A large proportion of the matter and even the method in his own books is *ab Aristotele*. Yet the changes which came about because men used the tool of logic in the ways toward which he pointed are such that I think not even English poetic imagery could remain unaffected by them.

[1] I need refer to only two books which have helped during the last decade to make these matters common knowledge to students: Hardin Craig's *The Enchanted Glass* (New York, 1936) (see chap. vi) and Perry Miller's *The New England Mind* (New York, 1939) (see esp. Book II and Appen. A). I make no attempt to give a systematic review of Ramus' dialectic; this has been done, and many of the more important differences from peripatetic logic are impertinent to the concerns of this book. The famous 'dichotomies,' for example, I shall scarcely mention. I am interested solely in what would happen when English poets wrote images *under the presuppositions* that became current as Ramist conceptions of the two disciplines of logic and rhetoric became prevalent. Ramist training the poets might not encounter; that they should escape the influence of these general presuppositions is close to impossible. The emphasis is thus different from that in the preceding sections. Actually all points there made about the direct influence of logical training would also hold for writers who went to school to a Ramist logician; I am not substituting but adding an influence.

The two striking differences I have mentioned are typically innocent. A Ramist logic does not get rid of the predicaments; and neither is there anything really new about exemplifying logical positions from poems, when rhetoricians had been pointing to the use of the places in nondialectical discourse for generations. The predicaments appear not as a separate list, but here, there, and again where their *utility* in the finding of arguments from the various places of invention is demonstrated. Granger says, in treating of the place *subject*, 'The Predicaments of substance, and place, site, or situation, belong to this Categorie.'[2] *Property*, *quantity*, and *habitus* are used for the place *adjuncts* (chap. 28). The places *Of unlikes* and *Of likes* (whereunder an abundance of poetic similitudes is given) compare things in *quality*.[3] The predicament *substance* is used in inventing from the place *material cause;* Ovid's house of the sun is an example, made of gold, etc. (1574; 1581; Milton). And so on.

But it is not precisely the same thing to regard Ovid's image as a noting of the substance of something (illustrating thus the first Aristotelian predicament) and to regard it as noting 'a cause of the which the thing hath his being.' Indeed, we have here precisely the same difference as obtains between Spenser's saying that the House of Pride was built of squared brick and

---

[2] In his *Syntagma Logicum.* I use the versions and translations of Ramus' logic listed or referred to under his name in my Bibliography, referring to them as simply as possible, in parenthesis, by date or by author of the recension if that is known or has any interest (as: *1574; 1581; Milton*). The consistently ordered treatment of the places, generally with a chapter apiece, obviates the necessity for page references. Phraseological differences are not important to the points I shall make; and examples are generously copied and exchanged about. Translations were no doubt important in popularizing the general concepts here examined, but there is no knowing when Englishmen used rather Latin editions printed in England, or the many Continental editions from Ramus' first, in French (1555) or the 1556 *Dialecticae libri duo.* Neither date nor language of edition used is important to my points; I merely identify for the comfort of the curious.

[3] Things are compared in *quantity* by one who invents from the place *Of the less* (exemplified, e.g., from Virgil's first Eclogue [1632; Milton]); or from the place *Of the greater*, or *Of equals*—exemplified from *Aen.* 2: Creusa's shade *equal with* the light winds; or from Ovid's *Trist.* 4: *As many* shells on shore, *as many* roses. . . . . *So many* griefs me press (Milton). Or, from Davison's Martial: why do you and your wife so ill agree, since you brawl *as much as* she scolds (Wotton).

Donne's comment on the substantial cause of lesser kinds of love, in

> Dull sublunary lovers love
> (Whose soule is sense) cannot admit
> Absence, because it doth remove
> Those things which elemented it.
>
> ('A Valediction: forbidding mourning,' p. 50)

But of this more later.

Othodox logics, too, had taught the use of the predicaments in inventing arguments from the places; but they do not imply, as Ramist logics do, that to see something in one of the predicaments, in whatever type of discourse, is to argue something. As we shall see, Ramists had careful definitions for 'arguing' and 'argument'; but no one could come away from the reading of a Ramist manual without the greatest awareness of the rational usefulness of these image-arguments. Each use of the predicaments would be designated as an argument or *ratio*, and large numbers of examples are simply images—seen, however, in terms of their logical functions.

In illustrating the places with poetic images, the Ramist manual of dialectic does something similar to what the preceding two chapters of this discussion have done—but it goes one important step further. It makes no distinction between a logical base distinguishable in an image and a dialectical function for that image which makes it identifiable with any other argument found from the places and used in dialectic. What I tried to define as the formal cause of an image is thus assumed to be its final cause. This is natural once one considers the predicaments only in so far as they are 'used,' and once one regards *all discourse* as obeying the processes uncovered in the *Dialectica*—a conception which goes very deep in Ramus' way of thinking about the disciplines and underlies his whole presentation. Indeed, the old-fashioned ways of understanding the didactic usefulness of poetry look positively slack and irresponsible in comparison with the Ramist's virtual identification of poetry with dialectic.

This is especially borne in upon one by the subtly convincing procedure of simply illustrating place after place from the poets. One does not thereafter need to be told that good poems are made by good logicians; and the logical complexity and conceptually functional use of the metaphysical image begin to seem like the norm toward which all images should strive. The impact of this constant stream of poetic illustrations is curiously powerful; I would defy even the twentieth-century reader, who scarcely shares in the prepossessions of the seventeenth-century one, to come away from a Ramist handbook still able to keep poetry and logic in separate compartments.

The examples are not always convincing, but one begins to share the excitement with which sixteenth- and seventeenth-century Englishmen heard Ramist proclamations of the unity of all the learnings, as one finds efficient cause *per se et per accidens* illustrated from Ovid's *Tristia*, Juvenal; matter from Ovid's *Met.*, Caesar; form from *Aen.* 1; effect from Horace; adjunct from Ovid, Cicero, Martial, Dido's setting out to hunt in *Aen.* 4; dissentany arguments from the *Ars amatoria*, *Aen.* 2; disparates from *Aen.* 1 (*o dea certe! Amoretti*, liiii would have done better); relatives from Martial and *Met.* 1; adverses from *Aen.*, Tibullus; contradictories from Martial, Terence; privatives from Martial, Cicero; equals from *Aen.* 2, 3, 6, 4, *Ecl.* 3, Catullus, Terence, Matthew, and three works of Ovid's; of greaters from Terence, Juvenal, *Aen.* 1, 5; of lessers from Ovid, Matthew, *Ecl.* 1; likes (similitude) from *Aen.* 1, 3, *Ecl.* 5, 2, *Tristia*, Horace *Ep.* 1; unlikes from Horace, *Aen.* 2; conjugates and notation from Propertius and Ovid; distribution or division of the various types from *Georgics*, Catullus, Ovid; perfect definition—the only chapter without a poetic example; description or imperfect definition from *Aen.* 4; divine and human testimony from *Aen.*, Terence, Ovid.[4] Any lingering sense that

[4] I have followed the recension printed in the Columbia Milton in choosing this string of examples, because it is the only conveniently accessible one in which readers may pursue the interesting point of which passages are used to illustrate what. My point is simply the cumulative effect of the method, and it is the same in any recension, though still more potent to an English reader when the examples are predominantly modern (as in Fraunce's two books of 1588), or when one suddenly turns up from *Troilus and Criseyde* or from *FQ* (Wotton, ii, chap. xix, and i, chap. xii). The translation of Milton's version, by A. H. Gilbert, is peculiarly valuable for its preservation of the contemporary

my illustration of the places with images was a *tour de force* may, I think, be dissipated by reading through the long analysis of the image of Fame, 'explained' by her adjuncts, procreating cause, nocturnal effects affirmed and denied, etc. (imperfect definition). Or by studying Ovidian and Virgilian images as Downham's students had to study them, a process one may follow in the *praxis* appended to the Milton text.

These examples are indifferently images or passages of 'conceptually stated' reasoning in the poems. The cumulative effect of them is to blur any distinction between these two, as to function. This would not trouble a sixteenth- or seventeenth-century reader, to whom, I am convinced, the distinction did not exist. The distinctions he knew were those between literal or figurative ways of stating conceptions, and between figures (images) of different basic *forms*—as a trope differs from a scheme.[5] The student met here no new *rapprochement* between poetic images which made men 'feel' and conceptual statement which made them 'think,' for he had not been taught to separate these two. He did meet with considerable emphasis upon the absence of any such distinction and with renewed emphasis upon the ways in which tropical language functions logically.

The old-fashioned rhetorician adduced his examples of figures best designed to help a poet move and delight and elucidate against the background of just such a conception as Ramus assumes—of the poem as a reasoned and reasonable whole, manifesting its 'cause' through a judicious and suitable formal expression of its matter. This relation between Wisdom and Eloquence may be overt or implied (Part I above abounds in examples of both), and it was no news to this century that the

---

terminology—words and locutions which anyone familiar with a group of English Ramist writings comes to recognize as weighted with special Ramistic meanings—and also for the fact that examples are frequently given as translated in other versions of the *Dialecticae*.

5 And between *figures of words*, oftenest schemes of sound, with functions like emphasis or moving of the affections, and *figures of thought* which by inventing or disposing notions in this fashion or that (in *sententia*, or *exemplum*) functioned to move or to convince or to elucidate. The admixture of *prose* examples in Ramist books discourages any distinction regarding the functioning of figurative language in the two forms of discourse.

poets were wise reasoners or that images embody concepts. Again, it is not that there is anything so new in Ramus. But the implications which follow from his way of using the old and accepted relations can lead to something new. No old-fashioned rhetorician or poet or critic conceived of any such sublime unity of all human thought as was argued by the Ramist, with every writer in every discipline valiantly engaged, at every level of composition, in the grand dialectical pursuit of distinguishing the true from the false. Nevertheless, one cannot fix precisely the point at which this conception actually differs from the traditional 'poetry pursues truth,' unless possibly it lies in the more narrowly rational conception of truth (determined logically by the *intellectus*). Chiefly, the Ramist's close relating of poetry and dialectic is just an attitude we must call new in so far as it is an old one emphasized almost out of recognition.

Ramist writings do not leave to mere inference and suggestion this conception of the unity of all writing and thinking, grounded as these are in logic. They state the notion boldly and insistently. Logic is the first and most general of the arts, since it teaches proper thinking. It is deservedly called the Art of Arts, says Fraunce in the *Lawiers Logike;* the precepts of 'artificiall' logic were first collected out of, and always must be conformable unto, those sparks of 'naturall reason' which do not lurk in the obscure headpieces of one or two loitering friars but manifestly appear in the monuments of excellent authors (i, 1).[6] In a preface to the Learned Lawyers of England, we hear of a 'raging and fireyfaced Aristotelean' who complains, 'Good God, what a world is this?' Ramus rules abroad, Ramus at home, and who but Ramus. Newfangled and harebrain boys will prate of Method that never knew order; hereby it comes that 'every Cobler can cogge a Syllogisme, every Carter crake of Propositions.' To which Fraunce answers that cobblers be men, why therefore not logicians? And carters have reason, why therefore not logic? The best thing in logic men make the worst—that it is so common.

[6] Unless the *Arcadian Rhetorike* is specifically cited, quotations from Fraunce are from his *Lawiers Logike,* by book and chapter except where folio number is needed for convenience. See Granger, p. 1, on this same point.

The best opportunity for maintaining the universality of the ways of thinking taught by logic comes in the chapters on 'Method' which generally appear at the end of Book ii (*Disposition:* Axioms, Syllogisms, Method).[7]

It is easy, say the Ramists, to illustrate the logical method of proceeding from the general to the special in poets, orators, and 'all sort of writers,' since they always really follow it, hidden though it may be with delectations (see 1581). Granger has a chapter 'Of Cryptike Method';[8] by Fraunce, this so-called concealed method is compared to the surgeon's hiding of his knife— yet even orators and poets, those 'people pleasing men,' must generally follow the method of logic, as most agreeable to reason (ii, 17). It would be easier to throw off remarks like Fraunce's, as those of a man who neither knew nor understood poetry, if he did not exemplify them by finding in contemporary poems elements which are indubitably there.[9] If I remark to a Ramist that I do not believe that the poet had any such laborious and deliberate intention, he will respond that he does not care whether the poet did or did not, for his point is not that it is deliberate but that it is natural. It may, of course, be both; this is the sixteenth, not the nineteenth, century. However, the Ramist adduces his examples to prove not that poetry is logically complicated but that logic is natural to poets—as to all other reasoning men. Even Spenser's shepherds, says Fraunce, 'by the light of nature, did, asmuch as in them lay, expresse *this methode* in their speeches.'

Thus the connection between poetry and dialectic is not only something praiseworthy though occasional; it is inevitable, not

[7] Method is defined as a discourse of diverse Axioms of the same kind, placed according to their manifestness in nature (Wotton); the 'naturall methodical order' which Ramist logic discovers characterizes all ordered thought, as well as nature's progress in all her edifices (Granger, Book iv). This notion that 'arguments' need only be placed in open, natural, manifest order will be seen later to have further connection with attitudes toward imagery.

[8] Whereby disposition is artificially obscured either to delight or to move effectually; this is most used in sermons, orations, epistles, and poems.

[9] In this connection, for example, there is no denying the fact that in Hobbinol's song in the April eclogue of the *Shep. Cal.* there is—just as Fraunce points out—first a general proposition declaring the intention of praising Eliza, then praises from *causes*, then *adjuncts*, then other arguments incident to Eliza.

necessarily planned out, but in any case the natural mark of the poet as reasonable creature. What poet will not note with pleasure the natural logic of his own images when such doctrines become the fashion of the day, screwing up their unavoidable logical relevance with an additional witty twist? So far, however, we have simply to notice: that such general conceptions take hold much more easily than special points of doctrine; that no denizen of the cultivated world of the 1590's and early 1600's could escape knowing about them or miss the excitement caused by the Ramist idea of a unity of all arts of thought, past and present; and that imagery is bound to be written differently by a man who makes no basic separation between poet and dialectician.

It would be pure pedantry under the circumstances to make any fundamental division between poet and rhetor. In so far as they were arts of thought, poetry and rhetoric had not been divided prior to Ramus, either. In fact, we are seeing just another example of the way in which the accepted could become the startling; the old co-operation between the disciplines is now so willing that marriage has made them all one. The co-operation was based on fundamental similarity of aim; so is the unity.

Another famous change made by Ramus in the organization of the disciplines is the natural result. However natural, it caused large disturbance.

Ramus simply sliced off the first two divisions of rhetoric. His dialectic, traditionally enough, falls into the two great divisions or stages, Invention and Disposition. These had been also the traditional two first divisions of rhetoric, after which it proceeded to the three which Ramus' reorganization still left to it: *Elocutio* or eloquence (the tropes and schematic figures), Memory, Pronunciation (delivery).[10] Rhetoric had never claimed that it could get along without logic. But rhetoric itself had taught in these first two divisions the methods of inventing

[10] The Ramist rhetoric by Talaeus (Omer Talon) came out in 1567; it was known and used by all who knew Ramus' logic, since these changes in organization are an essential part of his doctrine. Besides omitting Invention and Disposition, it shears down the number of figures, dividing them still into tropes and schemes, but ordering them more severely and simply.

and disposing that were peculiarly useful to the writer as persuader, and, in so far as the poet was 'moving' anyone, it had taught him his methods, too. Rhetoric had taught him to 'demonstrate' (commend or vilify) and to 'deliberate' (persuade or plead), and the ways to organize certain types of discourses with certain purposes in mind. But under Ramus' rearrangement none of all this was any business of rhetoric.

This does not mean that orators and poets no longer were supposed to invent and dispose matter. It meant that they were to learn to do this from the discipline to which Ramus said it properly belonged: *dialectica*. Awareness of process might vary, but, given the structure of man's mind, there was but one way to 'invent' or think out what one wished to say—logically, and but one way to dispose thought—reasonably. As all reasonable men including poets followed these methods, more deliberately or less according to their lights, so the way to learn how to exercise them more skilfully was to study dialectic. Rhetoric is far from useless or trivial; it must still handle, alone, all those formal helps to clear, pleasing, *and suitable* expression through which a framework of thought can come to be articulate and powerful. It is simply that the rhetor is a logician, just as any other writer of anything must be, *in the first stages of composition* —those dealing with the finding of matter for a discourse and with organizing it.[11]

Neither is this removal of rhetoric's first two sections so profound a change, on the face of it. Plenty of rhetorical handbooks had appeared which dealt simply with the third division, with the figures of Eloquence which can scarcely be remembered without some manual. It is the implications again which are to be influential. If finding matter and arranging it are taught, and thought to be sufficiently taught, as the logician teaches them,

[11] As Fraunce says: what precepts soever the common Rhetoricians put down for ordering of exordiums and framing and disposing the whole course of their speech according to 'cause,' auditors, and so on, 'all those I say, are altogether Logicall,' not in any respect pertaining to rhetoric *but as* a Rhetor may be directed by Logical precepts of judgment and disposition. I.e., he learns, and uses, all precepts touching framing and ordering, *qua* dialectician (see *L.L.*, ii, 17). One must bear in mind that in the sixteenth century this does not necessarily constitute, as it would today, a threat to the unity of the whole process by which an 'oration' or a poem is conceived-and-ordered-and-expressed. See below, chap. xiv.

we may expect a conceptual strictness in poetry which was not there before. If the old separation between demonstrative and deliberative 'orations' goes into the discard, and with it the conception it preserved of different structures and ornament for differing purposes, in lyrics, and if all pieces have instead a dialectical base, we may expect to see some changes in lyric theory. The user of the old-fashioned rhetorical handbook knew he was learning about one stage only of the whole process of composition, and so did the user of Talaeus; but only the latter was told that the earlier stages could be no other than dialectical. Any poet who believed what he was told would look to the strictness of his logic; and no reader who had come to expect the intellectual toughness of good upstanding dialectic in all kinds of discourse could be put off with the old ambling pace. Nothing new had to be mastered; no Englishman who had been through school or university was untrained in dialectic (and, indeed, if no study of technical logic had been done outside the universities, I should probably have had no translations to use in these chapters). But when a background becomes the foreground, there is a change in the picture.

If the Ramists had meant, by their stress on dialectic, that all discourse is disputation, perhaps fewer literary men would have listened to them. But they did not mean this. Herein lies another of the insinuatingly important general conceptions which altered men's attitudes and which made those Ramists who had never read Ramus' books. In this case what changes is the general conception of the nature of proof. The Ramist objects strenuously to the notion that all dialectic is argumentation, in the ordinary sense. Logic has been a long time untolerably abused, says Fraunce (i, 1), by those miserable Sorbonists who thought there was no reasoning without *Arguitur quod sic: Probatur quod non*, no part of logic without *Ergo* and *Igitur*. Whereas the true use of logic, says he, is as well apparent in simple, plain, and easy *explication* as in subtle and strict *probation*. 'Reade Homer, reade Demosthenes, reade Virgill,' Cicero, Bartas, Tasso, and the Countess of Pembroke's *Arcadia*, and therein see the true effects of natural logic.

If logic is no more concerned with proving strongly than with 'framing orderly' and 'expounding playnly,' we see that we must understand the Ramist extension of dialectic to cover all forms of discourse not as impelling a poet to 'prove something' in every poem, but rather as impelling him to declare reasons and causes, to examine the nature of something, to consider from various sides, to figure out, look into, mull over.

I might remark that this is precisely what most Metaphysical poems do and that the deliberate use of intellectually acute and strong images is bound to accompany such purposes, but another closely related element in Ramist conceptions of 'reasoning' claims attention first.

It is true that the Ramist is anxious to have it understood that dialectical invention (i.e., all invention) is concerned with 'declaring,' setting out, making known, not just with the devising of arguments to prove (Wotton, p. 4). But he is also convinced that the mere orderly setting-out of matters does demonstrate truth or falsity. That is, an orderly disposition of 'axioms' does constitute proof; in *doubt*, one has recourse to the syllogism.[12] The Ramist's profound belief in a reasonable order in nature allows him to have things both ways. Dialectic is just concerned with orderly thinking—every man's province; thoughts placed in order, however, will demonstrate the truth of a matter without the use of other dialectical tools. Dialectic is not synonymous with disputatious 'proving'; dialectically sound statements do, nevertheless, 'prove.' Apply this to poetry—and that it should be so applied is at the very heart of the doctrine—and you have a poem that has but to examine and state, with due care for dialectical soundness in the reasoning, in order to argue the truth or advisability of something.

Add to this one other Ramistic concept, and it seems to me that one comes out with the description of a Metaphysical poem. The other concept is that images (tropes, concretions, metaphorical epithets, descriptive definitions) are 'arguments.'

---

[12] Milton's Book ii furnishes a typical exposition of this; Wotton's is similar, as he handles the joining-together of arguments according to the rules of an axiom, in order to judge of truth or falsehood (see esp. chaps. 1 and 2 of Book ii); or see Granger, ii, 16, on axiomatical doctrine, and the need for syllogisms if fools cannot get wisdom in their hearts by declaration and illustration.

I do not suggest that Ramistic attitudes must produce none other than Metaphysical poems, but only that in an intellectual world where such attitudes toward imaginative literature became every year more prevalent, no result is more natural than the dialectical toughness of the Metaphysical poem, its substitution of intellectual probing for rhetorical persuasion. Donne is not hortatory after the old fashion; he sets out, examines, makes known the true nature of a subject, with axioms in the form of images that go to their mark like bullets. Carew and Suckling only occasionally plead outright with a mistress; they state with apparently unassailable logic that such is the state of affairs, and such the natural conclusion. King amplifies his grief not by calling out upon the high heavens but by showing exactly whence his grief depends and how it operates. Sidney does not need to orate in order to argue with his mentors touching the reasonableness of his love for Stella; he simply has to state certain self-evident truths about love, reason, and Stella. So Donne 'argues' the frailty and decay of the world in the 'First Anniversary'; so Marvell allows the Resolved Soul to vanquish Created Pleasure.

This is no more 'new' than Ramus is new. Poets had used the methods of dialectic before Ramus was heard of; but then they had done so much else, had used so many other methods, that one scarcely noticed this element in the whole. And so did poets go on using the old methods; in all these poets I have mentioned, the old 'demonstrations' and 'deliberations' and skilful rhetorical schemes occur. They suffer a certain eclipse, and one of the reasons they are hidden to us is that a special brilliance lightens one particular element in all this poetry: the imagery. Neither is the Metaphysical conceit a new phenomenon. But the images in Metaphysical poetry are more numerous, more consistently of one kind, and (this is the same point as the last) used for a narrower variety of functions.

The Ramistic notion of figures in a discourse—that they are 'arguments'—contributed, as usual, nothing but an emphasis. That figures are functional had been the accepted basis of advice, praise, and warnings concerned with them in orthodox

Renaissance poetic. But the understanding of their functions had been in the highest degree delicate; like a single brush stroke in a painting, a figure might cast but the shadow of a shadow upon the meaning and yet be part of it. That multiplication of divisions and complex classification of figures which the Ramists deplored resulted largely from this idea that, of the infinite variety of minute formal characteristics, none was too small to make a difference. To the Ramist, nothing was too small to make a *logical* difference.

'Argument' is a special, technical word in Ramist writings. The best I can do with it is to say that it seems to indicate the relatable*ness* of a word or thing; that aspect by which we conceive of it as relatable to another word or thing. It is that which has a fitness to argue something;[13] every several 'respect' (relation, reference) is an argument—as man referred to God is an *effect*, referred to sickness, is a *subject*, referred to a place he dwells in, is an *adjunct* (Wotton, pp. 5–6).[14] Any two such 'arguments' combine in readiness to be juxtaposed to others and form concepts.

A word, a thing, a relation, a concept—all may be seen as arguments; the moment I look at any of these, seeing its fitness to be related to another, I see it as an argument (*ratio*, reason). I may look at a tree and see it as an argument of the Creator; if I use a trope and compare it to a young man in his first strength, I adduce yet another argument of God's power—as the Cambridge Ramist Richardson says in his commentary on Talaeus' rhetoric, a trope is sweet not only because it gives 'a splendour, but besides that *it carrieth us to another Argument* from whence it was drawn' (p. 50). All images which have any reason for

[13] *Argumentum est quod ad aliquid arguendum affectum est.* The explanations and illustrations in Miller, *op. cit.* (in n. 1 above), esp. p. 124, are helpful. My metaphor of *hooking* arguments together so that the 'affection' to argue caught into a juxtaposed argument, is from Richardson (p. 76), who, though late for my purposes, often uses clarifying similes in his exposition.

[14] Thus the 'affection' of arguments may be altered, diversely considered, as Fraunce says, so that he can draw 'Man' through the whole string of places, showing the disposition of the 'argument' *Man* to argue something different according as man is referred to this or that other 'argument' (i, 2). I should remark that dangerous falsifications of Ramistic theory result, if the reader reads his ordinary definition of an *argument* into sentences in which I shall use the Ramist term.

being in a piece of discourse function therein as arguments (in the Ramist sense, not ours); any single word is on its way to a concept. Every image or term of an image has a fitness to argue many different things, and authors differ in the skill they show in ordering arguments reasonably and powerfully. This conception of an infinite progression of logical relationships is at the very core of the Ramist idea of *all* thinking as a vast orderly arrangement in which argument was hooked into argument, lesser attached to greater, word to concept, concept to larger concept, in an unbroken reasonable pattern. The inevitability of a conception of imagery as logically functional, given this understanding of the nature of thought and hence of all discourse, is obvious.

I am scarcely in a position to claim that it was Ramistic ways of thinking which caused men to think of imagery as logically functional in a poem, having spent large numbers of pages in trying to demonstrate that this was an orthodox sixteenth-century attitude. Having suggested also that much imagery cannot help functioning so, I should be quite willing to stop off and notice the presence of logically functioning images in Chaucer or in Yeats—images which define, differentiate, explain or support by similitudes. The deliberateness with which poets utilize such possibilities of imagery does, I think, vary with period, varying as it must with training and with habitual attitudes taken toward poetry's aims and toward the poet's medium and tools. All that is peculiar about the Ramistic understanding of these matters is the high-powered searchlight which it threw upon imagery's capacity to function in this manner.

Particular remarks made in Ramist discussions would cause us no surprise if we met them in Peacham or Puttenham. We have heard time and again that the 'innumerable *Epithits* of the Orators and Poets,' indicating *adjuncts* of something, afford more perfect understanding to the mind, since they are 'briefe explications, descriptions, &c.,' or since they can be used to 'confirme, or give a reason' (Granger, pp. 68–71). No orthodox rhetorician was surprised to hear that the arguments he

'fetched' from *Honestum* and *Utile* were for the most part derived from the end or *final cause* (Fraunce, i, 4). The same holds
for various other statements recognizing the 'logic' of images.[15]
But these traditional ties between logic and the poet's methods
take on a new force against the background of the Ramist conception that *every* unit in *every* type of discourse must, the moment it is seen in relation to any other unit, inescapably make
some minute step toward a true or false disposition or pattern.
Logic no longer merely offers the poet helps; he cannot but take
part in the universal and natural attempt to trace out the reasonable pattern of reality, and since every word he uses has its
modicum of conceptual gunpowder, it behooves him to notice
the exact direction in which he points it.

These ideas do not look 'merely academic' when one sees
where they led. There is a certain excitement about a minor
result like Richardson's statement in his commentary on
Talaeus that poetry is a branch of rhetoric (p. 70). It is a
branch of a branch, of course; dialectic is the trunk, presumably, but the tree upon which the Ramist's eye was fixed was
that universal reasonable order which it is the business of all
disciplines to assist men to perceive. That this order was the
pattern in the mind of God, that men might thus have knowledge of that pattern, that pursuit of the 'arguments' or
'reasons' in the universe would with proper dialectical safeguards lead one to indisputable knowledge of reality—all these
further ramifications are beyond the bounds of this discussion.
They furnish a tissue of old and new which requires discriminations of extreme subtlety; one may look at a sentence and be
struck simultaneously by its being almost identical with some
scholastic commonplace *and* by its being so phrased that it
could support the position taken by the Moderns toward the
rising sciences (e.g., the definition of truth as the adequation
between the thing as indeed it is and the understanding,
Wotton, ii, chap. 3). Luckily the two remaining points I shall

[15] Ramists did not discover the fact that 'Matter of praysing and dispraysing commonly is set from' the place *effect* (Fraunce, i, 5). Ramists warn one in the traditional
fashion against the 'weakness' of arguing by similitudes (Granger; Milton); it is the
warning any medieval or Renaissance student could have given Marlowe's Hero.

mention, at which Ramistic conceptions of reality touch imagery in a way directly affecting poetic practice, offer no such complications.

One is the great stress on the capacity of 'specials' to *state* 'generals'; when this is exemplified by poetic passages, the net result is an emphasis upon the power of an image to convey a concept, the power of a particular to 'say' or make manifest a universal. I have tried too hard to suggest that Elizabethans thought of particulars in terms of their 'significance' to be willing to call this new. The relation of Ramistic thinking to orthodox thinking is the same in this case as in others; emphasis and new contexts give new implications to old notions. When Puttenham describes the use of *exempla* (III, xix, p. 245), we seem to be reading about a poet exemplifying what he is saying by giving a concrete 'case' of it. But when Wotton in his version of Ramus gives us a passage from Ovid using 'examples,' we are left in no doubt that the Ramist saw something more: 'Here the *Poët* proveth the generall, that Adversitie sheweth true vertue; by three specialls: Hector making known his valour, Typhis shewing his skill in storms, Phoebus his art in sickness' (i, 26).

More than one type of image is affected by this general attitude; similitudes, examples, supporting concrete detail (such as that Fraunce adduces from *Shep. Cal.*), must all be seen as inevitably important to the conceptual structure.[16] This is at bottom an attitude toward the nature and structure of reality, like so many of the reasons which lie behind the nature of images in any given period. The influential part of the notion is that which receives emphasis elsewhere in Ramist doctrine— that the tiniest unit functions in a structure of thought by virtue of something in *its* nature; that, since the tie is essential, the special cannot help but 'mean' the general.

[16] Nor need we attend to all the logical distinctions which could be involved. Though it is important for images using simple particulars that Fraunce should claim (fol. 34^v) that no one before Ramus 'durst absolutely pronounce an Individuu*m*, as Socrates, to bee a speciall.' The influential point for imagery is that since specials *state* generals, every such image has validity as a logical argument; this does not imply that knowledge of a few specials necessarily constitutes full knowledge of generals (which the Ramist warns against). Man might still misread this relation, and he must still attend to warnings regarding insufficient data.

It does not seem necessary to make a new heaven and a new earth (as modern criticism has been quite willing to do) to account for the Metaphysicals' habit of embodying the statement of a concept in an image, if one picks up such a poem just after reading in Fraunce that 'If you put downe one, more, or all the specials, you also put downe the generall, for that the nature and essence of the generall is in every of the specials' (i, 6). I have suggested earlier that Donne is merely emphasizing a typical Renaissance understanding of the relation between particular and universal when he remarks that the brittleness of the jet ring can *say* or *speak* a property of his lady's heart. Nevertheless, Ramistic thinking gave new force to such ideas. It reinforced their logical validity, making this aspect of language's mode of operation clear cut and reasonable rather than undefined and mysterious. The conceptual contribution of metaphor[17] had always been pretty clearly seen; when even the lowly 'example' as used by a poet is seen to have logical *vertu* or strength, the ties between poetic method and logic are becoming close indeed.

For it is not unimportant that particulars or concrete cases are introduced as arguments from *special* to *general*, rather than as arguments from *testimony*. I am inclined to think that modern distaste for the 'mere illustration,' especially from the past, rises from our thinking of it as a mere expository flourish, a simple mentioning of a case in point which lends an air of authority and swells the volume of a passage but adds nothing. So seen, in so far as it has any structural relevance, the 'example' is just another witness and resembles the citation of authorities. When Spenser (*S.C.*, July, 149) fetches in Paris as an example of shepherds who were proud, we feel annoyed at the weakness of an argument which seems to run 'Paris should not have been proud; our shepherds [churchmen] had better not be proud either.' We dislike this easy appeal to the authority of the past

[17] As in the Donne example (see above, p. 290), the capacity of a single brittle thing to lead us to the notion of brittleness which links all brittle things; we ourselves make the predication not otherwise stated than *by the image*. Full *recognition* of metaphor's capacity to function thus (and of related but more complicated conceptual functioning natural to tropical language) is completely traditional.

to settle the problems of the present. But we may be quite certain that the Ramist at least did not think this was what he was doing when he adduced examples. He was *stating* his general point.

I should not be surprised if the Elizabethan who read Spenser's passage apprehended the relation of Paris to the point at issue in a way that is much closer to the Ramist way of regarding examples than to ours. I am quite sure that, when he read of Paridell's descent from Paris, he felt the *universalizing* power of this attachment of the Paridell seduction episode to a well-known specific story which had wide general meanings (*FQ*, III, ix). Again the Ramist understanding of how single units operated in poetic discourse reinforced habits of mind already well established in sixteenth-century thinking. The unequivocal sureness of the Ramist emphasis on this dialectical responsibleness is what counts for later poetry.[18] The seventeenth-century use of concrete example and ancient allusion is seldom logically loose. Like other figures, these see their duty and do it. Otherwise they do not appear.[19]

The logical duty of an extended exemplum is frequently to argue by analogy.[20] A great number of the images which have been pointed to in Metaphysical poetry as themselves constituting conceptual meanings without further 'general' statement are similitudes (as is Marvell's, praised for this power by Dobrée; see above, pp. 325–26). That similitudes are capable of

[18] Given the absence of poetical exemplification, it is not possible to say precisely whether a given orthodox peripatetic logician thought of poetical use of exempla and allusion as logically valid argument from special to general.

[19] The mere absence of narrative partially explains this, of course. The factor of genre is never to be disregarded in noting the character of a poet's imagery; its ties with decorum according to a poem's 'cause' are of the closest. I think that the growing prevalence of Ramistic ideas (concerning the relation of poetry to dialectic, for example) had something to do with shifts in the 'kinds' favored by poets. But this is the sort of point for which proper evidence cannot be furnished; we shall never have the knowledge which would enable us to isolate factors in such choices.

[20] Puttenham recognizes this. Ramist expositions of argument from *special* to *general* make it especially clear that 'examples' may simultaneously argue both from this logical place and from 'similitude' (see Milton, i, 27; or 1632). Images with such double logical functions are especially dear to Metaphysical poets, writing with dialectical sharpness in forms of short compass.

stating concepts is the orthodox defense of their use. Seen by Ramistic light, their ability to delineate the form of truth without the aid of abstract statement is all the better noted.[21]

The other point of Ramist doctrine which I wish to mention is its emphasis upon the disjunctive syllogism and upon the various kinds and degrees of diversity in things. I do not think that this is unconnected with the increased popularity of an important type of image—the 'figure of difference.' With respect to the 'doctrine of diverse things,' the Ramists claimed to have made an actual contribution to logic.[22] Ramists seem to be quite as interested in knowing what a thing is not as in knowing what a thing is, and the places through which they pursue the precise nature and extent of differences between things are numerous and carefully distinguished. Ramist logic was unorthodox in regarding the disjunctive mode with favor; and the extra importance which controversial points always receive gave extreme prominence to the careful distinction of diversity which this mode requires. The first example in Milton (ii, 15) is *It is either day or night, but it is not day, therefore it is night.* This is a familiar type of poetic argument; and, when it attained to dialectical respectability, the kind of negative definition which it encouraged became more popular still.[23]

The practical result of all such emphasis upon the doctrine of diversities, as far as imagery is concerned, is greater and more acute use of images which distinguish or differentiate. The apt and witty use of images with such functions is characteristic

[21] The understandings which these last paragraphs expound merely exemplify again the workings of the basic realism of the Ramists, their willingness to identify thing with *ratio*, idea with thing-as-it-is. Various quotations which make this philosophical alignment clearer may be found in Miller, *op. cit.* (in n. 1 above), pp. 147, 149, 151. Part I above is as important as the present one in showing why it was of importance to imagery that this attitude was reinforced by Ramistic thought.

[22] Their notion of what they contributed may be examined by reading Milton's recension, Book i, chaps. 12 ff. Or see, e.g., Spencer on dissenting arguments, for Ramist emphasis on negative definition.

[23] Poets were thoroughly accustomed to the use of arguments from difference to *illustrate, explicate, declare* (Granger's terms, p. 82); poets were as pleased as were any other writers to use them, with the blessing of the logicians, to *prove* and to *enforce* (as Granger recommends). Satire, for example, gained greatly in force under such understandings of what constituted good logic.

of early seventeenth-century verse, as it is of Sidney; the very many such images to be found in Donne's verse are of an extreme dialectical subtlety.

The relations between Ramist logic and poetic practice are seldom of so particular a character, and, although this last point could be demonstrated with accuracy and convincingness from a known Ramist like Sidney, I should rather suggest certain vaguer and more deep-going relations. One is dealing here with a slow realignment of attitudes toward poetry. That this realignment affected imagery is, I think, indisputable; yet it is both dangerous and unprofitable to say where such effects began or left off. Moreover, what poets were discouraged from doing, because Ramistic notions were prevalent, is as important as any positive effect. I have preferred therefore simply to present the differences in Ramus' conceptions of thought and of discourse which must affect the way a poet conceives of images and their functions; I shall not draw the lines of influence much tighter than that. It is sufficient if we realize that many of the qualities which we have been puzzled to account for, in the Metaphysicals especially, are better understood if we connect them with an undoubted fact: that these conceptions of Ramus' entered the intellectual world of England during the latter years of the sixteenth century, under the auspices of circles like Sidney's and to the accompaniment of such enthusiasm or such controversial discussion as insured their quick and wide dissemination, and that Ramus' ideas gradually took the field during the first half of the seventeenth century.

Such understandings as I have outlined help to account for qualities of images which are not new qualities but rather old ones highlighted; the light falls precisely upon those characteristics and those functions which Ramus' conceptions could not fail to emphasize. The English poetic tradition, so far as images are concerned, seems to me so much of a piece from Marlowe (or Wyatt) to Marvell that I do not care to press the points I have tried to make. A little pressure goes a long way in this case. I do not think that it is possible to read through the major contentions in any Ramist handbook, and follow this with a re-reading of Donne's poems, without arriving at the notion that these intellectual developments of Donne's day explain his processes of thought and his own attitudes toward such processes far more satisfactorily than any of the current popular phrases about 'feeling' his 'thought.' Except for such general caveats, I am little interested in providing a new 'explanation' of the Metaphysical image (no new creature). Any literary problem involving thousands of minute choices and infinite numbers of unconscious influences is so complex that all correct explanations together can point to but a part of a part of what went into the forming of any single image. The reader may hence choose for himself the extent to which he applies specific concepts of Ramist logic in the interpretation of any given single image.

Certain possible connections, general in nature, seem to me important and interesting; and recapitulation of them may serve as concluding summary. The dialectical acuteness and ratiocinative temper of early seventeenth-century poetry are commonly recognized; during the same decades Ramistic ideas were taking down the barriers between poetical discourse and dialectic. Metaphysical poets handle philosophical and ontological problems directly in poems, not denying themselves the use of methods which many eras have found too intellectually agile for verse; meanwhile, Ramists were propounding the unity of all discourse and exemplifying the methods of logicians from the works of poets. Ramus cut off from rhetoric the old divisions of invention and disposition, with their exposition of the ways to present 'demonstrative' and 'deliberative' 'causes'— intentions which pretty well cover the lyrical output of earlier years; the years which saw the gradual popularization of this change are the years in which we see the development of the typical Metaphysical lyric. The authors of such lyrics deliberate in the 'middle' philosophical style and in a somewhat novel fashion—examining, meditating, pursuing differences and essences and causes. Dialectic, which had been popularly thought of as disputation, came under the Ramists to include any reasonable 'explication' or attempt to distinguish truth and falsity

—and logically careful axiomatic statement, general *or* particular, was its primary instrument, rather than the formal syllogism. The reflective poetry of the early seventeenth century (and this includes much of the love poetry) is generally concerned to make this attempt, using this instrument.

Under Ramistic conceptions of the nature of thought, of the functions of discourse, and of the operation of language, poetic imagery would possess in emphatic and exaggerated form certain normal characteristics of images. Imagery seen in the light of these conceptions would be indisputably functional. 'Decorative' images would not be a desideratum; they would indeed scarcely be a possibility. Functioning as units in a 'dialectical' discourse, images would have a logical toughness and an intellectual fineness which could stand to the tests of such discourse. Images would be many, and oftener tropical than schematic, for their usefulness and dignity as 'arguments' were unquestioned, and they could reach outward by the use of trope to further and deeper arguments. The nature of their terms might range from the most subtle of abstractions to the most ordinary of daily objects, for their logical function outweighed the old considerations which dictated the terms of 'amplifying' imagery, while emphasis upon relations to dialectic impelled poetry toward the middle style and relaxed certain kinds of decorum conventionally observed in the two extreme styles. Images framed and used according to these freshly emphasized conceptions of their functioning would not disdain hyperbole or potent suggestions, but their chief characteristics would be aptness, subtlety, accuracy of aim, disregard of the superficially pleasing, logical power, ingenious or startlingly precise relationships or parallels, a certain 'obscurity' due to logical complexity or tenuous attachment—but an obscurity capable of becoming sharp 'clarity' upon thoughtful reading.

These are normally the characteristics of Metaphysical imagery.

CHAPTER XIII

EFFECTS OF SPECIFIC LOGICAL FUNCTIONS
UPON THE POETIC CHARACTER
OF IMAGES

THIS chapter must simply run the risk of oversimplification. The risk would be but little lessened by tedious
reiteration of the fact that we deal with poems, not
logical exercises. Here, as elsewhere, each image represents an
aesthetic choice, made by a sensitive mind and made against the
background of a whole life of experience and training—so that
our ignorance of many factors operating in that choice is very
great and is without cure.

The matter can be treated with a little more of the delicacy
which it merits if most of the examples are chosen from one
poet. To illustrate with images from all over the period would be
easy, but it would be endless. Only one thing would be easier:
to exemplify from Donne. But perhaps the application of relevant points to the strictest poet-logician of his times is so simple
and so obvious that it may be left to any unprejudiced reader in
his own next encounter with the images of the *Anniversaries,*
or of the shorter reflective pieces, or of the *Songs and Sonets,*
those masterpieces of dialectic lyrical, satirical, panegyrical,
comical-tragical-pastoral, trope undividable and invention unlimited. I shall illustrate most largely from the poems of Bishop
King. The body of his work is manageably small; the genres he
favors are those to which some of the best seventeenth-century
poets narrowed their work; useful sidelights are provided by his
use of images in a group of sermons from 1621 to 1664 which are
interesting and little known by readers of his poetry; we have
one of the few literary credos of any length published by a
Metaphysical poet, in his visitation sermon preached at Lewes

in 1662.[1] By centering temporarily upon King, I do not wish to prove that the logical functioning of images is peculiarly Metaphysical. In fact, this chapter will not prove anything. Its dialectic is Ramistic.

I shall attempt to 'explicate' and 'declare' the poetic effects of only the most omnipresent and influential logical functions of images. These seem to be: to define or elucidate the nature of something; to differentiate or discriminate; to support convincingly or even adduce proofs—usually by that method not entirely trusted by logicians, the similitude.

1. *Images Which Define*

Naturally, many images which define or elucidate appear in any sermon of King's, as in any other prose type. Their number and excellence are increased by a tendency to substitute vivid explanation for direct exhortation; this tendency King shares with various other seventeenth-century sermon-writers.[2]

In a sermon published in 1627[3] a long image with many parts

[1] This sermon, published in *1663*, will be referred to by that date. The fact that King intends his remarks to be applied to writing in a particular prose kind (sermons) means that his critical generalizations must be related with caution to his poetic practice. The two suit very well, however. This literary credo comes late in his life, and a man might well change his mind on critical principles between the 1630's and the 1660's in England. Yet the orthodox positions which King upholds in 1662 *must be understood in the same way* to account for his own practice *both* in his poems (mostly early) and in any of his sermons, late or early. To see his own work in both types as his way of applying his own critical pronouncements—which amount to a restatement of good orthodox sixteenth-century principles—is to make a neat demonstration of the flexible way in which orthodox aesthetic was able to take care of Metaphysical habits and fashions in writing.

[2] See the Appendix, Note U, for references touching the difficult problem, here unattempted, of relations between Ramistic ideas and prose style in sermons.

[3] On the text 'Remember now thy Creator in the days of thy youth'; the third part of what King generally calls his 'Division' springs from the words '*Thy* Creator' and treats of the proper end to which man should direct his knowledge and memory: his own cause, God. The sermons are listed chronologically in the Bibliography. This one was preached in 1625. Date of composition often antedates publication by a year or so, but I shall save frequent footnotes by conventionalizing references, to date of publication and page upon which an image commences (e.g., 1627:15). References to images in the poems are simplified to mere page numbers in Sparrow's edition. Paraphrasing is a falsification of any image, but I preserve crucial wording as conscientiously as possible.

It is improbable that King wrote the passages I quote without remembering famous similar ones in Augustine (*Conf.* x. 8) and Petrarch (quoting Augustine, *Fam.* iv. 1).

(King's frequently take half or a whole page) helps to define more carefully that general vice of man, that he loves not to be acquainted with himself. Like a humorous Novelist, man travels other countries, like the elephant abhors to see himself in the stream; we love to study other men, we who should rather make our own bosoms our chief libraries, seeking knowledge of causes by tracking God our cause to his retiring chamber within ourselves (1627:15). King begins 'An Elegy Occasioned by sickness' (96) with the Prophet's question *Lord what is man*, and meditates throughout an image-series of fourteen lines on 'Man is a stranger to himself.' He 'loves to travel countreys,' 'Delights to sit in Nile or Boetis lap / Before he hath sayl'd over his own Map,' returns knowing less of himself than when he went. 'Therefore might I advise,' concludes King, make man 'into his proper Opticks look, / And so become the student and the book.'

All writers repeat their own images. What is interesting here is that similarity in function (to elucidate a general idea strikingly enough so that it takes hold) produces, in both prose and verse, images with the same tone, the same witty compression, the same relation between concrete and abstract, the same reasonable advising as the image is pointed to its conclusion. The final twist is given by a metaphor of which King's most famous use is in the 'Exequy' (38): *'thou art the book, / The library whereon I look.'* Obviously this metaphor comes up usefully in King's mind when he wishes to talk about serious contemplation, whether contemplation of one's Creator, one's own nature, or a mourned woman. His use of the image in different contexts and literary forms warns us that he attends first to its logical usefulness in stating some variant of this notion; if he chose images primarily for the connotative reach that poetry needs more than prose, for their witty dissonance in an exequy, and so on, then we ought not to find virtually the same terms in these several places.

The tropes by which King 'opens' some *general* like Sin or Resolution or Hope are magnificently plentiful, imaginative, and economical; they seem to me very similar in conception in the prose and the poems. This is not a new function for trope; the traditional descriptions are 'light up,' 'make clear,' 'illustrate.' 'The Labyrinth' (91) is a 'deliberative' piece, that is, it pleads with Christ for help; but it does so by considering the nature of that 'homebred tyrannie,' the conflict between will and desire. The crooked labyrinth is life (vs. 1); it is also sin (vs. 37), since the poem's first point is the lifelong confused ineptitude with which man wanders daily into new sins, the most discerning eye being dark and blind in our own ills' prevention, unless we are helped by the clue of God's grace. Image and abstract statement combine to search into the labyrinthine workings of man's affection to sin; the poem is not a description of the state of mind of Henry King. Defining images which clarify the nature and workings of the passions are scarcely new to English poetry. They show similar characteristics when they appear in poems like this one, in the *Faerie Queene*, in King's sermons.

We may look at a few images defining such 'generals,' from prose and from poetry. Sin is a *fruitful parent* and never yet wanted issue, one misery calling up another as word will pass from sentinel to sentinel in a camp (1621:43); sin is an *epidemical sickness* whereof the whole world labors (1625:8). *Unconfessed* sin is the weightiest of sorrows, lodging misery in the heart like an *exhalation enclosed* in the earth and causing a quake (1625:6); sin is a *loud argument*, which if it want other tongues will relate itself.[4]

Repentance is an antidote for sin (1627:30, sermon 2); the sick soul poisons even that antidote ('Labyrinth,' 92). Jealousy once lodged, the heart weakens through *feeding* its own self with *self-consuming* smart, for this passion is a snake, nursed up on bitter milk; a pain bitter in root and stalk is engrafted in the heart by

---

[4] The completion of this image does not define, but one 'amplifying' continuation is too admirably phrased to omit: For sin is the worst of secrets—no bosom where it is safe, to make it manifest *'Night* would convert it selfe into a *Noone*, and *Silence* prove a *speaking evidence* against thee' (1625:16, 18; author's italics). Compare with the majesty of this threat the defining neatness of: Man's own body is like a *net*, cast over the soul, entangling her, so that the more he struggles the more he is implicated (1626:43); if man does not call upon Christ, he will be wrackt on his *own coast* (1628:265).

love frustrated, and if the fruit have no more sweetness than the plant, death must ensue; grief and jealousy are huge waves into which a man is plunged deep, inward grief a cud he chews, consuming his own gall.[5] Doubt treads with nicety, as though thorns lay underfoot, the reed it leans upon shrinks when weight is put hard upon it; grief's pincers pinch through to the heart, to kill slowly with inner wounds. Hope is a mere voice, a dream of nothing, a smooth quicksand; thou shalt not *bury* me in thy false *smiles*, says King (11), get rather to fools that can feed fat with noise, persuade the hopeless—the wretches marked for death, men broken on the wheel.

All these images function similarly, clarifying the nature and mode of operation of these abstractions by drawing resemblances to more familiar or tangible things on the basis of *manner of doing, quality, effect*. All are tropical, pass easily from concretion to abstraction, from straight statement to paradox or to wrenched metaphors very nearly 'mixed.'[6] This is quite simply a similarity in image-technique, caused by similarity in function, and argues no special affinity between poets who use it.

If it be thought that this is an easy game to play, and that amid the hundreds of images in English poems dozens are bound to resemble one another whether they serve similar functions or not, one has only to look at some which do serve a different function. Be the difference ever so slight, method of framing the image and hence its character and aesthetic effect will differ, though the images be found in the same poet and in similar genres. In stanza 2 of 'My Midnight Meditation' (94), King does not occupy himself with explaining the concept introduced with a sharp two-line definition in verses 3–4, but with 'diminishing' or making negatively impressive the puny length of 'lifes

---

[5] These three images come from *FQ*, III, xi, 1; ii. 17; x, 17–18; the next two from III, xii, 10, 16.

[6] Effects got by crossing the logical bridge swiftly to that which holds with most force *of the abstraction* defined through the image: e.g., King's smiling hope (sand) which can *bury*, Spenser's nourishing that *consumes*. Naturally, the whole pieces from which all these images come must differ by virtue of the extent to which they contain other very differently functioning images, by virtue most of all of the differences in form which arise from difference in intention (genre, stanza, line length, prose or metered rhythm, rhetorical figuring).

short Kalendar.' The logic becomes looser, our senses are more active in imaging the listed adjuncts: the beating of thy pulse is just the tolling of thy passing bell, the weeping dews but thy funeral tears, night is thy hearse, its sable canopy covering deceased day and thee. Each flower cries 'Fool! as I fade . . . . thou must dy.' The tone and images are less like those of King's 'Labyrinth' than like Herrick's, whose numerous poems with this 'cause'[7] display a great variety of images framed similarly to these.[8]

Any approach to the purposes of definition affects the imagery, even though the image has another than this logical *raison d'être*. When King tells 'his unconstant Friend' (24) in full detail just how he does not intend to die of her neglect, he is really concerned with 'diminishing' her powers; the end result is a description or 'imperfect definition' of a lover wasting in despair, presented as a diminution or meiosis. (He does not intend to weep when he should eat, sigh when he should sleep, fall upon his pointed quill, bleed ink and poems, despair in prose and hang himself in rhyme.) This could be matched in many a sonnet (of any date) showing a similar combination of aims, and is very different from the grave explanations of 'The Surrender' (17). Meiosis may, of course, diminish a subject *by* defining, and when it does is not like King's leisurely satirical description of the foolish *inamorato* but sharp and biting, like the definitions of false hope, above, or like Donne's elucidations of the body's worthlessness—it is a prison, a poor inn, a province packed up in two yards of skin (*Second Anniv.*, p. 256).

I have remarked that variety in kinds of images needed was gradually restricted as the list of preferred genres narrowed down and as sharpened attention to the similarities between poetry and other forms of reasonable 'dialectical' discourse made some of the old rhetorical 'kinds' seem old-fashioned. Thus some

---

[7] In this and the following chapter this Elizabethan term is again especially useful for its convenient succinctness; see above, chap. i, n. 7, if frequent intervening uses of it in its logical senses have clouded its meaning in sixteenth-century critical usage.

[8] Similar differences from the defining images quoted obtain in the closing figure of King's 'The Farewell' (3–4)—because it *amplifies* the lover's sorrow by a feigned situation, complete with 'circumstances' of cell, knell, epitaph, and hollow echo.

types of images which are most *un*like defining images are seldom exemplified in King, being most congenial to 'kinds' he does not touch. Some such are: (1) the quick descriptive comparison making appearance or action vivid—Florimell's face 'white as whales bone' through fear (*FQ*, III, i, 15); the stroke so powerful that Red Crosse might have been powdered as thin as flour (I, vii, 12). Or (2) the more leisurely simile of the high style, serving similar purposes—Red Crosse annoyed but not hurt by the spawn of infant errors, like the famous cloud of gnats about the shepherd (I, i, 23); Una in the situation of a lamb which, expecting to be a wolf's dinner, sees a lion approaching and quakes 'With chaunge of feare' (I, vi, 10). Or (3) the suggestive image used to intensify the mood of a whole scene, powerful sometimes through subtlety, sometimes through allusive spaciousness—e.g., the insidiously amorous seduction of Danae when Jove 'Did raine into her lap an hony dew' (III, xi, 31), or the whole great Circe-image of the Acrasia canto (II, xii). Or (4) the simple narrative type of amplifying image to magnify a character's importance—Florimell's flying hair like the locks of a blazing star that makes the people stand aghast, importuning disaster (III, i, 16).[9] King does not write poems whose 'causes' are best opened and assisted by such images.[10]

If an image which helps to define the nature of something differs much from the more usual tools of the narrator such as these last, it differs also from the image which helps disputation

---

[9] Several of these types could be turned up on any page of any novel, and the reason is not far to seek—the demands of narrative. Like King, Donne prefers other genres; but when occasionally some subject requires a descriptive passage, for example, as in 'The Storme' (pp. 176–77), the images are unlike his typical conceits. It rained as if the sun had drunk the sea and was sending it down, men peep forth from their cabins like souls from graves on the Last Day, the mast shakes with an ague, the hold is clogged with a salt dropsy—these could be images from Nashe's *Unfortunate Traveller*, for the quite ordinary reason that both men have similar tasks in hand.

[10] The moment Spenser approaches purposes which come closer to those in short reflective poems, he uses images for which we might find analogues in King. He may wish to give a reason for that tiny human perversity which makes one contradict what one likes to hear—a heart that is 'inly hurt' is eased by hearing of some slight hope, yet Britomart pretends to gainsay Arthur, 'So dischord oft in Musick makes the sweeter lay' (III, ii, 15). Or he describes Malbecco's wounded *amour propre*, the lingering resentment 'That as a Snake, *still lurked* in his wounded mind' (III, x, 55; probable pun).

by offering proof. Defining images used to explain are neat rather than cunning or subtly complex. King may wish (preaching on 'I said I will confess my sins') to expose more carefully the operation of good resolves, to explain that words are the introduction to deeds in God's method, the molds wherein actions are cast. Every purpose is a *silent dialogue* between the soul and her faculties; man is a *theater* with many subtle spectators waiting on every action. Thoughts are words' *elder brothers*, the most unalterable dialect, original and unconfused at Babel. But words are the *midwives* that deliver our thoughts (1625:3–5). This series of images rather clarifies than exhorts. I give examples from a poem in a note;[11] the same qualities appear. Images which explain, or by defining show the reasonableness of a position taken, are usually witty and compressed; they do not generally have the logical tightness and vigorous thrust of images used to prove.[12]

The quick 'bare' similitude is much used in both explanatory and argumentative images, and the first, like the second, must give the impression of logical competence to be effective. A Ramist would remind us that the same kind of argument 'may commonly serve both to declare and to confirm.'[13] The whole

[11] King explains ingeniously why he 'held it some allegiance not to write' joyful compliments to the King upon the occasion of the Prince's birth. Children are pledges of eternity, yet so are they reminders of mortality, for seen in the perspective of a longer view they seem 'The *smiling Preface* to our funerall,' and 'Like *succours in a Camp*, sent to make good / Their place that last upon the watches stood' (30). 'By this Grammar,' rejoicing over the child is no such compliment to the King.

[12] The contrast will show up if we watch King proceed from a mere *expounding of* the nature of sin (a snare only untwisted through repentance) to a direct *exhortation* arguing the dangers of that nature. Riches are most a snare if won by extortion, for the living of the poor is their very life—take heed then how you make your chests *cemeteries to bury* men quick, lest they become *gulfs to swallow* you too, and like true *tombs*, cause the *golden body* of that *saint* which lies there enshrined to *crumble* (1626:50). The conceited nature of this, with its double meanings and the shock of the apt, rapid parallels that seem found by elliptical leaps of the thought, is typical of images which try to convince, whether in prose or in poetry.

[13] Fraunce, fols. 9ᵛ–10ʳ; he who takes the word Argument only for a 'proofe or confirmation' deceives himself and bereaves logic of half her dignity. Let no man 'thinke there is no Logike, where there is no syllogisticall conclusion.' Fraunce's examples are from *Shep. Cal.*, Jan. and Sept., where arguments of *cause* are used 'onely for explication sake.' It is typical of the Ramist's way of thinking for Fraunce to add that, nevertheless, Diggon Davie does prove his point by clear asseveration and exposition.

force and virtue of Logic 'consisteth in reasoning,' which may
well take the form of 'solitary meditations and deliberations
with a mans selfe' (fol. 1ʳ). Like other Metaphysicals, King
frequently multiplies similitudes which keep the tone one of
meditative, unsentimental reasonableness though the situation
is charged with feeling; like them, he elucidates where earlier
poets might exclaim. Our hearts are tough as adamant, and as
nothing will cut it but diamond dust, so only our own dust,
misery, can cut our hard hearts to obedience (1627:9). Or see
the elegy on Gustavus Adolphus (75):

> Thy task is done; *as in a Watch the spring*
> Wound to the height, *relaxes* with the string:
> *So thy steel nerves* of conquest. . . . .
> . . . . *lie slackt* in thy last sleep.[14]

The resemblance may be rather fully indicated, or merely intimated, but the explanatory simile seems to declare unobtru-
sively that there is a certain reasonableness and order in the
whole sorry affair. This happens even when the basic similitude
is unstated, as in the military figure which constitutes a comment upon an unseasonable death: '. . . . nor are we *billited in
one clime*. / Nature hath pitch'd mankind at several rates' ('The
Departure,' 49). The very figure argues acceptance of the anomalies of our life and death.

Although it seems contradictory, the nature of something
may be declared and 'opened' by similitudes never openly
stated, if these be conventional enough. In the poem on His
Majesty's ship the 'Soveraign,' King allows for solemn and deep
reverberations of meaning by an implied comparison with something equally portentous and powerful—a planet and its influences (35; the 'aspect' and 'warring opposites' of vs. 8 establish the figure with perfect clarity). Or compare the hidden
simile of *life:stormy sea*, underlying the image of a coffin as a
safe harbor, land-bound, below cross winds or churlish tides
(90; 'Essay on Death and a Prison'). Both of these figures
amplify, besides declaring the nature of a thing by a concealed

---

[14] Or, 'It is the common fate, / Of greatest duties to evaporate / In silent meaning,
as we often see / Fires by their too much fuel smother'd be:' ('The Forfeiture,' 48).

similitude. But the different effect of a *purely* amplifying figure is apparent in the rash and powerful extravagance of

> At length (I fear) thy perjur'd breath
> *Will blow out day, and waken Death.*
>
> ('The Vow-breaker,' 2)

An unstated similitude is likely to lend subtlety; the compression of a resemblance into a metaphor lends, rather, terse sharpness to a defining image.[15] A single word is enough to convey an explanatory notion with extreme accuracy if the metaphor's terms have a significance so much part of common knowledge that 'translation' is immediate. This is exemplified also in images using the 'ecliptic line,' both in sermon and in poem. King, a constant defender of the King, writes in 1640 that those two jarring extremes, Papacy and Presbytery, whose opinions are opposite as the sides of the diameter, 'meet *in this one Ecliptick line*, to *darken*' the authority of God's anointed (1640: 29). Compare the much-praised image in 'An Acknowledgement' (47):

> Whose life your absence clouds, and makes my time
> Move blindfold *in the dark ecliptick line.*

King is not being daring, or dissonant, or penetrating tentatively into obscure reaches of the sensibility, in either case; he is being exact. Both images are admirable, but not for any new psychological discoveries they make. The second utilizes with beautiful delicacy that conventional figure of *the lady:the sun* which King has transposed into every key and elaborated in every mode, and always with exquisite restraint and tact.

The terse delimitation of an idea which King can secure with a single sharp metaphor is less apparent when he multiplies his comparisons, as in the definitions of man's nature in 'An Elegy Occasioned by sickness' (98)—a tree that withers faster than it grows, a torch puffed out by every wind, a web of forty weeks spun forth in pain and raveled out in a moment. Another varia-

---

[15] Such is the use of 'Grammar' in the poem about the Prince's birth (above, n. 11), or a similar use in speaking of wishes as springing from penury—the only 'grammar' by which they are taught to speak is want (1627: p. 9 of sermon 2). Or compare 'Natures true born child . . . . summes his years . . . . with no Arithmetick but tears,' in 'The Anniverse' (42).

tion appears when both tenor and vehicle are abstractions or 'generals' (this holds of the examples in n. 15). A yet more noticeable variation in effect results from definition according to the ancient pattern of a series of similitudes, stanza by stanza —e.g., the definition of man's life in 'The Dirge' (99–100): it is a storm (explained by *circumstances* and *effect*), it is a flower (*manner of doing*), a dream (defined by *qualities* and *effects*), a dial (*final cause* and functioning), an interlude.

Yet all these types of figures shed light on the nature of something, clarify our ideas of its essential cause, way of working, or substance, set its limits. All share the characteristics to which I have pointed, because these are required of images which are to accomplish such functions effectively and with that aesthetic fitness which comes of suiting form to intention.

These same characteristics are shared also by defining images written by poets of very different date and temperament. General developments in the history of thought sometimes cause poets to emphasize such functions more than is usual.

2. *Images Which Differentiate*

Assistance in making discriminations is a fairly common service to which images can be put. We do much of this without realizing it. To an Elizabethan it would have been a more conscious process, for he was accustomed to defining by noting the class to which something belonged and adding its 'difference.' The ultimate usefulness of differentiating images in a discourse is often, then, better definition. As open an example as one could find occurs in King's poem 'Being waked out of my sleep by a snuff of Candle which offended me, I thus thought' (93). '*Man* is *a Candle* . . . . Here is *the diff'rence*.' Man, too, hastes, by degrees of wasting, to darkness—but his snuff and ashes are not his end; 'God will restore those fallen lights again / And kindle them to an Eternal flame.'[16]

[16] Donne begins his 'First Anniv.' by differentiating between possessing a soul and lodging 'an In-mate soule' (p. 231); a soul sees and judges and follows worthiness, etc. (definition by *manner of doing*), and thus only is one 'sure he hath a Soule.' In a few lines the difference between a lethargy and health after a spent ague helps him to characterize the world as really sick though deceptively appearing well.

The difference which points up the nature of something is often conveyed solely or almost solely through the particulars mentioned, which gives a special concision and neat concreteness to passages using such images. Speaking of the impermanence of man's glory, King says that we have not *freeholds* but *farms*, are not *inheritors* but *tenants*, whereas the great landlord of Nature has everlasting titles, Eternity is his freehold (1628: 349).[17] Or he speaks of man's perverse ingratitude: we write *benefits* received *in water*, but print *injuries* in *capital letters* (1627:7). Daniel writes 'To Lord Henry Howard' and distinguishes between the '*right line* of Honor' and the '*by-path* of cunning' (p. 108). Donne writes 'To the Countesse of Bedford' that 'Reason is our Soules *left hand*, Faith her *right*' (p. 189).

Despite the natural tendency to concreteness in such differentiating passages, there seems to be no self-conscious attempt to avoid generalized phraseology, nor can I distinguish a different attitude in poems and in prose, toward writing 'concretely' or 'abstractly.' King's sermons and poems are strictly comparable in this respect. The concreteness of such passages seems rather to result from the convenient fact that ideas can be carried by concretions if those have significances either well known or easily indicated. It should also be noted that one does not find, in the seventeenth century, figures of difference like those in poems written under the influence of Symbolism, in which one remains quite unsure of the *reasons* for introducing certain distinctions conveyed by images.[18] The earlier poet, unlike the

[17] There is a somewhat similar distinction between possessors and proprietaries in the sermon preached at the funeral of that Lady Leinster to whom King wrote a poem and whom he knew well. On the authenticity of this sermon, which is to be found in fols. 87ᵛ–105ᵛ of Bodl. MS. Eng. poet. e. 30, see Percy Simpson, 'The Bodleian MSS. of Henry King,' *BQR*, V (1929), 325. I think that the point could be settled in this case by study of the images; the whole technique of the imagery is very like that of King, in both his sermons and his poems, and there are undoubted parallels with images in King's *Exposition* of the Lord's Prayer (1628) and his sermon for Bryan Duppa (1662). These are not adventitious parallels, but images whose similar functioning in a similar argument calls forth identical terms: we pay God out of his own exchequer, God in his pity bottles up our tears, decent solemnity at interment is contrasted with the indignity of going to one's long home with the burial of an ass.

[18] Such contrasted details as the following are obviously meaningful, in Yeats's 'Cap and Bells,' for example; yet they have no sure meaning, and, as Yeats stated, no constant meaning, even to himself (p. 72; 1899; see note, p. 444): 'She opened her door

modern, is quite willing to indicate the logical functioning of his images by passages of abstract statement.

Most common in both prose and poems is a tissue of concretions and abstractions which together convey distinctions that have a logical place in the discourse. In Donne's poem to Lady Bedford, such a passage is that in which her birth and beauty are compared to a *balsamum* which naturally keeps things fresh and new, whereas she has made of learning and religion a *methridate* to cure and keep off extrinsic blows (p. 190). Another is Daniel's long image with generalizing interpretation at the commencement of his poem to the same lady; virtue may be the same in obscurity or clad with authority, but its 'abilitie' to work is different—and the difference is clarified by an extended image of arms enwalled within a living tomb, of abortive thoughts, of newborn worth straight become full-grown (p. 116).

Like that of his poems, the style of King's sermons seems dense with images;[19] these come close-packed in little pockets like the seeds in a pomegranate. A moment's examination is generally enough to show how firmly they are attached to an underlying conceptual structure. In sermon and in poem, his differentiating figures show the same willingness to allow this structure to protrude in abstract statement, and hence the same interwoven tissue of particular and general. He speaks of ornaments in style, in his Visitation sermon, using images to help make his distinctions: for mine own part, he says, I never liked him who served up more sauce than meat, more words than matter, or wit than religion—but yet I have ever thought choice matter ill dressed like good meat ill cooked, which is neither a credit to the bidder nor a pleasure to the guest (1663:23). In his poem on the Prince's birth (30), nothing could be more direct than his statement that it saddens him to think that the King,

---

and her window, / And the heart and the soul came through, / To her right hand came the red one, / To her left hand came the blue.'

[19] So much so that the scarcity of images is the most immediate argument against King's authorship of a sermon on Ps. 101:1 by 'H. K.' D.D., and attributed to King in the British Museum copy: *A Sermon Preached Before the Kings Most Excellent Maiesty at Oxford* .... London .... 1643.

'he / Who now makes Lawes,' must sometime obey the decree which summons all men finally from this world. He praises the King rather than his heir and differentiates between those who truly love the *present* light and the malcontents or giddy men who, like the Persian, adore the *rising* Sun (pun and metaphor), worship 'not what is *best*, but what is *new*.' Such use of images does not show the effort to 'be concrete,' but the effort to be at once economical and clear.

It must be emphasized that the incisive compression which differentiating images bring into poetic discourse was not seen as a departure from orthodox conceptions of decorous eloquence. The sermon-image quoted above is part of a passage which declares firmly for decorum as it was traditionally understood. Flashes of unseasoned wit are not 'fit,' 'decent,' 'discreet,' in the pulpit. Yet a page or so earlier one of King's images calls knowledge a nice Venetian who never shows herself undressed; a few pages before, he argues for an eloquently articulate clergy by saying that he may know his heart to be his portable oratory, but if his tongue is tied to the roof of his mouth, he is only a chapel without a service (1663:13). We have no choice but to consider that these conceits did not seem to the man who wrote them 'dissonant' or startling by their apparent disproportion. These have a relation to their subject and genre precisely like that in the images which modern critics praise because they dare to flaunt decorum. Their author meanwhile is occupied with exalting proportion and decorum.

On his own testimony, King's determining principle in a style is a proportioning to the needs of the subject; and there is no reason to suppose that in poetry he was willing to supplant this ancient principle by some more modern exaltation of the poet's sensibilities as determinant. His poetic images, including those frequently very unconventional ones which discriminate concisely, obey the needs of his subjects quite as carefully as do those in his sermons. The Metaphysicals would, I think, have had a ready diagnosis for that willingness to crash through the rules of decorum in order to record their feelings, which we have imported into their poetic creed; it was well

known in their day, and was designated as a fairly simple form
of Pride. King declares against the 'factiously proud and
phantastical' persons who make themselves ridiculous in an
affected Plainness (1663:24). Singularity and affectation must
always offend decency, and *both* 'affected Plainness' and 'studied
Curiosity' are modes of it. If anything, King leans toward support of 'curiosity,' defending Eloquence in a style which shows
all the 'strong lines' and bold imagery we are wont to attribute
to the revolt against eloquence.

We have no choice, I think, but to believe that the ingenious
differentiating image, like the aptly brief defining image, was
genuinely regarded as an eloquent figure, the more poetically
fit for its logical usefulness. It can amplify powerfully, is sometimes indeed just a kind of hyperbole. So it is in the poem
'Upon the Kings happy return from Scotland,' which plays ex-
tensively upon the distinction between the King as Sun and his
Partner-Light and children-stars; 'Heavens greater lamps il-
lumine it; each spark / Adds onely this, to make the sky less
dark' (32).

However hyperbolical, figures which point a difference generally have the effect of sharp wit, since they cannot be framed
without the use of multiple predicaments and are usually found
from more than one of the places of invention. An example is
that image which King uses of the martyred Charles, in a sermon, and of Ben Jonson in a poem. Charles needs no sheet of
lead to enwrap him; his own precious *sheets* will preserve him
(1665:35). In the poem to Jonson (d. 1637), the image not only
has the pun based on use, efficient cause, and different substance, but adds the logical complication of a further differentiation through extension of the similitude (65):

> And *when more spreading Titles are forgot,*
> Or, spight of all their Lead and Sear-cloth, rot,
> Thou, wrapt and *Shrin'd in thine own sheets*, wilt ly
> A Relick fam'd by all Posterity.

Even in an amplifying image with a conventional base, the function of drawing a distinction will sharpen the tone ('Sonnet,'
13):

> Go shine on happy things. To me
> That blessing is a miserie:
> Whom thy fierce Sun not warmes, but burnes,
> Like that the sooty Indian turnes.

A figure of difference may cheer, complain, explain, or argue; any of these purposes will affect its formal character and hence its effect, especially upon tone. One may watch King use a similar image for three purposes, and watch these changes.

In an elegy on Lady Anne Rich's premature death, he uses merely as a complaint the notion of Death's confused choices of victims, which make autumn where nature meant a spring (59); the contrast is with the disciplined order of a camp, in which those who came last do not thus march off first in the van:

> We *fall in such promiscuous heaps,* none can
> Put any diff'rence 'twixt *thy Rear* or *Van;*
> Since oft the youngest lead thy Files.

In a sermon touching deliverance from the plague, a more complicated twist to the notion makes the image serve to hearten those who have seen multitudes in the 'communion' of Death: 'And although *like a tempestuous Autumne,* it shakes us *by heaps* into our Graves, our Extraction *will be more orderly,* in better Method then was our Buriall' (1626:79). The tone has become that of the reasoner, the image more economical, avoiding the explanatory particulars. In the elegy upon Lady Leinster (i.e., Katherine Cholmondeley, d. 1657), the image is compressed into a sharp interrogation, and the disputer's tone is evident in the curt antithesis which is all that remains of the original extended consideration of Death's disorder:[20]

> O wherefore since we *must in Order rise,*
> Should we not *Fall in equal Obsequies?*
> But bear th' Assaults of an uneven Fate. . . . .

Very numerous striking examples can be found, in sermons and poems both, of the differentiating image used to support a position in argument. Frequently only an image is needed to make the point, though the dialectic (often based upon an in-

---

[20] 'An Elegy Upon . . . . L. K. C.,' p. 105. There is a similar image in the *Exposition* on the Lord's Prayer: God hath stampt a method in the grave and made the parent of confusion, Death, sensible of order (1628:181).

complete disjunctive syllogism) would not pass muster. King, in defending formal prayers, remarks that Cartwright 'termes our Collects, *Shreds*'—even so, these are worth a whole piece of his followers' ill-spun meditations; does man think God is asleep? (1628:23, 21). He argues again against 'course and un-study'd stuffs' in the poem complimenting Sandys upon his biblical paraphrases, using against uneloquent writing (although a quarter-century earlier, 1638) the same arguments as those he puts forth in the Visitation sermon; there is even the same ridicule of an affected 'rustick' plainness (84).[21]

An image which discriminates may embody or be used in an argument from any of the places of invention which depend upon diversity—e.g., that from the greater to the less. The funeral sermon for Bryan Duppa 'begins where all must end'—at Death; this thing of no being, this privation, devours all things; tombs themselves have their dying day, marble quarries molder to dust like the bodies under them, how, then, can fragile man escape? (1662:8).[22] One might illustrate all the places using diversities with images from King, chosen indifferently from the prose or the poems.

The 'differences' which figures of difference single out are turned to use by poets in almost every conceivable way—to magnify, to belittle, to make more affecting, to define, to explain or reason out. There is a very natural relation, however, between images which make distinctions and the dialectician's task of supporting a position or discriminating between true and false. Hence a strict division between figures which mark differences and figures which attempt to bring proof would be incorrect. Most images have multiple functions, one of which may usually be distinguished as primary; moreover, these particular

[21] There are various similitudes used to point up a stylistic difference, none perhaps more neat than 'Who would not laugh at one will naked go, / 'Cause in old hangings truth is pictur'd so?'

[22] One may note in Herbert's use of a similar image in 'Church-monuments' (p. 65) the different nature of images which do not use the places so, not having to argue a position; Herbert is more meditative than sharp as he ponders the question of what monument shall memorialize these stones doomed themselves to molder: '. . . . What shall point out *them*, / When *they* shall bow, and kneel, and fall down flat / To kisse those heaps, which now they have in trust?'

two functions have a necessary logical affinity. Any sixteenth- or seventeenth-century poet knew this; he was entirely accustomed to 'diversities' as bases for several of the dialectical places for inventing arguments.

3. *Images Which Bring Proof or Support a Position*

The basic formal type for images with this function is of course the similitude. The fact that the 'argument from similars,' analogy, similitude, was taught among the places of invention in all logics is partly responsible for the enormous favor in which such images were held and for the fact that similitudes are generally advanced not as illustrations but as arguments. Similitudes may be full or 'bare'; worked out almost syllogistically, or briefly advanced to support points by implication and inference.

The number of such figures appearing in poems written during this period is amazingly large. This is not because poets had not been taught the dangers of argument from analogy. But the place of the similitude in rhetorics as well as logics is simply a recognition of the fact that, warnings or no warnings, the argument is powerful. Certain general tendencies in the Ramists' ways of thinking bolstered it; their conception of 'arguments' and their faith in proof through the axiomatical disposition of truths gave the poetic analogy more dialectical validity. The particulars of a similitude 'argue' their generals; the similitude can be an axiom. When these and similar attitudes are imposed upon the general Elizabethan willingness to see universals in particulars—in a period before scientific developments and habitual use of inductive reasoning had lessened men's respect for single 'significant' particulars—then the image functioning as analogy is bound to have considerable force to convince.

Almost innumerable examples of the quick, incomplete similitude used to support a position with swift effectiveness can be found, in many poets of the period. None offers them in more tumbling plenty than Donne. A typical passage would be that one in 'Satyre III' which begins with the famous analogy between the pursuit of truth and the winding ascent of a huge hill, cragged and steep (p. 157). Two 'circumstances' (the hill's suddenness, night's approach) provide a way to urge two similar manners of acting in both situations (resist by going about and about; strive untiringly). Donne proceeds immediately to a defining simile (some mysteries are like the Sun, i.e., dazzling but plain to all), to a similitude arguing for fortitude in maintaining truth (by means of a figure of difference: kings are but hangmen to Fate, not its vicars); thence to a similitude persuading men to attend only to the laws of God who is the fountainhead of Power, since otherwise they will dash themselves to pieces in the tyrannous rage of the stream in its lower reaches—only flowers which dwell at the rough stream's calm head thrive and do well. Kinds like satire, and epistolary pieces or reflective elegy, tend to show this functioning of images most unabashedly, as is natural, since these kinds are traditionally written respectively in the base and the philosophical middle style.[23] Yet the use of acutely argued similitudes in lyrics also is characteristic of Donne and of his period; this is but one of the ways in which closer ties between poetry and dialectic tightened the sinews of the old 'deliberative' piece.

Functioning similarly and formed similarly, the similitudes in King's sermons or poems have much the same sharp thrust. Is temptation to be sought after? he inquires in discussing that petition of the Lord's Prayer; that man would be mad who

---

[23] To open Donne at the *Letters to Severall Personages* is to pick similitudes like ripe fruit in full season; it is natural also that Daniel's *Epistles* and the epistolary pieces in Drayton's *Elegies upon Sundry Occasions* provide examples in plenty, while the *Civil Wars* or *Endimion and Phoebe* do not. It is unfortunate that Spenser has left us no evidence of what his imagery would have been like in this genre. That Davies needs and uses great numbers of all such figures as suit logical functions, in the *Nosce Teipsum*, is so obvious that I have preferred not to exemplify from it. Naturally, the latter, like the *Musophilus*, *must not* maintain the same tension of style as does a philosophical epistle of fifty lines or so. The question is not one of the 'intensity' of the poet's 'imagination'—in fact, the critical uselessness of such Romantic terms in dealing with works of Renaissance poets is only re-demonstrated when one considers their imagery carefully. More useful are their own terms, which regard the poet's product and his craft and forego noticing his psychological condition. The most heightened style the Renaissance knew—the heroic—is not hospitable to images which function dialectically like those here considered, and luckily the greatest poet of the seventeenth century was not above suiting his style to the length of his poem. The slow *reader's pace* necessary in poems which emulate the acuteness of dialectic cannot but make us rejoice that Milton was too levelheaded to think that a follower of Ramus must toss out Mazzoni.

would poison himself to try out an antidote (1628:286). Or he argues in a poem: forbear to reap 'Loves Harvest' before it is due—on the marriage day; Love's fruits are legal use, 'Who for this interest too early call, / By that exaction lose the Principall' (10). The sermon on 'Remember now thy Creator in the days of thy youth' uses metaphor and simile to explain and move, then turns to proper similitudes to urge a course of action.[24] Both the expository and the argumentative images, having functions primarily logical, differ from near-by images which amplify God's power or move hearers by methods best studied in rhetoric: *Now* lasts no time, thus doth Time incessantly feed on us, eat up all our days (1627:37); the numberless atoms of dust on which we tread bid our feet inform our heads of the infinity of Him who is no more to be numbered than they (10). These last are logically simple images; a slight complication interrupts the latter one when the process of this 'informing' is more accurately defined (the atoms are arguments of God's infinity). Certain following images which amplify *by defining* show how natural it is for witty sharpness to enter an image when a defining function leads to the use of tenuous links or multiple predicaments.[25] Yet all these last-mentioned images differ from the similitudes proper, which have greater formal complexity and demand of the reader a different and a more rapid process of inference.[26]

Such differences are radical, being rooted in the formal cause of the image; they are unaffected, for example, by length, while

[24] Man forgot quickly, when new from the mint and hand of his composer, when the articles between God and him were not yet fully dry; the puddled waters of adversity are the best perspective to see God (1627:4, 9). Later come the similitudes providing advice to the young—a newly planted tree bears the best fruit; granted, one can *walk* by a candle in a lantern, when age dims the sight, but one can *read* by a free taper (22). There are advices to the old, to prepare those younger (manure the garden while it is spring) and to watch themselves (winter voyages are dangerous; 26, 29).

[25] The whole universe is God's ledger-book, every species a line in it, its style curious, its story varied; the map of the created world is a geography to contemplate the Creator (14).

[26] Any reader who will analyze his next piece of writing will see that, as far as composition goes, the variations described in this paragraph are natural rather than mechanical —as the Ramists never tired of pointing out. He will also see, however, that Renaissance writers, trained to the observation of such distinctions, maintain them more aptly.

differences in terms (homely, elegant, decorative, etc.) are by-products rather than causal factors. The homeliest adjective will pass unnoticed in an amplification of something we are used to hearing praised; and no amount of 'extension' could make a Donnean conceit out of a descriptive simile *unless* the extensions multiply the logical parallels. It will then almost certainly cease to be a descriptive simile. King can fill a page with images which adumbrate the general idea that there is no gluttony like death's; the passage will remain a violent but simple amplification (meiosis: no surfeit chokes him, no meal is competent to satisfy his palate, he must have a feast of saints roasted, broiled, done all ways, a horrid bill of fare; 1662:9). On the other hand, a similitude proper will have the same logical acuteness and dialectical force whether extended or shrunk, in a sermon or in a poem. King may argue that we should strive to know God ourselves and not only by report, by asking: Were any ever fed by a mere report of a feast? Did a physician ever simply talk a patient into health? (1627:18). These images operate precisely as does that with which, in 'Silence,' he supports an argument (with himself) against treating of his griefs with others: 'Was ever stomack that lackt meat / Nourisht by what another eat?' (9). In a sermon the same image-argument assists him to conclude that mere wishes are of no use; he adds another set of terms without changing the nature of the image (that a contemplation of liberty never bailed a prisoner; 1627:8 of sermon 2).

It has sometimes seemed to me that the use of 'radical' figures increases in passages which dispute, that the priority of this dialectical function for images encourages the use of figures in which one term is of 'low imaginative content.'[27] For example, King exhorts us to pray however prosperous we be and tells us not to fall off *like a horse-leech* when we abound (1628:26); or argues that the rich should give freely, all parts of a state being made for the whole, and the rich man being *the stomach* of the commonwealth, receiving that he may disperse (1628:200).

[27] This characterization of a 'radical' image has been popular since H. W. Wells's *Poetic Imagery* (New York, 1924).

Or he supports the proposition 'That Fruition destroyes Love' (54) with the argument,

> Glow-worms shine onely look't on, and let ly,
> But handled crawl into deformity:
> So beauty is no longer fair and bright,
> Then whil'st unstained by the appetite. . . . .

Or he arrives at the amazing notion that God is being forced to father children which are none of his, when unrepentant men say the Pater *Noster* (1628:52, pursuing an argument that sin dispossessed man, and Christ repurchased man's title of son); this is, of course, meant to reduce to an absurdity such men's right to this prayer. The horse-leech and the image of God-as-wronged-spouse are meant as diminutions; the comparisons of beauty to a glowworm and the rich man to a stomach probably carried no belittling force.[28] At least there is nothing to indicate that we are supposed to pay any attention to 'lowness' in the terms. The fact of the matter seems to be that, where 'low imaginative value' was intended to be remarked at all, the image will always turn out to be used as meiosis, consciously employed to libel or diminish or deprecate.

Possibly, contentious writing of any type or date requires more meiosis, more images whose derogatory connotations lower our estimation of this or that thing or idea. I offer no statistics based on counting of images either for this point or any other, because I think these inescapably inaccurate. No system of sub-subclassifications is fine enough to take care of facts like the different aesthetic effect of (1) two simple diminishing similitudes based on *quality* in a longish poem, compared with (2) one complex one based on *cause* and another on *relation*, in a shorter poem. The method would wag the conclusions reachable by it. The chief results of my own attempt to examine the problem are two warnings, which we need only because we are not seventeenth-century readers. One warning is that if there is no indication that 'diminishing' is intended, it is wiser

[28] Of course, line 2 of the poetic image quoted does intentionally belittle—*much-handled* beauty only. *Unstained* beauty can as shiningly glow like a glowworm as sparkle like a star. The skilful poet denudes his terms of impertinent connotations, especially in the similitude, an intellectually rapid figure.

not to endow poets with reasons for pulling in connotations which look 'ironically' derogatory to us. The second is that tentativeness is the best policy when it comes to assigning connotations carried by seventeenth-century words to seventeenth-century readers. When King (59; on Lady Rich) says to Death, 'The whole world is thy Factory, and we / Like traffick driven and retail'd by Thee,' the thought-structure of the whole poem enables me to recognize intended diminutions in these images, though I must be aware that 'factory' has to be investigated before I call the image 'radical.' But when, in a short poem with a good deal to do, in a passage stating four concepts clearly in eight lines, King says, 'We must in tears / Unwind a love knit up in many years'—then I had best say nothing of the homely connotations, to me, of the word *knit* ('The Surrender,' 18).

Such cautions as these are not applicable generally to the reading of modern images. The poet is seldom interested that we should observe them and takes far less care to enable us to do so. Renaissance poets are adept at indicating what is the 'pointed end' of an image, partly because of the kind of training I have outlined, but even more because they are none of them unwilling to make the rationally apprehensible *raison d'être* of an image clear. If one would avoid misreading, it is necessary to match this with an equal willingness—which means careful attention to the functional relation of single images to the logical structure of the whole.

For example, it may seem almost brutal for King to write, in 'On two Children dying of one Disease, and buried in one Grave' (43):

> When once I have discharg'd that mournfull skore,
> Heav'n hath decreed you ne're shall cost me more.

But he makes no pretense that his images are designed to elucidate the relation between parents and their dead children; the whole pattern of the piece shows that this is a poem about the sad shortness of these babies' lives. One statement after another is an application of the predicament *quantity;* several of the statements are images, and nothing could be more natural than their arithmetical reference—not many years in these babies' *account, few* days—but hence without the *loss* of innocence, no *dower* asked beyond what eyes can *lay out*, a borrowed *trust* quitted by early accepting the common *inheritance* of dust. The witty couplet quoted is a remark about the shortness of this trustee-ship, not about the financial aspects of having children.

Again, it would be very unfortunate if one took as *elucidation* of the *nature* of prayer certain images which King presents as *arguments* for the *necessity* of prayer: we have no other commod-ity to traffic or exchange with God but prayer; it is the current coin in his exchequer, the peppercorn without which we forfeit our estates, our quit-rent (1628:4–8). Noticing the different operation of images which define and images which argue de-termines here whether or not one understands what the man says. An accurate judgment of the logical functioning of the images in a poem often determines our realization of its precise subject; it is by means of the images used to support arguments that we realize 'The Anniverse' to be a poem arguing God's justice and not a poem about his love now six years dead (41).

Though the similitude proper is the clearest example of an image serving a dialectical use, any image can so function if it embodies an argument found from the places as demonstrated earlier. Any which does so is almost certain to be pointed rather than casual, economical rather than leisurely, and more intel-lectually subtle than sensuously rich—*in any poet.*

That no startlingly new conception of the functioning of images is needed to make men use them to prove and to convince is quite obvious. Men have always used them so. Moreover, the relation of such image-proofs as I have here exemplified to the old rhetorical aim of persuasion was apparent to everyone. Certainly an honest reader has a hard time telling when a writer's images have persuaded him by moving his affections, and when convinced him by well-taken arguments. The com-monplaces of Elizabethan psychology made men less definite about the line dividing 'feeling' from 'thinking' than the aver-age person now is; nor does any early theorist to my knowledge divide rhetoric sharply from logic on any such basis. It would accordingly be inaccurate to erect a neat wall between rhetorical and logical functioning of images used to convince. All we can do—and I believe this to have been done by the ordinary sixteenth- and seventeenth-century writer and reader—is to distinguish degrees to which the effectiveness of a figure depends on subtle logical ties, found as a dialectician finds them because the aim which was uppermost in their invention was similar to the dialectician's aim.

I have cited images of which this seems to be true; these and images like them could equally well be cited by the rhetorician to illustrate the ways in which figures can move the affections and affect the will. When King argues that it is not reasonable to be proudly secure in times of our prosperity, saying that God by the battery of one hot disease can beat the soul from its citadel in a single night's skirmish (1628:203), his argument speaks to the reason. So does it when he uses the same argument in 'An Elegy Occasioned by sickness' (97):

> Yet as the mounted Canon batters down
> The Towres and goodly structures of a town:
> So one short sickness will his force defeat,
> And his frail Cittadell to rubbish beat.

Yet both of these are very moving images. King himself makes one of these rule-of-thumb divisions which hold only partially, when he says that a certain text is fit rather for meditation than for proof—the text is Christ's 'If they have persecuted me, they will also persecute you.' The 'meditation' which follows presents Christ's sufferings with pathos. In so far as the images have more than narrative significance, they do more than move; they persuade to a point of view. Yet it is possible to see a difference as King turns to disputation and frames an image-argument from the whole to the parts (or greater to less): when the principal is slain, the partakers must look to bleed (1621:42).

It would certainly be perverse to claim that King was other than perfectly conscious of the uses he makes of logic in his writing. When he reveals his structural plan, as in the sermons, rhetorical and dialectical terms and methods mingle in the unself-conscious co-operation we have come to expect. The metaphysical conceits which liberally punctuate both sermons and poems seem to me but another aspect of that co-operation; they possess rhetorical *efficacia, perspicuitas, energia,* in whatever proportions the context requires, meanwhile they are found by processes which only the trained dialectician had learned to practice with such acuteness and quick ingenuity. When their function is to bring proof, these latter qualities are naturally intensified.

I may conclude this examination of some of the qualities shown by images with primarily logical functions by noticing the entirely orthodox character of the critical principles subscribed to by the poet from whom I have taken most of the images. There is nothing to indicate that other Metaphysical poets had need of any other aesthetic than King's to justify their precisely similar uses of imagery.

King is no less a believer in traditional rhetorical virtues for all his dependence upon dialectic. His references to the former discipline are uniformly respectful; one may safely label it respect when he remarks that even the Jews acknowledged Christ for the best rhetorician that ever was (1628:48). He happens to be commending studied orderliness, brevity, elegance, and perspicuity—and it is amusing to range these substantives over against those which moderns commonly choose, to commend the style of poems he was even then writing. True, he is speaking just here of prayers, but the stubborn fact of stylistic likeness stands between us and any theory that the Metaphysicals had one aesthetic for their poetry and another for their other writings. And, in any case, these are not qualities which belong to single genres or to prose as against poetry, though methods of achieving them might vary. Modern criticism tends to deny these *aims* to the Metaphysicals; I should prefer to say that the opposition between these traditional aims and the Metaphysical style is a false one, that we ourselves have erected it, and that if such writers think they are being orderly, elegant, and perspicuous, we should avoid reading into them the intent to be divinely and imaginatively alogical, rashly colloquial, and obscure.

For images, this involves our allowing the logical functioning of Metaphysical figures to shine out and declare their purpose. It also involves our accepting, simultaneously, as intentional, their rhetorical eloquence. King's remarks about style are in line with what seems to me evidence from his poems and those of others; I use his remarks because they are at once convenient and symptomatic. His most outright defense of eloquence comes in the Visitation sermon published in 1663.[29] In it the framing and functioning of images is entirely similar to the habits shown in the first printed sermon of 1621, and in the poems of the intervening years, so that if we think his theory and practice are at odds, this is something he never discovered, himself, from first to last. His positions are just those of orthodox sixteenth-century poetic as outlined in Part I above; we could refer them indifferently to Quintilian, to Peacham or Puttenham, or to Jonson.

These positions, then, we must interpret with sufficient flexibility to take care of the 'dialectical' imagery of a Metaphysical like King—for he himself was able to do precisely this. His conception of decorum is exactly the conception outlined earlier in this study; he notices the proportioning to genre, to place and audience, above all to the nature of the 'cause' of any piece of writing. Good matter clad in very thin or ill words is one of the strangest, most misshapen things that may be (1663:21); to put on a small body more clothes than it can bear is to smother our conceptions, but to put on none at all is to dogmatize nakedness (20). His attitude toward ornament is that moderate one which furnishes the theme song of every ordinary rhetorical handbook; tinkling words are ill husbands (20), but knowing

[29] That King's sermon has a place in the current quarrel over plain and elaborated sermon-writing only strengthens my points. See Note U in the Appendix for references —but unfortunately nothing serves but reading the sermons themselves. The reaction against Victorian piety has reduced the sermon-reading of critics; this would matter little if it had not succeeded in splitting certain Metaphysicals into two men. Though scholarship has partly readjusted the balance, Humpty-Dumpty cannot be put together again without the glue of a sympathetic as well as a studious reading, by many and not by a few, of the *complete* works of seventeenth-century poets. A session with the elegies for Donne is enough to show how much easier it was for the seventeenth century, than for us, to allow a poet and a divine to be one man. Herbert we have found a little harder to unstick, but, by pressing 'The Collar' tightly, have gone as far as could be expected.

arguments are not to be sent abroad without decent apparel (21); the ceremony we are to use is that which 'becomes the subject.' His understanding of the relation of verbal clothing to thought clothed is that which I have called *making manifest* or *evident;* words are the robes of knowledge without which *it will not appear* unto the world (22). Sincere men must be realists, and 'speak Things' (20), yet bodies are allowed their shadows, the dress of decent circumstances. In a figure, he declares for an attitude toward language which is flatly opposed to that which became current with the spread of Symbolist poetic: words are excellent tinctures, so that (i.e., provided that), like metals in the alembeck, they have their just fixation; else, like unclosed distillations, they breathe out in fume. One cannot but reflect that this disciple of Donne's would have detected a considerable evaporation of meaning into fume, in some of the twentieth-century disquisitions explaining the images of his master and himself.

The upshot of all this is that King, whose place among the Metaphysicals I have never seen questioned, intended at least to maintain a conception which is of all notions now most unfashionable—the old and traditional relation between Eloquence and Wisdom.

CHAPTER XIV

IMAGES AND A REDEFINED
DIDACTIC THEORY

IT HAS never, I think, been questioned that theorists of the
Renaissance agreed in accepting the didactic usefulness of
poetry. English critical documents are quite in accord on
this; they are also in accord with ideas enunciated by a host of
Continental writers, and such rebels as one can find left few
traces on English thinking. Indeed, although it sounds promis-
ing when such a one as Castelvetro says that 'delight' is
poetry's cause, his definitions for that cause scarcely range him
with modern objectors to didactic poetry, who would be equally
uncomfortable in the presence of the kind of poetry he seems to
be thinking of.[1] In the main, and counter to modern desires in
the matter, it has not been possible to deny didacticism in the
theory or do more than read over it with generous swiftness in
certain major poets.

Modern attempts to see an antididactic revolt in early seventeenth-century poetry have found their strongest arguments in
the nature of the poetry itself, which to many seems to retreat
further and further from the 'teaching' which all admit in a
Spenser. Most modern commentary on the imagery of the
Metaphysicals, setting it off from that of 'the Spenserians,' attempts explicitly or by implication to endow the later group of
poets with aims more congenial to modern thinking, thus re-

---

[1] Modern objectors do not object to the didactic because poetry is thus made so hard
to understand that it does not 'recreate the minds of the crude multitude.' Neither do
most poets now writing in defiance of the didactic theory rebel because they consider
it instead 'the poet's function . . . . to give a semblance of truth to the happenings
that come upon men through fortune,' and because they consider that the 'delight'
they give should be 'by means of this semblance.' See *Poetica d'Arist.* (1576), trans.
in A. H. Gilbert, *op. cit.*, p. 307 (see Bibliography; in this section, since I wish merely
to make use of common notions, I shall use non-English texts only from this anthology
of translations).

moving the onus which traditional didactic aims have been felt to confer ever since the late nineteenth century. The motive is generous enough, for such criticism tries to pay the Metaphysicals the extreme compliment of bringing them into the fold of 'adult sensitive moderns.' But I am inclined to think that this is a form of buttering their hay. It may even be a kindness which will do damages hard to repair, like those done to Spenser when the nineteenth century read him for the Keats in him, and turned the *Faerie Queene* into a picture gallery hung with fine 'pieces,' with moralizing 'added' to the 'beauty'—damages which two generations of scholars have not yet succeeded in mending. Moreover, the cleavage thus made in the period, setting 'Elizabethan' against 'Jacobean' (with considerable violence to the chronology of the poems involved), seems to me to favor highly inaccurate understandings of both types of poetry.

I shall not enter this controversy with direct argument. My exemplification throughout has been chosen to demonstrate, against the background of orthodox theory, the consistency with which images from Marlowe or Sidney through Marvell were designed to achieve similar aims by similar means. Differences in poetic effect, which there is no slightest need to minimize, but which obey no simple chronological or 'personality' pattern, seem to me to depend from factors which we have been glad to forget, since they entail an understanding of the complicated Renaissance craft of poetry and of the disciplines of rhetoric and logic, things foreign to certain ideas we have inherited of how poetry ought to be written. When we embark on the assigning of causes and the comparing of talents, however, we must take cognizance of these factors. More than that, we must attempt a sympathetic understanding of the didactic aim as Renaissance writers conceived it.

To retravel all the devious paths down which one is led by the minutiae of sixteenth- and seventeenth-century advice concerning imagery is to realize that *our understanding of what they meant* by 'useful' poetry has become what Bacon would call a poor shrunken thing. It is no wonder we have had to deliver them from what we have defined so crassly. The defining of didactic aims for poetry in the period itself seems to me on the other hand extremely delicate. Their definitions made for a poetic at once flexible and stable, changing to admit new insights like those the Ramists claimed but never denying certain basic conceptions—now denied. Modern quarrels over alleged differences in images as the sixteenth century became the seventeenth are not my main business; an attempt to draw together the main points in the Renaissance understanding of poetry's didactic aim will take us, sidewise, into and out of the modern quarrel and will enable me to sum up that which is my main business: the functioning of imagery in relation to ultimate poetic aims, as this was seen and practiced in the century itself.

I suppose that the bluntest statement one could make of the didactic aim would be: poetry teaches. Fraunce has an interesting definition of what it is to teach:

> Melanchton useth this woord, *docere: Docere*, is to teach, and Logike is an art of teaching: but then marke what I meane by teaching, for you must not restraine the signification of it in such sort, as though there were no teaching but onely in schooles among Philosophers and schoolemaisters, or in pulpits among doctors and divines: but generally, *hee teacheth, whosoever maketh anie other man know that, whereof before hee was ignorant,* whether hee doo it by explication and illustration, or proofe and conclusion: . . . .[2]

Fraunce is trying to knock down certain vulgarized conceptions of the didactic: that it must needs be schoolmastering, or preaching; that it encourages writers to desert unargumentative or artistic methods for the direct method used by the philosopher (i.e., the moralist, scientist, and metaphysician); that it must always be concerned with lecturing at others. It happens that he also knocks down at one sweep all the popular present-day objections to the didactic in poetry. He does not knock down certain sophisticated objections—for poetry which teaches,

---

[2] *Lawiers Logike*, fol. 3^r. Fraunce adds a description of self-teaching through dialectic which (typically Ramistic) has interesting relations with certain types of poems: '[Logic's] vertue is seene not onely in teaching others, but also in learning thy selfe, in discoursing, thinking, meditating, and framing of thine owne, as also in discussing, perusing, searching and examining what others have either delivered by speach, or put downe in writing. . . . .'

under this definition, would still be primarily framed under the control of, and addressed to, man's rational faculties, and even these luminous presentations and self-discussions would hopefully look toward getting at the truth of things. But even the most enlightened Common Reader has never objected to a poem's making him to know that whereof before he was ignorant, nor has he objected to images 'illuminating' for him something he did not 'know' so fully before. Indeed, much of the best criticism in English consists of demonstrating how poems have done this. I shall let the sophisticated objections drop for the moment, in order to consider whether Fraunce is just speaking for himself here.

He is certainly speaking for Ramists, at the least. Such a conception of the approach to and the communication of knowledge is the very core of their way of thinking about the nature of dialectic and its relation to all the disciplines. The Ramists' use of poetic examples shows that we invent no connections for them when we relate such notions to poetic.

Ramists considered that their reorganization of the disciplines clarified and re-established the ancient and proper relation between Wisdom and Eloquence;[3] they redefined the relation of every province of thought to the didactic. The implications of their thinking, for aesthetics (for there is no systematic Ramist aesthetic), make all the arts very purposeful. Only, however, because they saw the universe as orderly, and men as incurably desirous of finding out that order—and *not* because they were intent on a particular order, and reality be hanged in case it disturbed the pattern uncomfortably. No one may be less forgetful of the pursuit of Wisdom than the Ramist, but no one must be more hospitable to those evidences of it which lie on every hand, which he does not himself make but only 'invents,' and which eloquently testify wise things by virtue of their essential nature in its relation to the scheme of things. It is thus

---

[3] This Ramist claim may be conveniently examined in Gabriel Harvey's *Ciceronianus*, ed. H. S. Wilson and C. A. Forbes ('University of Nebraska Studies' [Lincoln, 1945]). Remarks to the undergraduates, here and in the *Rhetor*, by a man not unimportant in English literary history, emphasize these points more forcefully for us than would a reading of Talaeus and his commentators.

that the Ramist finds particulars eloquent, rather than by virtue of some tricks of Elocutio with which arrogant man dresses them. A toothache is an eloquent argument for the proposition that it is better not to neglect decay, and no reasonable man is impatient when he discovers this relationship; an era which took moral law to be as natural as 'natural law' in the physical world was equally willing to have images point eloquently to concepts and values. That eloquence should make wisdom manifest did not seem so much a desideratum as a legitimate and universally discoverable connection; the possibility of a gap between the two results from the falsifications which imperfect man is always likely to fall into. The Ramist is against deceitful and frivolous and vainglorious eloquence which does not delineate the true nature of things. And so had been every great writer on the subject, from Quintilian down. Ramists were redressing a balance, but they were correcting the abuses of the hundreds of forgotten writers we have never read, not those of a Spenser or a Sidney. These writers they saw as in the great tradition to which they sought to bring back English rhetorical practice.

It was a tradition which had never been without spokesmen in England. The old generalizations about the responsibilities of a Wise Eloquence, which preface the figures of Elocutio in the handbooks, were not copied and recopied because men had stopped subscribing to them, and our lesser familiarity with the complexities of those figures gives us no right to label as mechanical and inhumane a conception of letters which sees Wisdom and Eloquence as the 'Ornamentes, whereby mannes lyfe is bewtifyed' (Peacham [1577], sig. A ii). Skeptical disbelief will not help us to see what a handbook writer means when he relates rhetoric to the other learnings by which man has tried to see to what end he is created (as no other animal does), the learnings in which man uses his intellective power to seek causes, and the secrets of nature, to study mathematical demonstrations, motions of stars, musical consent of harmonies, to conceive trim devices and profitable and pleasant inventions ([1577], pref. letter). It is a didactic theory, certainly, which sees speech as the instrument of our understanding,[4] and key of conceptions, but it is not an empty theory, nor one for pious fools.

The emphasis on man's intellective power, like Sidney's emphasis on poetry's concern with universals, is characteristic of this whole period; throughout it, writers unhesitatingly refer man's literary activities to the contemplating intellect which was thought to apprehend the true nature of things. This is quite different from referring them to that part of Edgar Guest's memory where he keeps moral platitudes until they come out in useful rhyme, or to whatever faculty in Joyce Kilmer enabled him to state that God had made the tree but he had made his own poem. Renaissance didactic theories of poetry are not to be confused with vulgarizations of such theories, whether by modern critics or by inadequate poets, Elizabethan or modern. Emphasis in early poetic upon man's 'rational' faculties is nevertheless not to be gainsaid. Like Tasso's statement that the poet's images are of intelligible, not sensible, things (Gilbert, p. 477), these emphases in Peacham are not very different from the Ramistic insistence on poetry's concern with the dialectical aim of distinguishing true notions from false. All really define teaching as any communication of a hitherto unperceived rationally apprehensible order.

For Sidney's remarks about poetry's concern with universals would have made his theory of poetry didactic if he had never mentioned teaching-and-delighting. It is the essential feature of the orthodox Renaissance theory of poetry's usefulness. We may call truth 'the real' if we prefer, but, given the conceptions of the mind's structure which were then current, no statement of poetry's concern with essential realities is possible except in terms which refer its operation to the intellect. If we expect to understand this, we shall have to define the functioning of that faculty as men of this time defined it. We find this emphasis on the poet's contemplation of the truly real in Fracastoro, in Minturno, in Tasso, in Mazzoni, in the English documents, in the rhetoricians' remarks about wisdom made evident and real-

---

[4] Enabling us to 'open the secreates of our hartes, and declare our thoughts to other' (sig. A ii). Statements like these are practically common property.

izable through eloquence, in the Ramists' relating of poetry and dialectic. Anything further from modern notions of didactic poetry, as an insinuating method of indoctrinating readers with moral commonplaces which will not stand the test of severe thought, it would be hard to imagine.[5] It has extremely little to do with modern clichés about the 'cold' intellect, set in opposition to the 'warm' emotions or the 'ardent' imagination, and still less to do with weak moralizing. The men I have mentioned would have thrown out the latter in a hurry because it was not reasonable.

The conception does, however, have certain links with modern notions of the didactic. One of these links is the fact that both traditional and modern conceptions of didacticism in poetry emphasize 'matter'; a poem must 'say something,' and accordingly its images should function in such a way as to help get the something said.

One would be at a loss to find a theorist or a poet in the whole period here treated who did not accept this. But, again, it was understood in a way foreign to our thinking; that it was universally so understood is apparent from the context in which such ideas are always presented. Men in this period commonly speak not of a poem's matter but of a poet inventing matter—the matter is pre-poem, the inventing a prenatal stage. Sections devoted to 'the invention of matter' do not deal with where to look up Staple Thoughts; they deal with ways of stimulating fertile thinking and imaging. Nor are these last two opposed, for this age did not share our prepossession in favor of the special reality of sensible objects, and what the mind shapes and operates with is conceptions of the real. Invention of matter is a stage which is several steps short of the actual formal organization which is the poem itself; by the time that has been born (cf. been conceived) we are not likely to hear much more about subject matter, but rather to hear about the poem's 'cause,' or subject, or what it achieves. Any mere manual, like Wilson's

---

[5] Mazzoni, in fact, defends the poet's didactic introduction of his own conclusions or judgments, by saying that perhaps *no less utility* is derived by the reader from considering whether the poet were mistaken (Gilbert, p. 393; see n. 75 on date; the whole chapter deals with a prevalent modern objection).

Arte of Rhetorique, will show the differences between this earlier era and ours in what I can only call loosely the mode of thinking on such questions.

The differences are chiefly to be detected not in specific statements but in presuppositions underlying the handling of invention (or underlying remarks about 'subject' or 'cause,' in poetics). First on the list of what Wilson says an orator must be perfect in is 'The *finding out* of *apt* matter, called otherwise Invention'; but he indicates clearly the unity of a process in which this is only a first step (and, as we shall see later, it would be psychologically impossible to halt after invention; possibly fleeting fantasies, as in dreaming, offer a special case). Although the Imagination is the faculty which enables man to do such '*searching out* of things true, or things likely' (p. 6), Judgment must immediately co-operate (as here in the determination of reasonable relations); Wilson commends the places of logic as giving 'good occasion' to find out 'plentifull matter.'

'But what availeth much treasure and apt matter, if man can not *apply it to his purpose?*' Therefore the orator must secondly be able to accomplish 'the setling or *ordering* of *things invented* for this purpose'—*Dispositio*, an '*apt* bestowing'; disposition declares 'in what maner every reason [i.e., the matter] shalbe applied for confirmation *of the purpose.*' Neither does this avail unless we 'commende the whole matter' or 'beautifie the cause'; hence follows Elocution, 'an applying[6] of apt wordes and sentences to the matter, *found out to confirme the cause.*' This is as schematized and simplified a statement as one could find, yet one cannot pick out in it the ordinary modern notion of some *content* as the *purpose* of a piece, or of a 'subject matter' (didactically important) divisible from the form (didactically negligible).

To what is the matter 'apt'? What does the distinction between 'matter' and 'purpose,' made several times, mean—if not

---

[6] *Apply* shows semantic changes which must be noticed. Cf. its precise meanings elsewhere in this paragraph, and see *NED*, meanings 5, 6, 18, 21—most meanings in fact except No. 1. Yet such statements as these are persistently used even by students of the period to support the idea that the sixteenth century believed in ornament *laid upon* a content.

that the directing conception determines my selection of things true and likely as well as my way of 'commending' or making impressive those things? How can words and sentences (probably figures of words and figures of thought) confirm the cause, unless the process is one of fit incarnation of an intention, just as I have suited my matter to my purpose by the way I have ordered it? I do not beautify my style; I beautify the cause. I do not start out with my matter; I find it. What I start with is a reason for writing, some significant conception, half-glimpsed *in* the raw material of experience, which is the 'cause' of my poem, its subject *and* its intention. What I find are thoughts and relations between thoughts. Yet the characteristic sixteenth- or seventeenth-century praise of a poet for his 'inventions' may well mean praise of his understanding of human feelings; these words *thought* and *feeling* are not the words which men of this period use, and it is a little dangerous to use them. The mind of man deals with forms; the intellect contemplates essential reality. Our terms and divisions as commonly understood do not take care of ordinary Renaissance understandings; they fall by the side and are not useful.

I have spent space on these handbook commonplaces because I believe that the root of much modern critical dissatisfaction with the didactic theory of poetry is its supposed identification of content with purpose—and I do not think that the Renaissance made this identification. Many of our quarrels with didactic poems turn out to be quarrels not with the poet's aim but with the subject matter and devices through which he has made his aim apparent—and no element in poetry is so subject to the changing fashions of different times as the first of these. Many who do not object to seeing vainglory come to grief in a Helen Hokinson cartoon can see little to look at in Braggadochio.

A related source of confusion lies in the fact that, whereas moderns seem unable to avoid a notion of 'content' as the non-poetic, logical, paraphrasable residue of a poem, the Renaissance man does not seem to run into this notion because he is looking at a different pattern, in which purposes are given body in suitable matter and made articulate through suitable form. This process he saw as a highly imaginative one. Because he had conceptions very different from ours of the mind's operations and of its relations to reality, any divisions which, like ours, separate 'imagination' from 'logical thought,' or which separate the judgment-pleasing 'cause' of a poem from its aesthetic value, do not really make sense. If we were to intrude such distinctions, we would make it impossible for a Renaissance writer to describe how he thought a poem was written.

When Puttenham defends the good poet as a man in whom the imagination or fantasy is well affected, he finds this faculty a 'representer of the best, most comely and bewtifull images or apparances of thinges to the soule and according to their very truth' (I, viii). This is the imagination in action, yet the contemplation of this very truth is the activity of the intellect. Persons with such a faculty of imagination are 'illuminated with the brightest irradiations of knowledge and of the veritie and due proportion of things.' Puttenham does not speak in these high terms because he has some airy notion of poetic fancy, but because he relates all insight in any field to poetic insight, and in all fields sees imagination as co-operating with judgment:

of this sorte of phantasie are all good Poets, notable Captaines stratagematique, all cunning artificers and enginers, all Legislators Polititiens & Counsellours of estate, in whose exercises the inventive part is most employed and is to the sound & true iudgement of man most needful.

This connection of the imagination with the matter-finding process, invention, is quite usual. If we forget it, we shall only succeed in reading meanings which are far too narrowly rational into statements of poetic theorists regarding the didactic importance of subject. We must simultaneously remember that matter-finding is a preformal stage and that the subject of a poem is an embodied purpose, not a subject matter as such.

The part played by beauty of poetic form in making purposes articulate (making subjects manifest) is integral, as seen by Renaissance didactic theory. When Daniel says that we need not copy classical measures, since we admire the Greeks and

Latins 'not for their smooth-gliding words, nor their measures, but *for their inventions*,' he is saying something much closer to 'for their imaginative ordering of reality' than to 'for their prose content.' And in fact this is part of a defense of just such formal poetic elements as smooth-gliding words; it is, after all, part of a *Defence of Ryme*. There is no inconsistency here, given the understandings I have outlined. These made it possible to see poetry as didactically useful through its aesthetically satisfying form; a thing cannot be useful if it cannot get born. Daniel's treatise is one of the most impressive and exciting critical documents in English because of his peculiar gift for seeing stability in mutability, without sentimentality and without compromise. His is a defense of '*whatsoever* force of words doth moove, delight, and sway the affections of men,' cogently argued on the grounds that these habits must change with times, conditions, and the different 'idioma' of different languages (in Gregory Smith, II, 363–65). Yet the purposes thus differently habited are the living souls of poems, and not mortal. To turn such understandings of the didactic theory into mere praise of 'the thought-content' of poems is foolishness.

Though it is fatal to forget the role of the imagination in bringing conceptions to birth, it is also falsifying if we forget the role of the judgment in writing and reading poetry. Daniel does not wish to see a poet 'smoothe up a weake confused sense' in order to delight the ear, 'seeing it is matter that satisfies *the iudiciall*.' That it is the reader's judgment which finds satisfaction in the conceptions which a poet can beget is not in the least inconsistent with high praise of the imagination such as Puttenham's. The writer's own judgment has passed his invented matter as satisfying, before the reader ever sees it, before it has found expression; it is the intellect which contemplates forms. Puttenham is simply talking about an earlier stage of the process of writing when he says that by the imagination as by a glass 'are represented unto the soule all maner of bewtifull visions, whereby the inventive parte of the mynde is so much holpen, as without it no man could devise any new or rare thing.' A man without judgment would never be able to see

the significance of his new rare things nor any relationships between them, nor shape them for the aesthetic contemplation of
others.

It is no accident that Puttenham's chapter proceeds to praise
poetry as an art of contemplation, which, like 'any other civill
or delectable Art of naturall or morall doctrine,' is one of the
few civilizing influences in an 'iron & malitious age' when
princes are overearnestly bent to 'the affaires of Empire &
ambition.' Poetry no more has to give up being a contemplative
art to be didactically useful than it has to give up being imaginative to please the judgment.

This kind of embarrassing reconciliation of modern irrecon-
cilables persistently occurs when one is pursuing sixteenth- and
seventeenth-century notions of the didactic in poetry. It was a
very roomy theory. There is room in it for the thinker whose
aesthetic theory emphasizes contemplation of the beautiful, and
for him who defends poetry as one of the useful learnings. There
is room for the poet who knows that it was his imagination
which carried him away, and for the reader who knows that he
must have had some hidden directing notion of where he was
going or he could not have got there in full sight of all of us.
There is room for poems which move, inform, open the eyes, set
the table on a roar, change men from Republicans to Demo-
crats, declare politics nonsense, say that Love is a fine thing, say
that Love is a cheat, argue that God is just, complain that He
seems unjust—for any poem that changes the mind in any
smallest degree and on anything, from the merits of spring to
the nature of the sin of Pride. There is room for every type of
image from Spenser's pictorially persuasive figure of Gluttony
to Donne's dialectically illuminating figure of the compass.
There is room for the poet as logician, as recorder of visions,
as craftsman, as child of Nature, as inquirer, as instructor, even
as full professor. There is almost room for Classical and Romantic. But this would be cutting it close. The fence goes up
just where certain modern objections to the didactic have
brought in conceptions of poetry as pre-eminently concerned
with the irrational and the unordered.

The most innocent-looking form of this antididacticism is that objective concern with particulars so universally thought of as a desideratum since the rise of modern science; Allen Tate, for example, praises it in Emily Dickinson: 'We are not told what to think; we are told to look at the situation.'[7] I am not sure that any Renaissance man's conception of the mind's functioning would enable him to speak of communication in these terms; writers of the period have an incurable tendency to assume that if anyone indicates some pattern of particulars as true,[8] he also inescapably indicates that it would be a good idea for others to accept the ordering to which it bears witness.[9] The closest approach to the modern notion is in passages talking about history's concern with the particular. Renaissance theorists would see as a confusion between history and poetry that modern predilection which comes out in Tate's further praise of Emily Dickinson: 'she speaks wholly to the individual experience.' Earlier theory is, of course, inhospitable to such conceptions, seeing poetry as one form of the highest activity of the intellect—the contemplation of universals (by writer and by reader). A by-product of this modern pleasure in particulars unaccompanied by general evaluative statement shows up in D. Daiches' reservation to his admission that Donne does usually state a universal problem; it appears to be to Donne's credit that he does so only 'through complexity of imagery and structure.' This is a common modern compliment and generally implies a certain separation between poetry and 'reasoning.'

The extreme point in poetry's flight from the rational is reached in certain attitudes encouraged by Symbolist poetic,

---

[7] Allen Tate, *Reactionary Essays* (New York, 1936), pp. 15, 24. For the Daiches quotation which follows see *Poetry and the Modern World* (Chicago, 1940), p. 56, where it is, however, part of a discussion showing the necessity for wider implications behind mere particular situations. These and the quotations from other modern critics are chosen simply as convenient statements of widespread modern attitudes; I discuss no modern critical position which is not propounded by a dozen writers and make no attempt to present fully the points of view of any single modern critic.

[8] See above, chap. ix, n. 32, on this possibly unmodern use of this word.

[9] The same writers are almost hypersensitively aware of the fact that selection of words inevitably betrays evaluations. The connection of language with the judgment (words with concepts) is universally assumed and frequently mentioned.

notably that described by G. Bullough as the 'direct worship of the unconscious, relying on the drifting undercurrents of the mind to give direction to a free play of association.'[10] Between this extremest form of antirationalism and that form which merely is nervous about universals there are innumerable degrees of concern with the irrational, all of them hostile to the didactic theory of poetry as the Renaissance defined it.

Anyone may summon his own examples from modern poems themselves, but I should perhaps peg down the discussion with one or two other critical attempts at phrasing of these conceptions. Such as Edmund Wilson's quotation from fugitive criticism by Valéry:

> There is absolutely no question in poetry of one person's transmitting to another something intelligible that is going on in his mind. It is a question of creating in the latter a state whose expression is precisely and uniquely that which communicates it to him.

Or see Bullough's exposition of the rise of a new technique in response to modern fear of the discursive and the expository, a technique in which association, symbol, and allegory took the place of logical or chronological sequence. Such methods are in line with Mallarmé's aim; they attempt to suggest 'complex emotion by an accumulation of direct images, each maybe by only one element bearing on the central idea, yet by its interaction with other images, evoking the final synthesis.'

These are no inconsiderable departures from a theory of poetry as concerned with rationally apprehensible order, and what they chiefly militate against, touching poetic method, is the logical functioning of images. A Renaissance man would find such modern desiderata difficult to accept not because he was less sensitive to the complexities of emotional and mental experience than we, or more piously moralistic, or more arrogant

---

[10] *The Trend of Modern Poetry* (Edinburgh and London, 1934), p. 116; pp. 69, 72; see also, on Pound, p. 88. The Wilson quotation comes from *Axel's Castle* (New York, 1932), pp. 81–82. Symbolism at second hand, in interpretations and in certain poets writing in English, has probably been more influential upon English poetry and criticism generally than the poems themselves of that school. The shorter and more explicit statements which I must choose are not always so justly phrased as more extended expositions; but I believe no one familiar with criticism of the last thirty years will consider that I have falsified general emphases.

as a writer, or more docile as a reader. What would chiefly stand in his way, and should prevent us from interpreting Renaissance poems, *late or early*, in terms of these conceptions, is an understanding of the mind's structure which did not allow him to conceive of images as working like this.

The elements in Renaissance psychological theory which are important here are the large general conceptions which went unquestioned, in all quarters, and over an extremely long space of time; they are the conceptions which we could find in the *De anima* or in medieval psychology, as well as in the numerous books on the subject which were currently produced and read in the sixteenth and seventeenth centuries.[11] The very divisions and oppositions accepted in modern writing, and nuclear to the controversial stand taken on these matters, are foreign to a writer used to thinking in terms of faculty psychology. Renaissance writers do not oppose 'an experience' and 'a thought,' or 'emotions' and 'ideas,' nor separate 'logic' from 'association,' nor divide 'imagination' from 'logic' in composition; nor do they identify 'reason' with 'intellect,' nor see the implications we see in 'rational' or 'expository.'

It is scarcely necessary to go into the role of the Common Sense, or the mode of working of the various 'spirits,' or into sundry disagreements here impertinent. The work of the Imagination or the Fantasy (or of the two together, when distinguished) was to receive, compare, and combine impressions of whatever the senses enabled man to perceive, and it was in continual and unbroken co-operation with the Understanding which judged of the truth or falsity of things (by logic) and with the Will which (if uninfected) moved man to favorable affec-

---

[11] I have chosen to introduce actual quotations from none of these many authors saving Sir John Davies, since again it is the large general differences between earlier and modern conceptions which matter, and since minor disagreements between various Elizabethan and Jacobean theorists do not touch the points here made. Useful treatments of Renaissance psychological theory, with references to the scholarly work now being done in relating it to literature, may be found in chap. v of H. Craig and in chap. ix of P. Miller (*op. cit.*, in chap. xii, n. 1, above); an item of first importance in any reading list on the matter must be Vols. I and II of G. S. Brett's *A History of Psychology* (London, 1912, 1921). Of early treatments of the mind's structure the most easily accessible are those in Davies' *Nosce Teipsum* and Burton's *Anatomy of Melancholy* (in Section I of Partition I).

tions toward the good, and unfavorable toward the evil. Although many distinctions are made in any treatment which now seem fantastic, the main impression one receives in reading of the process of rational activity, in any typical treatise, is an impression of the unity of the total mind-act. Once started, it went inexorably on, and all the faculties must be involved; one could no more have a thought without the prior operation of imagination than one could have a thought without having one's affections moved, however slightly, toward this or that conception which (to an uninfected mind) seemed desirable because good, and good because true. The true images of things which Puttenham says are in the Imagination of the poet must come to the bar of the Judgment (understanding, wit) if their truth is to be apprehended or examined—and no sooner are they formed in the mind than this process takes place. The understanding, looking in 'the mirror of the Fantasie,' abstracts the 'formes of single things,'

> But after, by discoursing to and fro,
> Anticipating, and comparing things;
> She doth all universall natures know,
> And all *effects* into their *causes* brings.
> (Sir John Davies, I, 76, *Nosce Teipsum*) (Author's italics)

Poetry's concern with universals is thus 'intellectual,' but it is dependent upon imagination just as, at the other end of the process, minute movements of the will and affections are bound to follow upon this 'intellectual' contemplation. One cannot confine 'the rational' to the activities of the *intellectus;* it cannot do anything alone. The pursuit of truth requires the interaction of all these faculties, and falsity or lack of discipline in any of them will hinder that pursuit. When one says that the didactic theory conceives of poetry's 'teaching' as the communication of any hitherto unperceived rationally apprehensible order, one must mean that this whole imaginative-intellectual-affective process has been gone through by both parties to the communication. The poetry cannot help partaking of all three characters, but the process may be refined or enriched in various ways, and methods peculiar to poetry as a special kind of rational discourse are the concern of poetic theorists. It shares ultimate aims, some immediate aims, and certain methods, with the other disciplines—simply by virtue of how the mind operates—and to this extent poetry's territory overlaps that of the other disciplines, as this book has tried to demonstrate.

All the disciplines use all the faculties, though the art of logic has been developed especially as an instrument to assist in the dialectical task of distinguishing between true and false, and though rhetoric concerns itself especially with moving the affections and the will. When we speak so, we must keep in mind that these disciplines did not teach men how to do (or cause others to do) two different and mutually exclusive mental acts, but how best to accomplish certain stages in a total mental process. The notions that poetry cannot but attempt distinctions between true and false, and cannot but move the will, result not from some obstinate confusion with logic and with rhetoric, respectively, but from the way the mind-structure was envisaged. However faulty we find this psychology, the way in which poetry operates to make the will reach out toward perfection was not crassly conceived in the Renaissance; in this province their interpretations seem to me to have an unexampled nicety and an extreme psychological acuteness. If the function of moving the will to good makes our century see poetry as an inhibited curate in blinders, one can say only that this is not what the earlier century saw—or recommended. Far from narrowing the range of poetry, this conception of its functioning gave it that place among the 'architectonic' sciences which Sidney claims for it, and without robbing it of its essentially contemplative character. Again this reconciliation of incompatibles (as modern writers see the matter) could obtain in the Renaissance because current conceptions of the mind's structure and working did not force certain oppositions with which we are very familiar.

Poetry's relation to the will, an integral part of the didactic theory, did cause images to be seen as active agents. Precisely here, Renaissance ideas come into sharp conflict with modern ones.

If I could quote all of Yeats's early essay on 'The Symbolism of Poetry,' for example, I might show with more fairness and less oversimplification the reasons for that conflict. I cannot, and of course Yeats later shifted in some ways from this position. But many will recall his description of the evoking of 'indefinable and yet precise emotions' through images, the Symbolist emphasis on the need for the perfect word in poetry—as compared with writing which 'expounds an opinion, or describes a thing' (and which can therefore get along with words 'not quite well chosen'), the distinction between emotional and intellectual symbols—a distinction surely totally incomprehensible in the Renaissance, though critics have used it to make contrasts between Donne's images and Spenser's. Especially pertinent is the phrasing of Yeats's wish that we would

cast out of serious poetry those energetic rhythms, as of a man running, which are *the invention of the will with its eyes always on something to be done or undone;* and we would seek out those wavering, meditative, organic rhythms, which are the embodiment of *the imagination, that* neither desires nor hates, because it has done with time, and *only wishes to gaze upon some reality,* some beauty. . . . .[12]

An opposition between rhetoric's concern with the will and poetry's concern with 'creating the inner meaning of experience' comes out with especial sharpness in Allen Tate's essays cited above; the *Faerie Queene* is a 'projection of the will' (p. 92).

It is characteristic of the Renaissance that most comments are in terms of what poetry achieves in a reader's mind rather than in terms of what poets feel and do.[13] But the point at issue here is not affected; there is no doubt but that the Renaissance poet willed to move his reader's will. Unquestionably, he, too, tried to convey the meaning of experience precisely as he saw it, the reality and beauty his imagination gazed upon; what is absent from his conception is the modern notion that this is at

[12] W. B. Yeats, *Essays (Complete Works,* Vol. IV [New York, 1924]), p. 201. Later poems would demonstrate his somewhat different later position, even if we had not such remarks as that made apropos of reading Mallarmé—that this was 'the road I and others of my time went for certain furlongs. . . . . It is not the way I go now, but one of the legitimate roads' (*Letters on Poetry to Dorothy Wellesley* [Oxford, 1940], p. 149).

[13] Except for direct advices on how to set to work, in the 'disciplines' of rhetoric and logic.

war with a 'useful relation to the ordinary forms of action' (Tate, p. 112). Unless he invented for himself a private science of psychology, I do not think that he could conceive of halting the mental process in mid-air before it reached the will; and certainly he could not think of the affective nature of poetry as disjoined from willing. I cannot imagine any astonishment more complete than that which one might have aroused by confronting any sixteenth- or seventeenth-century poet whatsoever with a statement of Day Lewis' ('this' refers to several quoted definitions of poetry, of the hackles-raising sort): 'There can be little doubt that this emotional disturbance in the reader is a reproduction of the disturbance which was the poetical impulse of the writer; and this reproduction is the first aim and effect of poetry.'[14] Renaissance thinking on the subject simply does not provide for emotional disturbances which just 'take place.' Some mental movement of acceptance or rejection thereupon *occurs*. And any hypothetical line between this and eventual *further* action regarding what one is thus impelled to embrace or repel is not, to my knowledge, drawn.

I am concerned not with the validity of Renaissance theories as against the modern theories here indicated but with the propriety of approaching Renaissance poetry with critical presuppositions like these. It seems to me as productive of misunderstandings as the converse would be—reading modern poems armed solely with the expectations which Renaissance theories provide. What these modern theories all share is an antipathy toward that moving of the will toward good or evil which is an integral part of the didactic theory as the Renaissance understood it. This antipathy is a ball-and-chain in reading some Renaissance poets and a fair-weather friend in reading others. Nevertheless, it is not easy to lay it by without going to the root of the reasons why the entire period of the Renaissance was so willing to accept a theory which sees poetry as speaking to the will.

Certainly one large and important reason lies in the fact that such a theory suited with the picture these men had of how the

[14] *Op. cit.*, p. 73; in chap. iv, n. 12, above.

human mind works, so that poetry's moral aspect is simply a natural part of its rational functioning. In the total process of perceiving, understanding, and taking an attitude toward reality, the final linkage in the normal chain of intellectual-distinguishing-of-true-from-false-and-moral-choosing-of-good-rather-than-bad was broken only by an 'infected will.' As Sidney says, 'our erected *wit* maketh us know what perfection is, and yet our infected *will* keepeth us from reaching unto it' (in Gregory Smith, I, 157). To be *moved* to do that which we know—there is the rub (p. 172). One came to be so moved by an 'intellectual' routing, however; modern clichés about a simple 'appeal to the emotions' do not fit.[15] When Sidney speaks of poetry as a 'medicine of Cherries' (p. 173), he is not advocating a cheap way of fooling people into virtuous conduct, a kind of propaganda in which any means will serve, given a good end. He is talking about the fact (or so the Elizabethans saw it) that goodness when it is contemplated in its essential nature—the intellect's task—is so lovely that men cannot but reach out after it. So even the hardhearted and blasé, reading a poem, 'steale to see *the forme of* goodnes (which seene they cannot but love) ere themselves be aware.' Thus the connection between intellectual integrity and moral soundness in a poem is assumed to be a far more necessary connection than we assume it; here falls one sword that divides the Mrs. Hemanses from the Daniels and Spensers. This conception of a necessary relation between seeing things truly (i.e., as they are) and choosing a right moral path is behind the pronounced emphasis upon intellectual discipline in the Renaissance, just as it is behind the Archimago plot-nucleus of *FQ* I. Red Crosse has considerable good will but insufficiently erected wits. Neither could do the work of the other in the united task of acting reasonably.

It is a great difficulty in interpreting Renaissance poetic or

---

[15] *Of course*, Renaissance thinkers took count of the fact that a man's passions sway his judgment—and many an image was written to do it. There is constant *inter*action between the faculties, *each* of which could falsify, in the total process of knowing and choosing. But a person does not do an undisciplined act because he '*didn't* think'; he thought, but not clearly. Right action argues a more nearly perfect knowing; there is no get-rich-quick route.

poems that one must get rid of modern usages of 'reason' and 'rational' and remember *simultaneously* that no amount of good will can make up for weak, undisciplined wits *and* that no excellence of wit can make a rational man out of one who does not feel the pull of attraction toward good. The combination of ratiocination and emotional power is the proper and normal character of didactic poetry, under such psychological theories, and what is peculiar about Donne's 'Holy Sonnets,' for example, is not that combination. Emotional power is striven for in all good Renaissance didactic poetry because the affections have a necessary place in *reasonable* action.

Similar notions and close connections are evinced by Tasso's phrases concerning love as a virtue or 'habit of the will,' and concerning certain romances which show lovers with 'such a disposition in the soul that no passion is able to take up arms against the reason' (Gilbert, p. 486). *Reason*ableness, in this instance, was constant love for their ladies. For Right Reason, that sixteenth- and seventeenth-century desideratum, does not involve the supplanting of the affections by intellectual activity, rather the 'rectifying' of them (*Nosce Teipsum*, p. 74). When we are impelled to use our tags of 'rational' and 'emotional' in differentiating between the various aims and methods in one Renaissance poem or another, it is useful to remember Sidney's remark that *moving* is 'wel nigh the cause and the effect of teaching.' And to remember also the reason he gives for thinking this: that a mind which 'hath a free desire to doe well' is the first evidence that reason has mastered passion (p. 171). Both *free* and *desire* are important words. Imaginative insight, keen and clear judgment, warmth of affection toward the good, mark the poetry man writes or enjoys as a 'rational' creature. This is not 'reasoning in poetry' as moderns think of it.

It is no wonder that poetry as contemplation can come so close to poetry as urging well-doing, against this background.[16] These conceptions offer the Renaissance man his answer to the

---

[16] That Mazzoni, for example, can say that the 'first seven books of the *Politics* speak of the civil faculty in action' and that poetics speaks of it 'as at rest' (*operante, cessante*), and can yet say also that the best poetry delights profitably, is actively useful, socially and morally (Gilbert, pp. 375, 381–86).

question, now so vexed, of whether poetry should ever 'propagandize.' When the contemplation of universals in truly judged relation to particular events urges a reader to a particular course of action, the poet finds himself a propagandist. Poetry moves to true knowing, and if knowing moved to 'the ordinary forms of action,' the Renaissance poet would not see that that put his poem into some meaner category. The theory erects bars against shoddy moralizing, wilful deceit, and the cheap short cuts of tricky appeals through the affections. Against other dangers—man's capacity for error and his insufficiently disciplined faculties—it simply takes its chances.

Two important reasons, then, why men willingly accepted a didactic theory for the most imaginative and the most affecting of the arts lie in their different definition of 'teaching' and in these current conceptions of the mind's workings (upon which that definition was erected). There are certain more ordinary and everyday reasons. These again have to do with what seem to me modern misreadings of earlier ideas. It cannot be mere chance that their poetic seems balanced, subtle, and aware of man's range of sensibility, when we read it in the Elizabethans themselves, and arrogant, inconsistent, and niggling, when we read about it in modern expositions. One cause for this is our persistent habit of seeing aims and methods as competitive which they saw as working together. Sixteenth- and seventeenth-century poets did not feel themselves faced with the grim alternative of teaching or delighting; they tried to be as thoughtfully witty or as deep-reaching as it was in them to be, on the understanding that intelligent men delight to be taught. They do not decide against the pleasing image in order to fetch in a brilliant analogy, or choose *between* sticking to the truth and 'persuading' through cunningly plotted rhetorical patternings; they rather try to teach truth through delightful persuasions in which analogies please by their brilliance and are didactically potent *via* their rhetorical figuring.

This absence of competition between purposes is observable on all levels upon which advice on writing is offered, from the most general discussion of aims to the *minutiae* of remarks upon a synecdoche or an *exclamatio*. Wilson's rhetoric notes the three aims—to teach, to delight, to persuade; his treatment of the first is concerned with being understandable and orderly, for, says he, what man can be delighted, or yet persuaded, if he does not know what you mean? If you do not the first, you shall not do the other (p. 2). And the most run-of-the-mill handbooks will give evidence of the close connection there was felt to be between the rhetorician's persuasion and the dialectician's distinguishing of the true.[17]

I have been able to detect no underlying habitual notion that some stylistic devices 'teach,' whereas others are irrelevant to meaning and only 'please.' Peacham takes it quite for granted that, if *schemates rhetorical* wake the ear, they assist the mind;[18] in contrast to this, many a modern comment on Spenser's archaisms (for example) seems to me to see no connection whatever between attention-waking variety and the clear and strong expression of meaning—as though Spenser had to choose either to be pleasing, with his old words and his patternings, or else to speak to the intelligence. In whole groups of Peacham's figures seemingly conceived to assist the aim of instructing,[19] it is quite impossible to separate off some 'didactic' what-is-said from the 'pleasing' how-to-say-it. There is not only no sense that attending to one of these cuts down attention to the other; the distinction itself is not made. Peacham is no genius, and neither are the men he copied from. Yet sharper modern minds are so caught in difficulties avoided earlier that one is almost persuaded that modes of thinking in one age are simply more congenial to the solution of some kinds of problems, in another age to other kinds.

Didactic aims for poetry must certainly be more acceptable to

---

[17] 'And to Perswade, is as much, as that one man should make others beleeve, that our talke, or the thing whereof we reason, is either True or False' (*The Welspring of wittie Conceites:* .... [London, 1584], trans. W. Phiston; Preface).

[18] If they take away the wearisomeness of our common speech, they will help us to strength, perspicuity, and grace, fashioning a pleasant, sharp, and evident kind of expressing our meaning (p. 40 [1593]).

[19] Such as his 'figures of moderation,' in one type of which the writer confirms by his own experience, in another rejects some authority, or he warns, or he emphasizes.

men who do not think of them as deflecting poets from that aesthetic delightfulness which a poem has by definition. Such a unity was only preservable, I think, because Renaissance writers took it for granted that all the faculties are involved in the kind of delight poetry affords, as well as in the process of writing it. Even careless or pedestrian remarks about the response of men to a poem seem to speak of a process that includes the whole gamut of the mind's activities, like the defense of figurative language which Puttenham throws off by the way—'which maketh that it sooner invegleth the iudgement of man, and carieth his opinion this way and that, whither soever the heart by impression of the eare shalbe most affectionatly bent and directed' (I, iv).[20] Puttenham tells the poet to be furnished with figures 'such as do most beautifie language with eloquence & sententiousnes' (III, xix, pp. 196–97); if one *beautifies* his *language* with *sententiousness* is he looking to the aesthetic or the didactic?[21]

Certainly there is nothing narrow about the range of delight afforded by poetry, as it was seen by the exponents of the didactic in this period. Men examined the nature and the variety of aesthetic effects possible in poetry with an unequaled meticulousness; the first part of this book was able to give only the barest indication of their willingness to observe almost infinite variations in artistry. Yet I used no writer who did not accept poetry's didactic usefulness—not giving it the lip service of a few general remarks, but making it the axis of his considerations. There were no others to use.

When Puttenham speaks of melody in poetry, he speaks of

[20] Minturno praises *sententia* for teaching by their acuteness, delighting by their wit, moving men by their gravity (Gilbert, p. 297); even *sententia* (general 'judgments,' p. 294) give pleasure to the judging intelligence by way of several of the faculties.

[21] Puttenham praises poetry for being 'briefer & more compendious' than prose (I, iv); Daniel praises formal restrictions, saying that they 'beget conceit beyond expectation,' for as in sonnets it is 'delightfull to see much excellentlie ordred in a small roome' (in Gregory Smith, II, 365–66). Yet we need not go outside the same paragraph in either treatise to see that pleasure in compression, which delights the understanding, prevents neither writer from urging the pleasures of musical language, 'currant and slipper upon the tongue,' falling with 'the certaine close of delight' as rhyme ends the period. Modern critics are given to separating these two pleasures especially, as though one must either think, when reading a poem, *or else* listen to it (Donne; cf. Spenser).

figures so delightful that 'the eare is no lesse ravished with their currant tune, than the mind is with their sententiousnes' (pp. 196–97). This 'ravishing' of the mind is one of the most usual of all Renaissance ways of referring to the didactic element in poetry. Since the experience to which the metaphor refers is one which none of us as readers would willingly give up, it is curious that Puttenham's phrasing of the same idea in another way is enough to frighten most of us straight into the arms of *poésie pure;* he repeats the familiar claim that 'by good and pleasant perswasions' ancient poets assisted in the establishing of civil society by 'insinuating unto' the ungoverned people 'under fictions with sweete and coloured speeches, many wholesome lessons and doctrines.' To modern ears this kind of remark has something we find ourselves tempted to call 'phony.' One supposes that this is not because we have more than the Elizabethans had of that kind of immaturity which resents wholesome doctrines, but rather because we have honestly become skeptical of man's capacity for attaining to and dispensing such wisdom. The whole business looks arrogant to us.

Moderns find equally arrogant the Renaissance willingness to call unwisdom roundly by its name and to expel its proponents from the domain of poetry. Modern criticism does not like to throw out poems on the ground that they bring us to no wisdom, are conceptually false.[22] A Renaissance critic could berate such an author for his untruths. But modern thought lost the stick with which the Renaissance beat the easy propagandist or the false rhetorician when it lost the right to call him a liar.

We pride ourselves upon this wide tolerance of other men's ideas. It has led not so much to careful willingness to examine all possible values presented in poems, as to easy acceptance of the tenet that poetry has no business with pressing men to action. Where the Renaissance threw out the abuse of poetry's didactic power, we throw out poetry's right to that power. There is a certain false humility in the modern position. Al-

---

[22] A reviewer might get away with condemning a poem for conceptual 'inadequacy' (though few try it without uneasy hedging). It comes easier to us to say a man thought too little than to say he thought erroneously.

though it fears the arrogance of stating 'true' insights into the order of the universe, or of calling other men's insights untrue, the modern position is the more confidently assured of man's central importance. The arrogance of the man who tries to expound what he can glimpse of the order imposed by God or 'Nature' cannot hold a candle to the arrogance of him who thinks that there can be no order but that imposed by man, or by successive groups of men. There is a fundamental humility in that Renaissance desire 'to know' which comes out in such an unabashed defense of didacticism as, for example, Chapman's preface to *Achilles Shield*, declaring Homer's 'chiefe holinesse of estimation' to be in his 'matter and instruction,' and finding pleasure simultaneously, and with passion, in the bottomless fountain of his learning and wisdom, in his wit, his elegancy, his disposition, and his judgment (in Gregory Smith, II, 299–300 [1598]). To the Renaissance, the presumptuous man is still he who will not learn, not he who teaches.

I do not imply that a more adequate understanding of the didactic theory can settle the modern problem of poetry's use or uselessness. It may be possible that poetry has no solid and consistent *raison d'être* under a conception of the universe which cuts men off from trying to arrive in a trustworthy fashion at a relative knowledge of absolute truths—which is all that any age has thought it could do. This is the problem of modern poetics, and I know of no profound or helpful consideration of it. We are still in the stage of calling other men's answers naïve.

Renaissance poetic belongs, to be sure, in the framework of Renaissance philosophy, but neither of these is naïve. The various considerations I have indicated unite to remove from Renaissance didactic theory the charge of oversimplification which we have laid upon it. They do not take from the poet writing under such a theory the burden of intellectual and moral responsibility which poets of our own day, like other men, can find no comfortable way of carrying.

The Elizabethans certainly made very light work of it sometimes. Their poems may sometimes seem too fragile to carry the heavy weight of what they say poetry should do; they seem so partly because it is so easy to forget that every least shift in evaluation is both 'rational' and 'moral' as the sixteenth and seventeenth centuries saw the matter. Many a modern poet would be alarmed to discover how many of his poems are didactic and useful by the standards of the Elizabethans. They were willing to admit that any judgment made a difference. Moreover, they rather co-operated with than fought against the tendency of language to convey general ideas, so that the relations of single judgments or particular experience to whole patterns of thought is clarified rather than obscured in them.[23]

The philosophical reasons why the didactic theory could be more palatable to sensitive and imaginative men of the Renaissance than it can be in our own day lie so deep that they are accepted rather than mentioned by treatises on poetics. Obviously, the conceptions I have outlined imply the notion of an order (of values) in the universe—so do the poems that were written. We must not confuse this accepted idea with certain other ideas which we find in the Renaissance as in much earlier times: distrust and disillusionment concerning man's ability to come at a sufficient working knowledge of this order, and discontent with orthodox ideas of the moral order. *Poems stating these attitudes do not come into conflict with the didactic theory of poetry* as we find it put forward in the period itself; the poems, especially if violently satirical, worried certain persons who did not think they told the truth. In point of fact, satire, which from the 1590's especially is the genre that shows discontent with the orthodox, is very closely allied to the didactic theory. We should be put to it to find any Elizabethan or Jacobean satire which does not attempt to recommend to men some change in the way they conceive of things. I use the word 'conceive' advisedly, to avoid the narrowly rational or the narrowly moralistic connotations with which changes in modern thinking have saddled the didactic theory.

In sum, much of Renaissance didactic theory is reconcilable

[23] Another kind of lightness, already mentioned, is harder to take sympathetically —the assumption that there is an aristocracy of the intellect, somewhat rigidly defined, which sets up the writer as the conscious leader (moral, even religious, political, social) of an ignorant multitude. There is a longer comment in the Appendix, Note V.

with ideas which can be entertained even by the modern man, surely the timidest host any century has produced. As sixteenth- and seventeenth-century thinkers conceive of the didactic use- fulness of poetry, that ultimate aim does not make of a poem a decorated sermon, or an informative exposition trimmed with metaphors, or a set of lecturer's precepts with examples to match. Least of all does such an aim ask poets to state, and make palatable, orthodox moral codes. (As always a few per- sons, not usually poets, or critics either, would like to have had it mean this.) The poets of the day, whether late or early, were not given to assuming that the unorthodox has some intrinsic and special relation to the true, and their works demonstrate this unexciting and un-Romantic point of view. But it is basic to Renaissance understanding of the didactic theory that poetry is concerned with truth, as carefully and sensitively seen as may be, and not with the Favorite Truths of the age. It may not be perfunctory and it may not be stupidly good.

There are yet some elements in the theory which the modern mind shies away from. This theory asks that poetry should be directed to the reasoning mind of man, and, generous as are the definitions of the 'rational' when we look closely at them, still they do not take care of those aspects of poems of our own day which use most fruitfully the close relation between poetry and dream. The didactic theory operates to lessen the emphasis upon the sensuous function of images and to subtilize and multi- ply the logical functions they are capable of performing. Both these habits of thinking run counter to what Romantic criticism and Symbolist poetic have taught us to expect of poetic imagery.

Nevertheless, whatever we may think of its virtues, a theory which asks poetry to undertake such large and noble tasks as this period asked of it was no small factor in developing imagery such as no period since has matched. The belief that the smallest particular is significant of ideas as large as the mind can inclose, and the constant habit of seeing the universe thus, helped to produce images of such profound reach that our own more self- conscious attempt to 'be suggestive' cannot rival them in penetration. The belief that poetry addressed itself to the distinguishing and judging wit, and training in such address, produced images of such intellectual brilliance that not even our own veneration for 'difficulty' in poetry has produced images to rival these in subtlety. If it had done nothing else, the didactic theory would have served us well in so stressing the significancy of tropical language as to encourage the development of an understanding of metaphor far more nice and more flexible than our own.

The theory of poetry as a useful learning gave it free right to all that had been preserved in the names of the two great disciplines which in that day governed thought and expression —logic and rhetoric. Without that free use of methods, formal helps, and basic concepts the imagery of the sixteenth and seventeenth centuries would have been immeasurably poorer. Images had to pay for all this with their independence. They were not regarded as ends in themselves, rather as units or elements in a larger process. They were viewed as elements in a pattern by which one man could change another man's 'mind.' I am not sure that this is so far from the truth.

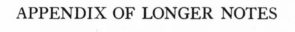

APPENDIX OF LONGER NOTES

APPENDIX OF LONGER NOTES

NOTE A (*To page 18, chapter i: The Problem and What It Involves*)

The added narrative function complicates the question in songs like 'Cupid, in a bed of roses sleeping' (Bullen, *Lyrics from the Song-Books*, p. 133); the 'poetical fiction' is a regular rhetorical kind, but it is present with modifications in all eras, whether or not the rules are known; this is one of the reasons, though only one, for the 'traditional' character of the images in many of E. A. Robinson's or Robert Frost's short poems (for example). There is further modification through the conventions of the pastoral genre or of the medieval *pastourelle* (as in Breton's Phillida and Corydon dialogue, p. 121) or through the use of conventional medieval forms like the *aubade* ('On a time the amorous Silvy,' p. 161). It is interesting to compare the generalized sensuous imagery of this last—'her fairest bosom showing, / Opening her lips, rich perfumes blowing'—with that in an *aubade* not meant to be *sung*, Yeats's 'Parting': 'The murderous stealth of day,' 'I offer to love's play / My dark declivities' (p. 313, from *Winding Stair* [1933]). Yeats's poem is one of a series, carries additional symbolic meanings attached to *night*, *day*, *moon*, and obeys Yeats's wish to preserve certain antitheses; and even so its images resemble those of many a Provençal *aubade* in tone as well as in content. Of course, the life of conventions does not depend on particular authors' conscious and calculated use of them; elements which depend chiefly on that are not of a nature to have become conventions at all.

NOTE B (*To page 27, chapter ii: 'Imitation' and Images*)

The predominance of rhetorical training in both schools and universities during the entire period covered by this study is a commonplace. It can be investigated through the bibliography on education by J. W. Adamson in *The Cambridge Bibliography of English Literature* (Cambridge, 1941), I, 364–80, or through the relevant chapters in Karl Wallace, *Francis Bacon on Communication and Rhetoric* (Chapel Hill, 1943); most specifically, for grammar schools, in T. W. Baldwin, *William Shakspere's Small Latine & Lesse Greeke* (2 vols.; Urbana, Ill., 1944) (this unfortunately appeared too late for me to use and cite in all pertinent connections). A general treatment which gives a convenient approach, with citations, is Hardin Craig's *Enchanted Glass* (New York, 1936), chap. vii. Late Romantic distrust of rhetoric, not yet dead, prevented adequate treatment of the actual rhetorical texts of the period in J. E. Spingarn, *History of Literary Criticism in the Renaissance* (New York, 1899; rev. ed., 1908), in George Saintsbury, *History of Criticism* (3 vols.; London, 1900–1904), more notably in C. S. Baldwin, *Renaissance Literary Theory and Practice* (New York, 1939); and to some extent in D. L. Clark, *Rhetoric and Poetry in the Renaissance* (New York, 1922). The influence of Quintilian's *Institutions* and of the three or four Ciceronian and pseudo-Ciceronian texts has been recognized, even when little attempt at unprejudiced interpretation of that influence has been made, but our knowledge of the use of roughly contemporary Latin texts as schoolbooks has outdistanced our attempts to relate such training to the character of the poetry written. Citations of some of the more recent attempts to restore the balance through a juster appreciation of the real character of rhetoric as a discipline will be found in Wallace's book, esp. chap. xi, and in the present writer's 'Critical Survey of Scholarship in the Field of English Literature of the Renaissance,' *SP*, XL (1943), esp. 236 ff.

Note to page 27

Some information on various rhetorics may be found in W. G. Crane, *Wit and Rhetoric in the Renaissance* (New York, 1937); but earlier lists are superseded by Wallace's bibliography, and in this special field currently appearing articles are important for the new materials and interpretations they present (for examples see H. S. Wilson, 'George of Trebizond and Early Humanist Rhetoric,' *SP*, XL [1943], 367–79, and on Aphthonius and Rainolde, 'Two Renaissance Textbooks of Rhetoric,' by F. R. Johnson, *HLQ*, VI [1943], 427–44).

NOTE C (*To page 30, chapter ii: 'Imitation' and Images*)

See A. H. Gilbert (*op. cit.* in Bibliography), p. 299, for a translation of the passage from Book iv, pp. 286–87 of Minturno's *L'Arte poetica* (1564) (paralleled in the *De poeta* [1559], pp. 445–46); the discussion concerns the use of 'sentences' to give *vim et lumen* to speech (for fitness and *chiarezza* see *L'Arte poetica*, pp. 301–2). The figure is frequently used in both works, as, e.g., in *L'Arte poetica*, p. 374, on lighting up the thought with figures, for deeper significancy. The same idea lies behind Sidney's remark on the 'woordish description' of the philosopher which cannot, like the poet's image, 'strike, pierce, nor possesse *the sight of the soule*' (in Gregory Smith, I, 164).

That penetrating piece of criticism, T. S. Eliot's *Dante*, remarks on the same quality, although he is speaking of a particular type of manifestation of it: 'The style of Dante has a peculiar lucidity—a *poetic* as distinguished from an *intellectual* lucidity. The thought may be obscure, but the word is lucid, or rather translucent' (in *Selected Essays* [New York, 1932], p. 201) (Author's italics). He relates this to the 'mental habit' of writing in the clear visual images induced by the method of allegory, and to universality—as do these other earlier critics. With this difference: that as the Renaissance did not distrust intellectual lucidity, nor set it apart and away from poetry, so too they were likelier to strive for and achieve a luminousness inhering in the whole structure of poems rather than in single images, with a consequent greater stress on the 'clear' *relation* of image to conceptual structure. I cannot think it an accident that the extraordinary luminous beauty which some of Eliot's own images possess accompanies an increasing (as cf. 1917) use of traditional symbols; these are not so much used with their traditional meaning, as so used that their traditional meaning gives us a first inkling of Eliot's meaning. This quality has become more pervasive, say from *Ash Wednesday* on, although already present in images like the Agamemnon stanza which with a startling and pitying flash of light universalizes 'Sweeney among the Nightingales.'

I do not at all refer here to the *content* of images; nothing could be more glowing, burnished, and swathed in varied lights than the beginning of 'A Game of Chess' in the *Waste Land* (p. 73), yet this does not cut out the shape of Eliot's thought in points of light as do the images of *East Coker*, for example: the wind that breaks the loosened pane, the falling light, the Summer midnight, the dancing feet, the late roses filled with early snow, the wood of brambles, the darkness, the blood and flesh eaten and drunk, the wave cry, the wind cry, the vast waters (*Four Quartets* [New York, 1943]). Even so, the influence of Symbolist ideas concerning the structure of a poem would, I think, remove this poetry from what the Elizabethan meant when he talked about the *clarté*, the illumination, of a work of art. Of course, it is not at all certain that this traditional attribute is a suitable criterion for the image-technique of poems with the untraditional 'causes' congenial to the modern poet.

NOTE D (*To page 33, chapter ii: 'Imitation' and Images*)

Certain nineteenth-century vulgarizations of didactic theory are partly responsible for present understandings of how that theory would necessarily affect imagery. Again

Note to page 33

it seems to me that the basis of the confusion is an ontological difference. Only when one conceives of the truth (of which the poet is expositor) in terms such as have been made most familiar by modern scientific rationalism and naturalism does the poet's responsibility as a truthful expositor cause 'the character of the imagery [to be] predetermined' in the direction deplored by Cleanth Brooks, for example (*Modern Poetry and the Tradition* [Chapel Hill, 1939], p. 35). That a poem must be a 'true statement' did not turn metaphor into a mere addendum, for poets who did not divide off the 'truth of the imagination' from 'logical' truth, nor conceive of the ends of 'poetry' and of 'science' as antipathetic. (I do not use the terms of systematic philosophy, preferring those in which these anxieties are generally couched in modern literary criticism. I select a thoughtful critic.)

The distinction between 'an imaginative decorum' and an 'essentially logical decorum' (p. 34) would have been meaningless to a Renaissance mind (in those terms, of course, since the imagination was considered responsible for initiating all those processes described as logical—but I cannot think of any terms which would have made it comprehensible). Renaissance poets would not see a quarrel here, and hence show themselves entirely willing to admit clarity in the *logical* structure of a work of art as an element in the *aesthetic* desideratum of *clarté* or luminousness. The whole body of didactic theory during the Renaissance—in poetic, in every twopenny-halfpenny rhetoric—takes a united stand, declared or implicit, on the premise that imagery and meter 'actually determine what is said by the poem' (p. 34). All treatments of metaphor deal with the *necessity* of metaphor to precise communication—but not because the poet deals in some a-rational way with some special kind of truth (I do not say this cannot be true but that I do not find Renaissance writers who thought so). Only if we can accustom ourselves to the Renaissance absence of self-conscious division between conceptual truth and imaginative (or nonscientific or nonlogical) truth can we understand their simultaneous stress on principles of formal design and on poetry as true statement.

The familiar sixteenth- and early seventeenth-century nervousness about the lawlessness of the imaging faculty does not indicate that these periods 'took the side of Logic' in the problem above described. This nervousness is related to a different stage of the poetic process and involves certain other meanings of 'Imagination.' For some references to discussions of this different sixteenth-century problem, see the book by Wallace (cited in Note B above), esp. pp. 37 ff., where an extreme position is presented (Bacon's). Semantic and philosophical developments did bring the thought of the latter third of the seventeenth century closer to modern divisions and distinctions (see D. F. Bond, 'Neo-Classical Psychology of the Imagination,' *ELH*, IV [1937], 245–64).

NOTE E (*To page 41, chapter ii: 'Imitation' and Images*)

Applications in dramatic theory of this one element within the larger concept of Decorum were bound to be a stumbling-block to the nineteenth century. Instead of seeing it (as Spingarn does, *History of Literary Criticism in the Renaissance*, chap. iii, pp. 85 ff.) as a somewhat reprehensible limitation of poetry to the 'formulae of rhetorical theory,' we are beginning to see it, I think, more as the Elizabethans must have—as a useful literary method. It is a kind of synecdoche carried through into characterization, to assist in ordering the mass of particulars in which the artist finds imbedded the universals he expresses. Theory offers the same justification for two apparently (but only apparently) different Renaissance literary habits: personified qualities of the Spenserian kind, and conventions of characterization in Elizabethan drama. Brilliant uses of the principle in the latter form demonstrate the fact that it need not involve

the substituting of formulas for reality, although anyone who has tried to teach Elizabethan drama to students who use 'just a *type* character' as a term of abuse knows
that such earlier ways of presenting 'the real' run counter to modern habits of mind.
'Late nineteenth-century habits' would perhaps be more accurate; one supposes that
fear of the 'stock character' is a heritage from what Professor Lovejoy calls Romantic
'diversitarianism.'

NOTE F (*To page 42, chapter ii: 'Imitation' and Images*)

Compare Minturno's statements (see *L'Arte poetica*, i, p. 39, for example); or Tasso's
(iii, p. 91; translation given in Gilbert, p. 492). Statements from Scaliger abound in
Gregory Smith's notes to Sidney; the clearest recent presentation of his theory I know
is B. Weinberg's 'Scaliger *vs.* Aristotle on Poetics,' *MP*, XXXIX (1942), 337-60. The
best help I have found to the discrimination of various closely connected senses in
which 'Nature' was understood, by Renaissance critics, is H. S. Wilson's 'Some Meanings of "Nature" in Renaissance LiteraryTheory,' *JHI*, II (1941), 430-48. A poet who
imitated 'Nature' in any of the thirty-five meanings he examines would write in harmony with the principles here discussed, with the sole exceptions of meanings 3 and 28.
The latter, illustrated from Aretino only, is possibly related to Harvey's scoff at the
'Aretinizing' pseudo-natural pamphlet style. Citations under meaning 3 chiefly concern the poet as natural philosopher (allowed by some, disdained by others); none of the
thirty-five meanings would turn the poet into an author of the naturalistic school.

It is obvious to those who know the remainder of the treatises from which I quote
that I support a single general conception from works of critics who were far from being
in entire agreement. But this is part of my point—that the larger lines of argument in
greatly differing theories would have similar effects as far as the demand for 'significancy' in the image is concerned, and that this is borne out by the evidence of the
poetry of widely differing groups, covering a wide range of dates.

NOTE G (*To page 49, chapter ii: 'Imitation' and Images*)

The unity, consistency, and workableness of Renaissance poetic are amazing, when
we remember the long time-span, the number of national literatures involved, and the
fugitive or polemical nature of so many of the critical treatises, or their instructional
(rather than philosophical) purposes, as technical manuals of the 'arts' of poetry and
rhetoric. The integrity of Renaissance criticism stands out when viewed against the
background of such a general exposition as T. M. Greene's (in *The Arts and the Art of
Criticism*), although the period itself was not given to making such syntheses of aesthetic
theory. Major tenets are held from Boccaccio and much earlier through Jonson and
much later; schools and fashions quarrel on a plane far below that whereon disagreements would bring about an important change in poetic creed; ancient theory and
contemporary problems were not merely linked but brought into harmonious working
relation.

Criticism of the period would find congenial, and indeed partly operates on, the
five levels of critical appraisal distinguished by Greene (p. 479). The second of my levels
above is his third: artistic integrity, 'a function not only of formal felicity but of ideational coherence'; for example, Drayton's corrections and removals in his 1619 edition of the sonnets (see chap. iv above) evince his discontent with the criteria of the
preceding levels of pure formal excellence and of artistic quality (Greene, chap. xxii),
and revisions touching images suit the criteria of the next level. My third level is
Greene's fourth—'artistic truth'; and Renaissance criticism of certain genres (notably
epic) further demands excellence on the level of 'artistic greatness'; a distinction be-

Note to page 49

tween the two could not really be formulated from Elizabethan sources. The law of Decorum operated on each level to provide criteria for images suitable to the ends thereon conceived.

Renaissance writers and theorists show understanding of and agreement with a very great many of Greene's distinctions and bases for analysis. They would similarly distinguish between which levels are *fundamental*, and which *important*, and in what order (p. 482). Their rhetoric is grounded on a similar understanding of the relation of form to expressiveness (chap. vii). It is grounded on an understanding of the nature of language which similarly takes account of the various types of verbal meaning (pp. 101 ff.), of the necessary core of conceptual meaning possessed by words (p. 105), of their 'metaphorical dimension' (p. 109), and, thence, of the distinctive type of referential specificity in literature (pp. 354–56). Much of their poetic is in fact based on a secure understanding of this last as a necessity and an advantage of the medium and upon acceptance of it as a datum.

Greene's discussion of the manner in which universals are particularized in concrete individuals (pp. 247–54) brings out conceptions justly parallel with those widely accepted in the Renaissance; the discussion of artistic specificity in its dual role of necessary vehicle and expressed content (pp. 313–15) could be given its Renaissance parallels. Theorists concern themselves with the artist's 'individual frame of reference,' but not because they see in this that which pre-eminently 'distinguishes artistic truth from scientific truth' (p. 459). This distinction was not one to which the earlier period gave much concern; even distinctions between the *methods* of logic, rhetoric, and poetry do not primarily fasten upon this factor, and similarly imagery often takes on (so far as words can) the 'scientific' character of 'concrete visual aids to abstract conceptual apprehension' (p. 260). I doubt if the statement (p. 264) that images are 'effective only *in proportion as* they are individualized' could find support in the period which would not prove equivocal.

But the relation of concept and image, the all-important 'polarity of literary quality' which finds its locus in the metaphorical relation and which is described as 'a fruitful interplay of the more general and the more particular' (pp. 421–22)—this is perfectly understood. Definitions and treatments of metaphor even in the most pedestrian of the rhetoricians are lucid and suggestive. The understanding and appreciation of the interplay between more general and more specific *concepts* which Greene thinks of (pp. 422, 356) as especially characteristic of the Metaphysical poets seems to me to underlie the rhetoricians' discussion of many tropes or combinations of tropes whose use would involve it: *ironia, allegoria, meiosis, ætiologia*. In losing (for practical critical purposes) the distinction between tropes and schemes, we have lost the most important and clarifying single distinction regarding ornament and its functions; modern discussions of imagery particularly suffer from confusions thence resulting.

The Renaissance emphasis on the didactic does not imply the critic's right to transform '*any one* specific pattern of beliefs . . . . into an absolute criterion of objective greatness' (p. 476); the answer of a Sidney to a Gosson is essentially the answer here made to 'the moralistic attitude' (pp. 472–75). I do not distinguish in Renaissance theory a stated willingness to allow the *self-sufficient* value of each level of artistic achievement (though a Castelvetro may be held to stop short with the third); I do not find that evidence from the practice, even of single poets, is conclusive. At least, although the teleological importance of 'means' is cautiously and far from naïvely interpreted (as on p. 482), the evidence that the first two levels were regarded as instrument, throughout the period, is rather formidable. Neither early nor late, however, is poetic 'truth' seen as identifiable with the formulation of propositions in a purely conceptual medium (p. 427).

Note to page 49

In general, Renaissance poetic stands up so firmly when correlated with a careful philosophical analysis of aesthetic theory, that it would seem time to withdraw our characterization of it as contradictory, immature, or ridden by certain inherited *idées fixes*. It is possible that, in examining the theory, we should be examining some of the reasons why poetry written under its flexible but stable laws, throughout the whole of this long period, achieved such variety and such lasting significance.

NOTE H (*To page 87, chapter v: The Criterion of Sensuous Vividness*)

Herrick, *Hesperides*, I, No. 142, 'The Vision.'

> Sitting alone (as one forsook)
> Close by a Silver-shedding Brook;
> With hands held up to Love, I wept;
> And after sorrowes spent, I slept:
> Then in a Vision I did see
> A glorious forme appeare to me:
> A Virgins face she had; her dresse
> Was like a sprightly Spartanesse.
> A silver bow with green silk strung,
> Down from her comely shoulders hung:
> And as she stood, the wanton Aire
> Dangled the ringlets of her haire.
> Her legs were such Diana shows,
> When tuckt up she a-hunting goes;
> With Buskins shortned to descrie
> The happy dawning of her thigh:
> Which when I saw, I made accesse
> To kisse that tempting nakednesse:
> But she forbad me, with a wand
> Of Mirtle she had in her hand:
> And chiding me, said, Hence, Remove,
> Herrick, thou art too coorse to love.

NOTE I (*To page 167, chapter vii: The Criterion of Significancy*)

Daniel, *Delia*, sonnet xlv.

> Care-charmer sleepe, sonne of the Sable night,
> Brother to death, in silent darknes borne:
> Relieve my languish, and restore the light,
> With darke forgetting of my cares returne.
>   And let the day be time enough to morne,
> The shipwrack of my ill-adventred youth:
> Let waking eyes suffice to wayle theyr scorne,
> Without the torment of the nights untruth.
>   Cease dreames, th'ymagery of our day desires,
> To modell foorth the passions of the morrow:
> Never let rysing Sunne approve you lyers,
> To adde more griefe to aggravat my sorrow.
>   Still let me sleepe, imbracing clowdes in vaine;
>   And never wake, to feele the dayes disdayne.

Note to page 167

NOTE J (*To page 173, chapter vii: The Criterion of Significancy*)

Donne's 'The Dissolution' (p. 64) uses very striking images: the four elements as 'my materialls,' paradoxically increased with her death, since they two were 'made of one another'; the elements translated into their courtly-love equivalents, but faster wasted as his fire doth with his fuel grow; the active kings who soonest break from greatest spending, as a later bullet may outstrip an earlier, as his soul will outstrip hers, though she set out soonest. C. M. Coffin, in his valuable study of *John Donne and the New Philosophy* (New York, 1937), p. 163, after a careful analysis of this poem, speaks of it as penetrating 'the region of consciousness where effects of experience are poignantly recorded but vaguely comprehended.' Yet when the poem is looked at as an integrated structure, it is seen to exhibit a full and clear comprehension; it implies and states certain understandings of the nature of human relationships interrupted by death, with an unhesitancy and clarity which is matched (secured, even) by the logical and forceful use of the images. Their relevancy and intended place in the structure is marked by Donne's own introductory particles and careful exposition. Naturally, a paraphrase boiling down this 'comprehension' of the experience simply fails to cover it; Renaissance poetic is adamant on that, as is any serious poetic. But for all that, since the rational coherency of the structure is carefully maintained, and each image clearly assists it, it seems only reasonable to read the poem with these helps.

NOTE K (*To page 182, chapter viii: The Criterion of Rhetorical Efficacy*)

Poets' notions of the fundamental achievement of 'rhetoric' appear to be much the same, at whatever date we choose to alight. Drayton says of Mortimer's letter to the Queen, in which every character wounded like a dart (*Mortimeriados*, 2797; I, 389):

> 'And every one would *pierce her to the hart*,
> *Rethoricall* in woe, and using Art:
> Reasons of greefe, each sentence doth infer,
> And evere lyne, a true remembrancer.'

King says in his 'Elegy upon Prince Henry's death' (p. 66):

> 'O killing Rhetorick of Death! two words
> Breathe stronger terrours then Plague, Fire, or Swords
> Ere conquer'd.'

'Henry's dead'—this 'were Epitaph and Verse / Worthy to be prefixt in Natures herse.' King liked the conceit; he speaks in a sermon published in 1627 of the 'rhetoric' of thunder persuading the Jews (see Bibliography; p. 13), and in another published in 1662 of the tomb as orator, the rhetoric of sorrow, eyes more 'fluent' than the tongue (pp. 2, 33). For a long Crashaw example see chap. xi, n. 48; and, of course, the famous Donne blood-speaking-in-her-cheeks image has the same base. Daniel uses it in a passage on Rosamond's beauty which I quote in full both for its explanation of that poetic power which poets thought of as 'rhetorical' and for the charming tumbled hurry of its close. The last image in it happens to be a 'Metaphysical conceit' from an unjustly neglected 'conventional' and 'prosaic' poet:

> 'Sweet silent rethorique of perswading eyes:
> Dombe eloquence, whose powre doth move the blood,
> More then the words, or wisedome of the wise:
> Still harmonie, whose diapason lyes
> 　　Within a brow, the key which passions move,
> 　　To ravish sence, and play a world in love.'

> ('Complaint of Rosamond,' 121; in HH, p. 251)

Note to page 182

NOTE L (*To page 190, chapter viii: The Criterion of Rhetorical Efficacy*)

I am afraid that both earlier Elizabethans and Metaphysical poets were all the things J. C. Ransom castigates in 'Poetry: A Note in Ontology,' *The World's Body* (New York, 1938); see also Allen Tate's related series of articles on 'Three Types of Poetry,' appearing in the *New Republic*, Vol. LXXVIII (1934), and with some changes in *Reactionary Essays* (New York, 1936).

These poets relate things to the human soul as a center of action; they can, I fear, be called sciencing, devouring idealists expecting to take a return from anything whatsoever, writing discourses on things on the understanding that they are translatable at every point into ideas (pp. 124, 130, 118, 122). If 'the poetic impulse' is defined by its struggle against the rational and practical impulses gratified by other modes of knowing, then quite possibly they did not have it; they are not even aware that image is *versus* idea (pp. 130, 114). I make these bold statements not through entire lack of sympathy with these critics' subtly persuasive arguments against 'Platonic poetry' but because these arguments serve admirably to help us distinguish what is 'bogus' in much poetry written during and since the Romantic period, whereas the oppositions they pose are not really pertinent to the interpretation of poems like Marvell's, or Herbert's, or Donne's, to say nothing of Spenser's or Ralegh's. The anti theses upon which these arguments are erected simply do not characterize the thought of these poets, or of their period.

The poet's world of 'stubborn and contingent objects,' rich in their *Dinglichkeit;* leaving us 'revelling in the thick *dinglich* substance'; with a sign up 'This road does not go through to action; fictitious'—Renaissance poets cannot be got whole into such a poet's world (pp. 123, 142, 131). Too much of what they insistently put into their poems is left unexplained by such a view of their world. To escape the slipperiness of generalizations, I illustrate with a much-used example; any would do, and none would bring in all the necessary points. The poem exhibits the typical and traditional relation of image to idea and of both to 'cause' or subject-and-intention.

One cannot even approach 'accounting for' Herbert's 'The Windows' (in HH, p. 743) in terms of 'reconstituting the world of perceptions,' 'holding out stubbornly against science for the enjoyment of its images,' having the courage of its metaphors (rather daring ones) for the sake of 'increasing the volume of the percipienda or sensibilia' (p. 130). Even the force of Herbert's sensuous diction is dependent on our interest in the relation of the *Dinge* to the idea. We enjoy somewhat the perception that a window uncolored produces a kind of flaring light, watrish, bleak, and thin; we enjoy more the pleasure of perceiving the aptness of the comparison between that sensuous percept and the preacher who has only speech, contrasted with the preacher that has God's life shining annealed in color, even in his brittle crazy glass, so that the light of doctrine comes through in glory, not vanishing like a flaring thing. More than this, verses like 1 and 3–5, and the tone deliberately given to the whole, are simply left on our hands as pointless or hypocritical, if we think Herbert was interested just to point out all the kinds of preachers a world thick with preachers could provide; we have to do the best we can, temporarily at least, to care whether it provides the first kind or the second, and to pursue not the fact of the difference but the idea which made Herbert bother to note it. We may not enjoy the value of the idea as 'truth,' although I think Herbert and his readers expected to, in poetry. But unless we enjoy relations to ideas, and the *possible* validity of ideas, more than *Dinge* or *Dinglichkeit*, the poet has used a technique very ill fitted to our enjoyment.

NOTE M (*To page 198, chapter ix: The Criterion of Decorum*)

On this question of the degree of mental upheaval caused by the new astronomy, a careful reading of the pertinent images presses one toward agreement with the general position taken by F. R. Johnson, *Astronomical Thought in Renaissance England* (Baltimore, 1937), esp. chap. iv, or A. O. Lovejoy, *The Great Chain of Being* (Cambridge, Mass., 1936), esp. chap. iv. In particular, I think that we import into our judgments of seventeenth-century images antipathies between 'science' and other disciplines which are a more recent phenomenon, thus attributing to 'scientific' images such as had characterized European poetry all through the Middle Ages a dissonant intention which they did not convey to contemporaries. See above, chap. iv, n. 12. Decorum was not disturbed by the connotations of images out of natural philosophy; and the final intention of an image must be sought by following it through to its end, in its relation to the demands of the subject of the whole poem. Donne's famous passage (so often quoted out of context), 'Poore soule, in this thy flesh what dost thou know?' has an Augustinian ring, and the 'metaphysical shudder' shakes most medieval poetry and prose written on similar subjects.

The flurry of popular interest in *libertin* ideas, which happened to affect several of these poets during the productive years of their youth, is more to the point here. But, again, hasty generalizations would be precluded if we studied certain shifts in rhetorical and logical fashions which affect tone but do not argue fundamental changes in poetic, and if we remembered to make the reservations due to considerations like genre, 'characters' of style, etc. Deliberative poems must differ from demonstrative ones in technique; and satire has in no era been notable for images producing a mood of enthusiastic affirmation. Careful parallel study of the images in parts of Jean de Meun, some Goliardic songs, the Pardoner's Tale, and the 'libertin' lyrics, would probably have a sobering effect.

NOTE N (*To page 204, chapter ix: The Criterion of Decorum*)

Meiosis is the figure used in the endearment 'duck' which gives I. A. Richards so much trouble (*Philosophy of Rhetoric* [New York, 1936], p. 117). The use of diminutives in endearment no doubt has obscure and deep psychological roots in the relations of love to protectiveness, in human attitudes toward the young of their own species, and so on, but at least it is a phenomenon occurring in all the languages with which one is familiar; and the relation between smallness and one of the kinds of tenderness is the basis for innumerable metaphors. Attempt to put 'duck' into the description of a moment of high passion and the basis of the similitude will reveal itself; a metaphor is indecorous when the *notion* at the heart of the similitude is irrelevant to desired context. Linguistic habits are, of course, too subtle to be seized by any such statements as these, and they are sometimes stronger than any poet's 'mastery' of language can control. They are not necessarily as irrational as they look, and the empirical data on which is founded *goose:stupid* but *rabbit:lovable* are probably sound enough, despite the fact that rabbits are stupid too and geese are pleasant to stroke. When a dumb bunny is a great goose, that is the other side of the rabbit.

NOTE O (*To page 225, chapter ix: The Criterion of Decorum*)

Hutchinson calls this one of the greatest textual difficulties in *The Temple*. His reading (like Sparrow's comment printed in the notes) is entirely supported by the pattern of the images, which (in accord with the intention as stated in the last two stanzas) include not a single example of a diminution of man's capacities or endowments, though many figures diminish the *Mundum magnum* (*cupboard, cabinet*, etc.). The parallel images of man as an unfruitful tree, adduced by Palmer, are not parallel unless we beg the question regarding Herbert's true meaning *in this poem*, and simply read *no* because elsewhere Herbert did state the concept the image would then convey; such evidence is not truly pertinent, for no one could maintain the unstated premise that poets consistently use certain objects solely to diminish rather than to amplify— both poets and other human beings constantly use the same objects for both purposes.

Note to page 225

The 'tree images' in these other poems (*Employment* [*ii*], *Affliction* [*i*]) are diminishing images used to support the notion that man does not sufficiently realize his capacities, a subject not treated in the poem *Man.*

NOTE P (*To page 226, chapter ix: The Criterion of Decorum*)

I have always found it hard to trace back this particular generalization about the Metaphysical 'rebellion' to a body of firm evidence from the lips of the primary witnesses; there must be a dozen anti-Petrarchan statements in the mid-sixteenth century to one from the Metaphysicals. If we wish to think of the Elizabethan poets influenced by mid-sixteenth-century French and Italian modes as Petrarchists, it is well to remember that the *Pléiade* was vociferously anti-Petrarchan, and that Du Bellay, like various others, wrote 'Contre les Petrarquistes' (1553). One quick reference to an article with citations will perhaps suffice; R. J. Clements, in 'Anti-Petrarchism of the *Pléiade*,' *MP*, XXXIX (1941), 15–21, notes how plentiful were these condemnations among French poets of the middle Renaissance, and in Italy, and how common were denials of being Petrarchist, by the 1550's.

We take facts like Harvey's praise of Petrarch's art and eloquence as a vote of approval for all the elements of Petrarchism which were misliked later (or earlier for that matter). As with all enduring influences (Milton's is another example) each later generation is influenced by a slightly different combination of elements, and each revolts against some which had come to be mechanically parroted by lesser minds. Spokesmen for sixteenth-century poetic ideals protest against whining poetry just as later spokesmen do, object to feigned exaggeration, mere silken words. So do we all. Concurrently, they remake the old conceits in their own way, as later poets were also to do. The conceits take less remaking in commendatory poems (as can be demonstrated in Carew), and reservations made above obtain here (see the analysis of Drayton's sonnet revisions, or discussions of meiosis and the decorum of satirical kinds). Yet to leaf through Donne or Sidney or Carew is to make a list of the old conceits—fire and ice, sighs and winds, heart wounded or besieged or made a temple, Cupid (Love with or without the capital), the eyes, the altar, and so on. But what poet (or lover) ever did otherwise than claim that the old ways of pleading his cause or praising his lady are insufficient? And, if he wishes to calumniate her, that the old ways are falsifications?

NOTE Q (*To page 227, chapter ix: The Criterion of Decorum*)

F. W. Bateson's argument does not center around the claims I try to refute in the section to which this note is attached. Yet his examples, though acutely analyzed, would not mean quite what he finds from them if read in the context of critical ideas of the period, treated in previous chapters. I cite without attempting full explanation: Spenser's psychological generalization (p. 32) is expressed through a 'similitude' (an *allegoria*, but declared); the pleasure *proper* to this figure resides in the multiplication of logical parallels. Herrick's *kind* of 'copie' differs (p. 42); if his figure really is the trope *allegoria* (as is claimed), the multiplication of sensuous detail with suggested further significance is normal, and can be matched in any period. The examples from Herrick, Tourneur, and Shakespeare (pp. 44–45) are all *tropes;* the reasons for the choice of tropical language would be complicated, involving several factors.

NOTE R (*To page 254, chapter x: Images Logically Defined*)

Recent studies of imagery have used almost entirely as a basis for characterizing and grouping images: the *kind of content* whence authors draw (1) descriptive detail and (2) second terms (things compared to, vehicles) of images. In the first place, 1 and 2 represent very different mental operations, differently caused. In the second place, the factor chiefly regarded in the drawing of conclusions is the author's predilection for certain contents. The number of other factors involved—and impossible to isolate—in the creation or choice of even the simplest image seems to me to throw this method out of court; Part I has demonstrated a few of these factors. Many studies in this kind have been made since C. F. E. Spurgeon's *Shakespeare's Imagery*; for other exemplification of the difficulties inherent in the method see the present author's article, referred to in n. 1 of this chapter. Or see L. H. Hornstein, 'Analysis of Imagery: A Critique of Literary Method,' *PMLA*, LVII (1942), 638–53.

One initial difficulty any reader may test for himself. It is seldom possible to determine except by an arbitrary decision the province to which an image's content allows us to assign it. Does the Marlowe image next quoted in the text belong under Mythology, or The Hunt? Yet this is a simple image in which semantic developments do not obtrude; these make insuperable difficulties as soon as image-content departs from mere naming of commonplace objects. Even objects are unsafe; for Marlowe, 'brass vessels' may belong to the province of 'commonplace' domestic objects, for me, to whatever province would include art museums in a remote and 'romantic' foreign country—and no reader of either of our images could ever tell it. Let the image mention not objects but things historical, religious, or political, and one is in far worse case. No *NED* could tell us the precise overtones of a particular 'vehicle' to a certain man in a certain region in a certain year, and our knowledge of social and political currents would have to be unimaginably delicate. But suppose we could surmount these difficulties.

We should yet have images ranged according to a basis of 'like-ness' which is almost completely irrelevant *to the effect of the image as an element of aesthetic form*. All that is *poetically* important about the image is yet undetermined. The best test of this is to try it with a few poems and notice what strange bedfellows any image must receive. Marlowe's brass-vessels image, for example, must range itself with St. Teresa's cup of death in Crashaw. I do not know anything that could be less illuminating to the critic of the two poems.

Moreover, images do not start and stop, in poems. They merge, are indistinguishable from the offspring they beget, refuse to be separated from a matrix of conceptual statement, and often turn out to be coterminous with the whole poem. It is often quite impossible to count the number of images in a poem; the number will differ *for the same reader* in different readings. We can frequently be entirely certain that an author is using language tropically; there are other cases where we do not know and can never find out.

NOTE S (*To page 294, chapter xi: Renaissance Logic and the Framing of Renaissance Images*)

The general method of expanding images by pursuing such a predicament as *quality* is variously used or variously combined with others. A favorite is the kind of 'testament-formula' found in Daniel's sonnet xviii: restore thy tresses to the golden ore, thy hands' pride to the ivory, thy blush to Aurora—and may Hyrcan tigers and ruthless bears be profited by the bequeathal of thy fierce and cruel mind. This formula is turned other-end-on in Carew's 'Ask me no more where Jove bestows'—the stars' brightness in your eyes, the golden sunlight in your hair, and so on. Some of Carew's images are complicated by other 'places' than simple quality; he states one outright in 'These flowers, *as in their causes*, sleep' (p. 141).

It should be noted that series based upon more tenuous logical relations produce images of a very different effect, as, for example, in Donne's 'The Will' (p. 56), which is an extended play upon the relations of subjects to adjuncts, using also the places of opposition and privation. The first stanza bequeaths gifts to those who do not need them ('had too much before'), the next to those who cannot use them ('have an incapacitie'), the third to those who would be insulted to hear they did not have them ('count my gifts indignity'), the fourth to those he got them from ('I did but restore'), the fifth to those to whom they would be useless. This is the wittiest possible reversal of a familiar logical exercise—for inventing adjuncts was as common a conscious method of amplifying as inventing qualities. As he says, 'disproportion,' instead of the usual careful proportioning, is his aim.

NOTE T (*To page 320, chapter xi: Renaissance Logic and the Framing of Renaissance Images*)

Sidney, *Astrophel and Stella*, xxvii.

> Because I oft in darke abstracted guise,
> Seeme most alone in greatest company,
> With dearth of words, and aunswers quite awry,
> To them that would make naked speech arise;
> They deeme, and of their doome the rumor flies,
>> That poyson foule of bubling pride doth lie
>> So in my swelling brest, that onely I
> Faune on my selfe, all others doe dispise:
> Yet pride (I thinke) doth not my soule possesse,
> (Which lookes too oft in this unflattering glasse)
> But one worse fault, ambition I confesse,
>> That makes me oft my best freendes over-passe,
>> Unseene unheard, while thought to highest place
> Bends all his powers, even unto *Stellas* grace.

NOTE U (*To pages 355, 380, chapter xiii: Effects of Specific Logical Functions upon the Poetic Character of Images*)

I cannot enter in this book into the complexities of seventeenth-century sermon styles, to which W. Fraser Mitchell's *English Pulpit Oratory from Andrewes to Tillotson* (London, 1932) is the best introduction. I shall not even enter the problem sufficiently to come to a clear statement of disagreement with some few of the ideas advanced in chaps. xi and xii of P. Miller, *op. cit.* (in chap. xii, n. 1, above), though my discussion clearly does not lead toward his statement (p. 345): 'It was, obviously, impossible to be a Ramist and still preach like John Donne.' Sidney is an example of the fact that it must have been possible to be a Ramist and still write like the author of *Arcadia*. Being a Ramist as far as the general conceptions affecting imagery are concerned did not involve what Ramism came to involve for later Puritans, especially in America. But the whole matter is one of extreme complexity, in which minor inconsistencies dog the footsteps of any simple theory; for instance, King's sermon organization was probably influenced by the anti-Ramist Keckermann, while his imagery functions in ways best demonstrated by Fraunce, except that it is 'plainer' when it ought to be fancier! This is no more of a puzzler than that afforded by trying to get Milton's Ramist logic and his prose style into the same box. And consistency is never maintained when ideas filter down to affect popular attitudes; in 1607 a book like Cleland's (*op. cit.*, in chap. xi, n. 20, above) can direct a young nobleman to get helps from Keckermann's logic *and* Talaeus' rhetoric (p. 90).

Our theories regarding Ramism and ornament in literature must be very complex and very flexible if they are to take care of considerations like: the great measure of orthodoxy in Talaean rhetoric; the consistency shown (from the earliest part of the period on, and by all authors of every stripe) in conceptions of the nature and functions of trope and scheme; the fact that poets certainly affected by ties between poetry and dialectic have left us literary pieces which are *not* rigidly all of one kind; the fact that Ramism offers no fundamental reinterpretation of the relations between Eloquence and useful Wisdom as we can follow them from Quintilian through Minturno and Sidney to Mazzoni and Milton.

NOTE V (*To page 408, chapter xiv: Images and a Redefined Didactic Theory*)

We find ourselves out of agreement with Renaissance theorists when it comes to their picture of society or their schedule of man's duties, and these necessarily furnish the context in which they explain poetry's didactic nature. The theory may look very crass when we read in Wilson about winning the ignorant through fables (*Arte of Rhetorique*, p. 198). The same idea will look less crass as Mazzoni builds it up through a long argument, though one is put off by innumerable differences in social outlook. If we can look through the accidental trappings, the specific definitions of social goods, which belong to a century very different from ours politically and sociologically, we shall perceive that he is asking poetry so to speak to men that it brings them to greater moral maturity, and that he is arguing for qualities in poems which shall insure sympathetic understanding and the possibility of seeing one's own case in those fictions which the poet presents (e.g., Gilbert, pp. 379–83). This again is not so distant from our own experience with poetry as the enemies of didacticism would have us believe.

BIBLIOGRAPHY

BIBLIOGRAPHY

This bibliography, a finding-list of editions for the convenience of readers, includes only texts quoted from or paraphrased in my discussion without the appending of bibliographical data.

ARISTOTLE   *The "Art" of Rhetoric,* ed. J. H. FREESE. 'Loeb Classical Library.' London and New York, 1926.

ASCHAM, ROGER   *The Scholemaster. See* SMITH, G. GREGORY.

BLUNDEVILLE, THOMAS   *The Arte of Logicke. Plainly taught in the English Tongue* . . . . London, 1619.

BOCCACCIO, GIOVANNI   OSGOOD, C. G. *Boccaccio on Poetry: Being the Preface and the 14th and 15th Books of Boccaccio's 'Genealogia Deorum Gentilium,' in an English Version.* . . . . Princeton, 1930.

CAMPION, THOMAS   *Campion's Works,* ed. PERCIVAL VIVIAN, Oxford, 1909.

CAREW   *Poems of Thomas Carew,* ed. ARTHUR VINCENT. 'Muses Library.' London, n.d.

CASTELVETRO, LODOVICO   *See* GILBERT, A. H.

CHAPMAN   *The Poems of George Chapman,* ed. PHYLLIS BARTLETT. New York and Oxford, 1941.

CINTHIO   *See* GIRALDI

COX, LEONARD   *The Arte or Crafte of Rhethoryke,* ed. F. I. CARPENTER. Chicago, 1899.

CRASHAW, RICHARD   *Steps to the Temple, Delights of the Muses, and Other Poems,* ed. A. R. WALLER. Cambridge, 1904.

DANIEL, SAMUEL   *A Defence of Ryme. See* SMITH, G. GREGORY.

Poems and A Defence of Ryme, ed. A. C. SPRAGUE. Cambridge, Mass., 1930.

DAVIES, SIR JOHN   *The Complete Poems,* ed. A. B. GROSART. 2 vols. London, 1876.

DAY, ANGEL   *A Declaration of all such Tropes, Figures or Schemes, as* . . . . *are speciallie used.* . . . . Part II of *The English Secretorie.* London, 1595.

DONNE   *The Poems of John Donne,* ed. H. J. C. GRIERSON. 2 vols. Oxford, 1912.

DRAYTON — *The Works of Michael Drayton*, ed. J. W. HEBEL, K. TILLOTSON, and B. NEWDIGATE. 5 vols. Oxford, 1931–41.

DU BELLAY, JOACHIM — *La Deffence et illustration de la langue francoyse*, ed. HENRI CHAMARD. Paris, 1904.

DU MOULIN, PIERRE — *The Elements Of Logick. . . . . Translated . . . . by Nathanael De-Lawne . . . . .* London, 1624.

ELIOT, T. S. — *Collected Poems, 1909–35.* New York, 1936.

ERASMUS, DESIDERIUS — *De duplici copia verborum ac rerum*, in *Erasmi Opera Omnia.* Lugduni Batavorum, 1703. Vol. I, cols. 1–74, 75–110.

EVANS, LEWIS — *[The Abridgement of Logique].* N.d.

FABRI, PIERRE — *Le grand et vrai art de pleine rhétorique ... publié ...* par A. HÉRON. 3 vols. Rouen, 1889–90.

FENNER, DUDLEY — *The Artes of Logike and Rethorike, plainly set forth in the English tongue. . . . .* [1584.]

FRACASTORO — *Hieronymi Fracastorii Veronensis Opera omnia. . . . .* Venetiis, 1555.

Naugerius, sive de Poetica Dialogus, trans. RUTH KELSO; introduction by M. W. BUNDY. 'Illinois Studies in Language and Literature,' Vol. IX, No. 3. Urbana, Ill., 1924.

FRAUNCE, ABRAHAM — *The Arcadian Rhetorike: Or The Praecepts of Rhetorike made plaine by examples. . . . .* London, [1588].

The Lawiers Logike. . . . . London, 1588.

GASCOIGNE, GEORGE — *Certayne Notes of Instruction. See* SMITH, G. GREGORY.

GILBERT, ALLAN H. — *Literary Criticism: Plato to Dryden.* New York, 1940.

GIRALDI CINTHIO — *See* GILBERT, A. H.

GOOGE, BARNABE — *Eglogs, Epytaphes, and Sonettes, 1563*, ed. EDWARD ARBER. London, 1910.

GRANGER, THOMAS — *Syntagma Logicum. or, The Divine Logike. . . . .* London, 1620.

HEBEL AND HUDSON (abbreviated as HH) — *Poetry of the English Renaissance, 1509–1660*, ed. J. W. HEBEL and H. H. HUDSON. New York, 1938.

HERBERT, EDWARD — *The Poems English and Latin of Edward Lord Herbert of Cherbury*, ed. G. C. MOORE SMITH. Oxford, 1923.

HERBERT, GEORGE   *The Works of George Herbert*, ed. F. E. HUTCHIN-
SON. Oxford, 1941.

HERRICK   *Hesperides: or the Works Both Human and Divine
of Robert Herrick.* 2 vols. 'Temple Classics.' London, 1899.

HOSKINS, JOHN   *Directions for Speech and Style*, ed. H. H. HUDSON.
Princeton, 1935.

JONSON   *Conversations with William Drummond of Haw-
thornden*, in C. H. HERFORD and P. SIMPSON,
Ben Jonson, I, 132–51. Oxford, 1925.
The Poems of Ben Jonson, ed. B. H. NEWDIGATE.
Oxford, 1936.
Discoveries: A Critical Edition, ed. MAURICE
CASTELAIN. Paris, 1906.

KING   *The Poems of Bishop Henry King*, ed. JOHN
SPARROW. London, 1925.
*A Sermon Preached At Pauls Crosse, the 25. of
November. 1621.* . . . . London, 1621.
*Two Sermons. Upon the Act Sunday, Being the
10th of Iuly. 1625.* . . . . Oxford, 1625.
A Sermon of Deliverance . . . . *Easter Monday,
1626.* . . . . London, 1626.
*Two sermons Preached at White-Hall in Lent,
March 3. 1625. And Februarie 20. 1626.* . . . .
London, 1627.
*An Exposition upon The Lords Prayer. Delivered
in certaine Sermons.* . . . . London, 1628.
A Sermon Preached At St. Pauls March 27. 1640.
. . . . London, 1640.
*A Sermon Preached at the Funeral of the R' Rever-
end Father in God Bryan, Lord Bp. of Winchester*
. . . . *April 24, 1662.* . . . . London, 1662.
*A Sermon Preached at Lewis in the Diocess of
Chichester, By the Lord Bp of Chichester, At His
Visitation Held there, Octob. 8. 1662.* London,
1663.
*A Sermon Preached the 30th of January at White-
Hall, 1664.* . . . . London, 1665.

LEVER, RALPH   *The Arte of Reason, rightly termed, Witcraft.* . . . .
London, 1573.

MACLEISH, ARCHIBALD   *Poems, 1924–1933.* Boston and New York, 1933.

MARLOWE

Marlowe's Poems, ed. L. C. MARTIN. London, 1931. (Vol. IV of *Works and Life of Christopher Marlowe*, ed. R. H. CASE.)

MARVELL

The Poems and Letters of Andrew Marvell, ed. H. M. MARGOLIOUTH. 2 vols. Oxford, 1927.

MAZZONI, JACOPO

Della Difesa della Comedia di Dante. Distinta in sette libri . . . . Cesena, 1587 (Books i–iii), 1688 (Books iv–vii).
See also GILBERT, A. H.

MILTON, JOHN

A Fuller Institution of the Art of Logic, Arranged after the Method of Peter Ramus (1672), ed. and trans. A. H. GILBERT, in *Works*. 'Columbia edition,' Vol. XI. New York, 1935.

MINTURNO

Antonii Sebastiani Minturni De poeta . . . . Venetiis, 1559.
L'Arte poetica. . . . . Napoli, 1725.
See also GILBERT, A. H.

PEACHAM, HENRY

The Garden of Eloquence Conteyning the Figures of Grammer and Rhetorick. . . . . London, 1577.
The Garden of Eloquence, Conteining the most excellent Ornaments, Exornations, Lightes, flowers, and formes of speech, commonly called the Figures of Rhetorike . . . . Corrected and augmented. . . . . London, 1593.

PUTTENHAM, GEORGE

The Arte of English Poesie, ed. GLADYS WILLCOCK and ALICE WALKER. Cambridge, 1936.
See also SMITH, G. GREGORY.

QUINTILIAN

The Institutio Oratoria of Quintilian, ed. H. E. BUTLER. 4 vols. 'Loeb Classical Library.' London, 1920–22.

RAINOLDE, RICHARD

A booke called the Foundacion of Rhetorike. . . . . London, 1563. (Facsimile edition, ed. F. R. JOHNSON. 'Scholars' Facsimiles and Reprints.' New York, 1945.)

RALEGH

The Poems of Sir Walter Ralegh, ed. AGNES M. C. LATHAM. Boston and New York, 1929.

RAMUS, PETER (PIERRE DE LA RAMÉE)

The Logike of the moste excellent philosopher P. Ramus Martyr. . . . . London, 1574.
The Logike of the Moste Excellent Philosopher P. Ramus Martyr. . . . . London, 1581.
P. Rami Dialecticae Libri duo, scholiis G. Tempelli Cantabrigiensis illustrati. . . . . Cantabrigiae, 1584.

The Art of Logick. Gathered out of Aristotle, and set in due forme . . . . by Peter Ramus. . . . . With a short Exposition of the Praecepts . . . . by Antony Wotton. London, 1626.

The Art of Logick, delivered in the precepts of Aristotle and Ramus. . . . by Tho: Spencer. London, 1628.

Peter Ramus of Vermandois . . . . his Dialectica . . . . Not onely translated . . . . but also digested into questions. . . . . By R. F. Gent. London, 1632.

The Logicians School-Master: or, A Comment upon Ramus Logick. By Mr. Alexander Richardson. . . . . whereunto are added, His Prelections on Ramus his Grammer; Taleus his Rhetorick. . . . . London, 1657.

See also FRAUNCE; GRANGER; MILTON

RICHARDSON, ALEXANDER *See* RAMUS

SCALIGER *Iulii Caesaris Scaligeri . . . . Poetices libri septem. . . . .* 5th ed. Heidelberg, 1617.

F. M. PADELFORD. *Select Translations from Scaliger's Poetics.* New York, 1905.

SHERRY, RICHARD *A treatise of Schemes & Tropes. . . . .* London [1550]. (Preface signed London, MDL.)

A Treatise of the Figures of Grammer and Rhetorike, profitable for al that be studious of Eloquence, and in especiall for suche as in Grammer scholes doe reade moste eloquente Poetes and Oratours. . . . . (Colophon: London, MDLV.)

SIDNEY, SIR PHILIP *An Apologie for Poetrie. See* SMITH, G. GREGORY.

The Last Part of the . . . . Arcadia, Astrophel and Stella and Other Poems, ed. ALBERT FEUILLERAT. Cambridge, 1922.

SMITH, G. GREGORY *Elizabethan Critical Essays,* ed. GEORGE GREGORY SMITH. 2 vols. Oxford, 1904.

SPENCER, THOMAS *See* RAMUS

SPENSER *The Poetical Works of Edmund Spenser,* ed. J. C. SMITH and E. DE SELINCOURT. Oxford, 1932.

SUCKLING *The Works of Sir John Suckling, in Prose and Verse,* ed. A. H. THOMPSON. London and New York, 1910.

TASSO *Discorsi del poema eroico,* in *Opere di Torquato Tasso.* Vol. III. Milan, 1824.

See also GILBERT, A. H.

VAUGHAN   *The Works of Henry Vaughan,* ed. L. C. MARTIN.
                       2 vols. Oxford, 1914.

WEBBE, WILLIAM   *A Discourse of English Poetrie.* See SMITH, G.
                       GREGORY.

WILSON, THOMAS   *Wilson's Arte of Rhetorique, 1560,* ed. G. H. MAIR.
                       Oxford, 1909.
                       The Rule of Reason, conteinyng the Art of Logike.
                       . . . . London, 1580.

WOTTON, ANTONY   *See* RAMUS.

WYATT   *The Poems of Sir Thomas Wiat,* ed. A. K. FOX-
                       WELL. London, 1913.

YEATS   *Collected Poems of W. B. Yeats.* New York, 1941.

INDEX

INDEX

[In this Index, *figures* (tropes and schemes) are indexed as a group under that heading. References by capital letters are to notes so designated in the Appendix of Longer Notes (pp. 413–25).

Numerals in italic type indicate: in the case of *poets* or of authors of *early critical treatises*, citations which include quotation; in the case of *figures*, citations which offer clarifying exemplification or commentary on the given figure; in the case of *subjects*, references to fairly full treatments. In references to a series of pages, one of the series of occurrences of an item may be solely in a note; if any one of the series includes quotation, the reference is italicized.

I have thought it to be of more service to a reader to include in the Index not every mention, but rather every description, or exemplification receiving comment, of a figure; a similar discretion has been exercised with respect to the extremely numerous references to single authors by name, but all commentary of importance and all quotations are indexed. For various topics which it would be impossible to index completely (e.g., metaphor, invention), the more important comments are indicated. Modern editors of texts appear only if materials from their introductions or notes are cited.]

sec. 2, passim; distributio, 306 n.; *divisio,* 120

enallage, 97; enargia, 29, 31–32, 114; *energia,* 29 n., 85, *114;* epithet, *10, 286; epizeuxis,* 154 n., *188; exclamatio,* 154 n., *188; exemplum,* 294 n., 301, 307, *347–49; expolitio, 141–42 horismus* (*see* 'figure of difference'); hyperbole, *150,* 224, 274, 301, *317–18,* 368

icon, 35 n., *54–55, 73–74,* 80, 82 n., 89, 93, 109, 297, 306, 312; *incrementum, 188; interrogatio, 188,* 313; *intimatio,* 143 n.; *ironia,* 16, 135 n., *184–85, 205–8,* 213–14, 260, App. G litotes, *204–5*

macrologia, 194 n.; meiosis, 131, *203–6,* 209–12, 215, 224–26, 280, 295, 301, 328, 359, 374–75, App. G, N, P; *merismus,* 300, *306; metalepsis, 62 n., 135;* metaphor (*see* Metaphor); metonymy, *129–30,* 270, *319 n.; micterismus,* 184; *mimesis, 73,* 94 n. onomatopoeia, 97

parabola, 73, 301; *partitio, 120,* 300, 306 n.; *periergia, 194 n.; periphrasis, 119–20, 276,* 301; *perittologia, 194 n.; pleonasmus, 194 n.; pragmatographia, 73,* 80, *97–98; pronominatio,* 157 n.; 301; prosopopoeia, 80, *94–96,* 98, 207; proverb, 9, 184

sarcasmus, 184; *sententia,* 35 n., 58, *88,* 160, *265; sermocinatio,* 83, 94 n.; similitude, 89, 102 n., 134 n., *183–84,* 255–56, *263–65, 289–90,* 295, 302 n., *311,* 324, 349, *361–64,* 370 n., *chap. xiii, sec. 3, passim,* App. N, Q; stichomythia, 324; synedoche, 54 n., 60, *104, 129–30,* 132, 136–38, *220–22,* 327, App. E; *synonymia,* 66, *119–20 tapinosis, 212; topographia,* 80, 88; *topothesia, 80–81,* 102; *traductio, 188; translatio, 100,* 107, 121–22, 169 n., 311 (*see also* Metaphor)

Forbes, C. A., 120 n., 385 n.
Fordyce, C. J., 291 n.
Fracastoro, Girolamo, *41–42, 56–57, 152, 195,* 387
Fraunce, Abraham, 139, 319 n., 332, 335 n., *337–38, 340–41,* 344 n., *346–48, 361–62, 384–85,* App. U
Frost, Robert, App. A
Fry, Roger, 57

Gascoigne, George, *28,* 62 n.
George of Trebizond, App. B
Gilbert, A. H., 90 n., 183 n., 214 n., 335 n., 382 n., App. C
Gilbert, K. E., 29 n., 139 n., 151 n.
Giraldi Cinthio, *38–39*
Googe, Barnabe, 96, *107–8, 240*
Gordon, D. J., 214 n.
Granger, Thomas, *285 n.,* 306 n., 333, 338, 342 n., *345–46,* 350 n.
Greene, Robert, 82, *147,* 302, 304
Greene, T. M., 49 n., 56 n., App. G
Grierson, H. J. C., 203 n.
Grimald, Nicholas, 302, 303 n.

HH (Hebel and Hudson), vii
Hard, Frederick, 135 n.
Harvey, Gabriel, 25, *29, 39,* 120 n., 332, 385 n., App. F, P
Herbert, George, *204, 217–20, 225,* 303, 313, *370 n.,* 380 n., App. *L, O*
Herbert of Cherbury, Edward Lord, *134,* 198, 282, *288, 290, 291 n.,* 294, 296, *304, 308*
Hermogenes, 83
Herrick, Robert, *11–12,* 28, 51 n., 83, *87–88, 93,* 97, *102, 105 n., 129, 141, 147–50, 204,* 228 n., 313, 359, App. *H,* Q
Holmes, Elizabeth, 291 n.
Hornstein, L. H., App. R
Hoskins, John, 32 n., *40–41, 66–67,* 89 n., *94,* 114 n., *120–24,* 127, *130, 140, 150, 188, 204–5, 211,* 213, *318*
Hudson, Hoyt H., 106 n., 120 n.
Hulme, T. E., 101, 152 n.
Hutchinson, F. E., 225 n., App. O

'Illumination'; *see* 'Illustration'
'Illustration,' *chap. ii, sec. 1, passim,* 51 n., 67, *94–95,* 123, 136, 219, 297, 357, App. *C,* D
Imagist, 5, 10 n., 13, 101, 314
Imitation, 13, 18, 23–26, *chap. ii, passim,* 78, 145, 251, *chap. xiv, passim,* App. B, C, *D,* E, *F, G*
Invention, 28, 31, 39, 286, 288, 291, 299–300, *chap. xi, sec. 3, passim,* 333–34, 339–42, 370–71, 378, *388–93,* 396–97, App. S
Irony; *see* Figures: *ironia*

John, L. C., 134 n.
Johnson, Francis R., 190 n., App. B, M